His Supreme Majesty
Chulalonkorn I
King of Siam.

TEMPLES AND ELEPHANTS

TRAVELS IN SIAM IN 1881–1882

BY

CARL BOCK

AUTHOR OF "THE HEAD-HUNTERS OF BORNEO"

MAP AND ILLUSTRATIONS

SINGAPORE OXFORD NEW YORK

OXFORD UNIVERSITY PRESS

1986

Oxford University Press
Oxford New York Toronto
Petaling Jaya Singapore Hong Kong Tokyo
Delhi Bombay Calcutta Madras Karachi
Nairobi Dar es Salaam Cape Town
Melbourne Auckland
and associates in
Beirut Berlin Ibadan Nicosia
OXFORD is a trade mark of Oxford University Press
First published by Sampson Low, Marston, Searle,
& Rivington, London 1884
First issued as an Oxford University Press paperback 1986
ISBN 0 19 582623 X

Printed in Malaysia by Peter Chong Printers Sdn. Bhd.
Published by Oxford University Press Pte. Ltd.
Unit 221, Ubi Avenue 4, Singapore 1440

PREFACE.

In the following pages I have endeavoured to give a faithful account of what I saw and heard during a journey from Bangkok through Upper Siam and Lao.

I trust that the record of my travels—in Lao particularly—will be of interest, as little or nothing is known in Europe of that country, the only European, so far as I can gather, who has traversed any portion of the same ground being Lieutenant (afterwards General) Macleod, who went into Upper Siam in 1837, and who succeeded in reaching Kiang Hung.

I regret that I can give but meagre information on many points on which I shall probably be expected to afford many details after a stay of fourteen months in Siam and Lao. The difficulty of extracting any information from the Siamese, and still more from the Laosians, who hate the sight of a foreigner, must be my excuse for any shortcomings in this respect. What I saw, however, I have described with fidelity; what I heard I have recorded as it was stated to me: I have, at the special request of the Siamese Government, refrained from any political allusions, but, with this obviously needful omission, I have endeavoured to " nothing extenuate, nor," I hope, have I " set down aught in malice."

To the many gentlemen, official and non-official, whom I met during my journey, and who rendered me valued services, I desire to convey my thanks for their kindness to a stranger.

Foremost amongst them I must express my deep sense of gratitude to His Majesty the King of Siam, without whose generous personal assistance, pecuniary and otherwise—by giving me letters of recommendation, and by placing steamers, boats, elephants, and coolies at my disposal—I should not have been able to accomplish the journey which it was my privilege and pleasure to make from end to end of the vast kingdoms which own allegiance to this enlightened monarch.

To H.R.H. Prince Devawongsa Varoprakar, for his many services and acts of kindness to me during my stay in Bangkok; to the Foreign Office in London, for its valuable letter of recommendation to her Majesty's representative at Bangkok, Mr. W. Gifford Palgrave; to Mr. Palgrave himself; to Mr. W. H. Newman, H.M.'s Acting Consul-general; to Messrs. E. B. Gould and E. H. French, of the British Agency; to Dr. Smith, the physician to the Agency; and to the American missionaries, Dr. Cheek and Mr. Jonathan Wilson, I beg to offer my sincere thanks for the assistance they rendered me.

I may, perhaps, be permitted in this place to acknowledge my sense of the honour which has been conferred upon me, in recognition of my humble efforts at increasing our knowledge concerning little-

known lands, by the bestowal upon me of the Order
of Franz-Josef, by H.I.M. the Emperor of Austria; of
the Order of the Rose, by H.I.M. the Emperor of
Brazil; and of its gold medal, by the Geographical
Society of Lisbon ; and by my election as an honorary
member of the Geographical Societies of Rome and
Samarang, and of the Anthropological Society of
Florence.

Finally, I have to thank Mr. Charles E. Fryer for
the care he has taken in revising my MSS., cor-
recting my imperfect English, and in passing this
book through the press.

My thanks are also due to Mr. C. F. Kell for the
reproduction of my coloured drawings, and to Mr. J.
D. Cooper for the manner in which he has engraved
the smaller sketches.

CARL BOCK.

CHRISTIANIA,
        October, 1883.

CONTENTS.

LIST OF ILLUSTRATIONS.

COLOURED PLATES.

ENGRAVINGS.

P.T.Mallings Boghandel.
G.Kr.Johs.Parmann.

J. Nordhagen del.
J.E.Irions Tryk.

Carl Bock

TEMPLES AND ELEPHANTS.

CHAPTER I.

At Singapore—Down the Malay coast—First glimpse of Siam—
Entering the Menam River—Paknam—Temples and Telegraphs
—Phrachedees—Bangkok from the river—Scene on the Menam
—A visit to the Kromatah—Albinoes—The Kromatah's palace
—A private interview.

In June, 1881, I found myself once more in the East,
sweltering in the moist heat of the island settlement
of Singapore, and longing for the signal for the
steamship *Kongsee* to start, hoping that her progress through the motionless air might in some
degree compensate for the absence of the slightest
breath of wind to temper the fierce rays of the equa-
torial sun. The shimmering sea seemed to intensify
rather than alleviate, as the presence of water
usually does, the oppressiveness of the atmosphere,
for its glassy surface, like a polished mirror, reflected
the bright light of the sun and seemed to focus his
rays as in a lens.

My only cabin companion was Senhor Prostes, the
newly-appointed Portuguese consul for Siam, who was
just about to take up his duties at the capital of the
Lord of the White Elephant. But in the forepart of
the vessel was a motley crew: Hindoos from Madras,
mostly tailors by profession; Chinese coolies going in
search of fortune among their co-religionists in Siam;

B

Burmese, tattooed all over in grotesque designs of
red and blue, bent on seeking wealth, but with the
greater probability of finding death, in the pestilential
climate of the famous sapphire-mines of Chantaboon;
with a sprinkling of Malays to complete the mixture.

As we skirted the eastern coast of the Malay
Peninsula, bound for the quaint and fascinating city
of Bangkok, Captain Uldall, accomplished sailor and
gentleman, pointed out the most prominent landmarks.

All the way up, the distant backbone of the long
tongue of land, ever varying in outline, and forming
a rich setting for the tamer foreground of the coast,
afforded a pleasing panorama. Four days' steaming
brought us to the mouth of the River Menam—or, to
give it its full name, Chow Phya Menam [1]—when a
pilot came aboard to take us over the treacherous bar,
and steer us through the myriad fish-stakes and traps
which fringe the shoals and banks like so many *chevaux
de frise*. The bar passed, we came to a small island in
the river, upon which is built a Wat, or temple, called
" Paknam Phra Che die Samundh Aprakan," whose gilt
spires, surrounded by those of several phrachedees or
topes, towering far above the tree-tops, shone resplendent in the evening sun. I felt that I was at last in the
land of Temples and Elephants, the land where sober
truth and strange fiction are so curiously interwoven
that it is often difficult to distinguish the one from the
other.

The first glimpse of Siam which the traveller obtains
at Paknam is a fair sample of what is to be seen pretty
well throughout the country. As Constantinople is
called the City of Mosques, so Bangkok may, with even
more reason, be termed the City of Temples. And not
in Bangkok only and its immediate neighbourhood,

[1] *Chow* = prince ; *Phya* = chief ; *Me* = mother ; *Nam* = water.

but in the remotest parts of the country, wherever
a few people live now, or ever have lived, a Wat
with its image, or collection of images, of Buddha, is
to be found, surrounded by numberless phrachedees,
those curious structures which every devout Buddhist
—and all Buddhists are in one sense or another
devout—erects at every turn as a means of gaining
favour with the deity, or of making atonement for his
sins. On the rich plains, in the recesses of the forests,
on the tops of high mountains, in all directions, these
monuments of universal allegiance to a faith which,
more perhaps than any other, claims a devotee in
almost every individual inhabitant of the lands over
which it has once obtained sway, are to be found.
The labour, the time, and the wealth lavished upon
these structures are beyond calculation. At Paknam
alone, as the steamer passes by, and temple after
temple opens to the view, the effect of the flashing
spires of gold is bewildering. The place is a favourite
resort of pilgrims, who go thither at the commencement of the dry season, taking with them offerings of
gold and other treasures, with which the priests are
enabled to keep up the decorations. Besides the tall
gilded spires, there is evidence of profuse expenditure
in the black-varnished doors, picked out with gold,
and decorated with gilded figures; and in the marble
flooring with which the whole of the temple-grounds
are paved.

" *Très magnifique !* " exclaimed my fellow-passenger
in raptures. " *Très magnifique !* "—and very magnificent was this little illustration of Siam as it is.
But, while at the temple at Paknam we have this
glimpse of what Siam has been and is, we have in an
adjoining institution a foretaste of what, in some
perhaps not distant future, Siam will be.

Opposite the temple, on the left bank of the river, are the custom-house, and, more notable still, the telegraph-office, whence information obtained from incoming vessels—for we are yet twenty-five miles from Bangkok—is sent to the king and other government officials for their private use. This is the first introduction into Siam of the electric telegraph, that destroyer of ancient prejudices, that leveller of the walls of mystery and ignorance and self-concealment which have so long surrounded the greater part of the Asian continent. This little line of five-and-twenty miles, however, is now being connected overland with the submarine cable at Saigon, and before the end of the present year (1883) Bangkok will be in regular telegraphic communication with the rest of the world— not the least of the results of the wise and enlightened policy which the present ruler of Siam has adopted ever since his accession to supreme authority.

Five miles above Paknam is Paklat-lang, on the western bank of the river, at the entrance to a canal which reduces by one half the rest of the distance— some twenty miles by river—to Bangkok. At present, however, this canal is only available for small boats, and we had to follow the sinuous course of the Menam. Arrived off the capital, we were boarded by two custom-house officers—a Siamese and a Chinese—who performed their duties very courteously towards the only two European passengers, but had to adopt a minute system of search among the other visitors, especially the Chinese, who are adepts in the art of smuggling opium and other contraband articles.[2]

[2] The import duties are not high, and yield nothing like so much to the revenue as the export duties, the export trade being greatly in excess of the import trade. The principal export duty is on rice —viz. 4 ticals (1 tical = 2*s.* 6*d.*) per picul (= 133⅓ lbs.) on cleaned

Immediately on landing I called upon the English consul, Mr. Newman, who with Mr. Gould, the first interpreter to the consulate, accompanied me on a visit to the Kromatah, or foreign minister, who resides in a spacious palace a short distance up the river. The roads being bad in Bangkok, especially during the rainy season, locomotion is mostly by boat, and, as the city extends for miles on both banks, the river is a busy highway, while numerous small canals serve as side-streets for conveying the traffic at different points into the interior of the city. Many roads have been constructed during the last few years, it is true, by the king's order, but they are all below the flood-level of the country, the city being built on the edge of a great alluvial plain, which is inundated during the rainy season, so that the roads will have to be raised to be of any permanent advantage. A certain sum of money—viz. that derived from the taxes on houses of ill fame, which the king will not allow to go into the treasury—is set aside for the purpose of constructing

rice, and half that duty on paddy. I was informed that the revenue from this tax alone is over 200,000*l.* a year, for the collection of which the Kromatah, or minister for foreign affairs, is responsible, receiving a percentage of ten per cent. It would be to the interest of the country if an efficient custom-house service were organized, similar to the Chinese Maritime Customs. On other articles of export, such as timber, dried fish—the famous *pla-heng* and *pla-salit*, of which enormous cargoes are exported—&c., a duty of three per cent. *ad valorem* is imposed. On certain articles, such as sugar, silk, cotton, pepper, salt fish (*pla-tu*), salt, tobacco, wax, &c., "inland" duties are levied, and these are exempt from export duties. The government derives a considerable revenue from the monopolies of salt, sugar, and opium, the last of which is the most important. Opium is also retailed out by the government officials. The late ex-regent received a commission of ten per cent. on the receipts. A monopoly almost equally remunerative with that of opium is the pork farm monopoly, *i.e.* the right to kill and sell pork, of which the Siamese and Chinese alike are very fond.

and keeping the roads in repair. In the meantime, until the level of the roads is raised, travellers will do well to keep to the river, and pay their visits from place to place by boat.

As a consequence of this, as well as of the desire among the European and wealthier native residents to avoid the not too savoury smells of the interior of the city, houses on the banks of the river are in great request, and house-rents there are accordingly high.

The view of Bangkok from the river, and the scene on the river itself, are both very striking. From the centre of the broad deep stream stand out the tall masts of large English steamers, their huge hulls towering far above the largest of the native craft that ply between them and the shore. Along the shore may be seen, in rows five or six deep—the inner row moored to the bank, and the outer ones connected with it by planks, or two or three bamboos lashed together, which serve as gangways—the native boats, with their deck-house covered in with a semicircular roof, under which the boatman and his family make their permanent home ; while beyond these, on either bank, as far as the eye can reach, stretches a wide expanse of the sloping roofs of the native houses, the monotony relieved at short intervals by the glittering spires of temples and phrachedees, or the pinnacles of the royal palaces, rearing their heads high above everything. There are said to be over 100 temples in the city, besides innumerable phrachedees, and on a sunny day the effect of the glistening towers, many of them gilt to the very top, is very beautiful.

The river itself is by no means a " silent highway." Here, in front of the residence of Mr. Alabaster, the king's interpreter, is a sort of aquatic Covent Garden market, where dozens of small skiffs are flitting about,

" manned" by one or two women, always in tight-fitting
white jackets, whose faces are barely seen beneath the
broad-brimmed hats of palm-leaves or straw, but whose
voices are resonant in all directions, bargaining with
their customers, and disposing of their fruit and
vegetables, their firewood, and varied up-country
produce. Scattered here and there are floating
Chinese eating-shops, little boats where John Chinaman sells for a few cents a frugal meal of curried
rice, boiled vegetables, bits of pork, or dried fish and
cakes.

Then there are the private pleasure-boats, shaped
like gondolas, in which languid officials or business
agents, forgetting for the time the cares of duty, take
the air in the approved Bangkok fashion on the river ;
for although the river-banks are fringed with green,
and the temple-grounds are always full of choice ever-
green trees, and even the narrow streets are often lined
with groves of cocoa-palms, betelnut-trees, plantains,
and other tropical growth, and the interspaces between
the houses are filled with clumps of vegetation, there
are no public parks or gardens, and the city finds in
the river its only " lungs." The king's garden is thrown
open once a week to the public, and an excellent
native band plays all the afternoon, but there is
nowhere for the few European and American ladies
to display their toilets, unless the minister for foreign
affairs or some other official takes compassion on them
and gives a ball or a garden-party. Boating is consequently the only chance of getting a little fresh air,
and nearly every one keeps a boat, with at least one
boatman in his regular employment. For visitors, boats
are supplied at the hotel—there is, by the way, only one
hotel, the " Oriental," now existing in Bangkok—at a
fixed charge of two dollars a day for a " four-chow rua,"

i.e. a four-oared boat, and half that sum for a "two-chow rua." The tide is very strong, and the boatmen have adopted a curious mode of rowing, by which they claim to gain greater power while going against stream. The rowlocks are very high, elevated as if on stilts, and the oarsman stands to his work, instead of sitting, and with his face to the prow, instead of facing the stern of the boat, so that he has to push instead of "pulling" his oars through the water.

In this style we went up to the Kromatah's palace, where, after waiting a quarter of an hour, we were led first through a series of large and lofty rooms, then into a long, narrow yard, filled with men, women, and children, apparently gathered there with the express object of staring at us. This yard contained quite a number of cages with live birds and animals, among which I noticed two fine white monkeys and a white crow. Albinoes seem to be quite the rage in this land where the "white" or albino elephant is a sacred animal. Turning to the left, we were ushered into a room with an elevated platform near the centre, the steps of which were of a fine dark wood, somewhat resembling rosewood, most beautifully polished; while from this platform sprang three magnificent and highly polished pillars, of the same rare and costly wood, supporting the ceiling. Although this wood was so hard that, his Excellency said, the Chinese would not touch it, the carving of these pillars had been executed by the Kromatah's native workmen.

His Excellency the Kromatah was a stout, well-built man of about fifty years of age; somewhat pock-marked, but with a pleasant face, the effect of which was, to European eyes, marred by his betel-stained teeth. I had expected to find him in a sort of semi-state; instead of which he was in a semi-nude state, with nothing but a cloth round his loins, while a slave was rubbing his arm and hand, and washing it with lemon juice, reminding me of the *pitcha* business of the Malays.[3] The minister, it appears, was suffering from the diplomatic complaint, the gout, and this was his bedroom.

On the raised platform stood an English brass bedstead, contrasting strangely with the rich native woodwork. Along the walls were various cabinets filled with all sorts of curiosities—quite a well-stocked museum—which his Excellency had collected in London on the occasion of his visit in 1880 to confer on the Queen and the Prince of Wales the handsome insignia of the Order of the White Elephant. It was somewhat embarrassing to make my first acquaintance with the powerful minister under these circumstances, but Mr. Newman assured me that it was a great favour to be received *sans cérémonie* in "private audience." Cigars and tea were handed round in Siamese fashion, but of course I did not stay longer than was necessary to explain to the minister the object of my visit to Siam, and to solicit an audience of the king, which he promised to ask his Majesty to grant.

[3] See my "Head-Hunters of Borneo."

CHAPTER II.

An audience of the king—The new palace and the old—Prince
Devan, the king's brother—A royal Amazon—A whiff of royal
tobacco—In the throne-room—The king's policy—Abolition of
slavery—The king's biography—His native and European
advisers—A big dose of medicine—Royal favours.

Two days later a note came from Mr. Newman,
that his Majesty would receive me at four p.m. So at
the hour appointed, with the consul to introduce me,
I alighted at the gates of the old palace.

Adjoining the old building is the new palace, called
the Chakr Kri Maha Prasat, the erection of which
has long been a favourite scheme of his Majesty, who
last year took formal possession of the building. The
style is a mixture of different schools of European
architecture, the picturesque and characteristic Siamese
roof, however, being retained. The internal fittings
of this palace are on a most elaborate scale, the most
costly furniture having been imported from London
at an expense of no less than 80,000*l.* One of the
features of the palace is a large and well-stocked
library, in which the king takes great interest—all
the leading European and American periodicals
and newspapers being regularly taken in.

Here the king transacts all state business, assisted
by his brother and private secretary, Prince Devawongsa
—usually called Prince Devan. These two are probably the hardest-worked men in the country:

To face page 11.

H.R.H. PRINCE DEVAWONGSA VAROPRAKAR.

[*To face page* 11.

nothing is too great or too trivial to escape the king's notice. A friend of mine who has had many opportunities of observing the king's actions, writes to me: "Every officer of any importance is compelled to report in person at the palace, and the entire affairs of the kingdom pass in detail before his Majesty daily. Although the king is obliged through policy to overlook, or pretend not to see, very many abuses in the administration of his government, yet they do not escape his eye, and in some future time will come up for judgment."

Prince Devan is the king's right hand, and well deserves the confidence reposed in him by his royal brother, discharging with great tact and ability the responsible duties which devolve upon him in his double capacity of private secretary and Chancellor of the Exchequer. Though quite young, he has the character of being as cool and reflective as many older heads, and his general intelligence is matched by his polite and kindly demeanour to all who have occasion to see him on business or in private life.

Inside the palace-gates were a number of soldiers in complete European uniform, *minus* the boots, which only the officers are allowed to wear. At the head of the guard, inside the palace-gates, is the king's aunt, who is always "on duty," and never allows any one to pass without a proper permit. Passing through a long succession of courts and courtyards, past a series of two-storied and white-washed buildings—the library, museum, barracks, mint, &c., all of which are conveniently placed within the palace-grounds—we were led to an open pavilion, furnished with chairs and tables of European manufacture, in which two court officers, neatly dressed in the very becoming court suit, consisting of a snow-white jacket with gold buttons, a "pa-nung"[1] or scarf, so folded round the body as to resemble knickerbockers, with white stockings, and buckled shoes. While waiting here we were regaled with tea and cigars, and Siamese "burees," or cigarettes, made from tobacco grown on the king's own plantation, and wrapped in the leaf of the lotus-flower, which imparts a curious fragrance to the smoke. Presently an aide-de-camp—one of the king's brothers—dressed in a neatly embroidered uniform, came to lead us to the king's presence. He took us first through the throne-room, the entrance to which was up a fine marble staircase, lined with beautiful palms, ferns, and flowering plants, amid which stood fine bronzes and rich candelabras. The room itself was a long chamber, containing many fine oil paintings, and an array of splendid ornaments, amongst which I recognized bronze busts of several European sovereigns; but we passed so quickly through that I could not take in any details. Adjoining this was the drawing-room, a stately and spacious saloon, furnished entirely in the European style in the most luxurious manner. As we entered I saw, at the opposite end of the room, his Majesty Chulalonkorn, King of Siam and Lao[2]—a very handsome man, of about thirty years of age, slim of figure and very erect, with a very fair complexion for a Siamese, and beautiful dark, beaming eyes—who, as we stopped to make the customary triple bow, advanced to meet us, his hand extended in greeting to Mr. Newman. As my companion introduced me, his Majesty shook hands, and invited us to be seated

---

[1] The *pa-nung* or *palai* is a garment, common throughout Siam and Lao, consisting of a strip of cloth or other material, fastened round the waist, with the end hanging, petticoat-fashion, so as to reach to the knees. *Vide infra.*

[2] A portrait of his Majesty appears in the frontispiece.

on chairs near the middle of the room, while he sat on a sofa which stood on an elevated platform near the wall. The abolition of the old etiquette, which required all who entered the august presence of the sovereign to prostrate themselves before him, was one of the first acts of the king on his accession in 1868, and all ranks and classes are now admitted freely to audience with the king, and may approach him standing erect.

Petitions to the king are generally presented personally—people watching an opportunity when his Majesty promenades in the palace-grounds.

In every respect his policy has been a progressive one, and he has spared no effort to increase the happiness and prosperity of his people. The greatest act of his Majesty's reign has probably been the abolition of slavery in his immediate dominions. The emancipation began to take effect in 1872, and is still being carried out by degrees. The children of slaves are free.[3] For this, if for no other reason, whether or not he is enabled to carry to a successful issue the important series of reforms in other matters, which he has

---

[3] All Siamese princes and officials, high and low, are surrounded with a large *entourage*, not of slaves, but of " slave-debtors," persons whose services are retained under much the same conditions as those known under the name of *pandelinge* in the Malay Archipelago. See my " Head-Hunters of Borneo," page 203 :—" ' Slave-debtor ' is the term applied to a servant who has got into his master's debt ; if he cannot pay the debt, the master may hand him over to another master, who pays the debt for him, and the servant then becomes . indebted to his new master in the amount so paid, and is called a ' slave-debtor,' giving his services till the debt is worked off. This very rarely happens ; on the contrary, the servant generally contrives to add to the amount of his indebtedness, and lives in a perpetual state of semi-bondage, with which his indolent nature fully harmonizes. I have seldom seen a slave-debtor discontented with his lot." These remarks apply to the Siamese " slave-debtors " as well.

initiated since the supreme control of the affairs of
state fell into his hands, he will well deserve the title
of " Good," or " Great."

His Majesty's full name[1] is " Phra Bat Somdeth
Phra Paramindr Maha Chulalonkorn Phra Chula
Chom Klao Chow Yu Hua," and this appellation is far
exceeded in length by the full list of the royal
official, and ceremonial titles, " Lord of the White
Elephant," &c.

The ninth child of his father and predecessor on
the throne King Mongkut, or, to give him his full
name, Somdeth Phra Paramindr Maha Mongkut, who
was himself a great scholar and an illustrious example
of an Oriental monarch, Chulalonkorn has profited
by the liberal education which his father was careful
to give him, and, with a mind fully impressed by the
advantages which only a large and varied store of
knowledge can afford, he has striven to give practical
effect to the ideas which a wide acquaintance with
Western civilization had early instilled in him ; and
his reign has opened a new era in the progress of
Siam. The education of his early days was entrusted
to an American lady, Mrs. Leonowens, while later
Captain John Bush, the present harbour-master of
Bangkok—a genial kind-hearted gentleman—had a
large share in shaping the mind of the future king,
and exercised a beneficent influence which his Majesty
has not been slow to recognize, and to reward by
many honours and other marks of favour.

Born on the 22nd of September, 1853, he was only
fifteen years of age when he came to the throne, and
during his minority his Highness the Somdeth Chow
Phya Boromaha Sri Suriwongse—an able and upright
statesman, the head of the most powerful noble family

[1] See chapter on Siamese titles, &c., in the appendix.

in the country, which practically rules the greater portion of the Western part of Siam —acted as regent : his only son is the prime minister or " Kalahome," who, however, has not inherited his father's great talent as a politician, nor has he any of the administrative ability for which the regent was noted, both in and out of Siam. One of the ex-regent's half-brothers is the Kromatah.

I had the honour of paying a visit to his Highness the ex-Regent during my stay in Bangkok, when he was in the seventy-fourth year of his age. Since my return to Europe his death has been announced, an event which will have caused the keenest grief to the king, and universal regret throughout Siam.

An important reform of administrative detail adopted by the king has been to encourage the princes and officers of the "Sanabodi," or council of state, to submit their opinions to him in writing, a practice which previous monarchs would have resented as an intrusion. In these and similar matters the king is a century in advance of his people ; but he is making the most strenuous efforts to bring his subjects up to his own level, by encouraging education, and granting the most liberal facilities for the prosecution of every form of research. For several years past he has sent a number of young Siamese noblemen to England, France, and Germany, to be educated at his own expense, in order that their own ideas might become enlarged by contact with Western civilization ; and one of his younger brothers, Prince Swatisobohn, is at the present moment being educated at Oxford.

Although the king shows great favour to Europeans, he does not display any undue predilection for them, and only avails himself of their assistance so far as their services are indispensable, and as a means of leavening the mass of native officialdom. Of the few Europeans in the personal service of the king, one, and perhaps the most intimately acquainted with his Majesty, has already been mentioned, viz. Captain John Bush. Another is Mr. Henry Alabaster, whose advice on the foreign relations of the state is held in high esteem, owing to his profound scholarship, his experience in the consular service, and, not least, his upright character. Dr. Gowan, the king's European physician, is also more of a friend than a mere professional adviser; and lastly, Captain Richelieu, who commands the royal yacht, *Vesatri*, is also a personal friend of his Majesty.

The example of the sovereign has not been without its effect on the minds of his native advisers, and the princes and officials by whom he is surrounded are rapidly developing enlightened ideas. This is the more important since many of the highest offices are hereditary, and there is consequently not the same scope for the choice by the king of men after his own heart which he would have if the appointments were at his free disposal. As one instance out of many, I may mention the case of his Highness Chow Sai, the king's body-physician (one of the last offices that one would suppose to be hereditary!). Chow Sai is one of those princes who are favourably disposed towards Europeans; he is well read, and some years ago sent his eldest son to be thoroughly educated for the medical profession in Scotland, where he has, I believe, just taken his M.D. degree. Chow Sai's father, by the way, was a great believer in European medicines—especially Holloway's pills—of which he ordered the enormous quantity of ten piculs, or over 1330 lbs., of which there is still a large stock left, with their qualities, no doubt, unimpaired.

But to return to my audience with this enlightened ruler. Asking us to be seated on chairs near the centre of the room, his Majesty sat down on a sofa which stood against the wall on an elevated platform, and at once asked Mr. Newman the object of my visit. With one exception the king spoke always in Siamese —and always, I may add, very loud—and Mr. Newman, who is a profound Siamese scholar, having been over twenty years in the country, had to translate his words into English for me. But there was no necessity for him to interpret my words to the king, who both speaks and writes the English language with ease. It is not etiquette, however, for him to speak in any other than his native tongue, and the only English words he uttered during the interview were when Mr. Newman explained that I was a traveller and a naturalist, anxious to see the country, to explore as far to the north as possible, to study the races, and collect specimens of the fauna. " Oh! a naturalist," exclaimed his Majesty, addressing me, and then, as if suddenly recollecting himself, resumed the conversation in Siamese, asking questions about the fauna of other countries. This led to an inquiry as to my nationality, and he seemed somewhat surprised when he heard I was a Norwegian, as I had a letter of introduction from Lord Granville : and the next question, " Did I not find it very hot in the East ? " brought up a reference to my previous travels in Borneo and Sumatra, about which he made minute inquiries, evincing a very close acquaintance with the position of affairs in those islands. His Majesty a few years ago made two trips abroad ; first to Singapore, Batavia, and Samarang in Java, and later on to Singapore again, thence to Malacca, Penang, Moulmein, Rangoon, Calcutta, and Bombay—visiting all the places of interest in India, including Benares—

C

his object being to make himself acquainted with the
neighbouring states, and to introduce reforms into his
own country, which has already reaped the fruits of his
enlightened method of government, and of the many
improvements he has inaugurated. Coming to my intended journey in Siam and Lao, he promised to grant
me every facility ; and gave instructions to his brother
that I should be allowed to see anything and everything
I wanted. Thanking his Majesty for the honour of
the interview and for his promised assistance, I then
bowed and retired, the king shaking me by the hand,
and again promising to afford me every assistance in
my projected journey into the interior.

When passing out through the throne-room, one of
the princes stopped me and said I must write my name,
together with the date of my birthday, in a book kept
for the purpose.

CHAPTER III.

The king's elephant stables—Royal tuskers—The white elephants—
A real white elephant—Reception of the distinguished stranger
—The astrologers—The insignia of Siamese nobility—A motley
crowd—The Siamese troops—The royal body-guard—An elephant on the rampage—The procession of the sacred pachyderm—
Christening the white elephant—Taking his portrait—The "lord
of the elephants"—How the white elephant was caught—Native
art and artists—Historic elephants—A sham white elephant.

ON the way back to the hotel I stopped to see the royal
elephant stables. Each animal—there were nine altogether—has a separate building to itself. Two of them,
which are driven out only on state occasions, are
celebrated for their enormous tusks, the points of which
cross each other and reach to the ground.

All the elephants wore heavy chains on their feet,
and were so hobbled that they could only move a few
inches; but we were warned not to go too near, as they
were apt to be savage with strangers, although they
had been over fifty years in captivity. I inquired for
the world-renowned white elephants, and Mr. Newman
pointed out two which were lighter in colour than the
others and had a few white spots on the ears. The
difference was so slight as to be hardly appreciable;
but I was informed that news had just been received
of the capture up-country of a real white elephant,
which was expected to arrive shortly.

The 21st of June was the date fixed for the actual
reception of this white elephant in Bangkok, and great
preparations were made for the *fête*, the king with a

numerous suite going some days in advance to Ayuthia, the ancient capital of Siam, to meet the illustrious and sacred beast.[1] Early in the morning of that day all Bangkok was in a state of the greatest excitement, authentic particulars received from Ayuthia having corroborated the rumours about the purity of colour of this latest addition to the Siamese emblems of royalty and divinity.

The astrologers had prophesied that his Majesty's reign would be exceptionally lucky, and that several white elephants would be caught, and they were right. Two or three white—or, as I should call them, " spotted "—elephants had already been caught, and now, to crown all, one of pure colour was to make its triumphal entry into the city.

The authority of the astrologers was accordingly in high repute, and, as the people were to share in the " luck " of the king, they were in the highest spirits, and the 21st of June would long remain a red-letter day in the annals of the country. These astrologers, or " Hones," have in times past played an important part in the history of Siam, and hold a high place in the estimation of the mass of the people. They are exempt from punishments of all kinds, and they are consequently in a position to exert a powerful influence for good or for evil upon a weak monarch. The present king, being a good Buddhist, and attached to the religion

[1] The sanctity of a white elephant dates from the earliest period of Buddhist history. Indra himself rode on a *three*-headed elephant. When Gaudama entered the womb of the queen to be born upon earth for the last time, it was in the form of an elephant, and, as albinoes are supposed to have sovereignty over their race (see p. 166), a " white " elephant, however few the pale spots he may have, is revered throughout the breadth and length of the land. One of the King of Siam's proudest titles, as is well known, is " Lord of the White Elephant."

of his forefathers, adheres to the old custom of "consult-ing the oracle," though he is entirely free from vulgar superstition, and retains the services of eight of these "wise men," more for the sake of their opinions on political events, upon which he frequently seeks their advice, than with the object of availing himself of their "prophetic" power.

Mr. Newman having kindly sent me a note, with a programme of the probable ceremony, I started early for the palace-grounds, at the gates of which I met one of the royal princes—one of the "real ones," as Captain Köbke whispered to me, *i.e.* a full brother of the king—being carried in a litter, in full state uni-form, a violet-coloured tunic embroidered with gold, his breast covered with decorations, and a huge gilt umbrella held over his head by an attendant, while another servant walked in front, bearing in outstretched hands a small bundle of rattans, an emblem of royal rank, reminding me of the *fasces* of the ancient Romans. More servants followed, carrying the usual array of betel-boxes, water-goblets, &c., which every grandee in Siam displays [2] whenever taking part in a

[2] No Siamese moves from his house, whether for a walk, or to make an offering at the temple, or to pay a visit, without two or more —it may be a dozen or more—"slave-debtors," according to his rank, carrying as the indispensable insignia of office, or of social rank, not only his umbrellas, but his betel and tobacco-boxes, tea-pot, &c., and, I believe, always in one of the betel or tobacco-boxes, his seal, for the Siamese attach great importance to seals, which take the place of signatures in Western civilization. These seals are mostly made of ivory, in the shape of a phrachedee, the devices represent-ing a Hoalaman or a Rachasee, an angel or a lotus-flower, &c., &c. No sealing-wax is used with these seals, but always a vermillion-red dye. If the master stops on the road, his cavalcade with their betel-boxes, umbrellas, &c. all sit down on the ground on their haunches at a respectful distance ; and when he enters a house these servants sit outside on the ground, or on the steps, or even in the verandah, some of them always quite near to overhear the conversation.

state-procession, or paying a visit of ceremony. Crowds of people came flocking towards the centre of attraction. In the palace-grounds were stationed soldiery in groups of threes and fours, while palace-officials, all excitement, hurried hither and thither on horseback, making the final arrangements for the reception of the illustrious pachyderm.

After watching for a while the streams of people, Captain Köbke suggested our walking down to the river to see the elephant disembark. As we approached the landing-stage we found the road lined with infantry and marines, all dressed in uniforms of European pattern, the marines especially striking me by their soldier-like bearing and smart appearance, and reflecting the greatest credit on Captain Richelieu, who has trained them and created this branch of the Siamese service. Then came the king's body-guard, both the old and the new corps, the former dressed in parti-coloured jackets and trousers of print, and with huge round hats, many of them carrying old flags and streamers; the latter, a much more military-looking body, with European uniforms.[3]

The ostensible object of the presence of the soldiery was of course to keep the road clear; but this duty was for a time very satisfactorily performed by a huge elephant, a splendid tusker, magnificently attired in gold trappings, which had been brought down to join the royal cavalcade, but did not appreciate all the ceremonies, and was showing off a bit of his not very small stock of bad temper. The carnac, or driver, was quite unable to control the beast, which roared and

[3] The Chinese and European army-tailors are continually hitting upon new designs and patterns for the clothing for the army, in which, it struck me, there must be an endless number of regiments, if the variety of uniforms is to be taken as a guide.

trumpeted his indignation, and every now and then filled his trunk with dust, blowing it out again with such fury that the carnac, to avoid the possibility of accident, led him aside into an enclosed yard.

Just beyond the king's body-guard was stationed a detachment of artillery, with field-guns and the king's favourite gatlings, and we were close to the river-bank when we met a number of natives, dressed in white, with tall sugar-loaf hats, with a broad gold band round. These were Brahmins, terrestrial angels, who, having satisfied all the requirements of the Buddhist faith, have attained the highest sphere of spiritual life in the flesh.

At that moment the brass band began to play the national anthem, so we stood back at the side of the roadway to watch the procession pass. Following the brass band came a band of Siamese musicians, dressed from head to foot in scarlet, and playing tom-toms, conk shells (a species of *fusus*) and other discordant instruments. Then the state-elephants, headed by three splendid tuskers, with trappings of gold, which shone resplendent in contrast with their lustreless skins, and bearing on their backs richly decorated gilt howdahs. Behind these came a few of the king's body-guard, the heralds, chamberlains, and other officials, and then his Majesty, carried—the king never rides, I was told—on a litter-chair, richly gilt, and inlaid with mother-of-pearl, on which he sat cross-legged, and sheltered beneath a huge gilt umbrella, the shade of which was needed that day beneath the scorching rays of the sun.

The king wore a white India helmet, and a coat of crimson and gold, the gold predominating, his breast covered with orders. His Majesty looked extremely well, and as I saluted him he acknowledged the

obeisance with a nod and a military salute. There
was no cheering among the crowd, the national and only
mode of salutation being to raise the hands together to
the forehead two or three times, bending the body at
the same time, and always to superiors using the word
" khorab " (equivalent to " obedience "), or " chow "
(prince)—this latter word being used even if the person
is not a Chow, but a high official. In Bangkok the
natives can now make their salutation erect, but

The king's gold betel service, &c.

throughout the country and in Lao, every one prostrates himself before his superiors.

Behind his Majesty followed a number of pages and
attendants, carrying a splendid array of rich gold
betel-boxes, teapots, &c., besides a number of presents,

to be distributed amongst the people, and especially the priesthood, in honour of this auspicious event. Then— amid a crowd of princes and dignitaries who brought up the rear, and among whom was conspicuous the Lord of the Elephants, H.R.H. Chow Fah Maha Mala,[4] uncle of the king, and, after his Majesty, the most important personage in the kingdom, upon whom had fallen the charge of all the arrangements connected with the reception of the white elephant—came the hero of the day, the white elephant himself, in company with three others, all so-called "white elephants," in comparison with which he certainly deserved the proud title. Were I to describe him as *white*, I should lay myself open to the charge of colour-blindness; but he was quite an albino, the whole body being of a pale reddish-brown colour, with a few real white hairs on the back. The iris of the eye, the colour of which is held to be a good test of an albino, was a pale Naples yellow. He looked peaceful enough, led, not ridden, by his carnac, and his quiet bearing was in great contrast with the excitement all around, as if he felt the importance of his position.

Hurrying forward, I now made the best of my way to the temporary shed or open stable erected for the reception of the elephant, just outside the palace-grounds.

Here he would be kept for about a couple of months, by which time, when sufficiently clean and devoid of devils, he would be allowed within the precincts of the palace. Here the animal was led on to a platform, and then fastened by a rope round his hind-leg to a white pole, H.R.H. Chow Fa Maha Mala closely supervising the operations.

Then came the ceremony of blessing and baptizing

[4] Also Minister of the north of Siam and Lao.

the beast, in presence of the king and all the nobility.
One of the high priests presented him with a piece of
sugar-cane on which was written the elephant's name
in full, and which the elephant very readily ate, although he had already been fed to such an excess on
sugar-cane that the natives said he had the " stomach-
ache;" at any rate he certainly had a touch of diar-
rhœa. Then on one of the pillars of the stall was
hung a red tablet with the name painted in gilt
letters in Siamese characters, so that all could read it.
A friend kindly gave me a transcript of this name in
good English characters, which I here reproduce for
the benefit of my readers :—

" Phra Sawet Sakonla Warophat ake udom chat
visute thi mongkon sri sama sakon loma naka net
adisaya sawet viset san komon la phan prom kra
khoon paramintara narane soon siamma tirat pha
hana nat mahan tadet kotchera ratana phiset chaloem
phop kiet kachon chop charoen sak phra chak phon
parun vibun sawat akka nakin ratana phra soet loet fa."

But, I shall be asked, what does all this mean?
His Highness Prince Prisdang, Siamese Minister to
England, has kindly translated the name into good
English as follows. It will be seen that its name is
really a description of the animal :—

" An elephant of beautiful colour ; hair, nails, and
eyes are white. Perfection in form, with all signs of
regularity of the high family. The colour of the skin
is that of lotus. A descendant of the angel of the
Brahmins. Acquired as property by the power and
glory of the king for his service. Is equal to the
crystal of the highest value. Is of the highest family
of elephants of all in existence. A source of power of
attraction of rain. It is as rare as the purest crystal
of the highest value in the world."

I applied to H.R.H. Chow Fa Maha for permission to make a coloured drawing of the white elephant, which he courteously granted, requesting me to be at the stable on the 27th, at eight in the morning, when he would be there to meet me. With his usual punctuality, the prince was there to the moment, superintending the six attendants while they washed the "Phra" elephant, by pouring tamarind-water over him, after which they brushed him with hair brushes. I noticed the attendants paid the animal great respect, and generally approached him on their knees with folded hands.

The elephant had for a companion in the stable a real white monkey,[5] which, however, kept at a respectful distance from him.

While I made my sketch of the elephant, H.R.H. Chow Fa Maha very kindly gave me the history of the capture of the animal, whose age he estimated to be between four and five years. Let me here say that his Royal Highness is *the* authority in Siam on elephants, both white and ordinary ones. One day when I paid him a visit he showed me quite a voluminous literature of elephants, with illustrations of them in all sorts of colours, which he had assiduously collected from many different sources.

Being a devout Buddhist, he has the profoundest belief in the sanctity of the white elephant, and is full of "elephant lore," and his *salon* is decorated with several excellent models of elephants made of clay by a native artist of no mean merit, and mostly either painted or gilded.

His Royal Highness—a powerfully-built man, half Siamese, half Laosian, about sixty years of age—

---

[5] The monkey, the natives think, never dies, but when he gets old he goes up into the air, and lives with the Hoalaman.

is a Siamese of the old school, and does not trouble himself about European etiquette and dress. At the time of my first visit he wore a white jacket with gold buttons and the customary silk pa-nung, but afterwards when I paid him visits he received me in his favourite " undress " costume, sitting naked with only the silk palai round his loins, and showing off his fine physique, smoking a cigar or chewing betel all the time. He is considered a good astronomer, and if he has a weakness for anything of European make it is for watches of all kinds. I was told he had over a hundred, and during one of my visits he showed me a very fine gold chronometer which he had just received, with a self-adjusting calendar, and a dial showing the changes of the moon. This watch was a source of great amusement to the old prince, but he was not quite at home in the mystery of winding it up or regulating it, and before he had had it a week it had to be returned to London for repairs, something being out of order in the machinery.

But to return to the new white elephant. " Phra Sawet Sakonla," &c., &c., &c., had been caught, it appears, as much as three years ago, by two poor men who were out hunting for a white elephant by order of the governor of the province. They had been out for some time in the jungle, and after a while had given up their hunting in despair, when suddenly they came upon this little fellow, all muddy and dirty, and appearing darker than the ordinary colour. One of them said, " We will take him home and give him a wash," which they did, and to their surprise and joy he turned out to be white. The fortunes of these two poor men were now made, for, besides being exempt from taxation, the king ennobled them and loaded them with presents : one received 400 ticals and a grant of 1000 acres of land, while his companion got 240 ticals and 600 acres. At the same time the governor of the province was made a Phya.

A few days later, when I had finished my painting, I took it to show to the prince, who examined it in detail, and then said to Captain Köbke, who accompanied me and acted as interpreter, "A European can paint an elephant." [6] He did not find any fault with the drawing, but a sore point was that the animal was too dark. I told him I wanted to paint the animal true to nature—though Mr. Newman had given me a hint beforehand to paint him as white as possible, in order to please the Siamese. Chow Fa Maha asked me to go with his chamberlain and have a look again at the elephant; this I did, and, to my surprise, I found the attendants

---

[6] Painting is on a low level in Siam. A few so-called artists are to be found, and their talent is employed in making fresco designs in the Wats. These are of a perspectiveless character, *à la chinoise*, and include all sorts of representations of incidents in the life and teachings of Buddha, of the monstrous animals which figure so largely in Siamese legends, such as the Hoalaman and the Rachasee, and of elephants, white as well as black. A Siamese artist, painter to his Majesty, both extraordinary and ordinary, showed me his latest productions, including portraits of the king and the late regent, and a series of elephants, politely informing me that his Majesty had bought several of his *chefs-d'œuvre*, and adding that he intended to send some of his pictures to the "Academy" in London, where he had a brother who could look after his interests. I advised him not to do so, telling him the subjects would not be suited to European eyes and taste. As for his Majesty buying several of his pictures, I am sure this was done merely to encourage the profession, for King Chulalonkorn has, I am convinced, a keen eye for the fine arts, and knows when a picture is out of drawing. But if its "painters" are not very advanced exponents of the art, Bangkok can boast of a sculptor or two of rare talent. Besides Chow Fah Maha Mala, both his Majesty and Prince Kromalat have in their employ native artists who can model and cast an elephant, or a rhinoceros, that would ornament any *salon*, and reflect credit on any sculptor, so true is the anatomy and so bold the modelling.

had really managed to give the animal a much lighter
colour, by washing him daily with tamarind-water;
the chamberlain pointed out several dark patches about
the feet and head, which, he said, would all disappear in
a day or two. So I made a second water-colour
drawing of the elephant as he then appeared, which
is here reproduced, so that my readers can form a
correct idea of a real " white elephant," for this was
acknowledged to be the " fairest " ever caught, at
least within living memory.

In the annals of Siam—translated by that distinguished Siamese scholar, Mr. Samuel Smith—there
are records of real white elephants having been caught,
from which I extract the following :—

" During the reign of Phra Narai, in the year
1658, which corresponds to the Siamese civil era
1020 (year of the cock), his Majesty took a boat-ex-
cursion to Nakhon sawan, and while there was informed by his Excellency P'raya Cakree that Kun
Sri-k'aun charin, of the province Sri-sawat, had reported that, while he was out gathering information
in the forests of Hui sai, Nai Ahnsui had captured a
white she-elephant, over sixty inches high. Her ears,
tail, and general appearance were beautiful. The
capture was made Tuesday, second lunation, second
of the waning. The king gave orders that his Excellency the Governor of Tanahwasee (Tenasserim,
now a British town in the province of the same name),
and all skilled in the management of elephants
should go and bring to him the white elephant. His
Majesty then returned to Ayuthia, the capital, whither
the white elephant was brought Saturday, second
lunation, fifth of the waxing, when a magnificent
boat-procession received her and brought her to a stable
near the royal palace. The king conferred upon his

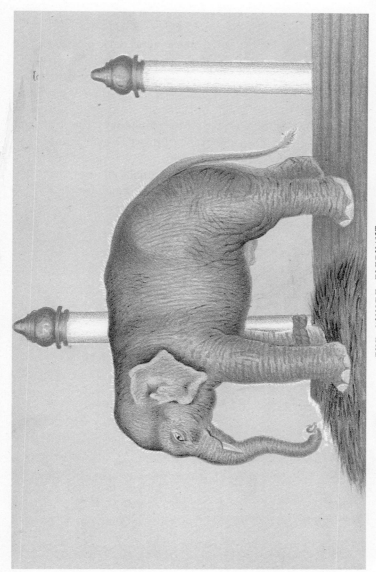

THE WHITE ELEPHANT

distinguished acquisition the following name, 'Phra-
intra - aiyarah - warna - wisutti - rahcha - kirinee.' The
astrologers, sages, princes, ministers, and nobles were
required to make demonstrations of gladness for three
days, after which, beautiful ornaments and utensils
were made for the decoration and use of the white
elephant, and Phra Sri-sittikarn was appointed to care
for the animal. Nai Ahnsui, the son of Kun Sri-k'aun
chahrin, who captured the elephant, received from the
king the title, ' Kun kachen-taun-aiyarah-wisutt-rahch-
kirinee,' a present of a silver box with a gold rim, a
cotton and silk waist-cloth, a silk coat, and ninety-
six dollars, while to his wife the king presented a
silver bowl with lotus-petal rim, a calico waist-
cloth, and eighteen dollars. His Majesty promoted
Kun Sri-k'aun chahrin, the father of Nai Ahnsui, with
the title ' Hluang Sawats Ka chentara,' and presented
to him a silver box inlaid with the figure of an
elephant's ear, and gold ornaments for his box, a
cotton and silk waist-cloth, a silk jacket, and ninety-
six dollars. As Nai Ahnsui, when he captured the elephant, thought her eyes were defective, and was about
to let the precious prize go, his Majesty gave only
such presents to him and his family. To the elephant-
driver, and the elephant-keeper his Majesty made the
presents usually given when a white elephant was
obtained. The bearer of the letter of information
reporting the capture of the animal, and the man
who delivered her, each received a present from the
king. The value of the presents made on this
occasion amounted to 846 dollars. The political
servants who were required to pay their annual quota
of block tin, and who assisted in leading to the capture, and the government servants who had charge of
the white elephants, and who assisted in the present

instance, each received some token of royal favour for their services."

Two years later, in 1660, there is a record of another white elephant—this time a male—being captured. The record runs much the same, except that it says that the Kun Mun who had charge of the beast "diligently taught it till it understood human language, and could do a number of deeds. All who were under sentence of severe penalties for grave offences, and were in prison, and for whom none could have interceded, prepared vows and promised votive offerings to this white elephant, and then presented to the elephant their written petitions. The elephant took those petitions up in his proboscis, raised it in adoration to the king, and presented them to him, and thus entreated for the petitioners' pardon, and out of regard to the lordly beast his Majesty granted to the animal the request of the petitioners."

Soon after the ceremony of receiving the new white elephant a performance of a rather different nature, and with very different motives, took place in the capital. It so happened that "Wilson's English Circus" was visiting Bangkok, and giving a series of performances, some of which had been witnessed by the king, princes, and nobility.

One day the proprietor announced in big posters and hand-bills sown broadcast in Siamese and English that a "real white elephant" would take part in the performance. The curiosity of the people was aroused, and on the evening in question the circus was crowded. After the usual "business" with the trained horses, in which the Siamese had the gratification of seeing European ladies "trip the light fantastic toe" on horseback, dressed in the conventional gauze, two clowns came in and began jesting about the white elephant.

" Have you seen the white elephant?" one asked the other.

" Yes ; of course I have. The king has got a stable full of them."

" Oh, no," was the reply ; " the king ain't got any white ones; his are all chocolate. I will show you the only genuine white elephant in the world:' and in came a small Indian elephant, appearing as white as snow ; not a dark spot could be seen anywhere.

The animal went through his performance, grinding an organ, rolling a tub, and so on; but the secret gradually leaked out. The elephant left white marks on everything he touched. He was chalked all over, and when one of the clowns told the other to " rub his nose against the elephant, and he will leave his mark on you," an ominous silence was maintained by the great mass of the people, only broken here and there by a suppressed titter.

The Siamese, it was plain, were annoyed that fun should be made of their religious beliefs. They did not, however, openly resent the profane performance, but merely expressed their confident belief that the circus-proprietor would be punished by Buddha, and that the elephant would die. And their prophecy came true. The elephant died at sea a few days afterwards, while on the way to Singapore, and Mr. Wilson himself, who had been ill for some time with dysentery, died almost immediately on landing there.

When the Siamese heard this, they said it was a manifestation of Buddha's wrath for the disrespect shown to the sacred white elephant, and I think every one will agree with me that the performance was, to say the least, in very bad taste.

D

CHAPTER IV.

The Wangna or " second king "—A birthday-dinner at his palace—
A Chinese garden—Shooting-fish—Fighting-fish—The Wangna's mother—A visit to the harem—Siamese dress—Taking tea
with a princess.

In striking contrast to his Majesty the King of
Siam is the Wangna [1] or second king, named " George
Washington," after the great American statesman and
first President, of whom his father was a great admirer,
and popularly known among the European residents
as " George." He is a mild-looking Siamese of the
old school, of stout build, and much above the average
stature of Siamese, with a genial face a broad forehead,
and fat cheeks. In the prime of life—about forty-
two years of age—he troubles himself little about poli-
tics, but devotes his time to scientific pursuits, being
a student of minerals, of which he has a fine collection,
and very fond of mechanical engineering, having a
model engine-manufactory, where he showed me a
small steam-engine he had just made. His official
position is that of generalissimo of the Siamese forces
—the duties of which it would be a grief to him ever
to have to perform in actual hostilities.

On the 2nd of July I had the honour of dining at
the palace of the Wangna with the staff of the British
agency, with whom it had been a custom for several
years to give a dinner on that day, in celebration of

[1] *Wangna* means " chief of the palaces of the front."

the birthday of the Wangna's mother, who on that occasion attained her sixty-fourth year.

On arriving at the palace I was conducted to an open gallery, where the Wangna was seated in his formidable armchair at a circular table, with Mr. Palgrave, the British agent, on his right, and Mr. Newman on his left. Here tea and coffee were served, while Mr. Newman performed the duties of interpreter. The gallery overlooked a garden ornamented in grotesque style *à la chinoise,* with trees trimmed to all sorts of fantastic shapes, fish-ponds spanned by quaint Chinese bridges, pagodas, &c. In one of these fish-ponds were kept a number of the curious " shooting fish," a species of *chætodon,* with the remarkable faculty of securing their prey by knocking it down with a drop of water ejected from the mouth. The attendant fed the fish by placing a number of ants on a tree growing in the middle of the pond. A fish at once rose to the surface, shot a drop of water at one of the insects with unerring aim, and, darting forward, caught it in its mouth almost as soon as the ant fell on the surface of the pond. I watched this performance repeated many times, and never once saw a fish miss the mark.

Another piscine curiosity, which affords much amusement to the Siamese, and of which the Wangna had several specimens, is the " fighting fish," a species of so combative a disposition that, like the " fighting cocks," whose combats the Malays are so fond of encouraging and wagering upon—a form of " sport " not wholly unknown in this country—it is only necessary to place two of them in close proximity to each other, and to irritate them, when they will at once charge at each other, with fins erect, and rapidly changing in colour, in the excitement of the combat, from the

dullest of grey-greens to the most brilliant of reds and
blues. Indeed, it does not need confinement in close
quarters to arouse their combative faculties. Place
two glass jars close together with one of these fighting
fish in each, and they will at once swim round and
endeavour to charge each other through the interposed
glass. Even a single fish, seeing himself reflected in
a mirror, will dart at his own image, and, irritated all
the more at his failure to reach his supposed enemy,
will assume the most brilliant hues, and, seeing his
shadowy antagonist doing the same, will redouble his
efforts to reach him.

After showing us these and other curiosities, the
Wangna invited us to go into the harem, and wish his
mother " many happy returns of the day." This unexpected invitation conjured up strange visions of all
the mysterious scenes of beauty and luxury of which I
had heard and read so much. I had known sultans
and rajahs who kept harems well filled with damsels
of all ages and all nationalities, but had never had the
privilege of setting my profane eyes on the jealously-
guarded interior. Even the Sultan of Koetei, whose
intimate friendship I had enjoyed, and with many of
whose secrets I was acquainted, had never allowed me
to invade the precincts of his *sanctum sanctorum.* But
now the second most powerful prince in Siam had
actually, of his own free-will, offered me, a visitor and a
stranger, this privilege ! I had just heard a story about
the Wangna and his harem, which gave additional
interest to the occasion. One day the king asked him
how many wives he had, as he was desirous of presenting each of them with a ring. The Wangna could
not for the moment recall the exact number, so
mentioned fifty, as a good round figure somewhere
near the mark. Fifty handsome rings accordingly

arrived a few days later, as a mark of the sovereign's favour ; but, when the Wangna came to measure fingers and fit rings all round, he found he was four rings short, and sent a polite message to the king to say that he had made a little mistake, having fifty-four wives, the last four of whom would be jealous of the other fifty if they, too, did not have a ring from the king.

However, towards the harem we were conducted, through two halls or antechambers, round the sides of which were a number of females, mostly old and grey-haired, as if to serve as a foil to the galaxy of beauty inside. Then we came to a long, lofty room, which appeared to be a kind of common boudoir or dressing-room for the ladies, for in it were a number of women —this time of less doubtful age—and children, who were undergoing the operation of having their hair dressed and decorated with flowers, the perfume of which was almost overpowering. The left side of this long room was partitioned off by an old but very handsome Chinese screen of carved woodwork, beautifully painted and gilt. Behind that screen, who could tell, perhaps the ladies slept ! The other side of the apartment communicated with a large courtyard. As we passed through this chamber, Mr. Newman whispered that we were approaching the central object of our visit. " But," he added irreverently, " don't deceive yourself by thinking that ' George ' will let you see all his pretty girls. They ought to be there "—pointing in front of us—" but they will be invisible." Here we approached a door leading to a handsomely-decorated apartment, on the floor of which reclined or sat a number of female figures—not with the beauteous faces my ardent imagination had pictured, but with wrinkled cheeks and grey heads. Mr. Newman was right. *The* ladies of the harem had been carefully secluded in antici-

pation of our visit, and replaced by others who a generation, or perhaps two generations, ago had been the concubines of the Wangna's father—if not of his grandfather. Amid them were two persons standing, one a
dignified old lady, with a pleasant smile on her face, the
other, apparently, a boy of about fourteen or fifteen
years of age. The former was the Wangna's mother;
the latter, her youngest daughter, whose slim figure
and short-cut hair gave her the appearance of a boy,
though she could not have been less than about
eighteen years of age.

The women and men, I may here say, dress very
much alike in Siam; and now that the fashion prevails
amongst both sexes to cut their hair short, and
to brush it back, the females often look for all the
world like men. Up the country the men and women
wear the hair in the old style; that is, the men shave
the head, except just from the middle of the forehead
to the crown, while the women do not shave, but keep
the hair cut short. The women often paint the eyebrows and eyelids, to give them a more marked and
distinctive appearance, and both women and men
powder their faces with white, which shows very con-
spicuously on the dark skin.

The main garment worn by both sexes is the *panung*,
a long piece of cotton cloth, or of silk with a gold
border, worn round the waist and passed between the
thighs, the two ends of the cloth being tucked up, one
in front, the other behind. The next indispensable
garment, among both men and women, is the *pahom*,
a long scarf, more than a couple of yards long, and
either white, or of a light pink or yellow colour, which
is passed over one shoulder, or under the arms, and
across the chest in a variety of ways. Many men and
women wear a tight-fitting white jacket of spotless

linen, which contrasts well with their olive complexion. When a jacket is worn, the pahom is thrown over it. Of late years the Siamese of both sexes, among the "upper ten," have taken to wearing white stockings and lacquered shoes, and at parties they even come out in dress suits, but never leave off the national panung. Only the soldiery and the princes in uniform wear trousers, but on state occasions the princes and high officials wear heavy gold-embroidered jackets, generally of blue silk, with patterns woven in gold thread. The Siamese women, like the women in every other part of the globe, are partial to ornaments and jewellery. Earrings are rarely worn, but they have a variety of rings on the fingers, and the rich ladies wear long massive chains of gold across the shoulder and round the waist. Children go naked up to the age of ten, wearing nothing but a silver (or sometimes gold) heart-shaped shield, which is fastened round the body by means of a string so as to cover the *pudenda*, with heavy anklets of silver or gold round the legs, and bracelets round the wrist. Adults and children alike are never without amulets or charms of some sort on the body.

But I am digressing. The Wangna's mother came forward and greeted her visitors with a hearty shake of the hand, while immediately afterwards some slaves entered with silver-gilt trays of bouquets, one of which was presented to each of us. Dr. Smith, the physician to the British agency, gave the Wangna's mother a smelling-bottle, with which she seemed much pleased, and then we were asked to be seated and tea was handed round. The room was brilliantly illuminated with hundreds of little cocoanut-oil lamps, multiplied again a hundred-fold by the profusion of mirrors which decorated the walls. At the extreme end was an altar-like arrange-

ment of glassware, covered with lamps, and surmounted by a gilt figure of Buddha.

Our hostess was very chatty, and kept Mr. Newman,
who sat between her and her daughter, in such constant
employment, as interpreter to the party, that he did not
seem to have time to deliver himself of half his com-
pliments to the daughter, with whom he seemed as
great a favourite as with the mother.

But a cup of tea will not last for ever, even in a
harem, with a charming princess to beguile the time;
while the mere fact that we were seated in the very
seat of love and beauty did not allow us to forget the
more substantial allurements of a dinner, for the loss of
which it is doubtful whether the beauteous presence of
even the whole of the ladies of the harem would have
compensated. So we returned presently to the room
where we had left the Wangna, who, as he had
preferred to be left alone while we went to pay
our respects to his mother, now excused himself from
joining us at dinner, which was served upstairs in
a separate building, with the Wangna's " ministers "
performing the duties of waiters, and an excellent
band discoursing a selection of Siamese and European
music.

CHAPTER V.

In the streets of Bangkok—The ubiquitous Chinese— A characteristic
scene—A liquor grievance—Convicts at work—In the prison — In
the great market—A Chinese gambling-den—Praying for luck—
A lakon performance—Siamese actors—Native music—A royal
band of musicians—Native instruments of music.

REALLY imposing as the view of Bangkok from the
river is, the contrast on landing and proceeding beyond
the principal roadway leading from the river to the palace
is very great.   The main road, or Krung Charoon,
which is several miles in length, is itself often partly
under water during the south-west monsoon, and the
back lanes and bypaths which constitute the principal
means of communication are in a chronic state of filth,
wet or dry.   The facilities for locomotion are on an
equally insufficient scale.   The carriages, kept for hire
by a few Klings and Malays, are generally in a most
dilapidated state, while the horses are still worse, such
as would not be tolerated in any part of Europe.   Sheds
of bamboo or wood form the bulk of the native habita-
tions; brick buildings are few and far between, and
all alike are in a state of general unrepair.   The nooks
and corners of the crooked lanes, being filled with cro-
ton-plants, or other vegetation, tend rather to increase
than to tone down the impression of general squalor.
On all sides are Chinese [1] joss-houses, Chinese carpen-

[1] A poll-tax, or as the Siamese call it *phuk-pie*, of three ticals a
head, is levied every three years on every Chinaman; but those who
are under European protection are exempt—an arrangement which
seems hardly fair.

ters' shops, Chinese cabinet works, Chinese carriage manufactories; wherever there is any work going on it is sure to be under the sign of a Chinese proprietor, though here and there may be seen a Siamese pottery works, where the brittle portable ovens, pots, and water-bottles are produced.

Suddenly you come upon a massive stone building of pretentious design, the architecture of which proclaims that it is a chapel. Of late years, however, it has been shut up, the European residents, with the exception of the Roman Catholics, keeping their Sunday "at home." The Roman Catholic church, with the palatial residence of the bishop adjoining, was formerly a Wat.

A little further on, across one of the light iron bridges which span the many creeks and canals which form byways connecting with the river, is a high brick wall, through which a wide and pretentious entrance-gate leads to a large brick mansion which is set apart for the special use of ambassadors coming to Bangkok. This is one of the liveliest and most characteristic quarters of the city, where in happy confusion may be seen Chinese pawnbrokers' shops; Siamese and Chinese eating-houses, between which there is not much to choose; Chinese duck-farms, where the ducklings are reared from the egg, and find plenty of rubbish to rout about in, if not much food on which to get fat; Chinese drug-shops; Siamese potteries; Chinese and Siamese dram-shops, where arrack [2] under the name of *samshu* is sold as a change from arrack under the name

[2] The government have arrack distilleries, and the selling of the spirit is a state monopoly. But the representatives of the various European states in Bangkok are entitled to issue consular licences to the subjects of the state they represent, allowing them to retail alcoholic liquors to the natives. The result of this has been that these licensees undersell the dealers licensed by the Siamese, thus

of *lao;* street-stalls, where John Chinaman offers his
home-made lemonade, or his dish of boiled vegetables
in which onions form the leading ingredient, with a
choice of bits of fat pork or lean duck, or where the
Siamese purveyor tempts the passer-by with a mixed
collection of rice and cakes, mussels and shrimps, and
dried or stinking fish. More numerous, perhaps, than
anything else, are the ubiquitous gambling-houses, with
a Chinese Waiang, or theatre, close at hand. The
State derives a considerable revenue from the licences
for these " hells," which abound in all parts of the city,
being largely patronized by all classes of both Siamese
and Chinese. All the gambling-houses I have seen in
Bangkok are of the commonest description : large
bamboo sheds, with an attap roof, devoid of furniture,
and many of them without even a floor, only the bare
earth, over which are laid mats for the players to sit
on. Over every mat, or at least over every gambling
party, stands a book-keeper, who watches over the
interests of his master, the proprietor of the den.

In company with my friend Mr. Solomon, or as he is
generally known, "Nai" Solomon, the obliging inspector
of police, whom I have to thank for his many services

spoiling one of their principal sources of revenue. Representations
have been made to the various European powers, as the Siamese are
anxious to have the treaties revised on that point. For instance,
a Chinaman from Macao goes to the Portuguese consul, and asks his
consul, the Chinaman being constructively a Portuguese subject, to
give him a licence to deal in liquors, and so on with the Dutch,
French, English, and American consuls. For the prescribed fee
the consul readily grants the licence, and thousands have been given
in this way. Latterly, however, some understanding has been come
to on the point, and the issue of these licences has been stopped,
pending the revision of the treaties in Europe. This matter has
been left to Prince Prisdang to arrange, and since my return from
Bangkok Prince Prisdang has informed me that he has succeeded in
getting all treaties with European countries revised in this respect.

to me during my stay in Bangkok, I visited all the
most characteristic scenes in the city, and was enabled
with his assistance to see a good deal of the " inner
life" of the people, which would otherwise have
escaped my notice. I could not have obtained a better
guide, for, besides knowing the Siamese thoroughly,
and being familiar with their language and with all
their customs, and having from his official position a
right of entry to many places which would have been
closed to a stranger, Mr. Solomon added a courteous
and genial manner which made it a double pleasure to
be in his company. As, like the rest of the Europeans
in the Siamese service, the calls of duty upon his time
and attention are not very pressing, he was generally
at my service when I called upon him. One day, under
his guidance, I paid a visit to the prison. Passing
along the main road one seldom fails to hear the clang!
clang! of heavy chains dragging along the ground.
Presently the sound is explained by a gang of prisoners
passing by, chained together two and two, with a heavy
iron collar round the neck of each, from which hangs
an iron chain connecting them together: heavy rings
are also round the ankles, with chains again connecting
the two feet of each prisoner, and one foot of each
prisoner to one of the other. I have, in many cases,
seen the flesh of the ankles quite raw from the galling
of the chains, in spite of the precautions which the
prisoners adopt of binding pieces of cloth round the
iron; and I think the Siamese inspector of prisons
might do something to alleviate their condition.

The prisoners are employed in making, repairing,
and cleaning roads. In the city proper—which is
walled in, and contains the royal palaces, &c.—the roads
are daily swept by the prisoners, and gangs of them are
seen everywhere at any time during the day, either at

this work, or sitting on the roadside making all kinds
of basket-work and fancy articles, such as cigar-trays,
&c., many of which, made of the finest rattan, are of
exquisite workmanship. The prisoners are allowed a
trifling allowance daily by the head gaoler, but, this
being insufficient for their bare necessities, they are
allowed to sell their handiwork, or, failing this, they
beg along the road as they go to work, though at the
risk of a blow from a long rattan, a symbol of authority
wielded by the man in charge of a squad, an under-
gaoler called a " Phokum," who is invariably a convict
whom somebody stands security for, more often
than not a confirmed drunkard or opium-smoker, and
ever ready on the smallest provocation to abuse his
authority by laying about him with his " staff " of office,
the only sign by which his rank can be distinguished.

But inside the prison the lot of the unhappy
wretches is even worse, and it is a mercy that they are
not compelled, however bad they may have been, to
remain there day and night. The prison is, I think,
the most filthy, foul, and fœtid place I have ever entered
in my life. It consists of a series of open sheds—fortunately, therefore, there is a fair share of air—in which
the prisoners sleep and eat ; but the stench from the
decaying refuse which is thrown upon the ground is
simply fearful, while there does not seem to be the least
attempt at drainage. Some of the prisoners were terribly depraved-looking objects, in whose countenances
crime could be plainly read. Mr. Solomon inquired of
the head-gaoler how many prisoners there were, and
he said about 650, most of them being murderers or
highway-robbers ; though, as Mr. Solomon remarked,
there were, no doubt, some whose guilt, to say the least,
had never been proved, while many others had only
been imprisoned for debt. Among the *détenus*, was a

prince—for what cause a prisoner, I could not ascertain
—who, however, seemed to enjoy a good deal of liberty,
and had a closed house all to himself, where he was
not obliged to wear chains. When he saw us he
endeavoured to hide himself, as if ashamed of his lot.

On another occasion I went, under Mr. Solomon's
guidance, through a part of the town called Sampeng,
where the great market is held daily—another district
thickly inhabited by the ever-industrious Chinese. As
we strolled amongst the bazaars, the narrow streets
of which are irregularly paved with big granite stones,
we went—it was eight a.m. on Sunday morning (31st
of July)—into one of the Chinese gambling dens, which
at that hour of the day was quite empty (for play
begins late in the afternoon and lasts half the night),
with the exception that there were five Buddhist
priests there, sitting on a mat, chanting some Pali
sentences !

Que diable allaient-ils faire dans cette galère? I
asked Mr. Solomon, who soon enquired and explained
that they were praying for luck for the proprietor
of the establishment. At one end of the gambling
saloon was an altar, on which numerous tapers were
burning, the light of which was reflected from the sides
of a dozen brass dice, polished with constant use. An
altar is always present in a Chinese or a Siamese house,
but I had begun to think such a structure was rather
out of place here, until I learnt what the priests were
doing. On the altar was a figure which I at first took
to be an ordinary statue of Buddha, but which Mr.
Solomon said was a figure of the god of luck. To
this figure a string was attached, the other end of
which was held in the priests' hands—a rather material
mode of communication with a spiritual being !

When tired of gambling, the Siamese adjourn to the

neighbouring theatre, where they spend an idle hour
or two in watching the lakons, or theatrical performances, in which only girls as a rule take part. The
amusement corresponds so closely with the Javanese
gamallang and tandak which I mentioned in my
" Head-Hunters of Borneo " that I cannot do better
than quote the following sentence from the description
of a *séance* given there :—

" The greater part of the performance consisted of
merely twisting the fingers and hands and arms in
such positions as to make them appear out of joint."

In Siam the gesticulations and contortions of limbs
are the same as in Java, but the costumes are different ;
the lakon girls wear gold-embroidered, tight-fitting
jackets, with a kind of epaulette on the shoulders
resembling horns, or, by a stretch of the imagination,
wings, while, on the fingers, they wear long artificial
nail-covers, with immensely long points, extending five
or six inches beyond the tips of the fingers, and curled
at the points, like miniature horns of " long-horned "
cattle. These lakons are, to Europeans, very uninte-
resting performances, but to the Siamese they seem to
afford perennial delight. The best in Bangkok belongs
to Phya Mahin, and I went there one evening to see
a performance. The girls, of whom there was quite
a large number, were all dressed alike—in complete
Scotch dress—the head-covering being a crown in the
form of a pradchedee. The girls' faces are always
powdered white, and they display some solicitude in
the matter of the due touching up of the eyebrows.

Possibly the lakons are patronized rather for the
sake of the slow music than for the acting or dancing.
The Siamese are very fond of music, and besides a
variety of native instruments, especially stringed instruments, which appeared to me to be of Chinese origin,

they are beginning to adopt those used by European brass bands. Every man of rank has at least one band, if not two, one exclusively of native and the other exclusively of European instruments. His Majesty has some excellent bands, in one of which the band-master as well as the members of the band are Siamese. In other cases the leaders are either Germans or Italians, though the rest of the musicians are all Siamese.

One of the king's brothers, H.R.H. Prince Kromalat, has a band of young girls, who perform on the native instruments all sorts of airs, including those familiar to European ears; they keep beautiful time, and it is quite a treat to hear them. One Sunday afternoon, Mr. Torrey, of the United States' legation—with that kindness which has made him so many friends among all visitors to Bangkok—drove an American friend, Mr. Libby of New York, and me to pay a visit to Prince Kromalat, who received us most kindly, and, while the usual ceremonial tea and cigarettes were being served, asked us if we would like to hear his band, which Mr. Torrey had already prepared me was well worth hearing. Of course we were delighted, and in a few minutes in came twelve little girls, from ten to thirteen years of age, all neatly dressed in white jackets and the Siamese pa-nung; they all had the head shaved, except a top-knot, which was held together with a gold pin, and all had gold bangles and anklets on. As they entered one by one, each with her instrument under the arm, they bent low, made obeisance by lifting their folded hands together to the forehead, and then sat down in a circle in a corner of the room.

Their instruments—all of beautiful workmanship, inlaid with ivory and mother-of-pearl—included a kind of guitar called *kayap*, Chinese fiddles called *saw*, flutes made of bamboo called *klue*, besides drums and gongs. They began by playing, with great musical taste, the Siamese national air, and finished with "Hail, Columbia," much to the surprise of my American friend, Mr. Libby. We were informed they had all been taught by Siamese teachers.

The Siamese prize their instruments very much, nor is there any shop in Bangkok where one can buy a set of them. An odd instrument or two I picked up in a Chinese pawnbroker's shop; but could not obtain a complete set. The princes and noblemen all have the instruments for their bands made on their own premises by skilled workmen.

CHAPTER VI.

NEXT to gambling-hells, theatres, and perhaps dram-
shops, the structures which are most numerous in
Bangkok are those whose tall spires have already
attracted the attention of the visitor from the river.
It would fill some bulky volumes to describe in detail
the temples of Bangkok alone, with their history, the
legends attached to the images, and the explanation of
the sacred frescoes invariably found on temple-walls.
I will therefore confine myself to an attempt to sketch
three of the principal Wats in the city.

As the reality of the interior of the city, in its filth, its
fœtid odours, and the poverty of its buildings, is very
different from the idea which the view from the river
conveys to the mind, so a close acquaintance with
the temples which look the most magnificent from a
distance shows them in a very different light from that
in which they reflected the brilliant rays of the midday
or the setting sun.

One of the largest temples in the city is the Wat

Poh, noted for its colossal gilt figure of the dying Buddha, said to be the largest in Siam. It is a recumbent figure, about 160 feet in length, representing the god reclining on the right arm. The figure is built of bricks, thickly coated with lacquer and heavily gilt. Hundreds of ounces of gold leaf must have been used, but here and there large pieces of the gilt lacquer coat have peeled off. The finest and most interesting piece of work on this Buddha, however, is on the foot-soles, which are most beautifully inlaid with figures of mother-of-pearl, illustrating legends connected with Buddha's life. The great teacher is surrounded by a number of figures and representations of monstrous animals standing between the open spaces of the columns. The floor of the temple is of tesselated marble. The grounds connected with the Wat are extensive, and are curiously laid out, containing fish-ponds, a crocodile-pond, in which the sacred reptile (I think there was only one) is fed and teazed by the Siamese youth; grotesquely-shaped granite rocks carved to represent pigs, dragons, and other monstrous animals; numbers of small phrachedees; quantities of deformed trees; a series of covered arcades for the priests to meditate in; and dirty-looking white-washed cloisters, where they reside.

The poetical idea that—

" Distance lends enchantment to the view "

has seldom been more practically exemplified than in the case of the famous temple Wat Chang,[1] which, as it towers its head above the low sea of roofs of Bangkok, as seen from the River Menam, looks like a grand and costly work of art, on the external decoration of which beautiful masonry, delicate painting or mosaic, with

---

[1] *Chang* = elephant.

precious stones innumerable, have been lavished. Tier
upon tier, row upon row, line upon line, this imposing
structure rises, gradually diminishing in beautifully
graduated proportions, till its curved apex reaches a
height of over 100 feet from the ground. Line upon
line of what, in the distance, looks like delicate tracery,
picked out with sparkling gems, follow each other in
bold array, marking the broken octagonal form of the
temple, while each important break in the outline of the
structure is marked by row upon row of pinnacles of
varied design. When the eye has followed upwards,
tier upon tier, for twenty tiers or so, this detail, which,
being in high relief, stands out in great prominence,
and with wonderful distinctness, owing to the brilliantly
lighted projections against the dark shadows of the deep
recesses, it is arrested by representations of the three-
headed elephant, of which there are four, one on each
principal facade of the temple, projecting some distance beyond the line of the tall pilasters which enframe
them, and which support four graceful turrets, from
between which springs the central spire. When examining in detail this imposing and effective structure, a
feeling of amazement that such effects could be produced,
with the materials employed, conflicts with a sense
of ludicrous incredulity that such materials could ever
have been employed with the object of producing such
effects. The general part of the structure is of brick;
the tracery is composed of bits of broken plates, glass,
cups and saucers, in fact, all kinds of broken pottery
and crockery, mixed with thousands upon thousands of
the common *cypræa* stuck into the brickwork, and
formed into designs of the lotus-flower, the monstrous
guardian angels and other figures. Only the immense
impudence, if I may use the expression, with which the
idea of utilizing such decorative materials has been

carried into effect, and the great boldness with which
the figures and flowers have been executed in high—
some in full—relief, producing the wonderful effect of
the deep shadows and high lights, redeem the structure
from the charge of being absolutely tawdry. I several
times examined this curious, if not unique, edifice, and
one day, in company with Mr. Libby, ascended it as far
as it was possible to proceed, up very steep steps,
eighteen inches at least " in the rise," and was rewarded
by a very fine bird's-eye view of the city.

But the finest view of Bangkok and the surrounding
country is obtained from the summit of the Wat Sikhet,
or rather of the great phrachedee connected with the
Wat, and one of the most remarkable structures I
have ever seen. The base of the phrachedee from a
distance resembles nothing so much as an ancient
castle built on and in a rock, where advantage
has been taken of every coign of vantage to erect a
substantial tower or fort, varying in shape according
to circumstances from square, through every imaginable change of angularity, to circular. The resemblance
to a fort is increased by the great baulks of timber
used for the support of stagings erected for repairs,
which project here and there, and look, from the distance, for all the world like ancient long cannon.
But a nearer examination shows that this rock-like
mass is a huge artificial mound of earth, the sides of
which are surrounded by massive brick walls, which
form, as it were, buttresses, binding the whole mass
together, rising one above the other, and gradually receding as the summit is approached, while every crack
and cranny in the ruined sides and the tops of the
thick walls forms a foothold for scanty vegetation.

A broad pathway, running round this strangely-con-
structed mound, leads to the flat summit, which is walled

in, and supported by bastions and gabions of brick-work
of immense thickness and height. From this eminence a
magnificent view is obtained of the city of Bangkok, looking more than ever like a sea, or rather like a flat desert,
of roofs, from which here and there emerge the glittering towers of the temples and palaces, or the white spires
of the phrachedees below, but with many an oasis of
green, the brilliancy of which contrasts strangely with
the neutral grey of the shingle roofs : while the River
Menam looks like a broad band of silver, stretching
with ever-increasing breadth in one direction towards
the sea, which is plainly visible, and, in the other
direction, with slowly-diminishing volume till it is lost
behind the rising ground, which gradually closes in on
every side, till the horizon is bounded by the summits
of the distant lofty mountains.

But this is not all. This curiously-constructed artificial hill serves as a vast pedestal or base for a
lofty tope, of which the upper part only can be seen on
a near view. Externally, the pinnacle is of the shape
usually adopted in the erection of topes or phrachedees
throughout Siam, viz. a circular or oval cone of rings
from base to summit, broken, perhaps—as in this case
—half-way up, by a square or nearly square formation,
which still, however, preserves the conical outline.
Immense treasure is said to be buried under this tope,
the custom being to deposit coins or other valuables
beneath one of the corners of the base of all phrachedees. There is not much of interest inside the structure,
which has four entrances, one on each side, the plan
of them being in the shape of a cross. On a large
altar, near the centre, are a couple of images of Buddha,
enveloped in priests' clothing.

Besides this pagoda there are numerous pavilions,
cloisters, crematory temples, on the roofs, or even

within the walls, of which, as well as on the branches
of the trees, sit quite an army of vultures, which, in
company with dogs [2] and carrion-crows, find many a
meal here, for the Wat Sikhet is a favourite place for
the disposal of the remains of the dead.

Cremation is the usual method in Siam of disposing
of the dead. When a person dies the body is placed
in a coffin, and four priests are sent for, who come
and pray all day and night until the body is taken to
the temple-ground. The period which elapses between
the death and the cremation entirely depends upon the
circumstances of the departed and of his friends. If
he is a poor individual his corpse is carried off next
day on a bamboo litter, to be burned; but, in other
cases, it may be from five to fifteen or thirty days, or
even six months or longer, before the ceremony of cremation takes place. During all this time the body is
kept, sometimes inside the house, sometimes outside,
in the coffin, from which a bamboo pipe, fixed in the
bottom, carries off the fluid products of decomposition.

I remember paying a visit to his Majesty's coach-
man, who, by the way, is a cousin of the king, and
whose father had already, at the time of my visit,
been dead six months, and still no date was fixed
for the funeral, which would be on a grand scale. I
asked the prince-coachman for permission to go and
see where his father's remains lay in state. Entering a
dark room, dimly illuminated by wax tapers, I found
two priests muttering prayers in front of what I took
for a richly decorated altar, but which turned out to

[2] There are few greater nuisances in Bangkok than Pariah dogs,
and, as the Buddhist religion does not permit the authorities to destroy them, it has become a grave question for consideration how to
get rid of them. A dog-tax might with advantage be imposed in
Bangkok, and no doubt people would find some means of getting rid
of all animals that were not worth paying the tax for.

be the *castrum doloris,* on which numerous figures of
Buddha, a profusion of artificial and real flowers,
and myriads of wax tapers, were piled up in the form
of a pyramid, beneath which the coffin was so hidden
from view in a mass of gilt and coloured paper that
only one end of it could be seen. Amid these ornaments the deceased had been resting pending the
completion of the formalities incidental to a grand
funeral, and yet there was no offensive smell, but
rather an overpowering scent from the flowers.

In the case of an ordinary individual, the corpse is
taken to the cremation-ground in a wooden coffin of
the commonest make, plastered outside with wall-paper
—sometimes with a loose lid, or sometimes merely a
piece of white calico serving as a covering. The body
is invariably borne two or three times round the cre-
mation-altar, which is prepared for the reception of
the coffin by a wood fire being laid, over which a kind
of gridiron is placed, upon which the coffin is finally
deposited. Sometimes a sort of canopy is constructed
over the coffin, of white and yellow cloth, supported on
bamboo sticks, and ornamented with tinsel. All the while
the priests murmur prayers until the signal is given
to light the fire. The process of combustion is eagerly
watched by the mourners, who are furnished with jars
or bowls of water, which they and the " undertakers "
pour over the burning pile, with the object of pro-
longing the ceremony as much as possible; for, at a
middle-class funeral, tea and sweetmeats are handed
round during the cremation, at the end of which the
officiating priests are presented with various gifts,
generally materials for clothing. Another object of
the use of water is, in the case of poor persons, to
prevent the complete combustion of the coffin, for,
although timber is plentiful enough in the country,

the coffin, charred and disfigured though it be, is used over and over again as long as a fragment remains.

But it is not always that the remains of the poor receive even such scant ceremony as this.

The first time I visited Wat Sikhet, as I entered the grounds, I met two Siamese coolies, carrying, on a bamboo stretcher, the dead body of a native pauper or criminal, followed by a couple of dozen of Siamese, some of them priests.

One or two of the group were dressed in white calico—the national garb of mourning—with heads completely shaven in token of grief,³ but they seemed to be mere lookers-on, and not to form part of the actual funeral *cortège*. The bearers of the corpse and the officiating priest were the only persons directly interested in the "last scene of all" in the unknown history of the dead man. But high up in the air hovered a dark group of aerial beings, who were to take a very active part in the proceedings. Circling and wheeling directly over the heads of the corpse-bearers was a flight of vultures, eagerly watching the scene, while the fluttering of wings close by, and the hoarse "caw" "caw" of carrion crows perched among the trees, showed that there were yet other beings anxious to participate in the mournful rite. Here and there the gaunt form of a dog would slink by, sneaking about the grounds and gradually coming nearer and nearer to the central group. When the coolies reached the selected spot they cast the dead man's body on the ground, and the next moment the air

³ The custom of shaving the head, which, with the white garb, is the national sign of mourning, hitherto universal among both sexes of all orders and ages, seems to be dying out among the better classes. I noticed that the princes and high officials copy the European fashion of wearing a piece of black crape round the arm.

was darkened by the ghastly, greedy vultures, as they swooped swiftly down and stood in a semicircle round the body, while the priests and spectators completed the circle. Behind the vultures came a flight of crows, and, outside them, again, the dogs ran round in twos and threes, snapping and snarling at each other and at everything that stood between them and the dead body. During a moment's delay, while an official, after sharpening a huge knife, approached the body, the vultures became impatient and impudent, hustling and fighting each other for a front place; once or twice they came quite close to me, and I had to keep them off with my stick. Then the official already mentioned stooped down and cut the body open, with a long slash down the stomach. The sight of the blood and entrails was too much for the filthy vultures, which began to flap their wings, and to utter their well-known sepulchral scream, jumping about in rest-less anxiety, and requiring the assistance of two other men to ward off their unwelcome advances from the officiating dissector. The flesh from the thighs, legs, and arms was then cut off, and the chest opened. A priest next advanced and chanted a few words, hold-ing a fan and a pipe in his left hand, and in his right a piece of bamboo with which he touched the body. No sooner had he uttered his last words than the vultures seemed to know their time had come, and, with a frantic rush and a horrible scream, swept for-ward, dancing a strange dance of death as they hopped and fluttered round the mangled corpse, each trying to get his full share of the horrible feast. Two birds, I noticed, at once picked the eyes out of the dead man, which, by the way, had remained open all the while, adding to the ghastliness of the spectacle: whether the birds did this from fear or because they regarded them as a dainty, I cannot say, but they always make a point of picking out the eyes first. The birds tore the body most dreadfully, sometimes actually lifting it off the ground, and fighting among themselves as one or another dragged off a piece of flesh. Once, when the birds seemed more intent on their mutual disagreements than upon their ghastly meal, a dog sneaked in and secured a morsel, but in a moment two vultures attacked him, one snatching away his mouthful, and the other giving him a bite in the neck which sent him away howling. Not more than ten minutes had been occupied in this horrible feast, when the vultures retired a few feet, and the human "butcher" came forward a second time and cut the back open, followed again by the priest, who performed the same offices as before, and then there was a second feast for the birds. By this time some of the vultures seemed surfeited, and the crows and dogs had a larger share of what was left of the body. Eight minutes later and little remained except the head and the bones, which were collected together by the attending friends, whom I left gathering a few sticks with which to burn them.

Strolling a little further, I came to another portion of the temple-grounds, a sort of yard in which stood a circular altar made of bricks, whitewashed, in the middle of which was fixed an iron post about four feet high, with a couple of iron hooks at the top used for hanging lamps upon. On this altar lay a number of human bones of all kinds, from a vertebra to a scapula, several skulls, and the bodies of a couple of infants only lately dead, but in an advanced state of putrefaction, round which buzzed myriads of flies busy as bees. Opposite this altar was a wall, on the face of which I observed the remains of a human skeleton plastered in. What could this new horror be ? I asked myself. Through a friend I afterwards ascertained that this was the skeleton of a priest who had, during his period of priesthood, violated his vows of chastity, an offence for which the punishment used to be death. This man had accordingly suffered the extreme penalty of the law, and his skeleton was now exposed as a warning to others.

From the above description it will easily be seen that the atmosphere of the charnel-ground of Wat Sikhet is not of the sweetest, and the sights are not of the most delightful. Even when bodies are properly cremated the foul stench is often sickening, both before and during the ceremony, for the corpses are nearly always in an advanced state of decomposition, even when the shortest interval has elapsed between deatn and cremation ; while the practice of keeping the bodies so long before the last rites are performed is productive of most unwholesome conditions of the atmosphere. That Bangkok is not the most salubrious place in the world goes without saying, and it is surprising that outbreaks of fever and cholera are not more frequent than they are.

While I was there a visitation of cholera occurred, during which the air of the whole city was tainted by a foul odour. At this time the ordinary modes of sepulture could not keep pace with the number of victims brought to the Wat Sikhet, and the bodies— sometimes as many as from 60 to 120 in a day—were piled upon each other, and quicklime thrown over, but this did not kill the terrible smell.

It is but right to say, however, that speaking generally the sanitary condition of Bangkok is, under the king's influence, receiving greater attention, and measures are being gradually adopted to mitigate the severity of the fearful epidemics of cholera, which in times past have from time to time devastated the country. When the outbreak just referred to occurred, his Majesty took prompt steps to check the spread of the malady. He ordered his own physician, his Highness Chow Sai, to run three small steam launches, carrying white flags as distinguishing marks, up and down the river, and in the creeks adjoining, each of them having on board a native doctor ready to render assistance and distribute medicine free of charge. The king also directed his brothers and principal officers of state to erect temporary hospitals, the cost of which was defrayed out of his private purse. Daily reports of the progress of the epidemic were laid before his Majesty, with full details of all the work done. Fortunately, six weeks or so saw the worst of the epidemic over, and, when the plague was past, medals were struck in commemoration of the event, and distributed among those who had rendered conspicuous and efficient service.

The people, of course, are hardly yet " educated " up to the king's standard. They place greater reliance upon their charms than upon scientific skill, and no doubt thought the measures they adopted were far more effective than those taken by the authorities. As a means of protection against disease, and particularly against the evil spirits or *Phee*, in which all kinds of misfortune are supposed to be personified, talismans of all kinds are worn by the Siamese. The most inexpensive, and therefore the most common, is a piece of ordinary twine, which, after being consecrated by the priests, is tied round the wrist. During the time the cholera raged I found it almost universally worn, even by persons of high degree, who assured me that they believed it would keep the disease away.

Another charm is the *takrutt*, a piece of thin gold or brass plate, about three or four inches square, on which a few Pali sentences are written, and which are then rolled up, with a piece of string through the centre, and worn round the body. Priests alone are allowed to distribute these charms. Then I have seen a heavy ball of tin with a hole through the centre, suspended from a piece of string and worn round the waist or neck. These are called *Luk sakhot*. Rosaries called *Luk phat* are also worn, consisting of a string of small beads or balls of resin, 108 in number, to correspond with the number of the well-known symbols on the foot-soles of Buddha. Every night during the prevalence of the cholera a lantern was hung at the top of a long bamboo pole placed in front of every house, so that Bangkok presented the appearance of a city illuminated in sign of popular rejoicing rather than a place where disease and death stalked supreme.

The Siamese have a curious theory of disease, believing that matter of all kinds is composed of the four " elements " of water, wind, fire, and earth, and that disease is simply a dérangement in the proportions of these elements. As the human system is, in their belief, constituted in the same way, the elements within are continually operated upon by those without, producing health or disease, according to the disturbance of the proper balance or proportion. There is no class of agents which is supposed to have so constant and widespread an influence in producing disease as that denominated " wind," or, to use the Siamese word," Lom." In nineteen cases out of twenty, when a patient is asked what is the matter, he will reply, " Pen Lom," " It is wind." The better class of Siamese now employ the European doctors resident in Bangkok; but among the mass of the people superstition takes the place of science, and, although they are beginning to learn the value of such agents as quinine, castor oil, and chlorodyne, their medicines are usually the expensive and worthless drugs sold by the Chinese, who do a lively trade in rhinoceros horn, rhinoceros blood, young deer horns, and the like potent remedies. But invariably whenever any one is ill, before medicine is administered, an offering is made to the "spirit."

During the time the cholera raged most virulently, I observed that the sky presented a curious appearance, being of a dull grey colour, mixed with patches of blue and white ; the sun was seldom if ever visible. Every now and then a rather cold wind would spring up, but not a drop of rain fell during the outbreak, although it was the " rainy season."

Although I got a slight attack of cholera, I was fortunate enough, by keeping indoors and restricting myself to a milk diet, to get over it in eight days.

Just about this time the general gloom caused by the cholera was, in commercial circles at least, lightened by the arrival of the Siamese corvette *Constellation,* with the tribute collected from the provinces down the west coast. She had 570 cases of bullion on board, each case containing 2000 dollars ; so there was some chance of the merchants and others to whom the state was indebted getting some of their outstanding dues. The Siamese as a rule are never in a hurry to pay, but there are three notable exceptions : his Majesty the King, the Wangna, and H.R.H. Chow Fa Maha Mala are known for the promptitude with which they discharge all liabilities over the payment of which they have any control. Even the Kromatah, who collects the export duties, often does not make up his accounts for a year or more. Just as I was leaving Bangkok, the king was pressing him to " square up," after an interval of nearly two years.

CHAPTER VII.

ALL this time I had been staying in Bangkok, acting
upon the advice to defer my journey to Upper Siam
until the advent of the dry season. But I was beginning to get impatient of the delay, and my attack
of cholera determined me to make some effort to get
away somewhere, so I decided to make a short excursion
down the west coast, returning to Bangkok as soon as
the season was more favourable to life in the jungle in
the interior.

So I set to work " servant-hunting "—that *bête noire*
of all travellers in distant lands—and had the usual
difficulty in engaging suitable attendants. I had
brought with me a Malay from Singapore, by name
Osman, and highly recommended. His engagement
was not of long duration, however, for one evening,
while sitting at *table-d'hôte* at the Oriental Hotel, we
were suddenly surprised by cries of "Thief! thief!"
from one of the Chinese boys. All the waiters, followed
by the people at table, aroused by the unpleasant

words, ran out into the next building, where the bed-
rooms were, and whence the sounds proceeded, to find
that one of the hotel-boys had caught Osman in
another gentleman's room in the act of ransacking the
drawers, so I had to discharge him. My next venture
was not more fortunate. Toke, Osman's successor,
was, I believe, half a Siamese and half a Chinaman, but
spoke some English, and was a " Christian " into the
bargain. Captain Köbke, whose servant he had formerly
been, said he was a " great rascal," but in the absence of
any definite complaint against him I engaged him. I
had only had him a few days, when I missed one of my
guns, and then missed Toke, who did not make his
appearance next morning. Captain Köbke, however,
was energetic enough to put the police on the scent,
and I soon got word to say he was safe in irons, in the
court of justice, so Captain Köbke and I went up at
once in a *carreta* or cab, and, passing through a dirty
lane, we came to a court of justice—a mere bamboo
shed, at one end of which was an elevated platform
with a few mats for the judge and his assistants.
Adjoining this open court of justice was the prison-
yard, where a number of prisoners, among whom we
saw Toke in the distance, were either in irons, or
sitting in wooden stocks.

Presently there entered an elderly man, followed by
a few attendants carrying a silver betel-box, tea-pot,
&c., who by taking his seat on the principal mat on
the platform proclaimed himself to be the judge. His
" robes of office " he had apparently left at home, being
entirely naked with the exception of a *pa-nung*
round the body and legs. The proceedings were short.
Captain Köbke gave evidence against Toke, and,
taking the word from " his lordship," said he wanted
him to be flogged; the judge said nothing beyond

F

asking us to come again to-morrow, to see the flogging executed. So the next day we went. Toke was brought forward in irons, and began to cry and implore Captain Köbke's pardon, but one of the prison-warders quickly administered the twenty-four strokes on his back; at the end of which Toke, although evidently smarting, did not forget to make the usual sign of homage to the judge by raising his hands together to the forehead. Captain Köbke was not satisfied, and asked that Toke might remain in irons till the gun was restored or the value paid in money. I thought, however, he had been pretty well punished, and, hoping he might profit by the exercise of a little leniency, proposed to take him back into my service. But Captain Köbke advised me not to do so, and I set to work to find a substitute. Then I met with Chin, a native of Siam, and also a " Christian," who had learnt a little English at the American Mission, where he had been employed. Him I engaged, but finding great difficulty in getting a second boy who was willing to travel in the interior, and who could talk either in Malay or in " Pigeon English," I went back to Toke, and, as he promised to be faithful and obedient, I asked for and obtained his release.

Toke brought another gun as security for his good conduct, but a few days later I found that this gun also had disappeared from my room, together with sixty-four ticals in money, and a watch which Chin, firm in the belief in the loyalty of thief towards thief, had lent him.

I offered a reward to the police for the recapture of Toke, and the next day he was again safe in irons in the prison. I sent word to say he was to pay the penalty of a further flogging and of remaining in irons if the value of the gun—twenty-two dollars—was not paid at once. Toke's mother then made a move, and the day after a Chinaman who said he was Toke's father-in-law came to me and paid the money, coolly asking for a "discount." I told him I could not allow him a cent. Then he complained that he had several times had to pay for Toke's *lâches*, adding this would be the last time.

By this time, however, Chin had begun to play his pranks. One day, when I asked him for the change out of some money I had given him to pay a bill, he coolly answered, "I have spent it; please put it down to my account, sir." And two days later he, too, ran away, taking a valuable chronograph watch, of the loss of which I was often reminded when I wanted to use it in my journey. Although I gave notice to the police, they never caught Chin, who, probably, had profited by the lesson which the double capture and double punishment of Toke had taught him. At this juncture Mr. Gould, who was just leaving Bangkok for England, offered me his servant Kao, who, besides having the character of being a steady, faithful boy, was also a good linguist for a Chinaman, speaking Siamese, Burmese, Malay, and somewhat broken English. He was of a somewhat timid disposition, and often found difficulty in screwing his courage to the sticking point, but he was thoroughly honest, and trustworthy in every point but one, viz. that he did not always correctly interpret my words at the very time when I was most dependent upon his services. I do not think he wilfully mistranslated; sometimes his knowledge was hardly up to the mark, at others his timidity tempted him to modify my language when he thought, probably, a "soft answer" might "turn away wrath," but when decisive language and prompt action were alone likely to have any effect, as the sequel will show. I also engaged one cook and two hunters.

An interlude to the petty annoyances incidental to engaging servants and to punishing their misdeeds was afforded by an invitation from Mr. Libby to join a party of friends on an excursion up the river to Ayuthia, the ancient capital of Siam. We left Bangkok early in the morning of the 4th of August, in the small river-steamer called, after the hotel of which she was a popular adjunct, the *Oriental.* Our party consisted of General Holderman, the United States minister, in whom the soldier, the scholar, and the genial companion were happily combined; Mr. Hamel, the Dutch consul-general, a humorous comrade; Mr. Richmann, the Austrian consul, full of anecdotes gathered during his varied experience; Mr. Xavier, a good Siamese scholar, with a fund of information about any object of interest that we passed; and last, but not least, our pleasant host, Mr. Libby, whose excellent company and choice conversation the European residents in Siam will always remember. I must not forget to mention, with such pleasurable recollections of the picnic, that Captain Salje the commander and part owner of the *Oriental,* who was a noted *gourmet,* had provisioned the vessel in the most perfect manner, and was always ready to give the most authentic particulars about any object of riverside history on which the united intelligence of the party happened to be at fault.

Ayuthia, the old capital of Siam, founded in 1350, was laid in ruins by the victorious Burmans in 1767. Of the former glories of the city only ruins are left, scattered far and wide over the low-lying rice-fields. The area of the old city was apparently of great extent. It is related that a certain Phya, when about to found the city, was directed to shoot an arrow from a bow, and where the arrow fell the city was to be. When he shot the arrow, the Hanuman [1] caught the arrow and stuck it in the ground. Meanwhile the Hanuman's tail developed to an extraordinary length, and the sweep of the tail was to be the limit of the city. There is a similar legend about the city of Lampoon. The Hanuman promised that, in case of any danger to the city, he would come to its assistance at the sound of the drum. There is in Bangkok such a drum. The legend runs that the Siamese being anxious to see the Hanu-

The Hanuman or Hoalaman, from a native drawing.

man once sounded the drum, and he really came, but, finding it was a false alarm, he became angry and swore at them, and has never since made his appearance.

The foregoing woodcut represents the Hanuman according to the Lao notion of the creature. It is taken from a coloured drawing made for me by a native

[1] The Siamese call this creature Hanuman, the Laosians know it as Hoalaman.

artist at Chengmai.   A festival known as the " Swinging Festival" is held at Bangkok in honour of the
Hanuman or Hoalaman, during the second Siamese
month.

The present city, which is reached after seven hours'
steam against a swift current, was built about sixty
years ago.   It is intersected by numerous canals,
and a peculiar feature is the large preponderance in the
number of floating houses over the number of houses on
the shore.   These with the many trading-boats—for a
large traffic is kept up with Bangkok, especially in the
rice season, when large cargo-boats come up by the
hundred to carry away the crop—make the navigation
of the river difficult.   There are some local industries
on rather an extensive scale, such as lime-kilns, a
number of brick-yards, where the brittle tiles and
bricks are made, and many potteries.

Of temples and ruins of temples, there are here as
elsewhere in Siam, plenty, but the most interesting
thing in the neighbourhood is the gigantic elephant-
enclosure, into which the wild elephants from the
jungle are driven, and where the princes come occasionally to join in a royal elephant-hunt.

The " enclosure" is surrounded by an " elephant-
proof" fence, composed of huge piles or pillars of teak,
firmly let into the ground at intervals of about a
couple of feet.   When one elephant is got through the
opening, all the rest of the herd follow, like sheep, though
with bellowings and trumpetings anything but lamb-
like.   A grand stand is erected outside the enclosure,
at a convenient spot, where the princes and others
who do not wish to take part in the " drive" can
witness the exciting scene ; and from this vantage-point
Mr. Richmann told us that he had witnessed one of
these great " drives," in which over 200 elephants were

PAVILION IN THE LAKE AT THE PALACE OF BANG-PA-IN.

[*To face page 71.*

driven into the enclosure, by an army of hunters under the command of Chow Fa Maha Mala.

Close by is an extensive palace, inhabited by the late king, but now falling into ruins, the present king having built himself a new summer residence at Bang Pa In, on the banks of the river a few miles below Ayuthia, which we visited on our return to Bangkok on the following day.

It is a large building, in semi-European style, painted white, with a *facade* of pillars painted a light-blue colour to relieve the monotony. The prettiest sight in connexion with the palace are the grounds, ornamented with fountains and statuary, intersected with canals which are spanned by neat bridges, and containing a fine lake, in the middle of which is a delightful pleasure-house in genuine Siamese style, with the triple roof in divisions, and many-pointed gables, and a spire in the middle.

The effect of this very characteristic structure, its broken outline reflected in the placid water, is so striking that I got a photograph of it, which is here reproduced.

I cannot help here remarking upon the very close resemblance between the style of Siamese architecture and that of the so-called " Stavekirker," of Norway, which date from the 11th and 12th centuries. The examples of this style to be seen, for instance, at Hitterdal and Borgund, which must be familiar to all tourists in Norway, bear a very close likeness to the better-class Siamese buildings, of which the pavilion at Bang Pa In and the Royal Wat at Lakon (see p. 168) may be regarded as typical examples. Both here, and in the instance referred to in Norway, we have the same high-pitched roofs, covered with scale-shaped shingles, with a tower in the centre, terminating in a spire, while the grotesque gables, and even the wood carvings, representing monstrous animals, are not wanting. It would seem that this style of architecture must have wandered centuries ago from the far East, across Russia, to north-western Europe.[2]

In strange contrast to this purely Siamese structure is the Royal Wat opposite the palace, which, curiously enough, is a copy of a Gothic church. On looking at it one for a moment fancies oneself to be in a Christian country ; even inside—quite contrary to Buddhist forms—the Wat is fitted with regular pews ; while the resemblance is still further enhanced by a stained-glass window over the entrance, representing his Majesty the King of Siam in his coronation-robes; but the altar with its many figures, especially the large one in the centre, at once proclaims the Buddhist temple.

In the rooms of the palace there is nothing noteworthy. In the dining-room I noticed a number of framed cartoons from *Vanity Fair*, conspicuous amongst them being the portrait of the Kromatah.

The king occasionally retires to this summer residence when desiring to throw off the cares of state. It was during a visit to Bang Pa In, about three years ago, that he sustained a great bereavement in the death,

---

[2] A fact which seems to lend additional point to the foregoing observation is that there exists in the palace-grounds at Bang Pa In a curious kind of "swing," the like of which I have seen nowhere but in Copenhagen. This consists of a sort of platform, built in serpentine or wave-like form with regularly curved depressions and elevations, along which a small carriage is made to run, with alternate upward and downward movement, giving the riders a sensation something akin to that of being in a boat rising and falling upon a regular swell at sea. The carriage is first hauled up a steep incline, of which there is one at either end, and the momentum gained by running down this is sufficient to carry it up and down over half a dozen, or more, of these alternate ascents and descents.

by drowning, of his first queen, Sunanda Kumaritana, and her infant daughter. Her Majesty was proceeding up the river in a picnic-boat, in tow of a steam launch, when the boat was upset, through swinging against the swift current while going round a bend in the river. More than half a year elapsed before the queen's remains were cremated, while a magnificent building of great size, known as the Pramene, was being erected for the express purpose of serving as a *crematorium.* This structure extended over an area of something like an acre, and in its many-gabled and high-pitched roofs, and the multitude of pinnacles and many-storied umbrellas with which it was furnished, had all the appearance of a permanent palace.

A portion of this extensive structure was still standing when I arrived at Bangkok in 1881. Some idea of the extent and costliness of the Pramene, and of the ceremonial connected with the cremation of Siamese royalty, may be gathered from the following account of the customs observed on the death of a king or queen.

Orders are issued for " general mourning," which consists, as already stated, in shaving the head. At one time the shaving was compulsory, under the penalty of a severe flogging, but, though it is generally observed, the practice is not now enforced. At the same time the people are called upon to make an offering to the remains of the king, which to many of them is in truth a great sacrifice ; and instructions are at once sent to the governors of the northern provinces where the large timber abounds, requiring them each to furnish one of the four large logs for the centre pillars of the Pramene. These logs must be of the finest description and very straight, 200 feet long, and proportionately large in circumference—which, I am

told, in the case of the queen's funeral was not less
than twelve feet.

Besides these large pillars, twelve others of smaller
size are demanded at the same time from other governors, as well as all the other necessary materials.   As
sacred custom will not tolerate the use of pillars that
have been used on any former occasion, new ones must
always be obtained for the funeral obsequies of a king.
Four pillars are very difficult to find of such enormous
dimensions, and, besides, they can be floated down to
Bangkok only at those seasons of the year when there
is plenty of water in the Menam ; hence the frequent
long delay in the completion of the funeral obsequies
of royalty.   Arrived at the cremation-ground, the four
principal pillars are planted in the ground thirty feet
deep, one at each corner of a square, and not less than
forty feet apart, and leaning slightly inwards so as to
form the framework of a tapering tower, about 170 feet
high, on the top of which is erected a pagoda-shaped
octagonal spire, adding from fifty to sixty feet more to
the height of the structure.   This upper part is so
covered with yellow-coloured sheets of tin and tinsel-
paper as to resemble a cone of gold, for at such an
elevation the deception is not apparent, and the effect
is said to be really very striking.

At each of the four corners of this lofty pyramid are
erected, by means of the twelve smaller posts, four
covered structures, extending out from the main pillars
about forty feet, one on each side.   Each of these has
also a pagoda-shaped spire, also decked with tinsel, of
the same general form as the central one, but not as
tall by fifty or sixty feet.   Between each of these corner
buildings is a gaily decorated porch, facing each cardinal
point of the compass.   The Pramene thus completed,
the receptacle for the body that is to be cremated,

JEWELLED URN CONTAINING ASHES OF THE LATE QUEEN OF SIAM.

[*To face page* 75.

called the " Pra Bencha," is erected inside. It is also a pyramid, overlaid with a thick sheathing of fine gold, elaborately wrought into the appearance of carved work, with small pieces of mirror cut into angular and circular forms, thickly set into the gold like gems in a ring. This primitive kind of decoration has a magic effect, especially in the evening, when the whole interior of the building is brilliantly illuminated.

The gold sheathing employed on the Pra Bencha alone for the cremation of his late Majesty weighed, I was informed by the late ex-regent, 190 catties, worth sixteen times its weight in silver, which would be 243,200 ticals, equal to 145,920 Mexican dollars. This sheathing was afterwards converted into an image of Buddha, and placed in the Wat Pra Kao as a memorial to the departed king.

On the Pra Bencha the royal remains " lie in state " for seven days, when the king starts the cremation himself, by lighting the inflammable materials beneath the Pra Bencha, and after him the princes, nobles, and priests all put candles in the flames. There is no unpleasant smell, but rather a strong perfume as of incense —an abundance of the choice-scented aquila, or eagle-wood, being specially used in the cremation of people of rank.

During the seven days the people take their part in the ceremony by indulging in all kinds of amusements, such as lotteries, theatrical performances, displays of fireworks, &c., while presents, both to priests and people, are distributed by the king in great abundance. During the festivities in connexion with the cremation of the late queen in 1881, the king most lavishly distributed presents—some of great value—to the public. Limes, for instance, were thrown to the multitude, containing either gold or silver coins, or a ticket for a lottery, amongst the prizes being an elephant, several horses, and cattle. The parties who won the horses and elephant had to ride before his Majesty and bow down three times with their hands folded as they came before the presence of the sovereign. The winners, I was told, were poor people, and knew nothing about riding on horses, upon which they sat most awkwardly, adding not a little to the fun by the difficulty with which they retained their seats. This distribution of

The Queen of Siam.

presents, &c., I may add, is not a religious observance, but a national custom.

When the cremation had been successfully accomplished, the queen's ashes were deposited in a magnificent gold and jewelled urn of the most costly and elaborate workmanship that the court jewellers could design and make, an illustration of which is given in the accompanying plate. The engraving gives but a faint idea of the splendour of this jewelled urn, which now adorns the hall of the palace known as the Pra Maha Prasat.

It is in this hall that the body of a deceased king is kept "in state," pending the erection of the funeral pile. When the late king died, on October 1st, 1868, the official "court circular" relates that "early

The King of Siam with the Crown Prince.

next morning his late Majesty's remains were bathed, dressed in regal attire, placed in a golden urn, borne in procession, and deposited upon a throne in the Maha Prasat that same day, in accordance with the usual custom."

I may here add that the present queen, Swang

Wadhana, whose portrait is given above, is a sister of the one whose funeral has just been described. I also give a portrait of the crown prince, the son of the present queen, sitting on his royal father's knee. His Majesty has already, by the way, a large family of no less than forty-two children, so that there is little fear of the royal family becoming extinct.

CHAPTER VIII.

On Thursday, the 11th of August, I made a start for
the west coast in a small steamer, the *Crocodile*, which
his Excellency the Kromatah had kindly placed at my
disposal. Kao asked for a day's leave to go and get
his clothing ready, and spend the last few hours with
his wife, while the cook went to pay his devotions
to Buddha. Both returned punctually to their duties;
but not so the two hunters, who at the last moment
were missing, while Chin was likewise still " wanted."
However, steam was up, and the *Crocodile* was snort-
ing impatiently to get down stream; so at 4.30 p.m.
we were off. In four hours we reached Paknam,
where we anchored, on the plea of waiting for a pilot.
It was bright moonlight, and I doubted the sincerity
of the plea, but resigned myself to the delay, and endeavoured to sleep through it. The mosquitoes, however, stung me to action, and, unable to rest, I declared my belief that the pilot was a myth, and urged

the immediate continuation of the voyage. After a
somewhat lengthy palaver, the captain and crew consented to go on, and just as day broke we were in
sight of the old white-washed residence of the king,
built on a commanding eminence and surrounded with
its temples and phrachedees, at Petchaburee.

We steamed slowly along, skirting the flat coast,
fringed with fishing-traps and V-shaped stakes or
weirs, and at nine a.m. reached the village of Ban Lem.
As it was low water we could not get over the bar,
and had to content ourselves with watching the natives
in their large, open boats, busily engaged in angling,
hauling in their finny prey as quickly as the rod and
line could be baited, or diving for mussels, which are
very abundant here, or collecting the fish left by the
receding waters in their cunningly-devised traps.

It was three o'clock before we got a pilot to take
us into the bay, and he managed to get ashore twice
before landing us finally and properly at Ban Lem—a
small village inhabited principally by Chinese duck-
farmers and Siamese fishermen.

A couple of small boats were obtained with
difficulty, and it was nearly midnight before we
reached Petchaburee, which seemed to be inhabited
principally by pariah dogs. These, at least, were the
only creatures that took any notice of our arrival;
and they were so vociferous in their welcome that I
wonder the whole village was not brought out of doors.
The yelling and barking of the dogs, however, is so
incessant that their silence would be a phenomenon
far more likely to attract the attention of the
people.

Late as it was I could get no assistance, and had no
alternative but to send Kao to find one of the officers
of the governor. After an hour's absence he returned

with a servant of the second governor, who told me that the first governor was at Radburee, on a visit to the ex-regent, whose summer residence was at my disposal —a white-washed building on the wall of which was a tablet with English letters engraved as follows : " His Excellency the Prime Minister of Siam, A.D. 1861." It was a small building of two stories, a very modest residence for so wealthy and great a man; and, judging from the dilapidated state it was in, it could not have been inhabited for years. The staircase was almost eaten up by white ants, and the air inside was foul, as if the windows had not been opened for ages.

On the following day I called upon the second governor, whom I found in low spirits, having just lost one of his children, and surrounded by his wife and servants, busily preparing for the cremation; then I called on the American Mission, where Mr. and Mrs. McClelland, and two evidently disappointed ladies of middle age, were doing some good Christian work in the way of teaching a few young Siamese.

Two of the governor's sons were good enough to show me the " lions " of the place, among which are two caverns, which, as usual, have been turned to account as temples. Entering the caves from the bright sunlight, they naturally appeared very dark at first, but after having penetrated some yards, we found several natural skylights, over which, to prevent the rain coming in, an attap roof has been built, so that the devotees can say their prayers inside, and make their offerings to the numerous idols, without getting wet. In the largest cave, on both sides, is a regular gallery of Buddha figures in various attitudes, while on the walls are a number of tablets with gilt bas-reliefs called *Sama*. On the top of the hill on the side of which the caves are situated are two temples with a large phrachedee between them.

Among the other sights at Petchaburee is the royal palace, also situated on the top of a hill, which we had seen from sea *en route* to Ban Lem. It was the favourite residence of the late king, but is now in a sad state of neglect.

It is a curious fact that the Siamese, though ever building, seem seldom, if ever, to take steps to keep their edifices, sacred or secular, in repair. And more often than not what they do build they leave uncompleted. It is quite an exception to see any building which has been completed " out of hand," and still more exceptional to find repairs going on.

The rooms of the palace were small, but fitted with an astonishing number of glass-fronted cupboards, in which were stored a miscellaneous collection of china and a number of bottles filled with French preserved fruits. From the windows one has a fine and commanding view of the country. Going down from the palace, we passed a small wat on the slope of a hill, which my curiosity led me to enter. No priests were present, but a number of old women were engaged in repeating prayers after an old man who sat in front of the female congregation, while others were making offerings of a flower called *lan tom* (a jasmine-scented flower, of a white and yellow colour, and sacred to the Buddhists), which they strewed round a T-shaped stand on which wax tapers were burning. The worshippers scrupulously avoided entering the space assigned to the priests—which was carpeted off and furnished with spittoons !—but they did not seem particularly absorbed in their devotions, for some of them came forward and offered my native companions some tobacco and sirih.

The natives in the district were all busy planting rice, so it was difficult to engage hunters, but the second governor was kind enough to help me in securing the services of a man named Pan as a guide and interpreter, giving me at the same time a letter of introduction to the chief of the village of Ban Kow Jai, directing him to assist me in collecting natural history specimens.

I left Petchaburee on the 18th of August, my luggage being conveyed in two bullock-carts, while the governor was good enough to accommodate me with a pony to ride on. The road was easy, being across flat country, covered with a thick tangle of prickly bamboo, with here and there an open space devoted to the growth of paddy, or with a clump of "ton tan," or sugar-palms, towering majestically above everything else. Up the lofty stems of these palms the natives climb to collect the fruit from which the sugar is extracted ; to facilitate the ascent they attach a thread-like ladder, consisting of lengths of bamboo fastened at intervals round the trunk of the tree in such a way that the climber can hold it with his hands while he presses his feet against the trunk, and so gets a firm foothold in mounting. Along the road I frequently noticed large square ponds or holes, called *Baw,* used for storing water.

After three-quarters of an hour's ride we came to the village of Tapanjihon, inhabited chiefly by Eastern Laosians, descendants of prisoners of war captured sixty years ago and permanently "interned" here. There are several such settlements in this part of Siam, lying to the west of Bangkok. After passing through Tapanjihon we had to cross a small river, which was full of water, it being the rainy season, but which the bullocks had to ford, although it was spanned by a small wooden bridge, suitable, however, only for bipeds.

The bridge was constructed of two rows of piles, increasing in height towards the centre, and shorter at each bank, each pair of piles being joined together by teak planks or beams. A row of three planks thrown longitudinally across these primitive piers completed the structure.

In the afternoon a heavy shower of rain came on, with thunder and lightning, and before we could reach the shelter of the nearest village we were all wet through. We put up for the night at another Laosian village, called Nongchick, where the king of Siam has extensive rice-fields, which the people have to cultivate for him, and where the chief—a very pleasant old man called Rung Ram—gave me his history; he was born, he said, in Saigon, fifty-six years ago, and when six years old came along with his father and the rest of his native village to Siam as prisoners of war.

As head of the village of Nongchick, Rung Ram said he got thirty-two ticals a year, government pay, and occasionally received presents, such as money, cloth, &c., from the king. Besides this, he exercised certain rights over his subjects, being able to command the labour of 1000 men for two months every year; formerly, he said, he used to be able to exercise this privilege for three months out of the twelve, but by a recent royal decree the period had been reduced to two. The population of the village is about 5000, but the old chief complained much of the large number of men— over 800—who had been drafted for soldiers during the last two years. In a couple of days, he said, he was going to Radburee to fetch a Siamese official who would mark the young men in the village for the king's service.

Every man in Siam is supposed, according to an ancient law, to work a certain number of weeks in the year for the king, but those who can afford to do so buy exemption.   For this service, which is called *tam rachakan*, they receive a small sum, sufficient to buy rice during the period of labour.   Every man is marked with a few letters, tattooed inside the left arm, stating for what particular purpose he has been selected.   Ka Hluangs (royal servants) are yearly sent from Bangkok to different parts of the kingdom, to mark the young men as they are drafted for service.   The different services have different letters, such as—

Kroma Wang, guardians within the royal palace;

Kroma Muang, a company in charge of the walls of the royal palaces;

Kroma chang, a company in charge of the royal elephants;

Kroma ma, a company in charge of the royal horses;

Kroma Sanom, a company in charge of the royal concubines;

Kroma Tahan, a company in charge of men liable to be called out to war; and so on through quite a long list of " Kromas."

The chiefs of each of the above-named companies reside in Bangkok, and rolls are kept of the men belonging to each, who are scattered all over the land.

The next morning we came to Ban Kow Jai,[1] also a Laosian village, situated on an open plain, on which the houses are scattered about, partly hidden from view by gardens and small plantations, and backed by a solitary mountain.   Here I and my men took up our quarters in the Sala, or public resting-place, one of which is to be found in almost every village in Siam and Lao—generally a large wooden shed, covered with

Ban = village ; *Kow* = mountain ; *Jai* = great.

a roof, but open all round, and mounted on posts. As it appears to be nobody's business to keep these places in order, they are generally in a wretched state, a receptacle for all kinds of filth, and a place of refuge for all sorts of vermin. Here, as elsewhere, the whole population was busy planting rice, only the old women being left at home to take care of the babies, and the younger children to attend to the buffaloes and cattle, while the pigs were trusted to take care of themselves.

The heat was intense, the thermometer registering over 90° Fahr. in the shade at three p.m., and the mosquitoes were unremitting in their attentions. Even the natives could not tamely submit to their attacks, and every evening would make fires under the houses, where the cattle were resting, to protect themselves and the animals from these pests.

The day following my arrival a couple of chiefs paid me a visit, each bringing me a fowl and some rice as a present, together with some *het*, or mushrooms, which the Laosians and Siamese both consider a delicacy, like others in the western part of the world. Seeing the women returning home in the evening from the woods, I was curious to know what their baskets were laden with. Kao said it was only *makkan* (food), but as that was a very indefinite answer, food varying in every country, I asked to be allowed to see for myself, a request which amused the women, who were shy of approaching a farang (foreigner). Among the most valued contents of the baskets were some frogs and mushrooms ; a quantity of *Mengda-na*, a species of *belostoma*, or water-beetle, belonging to the order of *hemiptera*, found in mud and ponds ; some of the large fresh-water shells, *ampullaria*, so common in the paddy-fields, and called *hoi khong* by the Siamese, who eat them with curried rice ; the stems of an arum (sp. of *amorphophallum*), also eaten with curry ; and a number of wasps' nests, containing the grubs only, which the natives say are very fat and oily, and which, when mixed with pork fat, are considered a *bonne bouche.*

Provisions were very cheap here, fowls only fourpence each, and rice and fruits in proportion, and the Karians —independent tribes inhabiting the mountain-chain which runs through Siam from north to south, right to the end of the Malay Peninsula—used to come down to buy rice. One day a party of them came into the village, with their clumsy ox-waggons to carry away their purchases. I called on them and managed, through Pan, to exchange a few words with them, when they turned the occasion to advantage by begging for powder and coral beads, which I gave them with a view of being well received when I paid them a visit in their mountain retreat, as I had all along intended to do. Their home, I found, was only a day's journey distant, in the roots of the neighbouring mountains, which were plainly visible from Ban Kow Jai, and I at once told Pan that I should not leave this part of the country without having seen the hill-tribes in their own homes. He said, however, that it was impossible at this time of the year : the jungle was dangerous, and, if four of us went, two would be sure to die on the road of fever. I told him we were no more likely to die than the Karians, and that go I should, and go with me he must, if only for one day. But day after day passed and still objections were multiplied, two fresh ones being started for every one that I managed to demolish. At last, however, he graciously promised to go with me on condition that I remained only one day amongst the Karians.

On Thursday, the 25th of August, I packed the necessary luggage ; it was not much, only a couple of

blankets, some provisions, and a mosquito-curtain,
weighing altogether less than forty pounds, but when
two coolies arrived on the following morning they
grumbled at the weight they had to carry between them.
I tried to shame them by telling them that in Borneo
and in Sumatra each coolie carried from fifty to sixty
pounds, without a murmur, and at last their scruples too
were overcome, and I left the Sala, with Kao and a
native guide who knew the way through the jungle,
to find Pan kneeling on the grass, engaged in earnest
prayer, and every now and then gazing at the solitary
mountain close by. When he had finished, he got up
and lighted a wax taper, and put it in the dead trunk
of a tree, laying a whole bundle of wax tapers higher
up in the fork of the tree, as an offering to the spirit
of the mountains, whose assistance he had invoked to
preserve us from illness and misfortunes on the road.
When Pan joined us, I asked him where the horse was
that I brought from Petchaburee; he at once, with a
calm countenance, told me the horse was ill and had
a bad foot. When I asked to see it, he said it had gone
astray in the woods ; but the fact was that he had
sent the horse away, thinking I should give up the
journey. It was no use parleying, so I quietly said,
" As there is no horse, I walk ; come, let us start ;" and
poor Pan had to throw himself entirely on the goodwill
of the mountain-spirit.

Most of the way the path—and a rough path it was
—lay over gradually rising ground, intersected with
small streams, and covered with low jungle, unrelieved
by big trees, but with occasional dense groves of
bamboo, or with patches of thick long grass, in some
places six feet high. But what made the travelling
especially unpleasant was the damp, hot, and peculiarly
foul atmosphere, putrid with the decaying vegetation,

and strongly suggestive of the fevers that had excited Pan's aversion to the journey.

I searched for insects and land-shells *en route*, but found only a few. About half-way we came across a big, hollow tree, the trunk of which I struck twice, to see if any reptiles or insects were lurking inside. Pan was dreadfully shocked at me for doing this, and begged me not to do it again, for fear of arousing the spirits in the forest. After a laborious ascent we came, about four p.m., to a plateau covered with forest and high grass, a perfect wilderness some 800 feet above the sea-level, where the Karian village was situated. Close by was a Laosian settlement, consisting of half a dozen houses where we arranged to remain for the night, as we were all of us pretty tired, having walked without resting since eight in the morning, and all uphill work. Going on to the Karian village, we first came to a hut raised on posts, and standing alone in the forest. My guide told me to enter it, so I did, mounting a shaky ladder, to find myself in the midst of three women and two young men. The females struck me as bearing a very strong resemblance in their features to gipsies, and this I noticed in all the other women I saw later. Like the Dyaks, the men, and especially the women, had large gashes in the lobes of the ear, in which the women wore circular wooden ornaments, while the men had the lobes distended by cylinders of bamboo three or four inches long, and about one inch in diameter. Both sexes had necklaces of beads, and strings of small round Siamese coins (quarter-ticals). The first words the spokesman of the party uttered, or at least the first that Pan interpreted, were : " This is not the chief's house." I inquired " How far ? " and the answer was, " If we sound our wooden drum, they can hear it at the chief's house in the village "—a strange way, I thought, of

reckoning distances. A walk of seven or eight minutes
more, through rice-fields, brought us to the settlement,
where we were directed to the chief's hut. As soon as
I reached the small platform outside, the chief at once
hastened to spread out a new mat for me to sit on,
while his wife and daughters came out of their retreat,
and looked and laughed at me with the greatest *non-
chalance.* Their quaint, gipsy-like features were in
striking contrast to his essentially ugly face, which accident and disease had still further marred. I wondered
how the Karians could ever have chosen him as chief.
His right eye was blind, with a great grey star covering pupil and iris; his face was terribly pock-marked,
besides being dreadfully dirty; his clothing consisted
of a piece of rag round his loins, and an equally ragged
jacket, which in years gone by had been white.

I asked permission of the chief to sketch his wife, and
he at once complied. Scarcely had I made the first out-
lines, when she turned round to see how the sketch was
progressing, and in order to get her back in the original
position I touched her chin. Immediately she altered
the expression of her face, got up, and hurried off into
an interior apartment. I looked at the chief, whose
face was full of passion, and who had difficulty in
restraining his anger, while he explained to Pan that
I had committed a grave breach of etiquette in
touching the woman's face. No one was allowed to
touch a Karian woman. Had it been a native, he would
have had to pay a fine for the offence. I thought
this was merely a ruse to extort a little money from
me, so I took no notice of what he said, appearing
not to understand, and asked permission to sketch one
of the young men, to whom I promised to give a
present of money. After a little parley the man's
anger seemed to cool down, and the bribe acted like

oil on the troubled waters. The woman whose dignity
I had unintentionally injured looked on round the
corner of the partition all the time, while I sketched
her son's face, and the chief left the hut, apparently
appeased; but no sooner had I finished the sketch
than the mother came out, demanding to see the
portrait. Looking at it a moment, she exclaimed
" It is an evil spirit; my son will be ill;" then,
rushing outside, she called loudly for her husband. In
the mean time a large crowd had gathered round the
hut, and, as the chief returned at the summons of his
wife, their demeanour seemed so threatening that I
foresaw trouble. Kao, Pan, and my guide all begged
me to pacify the natives by giving up the sketch, but
I was unwilling to lose the fruit of my labour, and still
more was I unwilling to make an unconditional
surrender. However, the chief listened to the half-
frantic entreaties of his wife, and then said that I had
offended the spirits by touching a Karian woman and
by putting the spirit of his son on my paper, and, if
I did not give up the paper to his mother to destroy
it, not one of us should be allowed to leave the place.
An ominous movement and suppressed shouts among
the crowd outside seemed to give additional force to
the ugly chief's uglier words, and I saw there was no
help for it but to give way. So I proposed a bargain.
" If you will order the crowd home, men and women,
I will return the sketch to the lad's mother." After
some demur, this was agreed to, and as the chief went
outside to send the people to their homes, I went
down with him, and, behind the friendly shelter
of a tree, I hastily made a duplicate sketch of the
youth, and, secreting the original, waited till the crowd
had dispersed; then, showing the second sketch successively to father, mother, and son, I tore it in half,

and gave the pieces to the mother. She completed
the work of destruction, and to her entire satisfaction
disposed at once of the evil thing, spirits and all, by
tearing it into minute fragments. The original sketch
is reproduced in the accompanying wood-cut, without,
I trust, any taint of the evil spirits which were aroused
by the innocent use of my pencil.

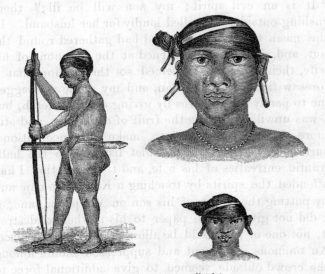

Karians of Petchaburee district.

The Karian men wear their hair long, just like the
Burmese, but, instead of fastening it in a top-knot on
the crown of the head, they have their knot on the side
of the head above the right ear, the hair being brought
low down entirely across the forehead, so as to conceal
the face right down to the eyebrows. Sometimes a piece
of red calico covers the hair, and finishes in a point
where the knot is concealed, though this head-covering
is not always worn. As nothing is seen of the forehead, the people look rather idiotic.

It was now getting dark, so we returned to the Laosian village to sleep, conjuring away all remembrance of the evil spirits by a distribution of money, tobacco, and beads; and next day returned safely to Ban Kow Jai, greatly to the relief of my timid attendants.

A few days later some of the Karians returned my visit to them, and begged for a further supply of powder and coral beads, which I gave them. In exchange I took portraits of a few of them, two of which are reproduced.

Although throughout Siam and Lao, up in the high mountains, settlements of Karians are to be found, many of them with quite a number of elephants, the real home of these people is right to the north-west of Lao, hemmed in by the mountains, and bordering on the west on British Burmah, where they are a frequent source of trouble, committing highway robberies on British as well as Siamese subjects. Before embarking on such an enterprise, they are careful to go first and pray and make offerings to the spirits in the jungle, asking for success in their undertaking.

Their weapons are crossbows and arrows. I met with tribes of them in the Lakon district in Lao, where I took another portrait of one of the men, and one of a girl, which will be found at pp. 174, 175.

On the 8th of September I left Ban Kow Jai for Radburee, on the bank of the River Meklong, or Menam Radburee. The country *en route* was thickly populated, and for two days nothing was to be seen but immense rice-fields, with groups of huts clustered here and there in every direction. The moon was just making its appearance as we came in sight of Radburee, about eleven p.m., and across the river were borne the sounds of native music from numerous lakons. I made my

way to the ex-regent's mansion, hoping to find my
friend Captain Hicks, secretary to the ex-regent, in
attendance on his Grace, who was seeking relaxation
and fresh air here. Fortunately, Captain Hicks was at
home, installed in a pleasant villa, where he gave me a
warm welcome. He took me at once into the residence
of the ex-regent, next door, where we found his
favourite grandson, Khoon An, playing chess on the
verandah. His Grace, however, had just retired to rest,
although the sound of slow music could be heard from
his private lakon, for it was customary to keep playing
till they had lulled the former ruler of Siam like an
infant to rest.

Next day I paid a visit to the ex-regent, and the
first question he asked was, "Had I many sketches?"
So I went and fetched those I had. He then asked if
there was anything I wanted, to which I replied that I
should like to go to Kanburee, and he very courteously at once gave orders to have a boat ready for me,
with men, and even provisions for them. After inviting
me to lunch with him and his grandchildren, he sent
me in the afternoon to see the king's palace and Wat,
built on the summit of a hill, half an hour's ride from
the town.

On the 13th of September I left Radburee in a
commodious boat, manned by seven men, for Kanburee.
At 3.45 p.m. we arrived at Potaram, a large town,
peopled almost exclusively by Chinese, many of whom
have large sugar and coffee plantations, which for
two days lined the river banks, with considerable
villages at short intervals on either side. On the
16th we came to a Wat where nine priests administered
spiritual consolation to the people, and, on going ashore
to cook our breakfast, we found it was a Siamese
holiday. First of all, the women and children came

and made their offerings of rice, fruit, fish, and betel-nuts to the head priest, and then they all went to the Sala, where they awaited the arrival of the priests, who were to perform service [2] there at eight a.m. As the ecclesiastical body entered, every one bowed to the ground two or three times, and then sat on their haunches, with their hands up to the forehead in a praying attitude, resting their elbows on the knees. Before the head priest began the service, several children came and offered betel-nuts, tobacco, and *burees ;* when this was over, the head priest, holding his big fan before his face, chanted some prayers : the congregation were not very attentive, and an old grand-mother attracted my attention by taking the opportunity of teaching a little girl, not two years old, how to make a curtsey before the priest. After a while the old priest himself began counting the cigarettes, some of which he distributed by throwing them to the left among his colleagues, while one of his coadjutors took up the duty of reciting some Pali sentences.

At four p.m. we arrived at Kanburee, pleasantly situated in a valley, through which the river flows, with high mountains close by on either side.

Kanburee was once a fortified town ; the old walls, over five feet thick, still remain, while here and there some old cannons peacefully show their mouths, in-side which serpents live and spiders make their webs.

Here, again, we find the industrious and ubiquitous Chinaman in full force, cultivating his plantations of sugar and tobacco, buying up sapan wood (the *mai fang* of the Siamese), which is plentiful in the jungle. The only native industry, though one of some import-

[2] Many Salas are provided with pulpits and other adjuncts to religious services.

ance, seems to be mat-making—an occupation of the
women, who sit under the houses, plaiting alternate
strips of bamboo and bark into mats of a chequered
pattern, the bark being brown, while the strips of bamboo are light yellow. These mats, which are exceedingly durable and cheap, are sent in quantities to
Bangkok. The Siamese call them *sua.*

I went at once with Kao to the house of the governor, who had only lately been installed in his office, and
resided in a large but dilapidated bamboo house. He expressed regret at having no accommodation to offer me,
but I said I should be pleased to stay in one of the
Salas, if he would get one swept clean and enclosed, and
guard it at night during my stay ; so half a dozen
prisoners were set to work to erect a plaited bamboo
screen round a portion of the Sala, and to partition off
a place for my attendants. The building was partially
occupied by a Burmese from Moulmein, who with his
three servants had already been here seven months,
waiting for the trial of a Karian who was charged with
murder under the following circumstances. In the previous year the brother of the Burmese had left Burmah
with about 800 ticals (100*l.*), to go to Chengmai to buy
an elephant, and on the way he was murdered. When
last heard of he was amongst the Karians, one of
whom he had for a guide, but who had returned to his
hut alone. His gun had since been found in the possession of this man, upon whom suspicion naturally
fell, and who had been arrested and brought here.
He was actually one of the men employed in erecting
the partition at the Sala for me. Of course he denied
the charge, but the evidence against him was very
strong, and there was little doubt that he was the
guilty person, and that robbery had been his motive,
for he could give no satisfactory account of the disap-

pearance of the Burmese trader, to whom he admitted having acted as "guide." The brother of the murdered man told me it had already cost him, since he left Moulmein, a considerable sum of money simply for food and other expenses of travelling hither; yet, though he was furnished with all the evidence he wanted, he could not get the trial fixed, and he might possibly have another seven months to wait before it came on. In the meantime the Karian, with the chance of the death penalty staring him in the face, was happier and better off in every respect—manacles notwithstanding —than his prosecutor. So "indifferently" is justice administered in this part of the world!

Next day I had a visit from the first and second governors, who brought some presents in the shape of fowls, eggs, and pork. In the afternoon I visited the principal Wat, "Chai Sumpun," under the charge of a high priest. On the altar lay, heaped together in great confusion, Buddhas, vases, candlesticks, paper flowers, flowers preserved in salted water, lamps, clocks, and lastly, hidden behind a large vase, a pipe made of a bamboo, and curiously carved into a somewhat indelicate figure which struck me as being singularly inappropriate for a priest, so I begged him to exchange it for an English pipe, which he was pleased to do.

H

CHAPTER IX.

Return to Radburee—A famous shrine—The ordination of Buddhist
priests—An illustrious novice—The government of the Church
—A visit to a high Church dignitary—Life of a Buddhist priest
—Return to Bangkok.

AFTER a few days' stay at Kanburee, and at a small
village called Radja, about eight miles in a north-west
direction, I returned to Radburee, stopping on the
way at the village of Tarua, the seat of a governor
and the nearest station to Praten, a famous resort of
pilgrims, who go there in thousands every year to
do homage to a noted sacred stone in the Wat, which
Kao was delighted to have an opportunity of seeing.
The governor kindly lent me a horse to ride, the road
through the forest being at this time of the year partly
under water. The "stone," which is preserved in a
small Wat, round which are congregated a number of
Salas to accommodate the crowds of pilgrims who
flock thither in the dry season, is seventeen feet and
a half long by six feet and three quarters wide, but
so smothered was it beneath votive offerings of clothing and other materials that I had some difficulty in
seeing it at all. The upper part of the "stone" is
undoubtedly brickwork, gilt all over, while the lower
part is ornamented with a small angular pattern, also
gilt. Inside the brickwork, the priests say, is a natural
stone. Over this sacred relic is placed a double
canopy, round the lower edge of which are suspended
rows of glass balls, and fancy fringe-work made of pith

and beads. In front of the stone is a copy of Buddha's foot-sole, with the 108 symbols, and below this is a small altar with a few vases and gilt stones upon it. Here the devout Kao lighted his matches, stuck them in the vases, and uttered his prayers. Outside the Wat were three old bells of fine sound, which called the faithful to prayer every morning.

When I returned in the evening to Tarua, the governor gave a lakon performance in my honour, which lasted till early in the morning; I got tired of the monotony of the play, however, and retired at midnight. During the evening one of the governor's boys offered me a cigarette, lighting it first in his own mouth, according to native etiquette, before handing it to me.

On returning to Radburee I found that Khoon An, the ex-regent s grandson, had entered the priesthood, so I went and paid him a visit at the Wat Suriwongse.

His admission to the priesthood was a mere formality, but he had to go through all the religious forms and ceremonies just as if the service of the temple was to be his lifelong mission. When a youth attains the age of twenty-one he is supposed, according to the canons of the Buddhist faith, to enter the priesthood, and although, of course, among the lower orders this practice is not adhered to, it is rigorously observed among the nobility. As soon as the youth has made up his mind what particular Wat to enter, he goes round to the princes, nobles, and elder members of his family, and makes known his intentions, and then, having paid all his debts, he invites a priest or priests to come and pray at his house. The first night is generally one of merry-making, and on the next morning the priest or priests are fed before noon. Immediately afterwards a procession is formed. First,

riding on a horse, comes a man with the all-important
rice-pot and fan for the novice; then, also on horseback,
a man carrying the yellow cloth for his clothes, called
krai set. Immediately behind, on a third horse, comes
the novice himself, clean-shaved, even to his eyebrows,
for it is a sin for a priest to appear unshaven.[1] I have
several times seen this procession, and have always
thought the intending priest looked the very picture of
misery, as, dressed in white, wearing a conical gilt crown,
not unlike the royal crown of Siam, and with a number
of rings on his fingers, he rides solemnly on the back
of a horse, whose reins he cannot hold, and which has
to be led by an attendant, because his hands are posed
in an attitude of prayer, with a lotus-flower clasped between the palms. Behind him follow his family and
friends, with more yellow cloth, umbrellas, lamps, shoes,
and many other odds and ends for his future use as
priest. This procession ceremony is called *Buat Nack*,
and the novice himself is called *Nack*. When the Nack
arrives at the temple, he dismounts from his horse, and
takes off his shoes, because the religion forbids the wearing of shoes in the temple, but retains on his head the
crown ; and, after walking with the other members of
the procession three times round the temple, he enters
the dormitory, where he changes his dress prior to
returning to the temple. Here the head priest and
two other priests, called *Koo suat* and *Hupacka*, invest
the Nack, one by one, with the robes of the priesthood,
during which ceremony they ask him a number of
questions, such as whether he enters the priesthood at
his own desire, or under the compulsion of his parents,
or for the sake of receiving money—for natives, when

---

[1] Buddha was shaved by Indra, under the banyan-tree in his
retreat in the Himalayas, and invested with the dingy yellow garments of priesthood.

in debt, often enter the priesthood as a means of getting rid of their debts; they apply to some one who wishes to make merit with Buddha, and induce him to pay the debt on condition of "taking orders," and so escape imprisonment for life with a pair of iron bangles and chains round their limbs. Other questions are then put as to his relationships, whether he has father, mother, brothers, sisters, or, more important still, wife, children, property, debt, &c. The interrogatories are put three times, and if the Nack answers the same every time, a prayer is offered, and a sermon preached by the priest to the newly-ordained *Phra*, whose name and date of admission are now registered in a book kept in every Wat. He has to live in the monastery, under the jurisdiction of the head priest of the temple, and to follow the example of his colleagues. His first daily duty is to collect alms, that is, properly speaking, his food. Every morning files of yellow-robed priests are to be met on the roads, or paddling along the river in boats, each with a fan in his hand and an iron pot under his arm, passing from house to house for "alms."

My Siamese informant told me there are 200 commandments to be observed by the lowest grade of priests called *Nane*, while 500 have to be observed by the highest grade, the *Phra Song*. The principal precepts are: (1) Believe in the only true Buddhist faith; (2) Obey thy father and mother; (3) Do not kill or injure any life whatsoever; (4) Do not steal; (5) Do not drink alcohol or smoke; (6) Do not eat or drink more than necessary; (7) Do not be lazy or effeminate, such as using perfumery, &c.

The shortest period of probation as a priest is seven days, but in practice the average time is about three months. I have known many priests who, entering only for a month or two, had remained in the service

of the temple for two or three years, waiting for a
favourable opportunity of marrying, or till something
else, in Micawber phrase, "turned up." My friend
Khoon An was going to remain in the priesthood for
three weeks only, but he had to submit to the complete tonsure, and his appearance was so altered by
the removal of his eyebrows and every particle of hair
from his face that I hardly recognized him. Besides the
necessary articles enumerated above, it is customary for
the novice to receive gifts, according to his rank; and
Khoon An, belonging as he does to the most influential
family in Siam, had received quite a number of beautiful
objects, such as inkstands, paper-weights, cigar-stands,
and other *articles de luxe*, with which to soften the
rigours of his not very prolonged or very self-denying
régime as a priest. The temple which he had entered,
the Wat Sri Suriwongse, built by the ex-regent himself,
was more completely and comfortably fitted with all
needful accessories than any I had seen elsewhere. The
temple, cloisters, belfries, &c., were all built of brick,
and kept clean and whitewashed. There was also, in
the grounds, which were nicely laid out, a pond with
lotus-flowers, so that the priests could have a constant
supply for their festivals. The head priest had a brick
house to himself, and so likewise had Khoon An—a
cosy little place, with two rooms upstairs and a sort of
kitchen below.

The priests have a complete code of laws, and a
government of their own, at the head of which is the
Somdeth Chow Phra, uncle to the present king, a
very short, mild, resigned-looking gentleman, who lives
at Wat Buromanivet, where I paid him a visit one day.
He is the head priest of Siam, in fact, the supreme
authority, and has to report on all religious matters to
his sovereign. After him in rank comes also a

" Somdeth " priest, whom, in company with the ever
courteous Mr. Solomon, who acted as my interpreter,
I often visited, to have a look over his " curiosity shop,"
as I somewhat irreverently got to call the two gloomy-
looking rooms which he inhabited in the Wat Sutat

A high priest of Bangkok.

Tape Pataram. The Somdeth Phra Tomoro Wodom,
that is his full name, has been forty years a priest,
and by degrees has risen to be the second highest
ecclesiastical authority in the kingdom. He is reputed

to be a very learned Pali scholar, of whom, by the way, he told me there were few in the kingdom.

We generally visited the Somdeth Phra directly after noon, and nearly always found him reposing on a yellow velvet mattress, with a number of cushions under and around his head, and a pile of Pali MSS. at his side, and a cigarette in his mouth. Though smoking by priests seems to be forbidden—or perhaps it is smoking to excess that is meant—I may say that all priests are smokers as well as betel-chewers. He never rose, but, with a pleasant smile on his face, offered us his hand—sometimes the right, sometimes the left—and pointed us to be seated on a mat near him. The room he lived in was crammed full with *bric-à-brac*, most of which he termed Phra, or holy, including a fine collection of vases, a number of china teapots, —for it is strictly forbidden to priests to possess any articles of gold or silver—and small cups and saucers; spittoons of enamelled brass or of china; common Bohemian glassware; lamps, all of European make; quite an assortment of sticks, from the highly prized black coral or heavy ebony stick to a slender cane; several small cabinets filled with Pali MSS.; and a varied selection of fans and almspots, his "insignia of office." On a small altar at the back of the room were a gilt figure of Buddha, a number of glass vases of old French manufacture, many of them empty, some filled with flowers; a number of cheap German and American clocks; and, what I most admired, a very old and choice cabinet, most beautifully and effectively inlaid with mother-of-pearl, in such profusion that the wood was scarcely visible, which contained the sacred MSS.: each volume, I noticed, was wrapped in yellow silk, and fastened with string. In the adjoining room, which was dark, and to which no sunlight was ever admitted, the venerable priest slept.

Attached to every wat are a number of boys who perform the menial services, such as cleaning, cooking, &c., but who also wear the dingy yellow garments, otherwise peculiar to the priests. The life of a Buddhist priest from a western point of view is one of indolence ; at sunrise they ring the bells, or beat the drum, when some of them go into the temple and recite Pali prayers ; they then go their daily round, either by land or by water, and collect their food for the day—rice, fish, fruit, and vegetables, not omitting tobacco and betel-nuts, being freely and generously given by the people, who know they will attain merit and reap reward, both here and hereafter, from their great law-giver, Buddha. When their pot is filled, they return to the temple to eat what they want at noon, throwing the " fragments that remain " on the ground, where they are speedily devoured by the hungry dogs, the fowls, and the crows, of which there are millions in Bangkok. After noon, no food is permitted till next sunrise, except a cup of tea.

During the rainy season the priests remain in the cloisters or temples, but when the dry season begins they wander about the country to different places of interest, especially the Phra Bat, where Buddha is supposed to have left his footprint. The full moon of the third month, corresponding with February, is the recognized period for the commencement of this pilgrimage, and then the priests can be seen going there by thousands.

On the 5th of October I left Radburee for Bangkok, as the time was getting on for me to commence my journey to the north. The ex-regent kindly ordered a boat and crew to take me back to the capital, but when I went down to the river in the morning I was surprised to find the governor had given me an ordinary trading-boat, without a cabin or shelter of any kind. As I proposed returning by way of one of the numerous canals [2] which connect the delta of the Menam with the Meklong River, where mosquitoes abound in untold millions, and where it is no uncommon thing for a heavy trading-boat to stick fast for days, I complained to Pra Maw, a grandson of the ex-regent, who said it was an insult to offer me such a boat, especially in face of the ex-regent's orders. He at once furnished me with a light boat and four men to take me and Kao to Bangkok, while my luggage remained in the trading-boat, to come on later; and two days later I found myself once more in the city of temples.

[2] Siam is, like Holland, well furnished with canals, which have been made mostly by Chinese coolies, and which are perhaps a trifle more malodorous than those in the Netherlands.

CHAPTER X.

The royal visitation of the temples—Procession of state barges – A magnificent scene and its contrast—A woman condemned to death—Proclaiming her doom—Awaiting execution—The last scene of all—The decapitation—Given to the vultures.

WHILE making the final arrangements for my journey through Upper Siam and Lao, I witnessed two sights which, varying extremely in their nature, were both characteristic of the city of Bangkok, and of great interest. The first of these was the annual ceremony of the *Kateen*, or royal visitation to the temples, or at least to those dedicated to or built by the king.[1]

[1] The building of temples is esteemed by Buddhists as very meritorious, and all classes vie with each other in this work. These edifices are of four general classes, viz.:—

1. Those made by order of the king, or dedicated to him, called *Wat Hluang*.

2. Those made by order of princes, called *Wat Chow*.

3. Those made by order of noblemen, called *Wat Koon Nang*.

4. Those made by order of the people, called *Wat Ratsadawn*.

Nearly all the temples erected by noblemen are eventually dedicated to the king, and hence fall into the first class.

Ratsadawn temples are built by contributions from the people. As a preparatory step, a crier is generally sent forth, proclaiming that a temple is to be built in such and such a district, and all who place confidence in Buddha are invited to join in this good work: "Come, yĕ rich! come, ye poor! come all, and contribute according to what ye have!" Sometimes a circular is sent round in which men and women are cordially invited to unite in this work of merit.

The grant of the site of the temple must be formally requested of the king, who alone has authority to devote any plot of ground irre-

The festivities in connexion with this ceremony commence on the 15th of the waxing [2] of the 11th Siamese month, *i.e.* about the 8th of October, and last for a month.

It is during these Kateen *fêtes* that the River Menam affords perhaps the most imposing spectacle which this magnificent river, ever full of life and interest, can afford—when the king with a royal procession of barges, proceeds in full state array to visit the temples on the western bank of the river.

First those on the " city " side are visited in rotation. The first of these was the Wat Buromanivet, so I drove up there early in the day to look round before the king arrived, in order to see the preparations made. The grounds were kept by marines and infantry in groups, while a number of Siamese officers, in their gorgeous costumes, and loaded with decorations, were waiting, surrounded by a crowd of men, women, and children, anxious to get a glimpse of their sovereign.

vocably to the purposes of a Buddhist temple. If the site is in any of the provinces, the application must be made through the governor. The site being duly dedicated to the purpose, eight round stones, called *luk nimit*, are taken, and a parallelogram marked out with them, one being placed at each of the eight points of the compass. Some indefinite time afterwards a small, round-roofed, brick structure, either square or hexagonal, from four to six feet across, and about five feet high, and having four porches, is erected over each of these eight stones. On the top of each of these structures is set up, endwise, a stone of red free-stone or marble, sixteen to twenty inches in height, and ten or twelve inches in breadth, and carved in the form of a leaf. These stones are called *bysema* (*sema* is Sanscrit for " boundary "), and mark the boundary of the *obosot*, which, though built separately from the Wat, may be said to correspond with the holy of holies in Jewish, or the chancel in Christian places of worship. This obosot is destined to contain the most sacred of the idols, and no woman is allowed to enter. It is here that the royal gifts are given away at the Kateen visitation.

[2] For Siamese system of measuring time see Appendix.

THE KATEEN FESTIVAL: THE KING CARRIED IN STATE.

[*To face page* 109.

The temple floor was covered for the day with mats, and a richly-gilt easy chair, borrowed from the palace, with a yellow silk cover on which the royal coat of arms was embroidered, was placed near the altar. By its side were a small, round, marble table, and a few chairs for the princes and suite. On an elevated platform opposite, where the priests of the temple would sit, the royal gifts to the priests were laid out, consisting mostly of bundles of yellow cloth, for garments.

Shortly before eleven a.m. the king, dressed in Siamese state costume, glittering with gold, was carried in on a sedan-chair, and distributed the presents; after which the high priest preached a sermon, and invoked Buddha's blessing on the king.

Similar ceremonies at other principal Wats occupied several days, but the " function " which carried off the palm for gorgeousness and impressiveness was the visit to the temples across the river, when the procession of royal barges, borne along the bosom of the great mother Menam, with all the accessories of splendour that Bangkok could produce, afforded a sight the beauty of which is hardly to be equalled in any part of the " gorgeous East."

After several fine boats conveying the princes and great dignitaries of the state, came the king's barge, an immensely long low boat, with high prow and stern, richly carved, and gilded throughout, manned by 120 rowers, who, every day for a month previously, had been practising the proper time and swing, up and down the river. The rowers kept time like clockwork, raising the blades of the paddles above their heads at every stroke, the time being marked by two men in each boat waving long poles decorated with tassels. In the centre of this state barge was a raised seat,

on which, sheltered beneath a golden canopy, sat—
looking, and no doubt feeling, every inch a king—
the sovereign, surrounded by attendants sitting at
his feet, bearing the regalia. Behind this came at
least fifty other royal barges, all of great magnifi-
cence and size, but of course not equalling that of
the king himself, bearing his distinguished suite,
and at a respectful distance on all sides hovered a
swarm of boats, gaily decorated with bunting. The
effect of the scene and its surroundings, the deep,
wide river reflecting the brilliancy of the sunny sky,
and doubling every gay object upon its surface, while
ashore, on either side, flags fluttered and gilt spires
glittered, will never be effaced from my mind.

A day or two after this, occurred the second event
which marked this period of my stay in Bangkok, and
which I have said offered so striking a contrast to that
just described. This, too, was an "affair of state,"
but of a very different nature. On the 15th of
October, just as I had returned from lunching with
my vivacious friend, Mr. Torrey, of the United States
Legation, and his hospitable wife, Mr. Solomon
knocked at my door, and said,—

"Mr. Bock, the execution is, after all, going to
take place to-day; make haste, I have a *garrie* (dog-
cart) ready, and we will drive down at once."

Bangkok had, a fortnight before, been startled by the
report of a horrible murder, committed by a noble-
man's wife on one of her servants. The details of
the crime, and how it was committed, are too shocking
and disgusting to relate here. Suffice it to say that
jealousy was at the bottom of the matter, and that the
deed was marked by diabolical inhumanity. The case
was fully proved and the accused sentenced to death,
and the king, who is rather averse to signing death-

warrants, in this case very naturally did so without hesitation. As is customary, the condemned woman had,
three days before the date fixed for the execution, gone
round the streets in chains, to cry aloud her horrible act,
and her righteous doom; but for some reason a rumour
had got abroad that the sentence would not be carried
out. The day, however, had arrived, and the law
was to take its course; so we drove quickly up to the
Wat Ko, on a field adjoining which the execution was
to take place. The whole main road was crowded with
people, men, women, and children, anxious to see the
execution, which was to take place at three o'clock. In
a narrow lane, leading from the main road to the field,
there was quite a crush—Siamese, Chinese, Malays,
and a few Europeans, all forcing their way through,
in the hope of catching a glimpse of the wretched
woman.

"Where is she?" was the question raised everywhere.

"In the Sala yonder, most likely," said Mr. Solomon, "for I see a company of soldiers stationed
there."

So we pushed our way as best we could through
the dense crowd—and a more solid mass of human
beings I never saw—surging around that Sala, the last
"resting-house" the condemned woman would ever
make use of.

Soldiers were there in plenty to keep order, but
order there was none, and orders, if issued at all, were
not obeyed.

The crowd gave way a little as Mr. Solomon, ·wear-
ing his full-dress uniform as inspector of police,
pushed his way through, and I followed him as
closely as I could stick to him. We went upstairs,
where the condemned criminal sat on the floor,

her neck firmly held between two long poles on either side, and two crossbars, one under the chin, the other behind the neck, so that her head could not get out. The ends of the long poles reached forward to the ground, where they were "braced" together by another crossbar. Her hands were locked with a pair of iron handcuffs, and round her feet were heavy irons and chains. I approached to within two feet of her, but she held her face to the ground; once or twice she slowly looked round, appearing as if an opiate had been administered to her, for she was very drowsy and most unconcerned. Three women, friends of hers, sat round her, telling her not to be afraid, and to think how happy she would be soon! A priest sat in front of her, and uttered some prayers, to which she did not seem to pay the least attention. The only tender part about her was her back, for on this she had received, in three instalments, the well-deserved ninety lashes—the utmost ever given, and a punishment so severe that many do not survive it.

Having seen all, and more than, we wanted, we passed on to the place of execution. The rush on the Sala was now so great that Mr. Solomon and I had, if anything, more difficulty in getting out than we had in getting in; and just as we were approaching the field we heard a tremendous crash behind us; a part of the flooring of the Sala had given way, and a batch of people were thrown down. Fortunately nobody was seriously injured, but, by the time the effects of this little accident had been remedied, the time for the execution was at hand. The prison warders, guarded by soldiers, appeared with the culprit at three p.m. precisely. An open space was formed and kept clear by the soldiers, in the middle of which the woman was placed. The two poles with the crossbars were now taken away, so that her head was free, and she was ordered to sit on the ground with her back against a couple of small wooden poles, to which her upper arms and body were tied by one of the executioners. Of these functionaries there were six, every one of them dressed in a scarlet waistcoat, trimmed with gold lace round the edges, and a scarlet cap on the head. On the forehead they all had put some white chalk or lime, the object of which I do not know. Each was armed with a sharp Japanese sword.

I asked why so many executioners were wanted. Mr. Solomon explained that it was in case the first or second executioner failed in their stroke.

I managed to get in the front row of the onlookers, among the officials, and close by one of the king's brothers, so that I could see everything that occurred.

The first executioner, after having tied the woman to the posts, prepared her for the loss of her head by cutting her long hair, so as to get a clear view of the neck. After this he took some clay, rolled it between his hands, divided it, and plugged her ears with it, so that she should not hear the noise going on ; her nose also was plugged. Then the executioner placed a piece of clay on the spot where he intended to hit her. During the preparations the woman exclaimed, " Take my life quick ! Take my life quick ! "

Now followed a sort of dance, preceding the execution, the executioners following each other at a short distance away from the victim, waving their swords in the air, and dancing backwards and forwards once or twice; then the first executioner rushed forward, and at a single stroke severed the head from the body. A fountain of blood rose from the headless trunk, while the head rolled along the ground right in front of us,

I

till it nearly touched our feet. The crowd now slowly
dispersed, here and there muttering " She got her
deserts." There was not a word of commiseration for
the woman, even among her relatives.

The executioners then set to work to complete their
task. Instead of unlocking the chains round the woman's feet, they simply cut off the heels from the feet
and the chains dropped. Then the body was cut up
into fragments—the flesh from the bones —much in the
same way as the bodies of paupers are treated, as
already described, at the Wat Sikhet, and the mangled
remains were left for the vultures to feed upon, while
the head, according to custom, was fixed on a tall
bamboo so that it could be seen from all parts of the
field.

CHAPTER XI.

Northward ho !—Bangkok from the river by night—A gigantic
Buddha figure—Paknam Po—" Poling " up stream—Ban Put
Pisai—How to find a governor—A dead chief awaiting crema-
tion—Diving for shells—A curious charm—Swamped—My
boat carried away by the flood—Praying for a safe journey—
Deserters and deserters—The view from the river—Arrival at
Kampheng Pet—Dining with the governor—Sham champagne—
An eclipse of the moon—A great ruined temple - Nature *versus*
Art.

ON the 9th of November, 1881, I left Bangkok in
a steamer under the command of Captain Richelieu,
and graciously placed at my disposal by the king, to
convey me and my men as far as the river was navigable. Besides Kao, my interpreter, I had a Chinese
cook who had an unfortunate weakness for strong
drink, and, as personal attendants, two Chinese boys,
by name Yang and Kien, who, though of a somewhat
timid disposition, both proved themselves faithful
servants. They both prepared themselves for the
journey by obtaining from the priests one of the
charms known as *luk sakhot*, which they treasured
above all their other earthly possessions. Kien was an
exceedingly good-looking boy ; though he called himself
a Chinaman I am sure he had European blood in his
veins.

I remember the day well : for, after delays which
had seemed well-nigh endless, and an illness which
had threatened to put a complete stop to my long-

I 2

projected journey, I was at last fairly started on my way, with the goodwill and practical co-operation of the supreme ruler of the land, while his Highness Chow Fa Maha Mala, the minister for the north, had kindly furnished me with an open letter to the officials of the districts through which I should pass, and to the chiefs of the tributary states, calling upon them to give me facilities for the prosecution of my journey.

Clear against the light blue sky floated the royal standard of England, displayed above the British agency in honour of the birthday of his Royal Highness the Prince of Wales. The day itself, I thought, was auspicious, and the weather was perfect.

It was evening, and, as the brilliant day gave way to the rapidly-falling shades of a tropical night, the bright full moon rose above the city of golden temples, casting a long silvery streak across the broad waters of the River Menam. As we steamed slowly up stream hundreds of lights twinkled from the windows of the long rows of houses lining the banks of the river for miles, while across the water here and there came the sounds of merry-making, and the faint echoes of the musical accompaniments to the dances and lakon performances taking place in the native theatres.

As the long line of lamps flickered and faded gradually from sight, the brilliancy of the stars in the dark sky, their steady beams reflected upon the still darker waters, and of the ampler flood of light shed by the rising moon was very striking. The scene was poetic in its peaceful impressiveness, but a sudden cry of " Rudder lost ! " was enough to bring back the most sentimental mind to the regions of prosaic necessity. The sound came from the men in charge of a boat which we were towing astern, and which his Highness Prince Devan had kindly lent me for the purpose

of continuing my journey when the river should become too shallow for the steamer. The engines were
stopped, and a man sent on board the boat to remedy
the mishap, when he fortunately discovered that the
damage was less than had been represented, and that
it was only the rudder-pin that was gone ; but half an
hour later another voice raised the same cry, " Rudder
lost ! "—this time with too much reason, and Captain
Richelieu had to send two more men into the boat to
steer her with oars.

Early on the following morning we saw in the distance, towards the north-east, the Phra Bat [1] Mountain,
so named from the famous foot-print of Buddha,
which forms the object of the pilgrimage of so many
thousands of Siamese during the dry season.[2]

About a day's journey from the spot we had now
reached is the Wat Tja Jo, with a gigantic white-
washed figure of Buddha, the head and upper part of
the body of which are distinctly visible from the river,
towering above the foliage of the dense forest-growth
with which the river is fringed.

Every few miles the banks are dotted with villages,
the river flowing through a low alluvial plain, thickly
populated, and studded with temples and phrachedees
whose conical spires serve to relieve the monotony of the
scenery. The country is very fertile, but from the river
no sign of cultivation can be seen, the rice-fields lying
out of sight at a short distance from the banks, behind
the villages and the forest-growth.

As we proceeded up stream the river gradually
became shallower and frequently obstructed by sand-

[1] *Phra* = lord or sacred. *Bat* = foot.
[2] An excellent article upon this Phra Bat, from the pen of Mr. Palgrave, British agent at Bangkok, appeared in a recent number of
Macmillan's Magazine.

banks. It was the dry season, the effect of which was seen, not only in the rapidly-decreasing volume of water, but in the shrivelled appearance of the foliage, which was beginning to lose its brilliant, glossy, green hue.

After four days' pleasant steaming, at the rate of about six miles an hour against a four-mile current, Paknam Po was reached, at the junction of the Menam with the Menam Jai, or Great Menam, which, notwithstanding its name, is the less navigable stream of the two. Here I took leave of Captain Richelieu and his comfortable steamer, and began the second stage of my journey in Prince Devan's river-boat, with a crew of nine men, followed by a second boat with four men and my luggage. No oars were used to propel the boats, but the tedious system of " poling " was adopted—a very laborious and slow mode of progression against a shallow and rapid stream. I was surprised at the swiftness of the current, seeing that the land on either side of the river for many miles still preserved the general character of a flat alluvial plain, and more particularly as it was the dry season. It took us two and a half days to reach Ban Put Pisai, only twenty miles above Paknam Po. Here I made my way to the governor's house. On the road I met some Siamese women, who informed me that the governor was dead, and that all the men of the place were away in the forest, cutting timber for the buildings to be erected in connexion with the festivities in celebration of the coming centenary of Bangkok. Still I determined to call at the official residence of the governor, which was pointed out to me as being distinguished from other houses by a huge archway formed of three immense square logs of teak, two as uprights, with a third placed across them. These simple but massive arches, which are high enough for the largest elephant to pass through, are always erected as a sign of his authority in front of the entrance to the house of the governor of a town in all parts of Siam. Sometimes they depart a little from the rigorous simplicity of the two posts and crossbar, and assume the form shown in the accompanying sketch, which was taken at Radburee.

The residence itself was composed of a series of bamboo buildings, erected on timber posts, and connected with each other by planks. In an open space in the centre of the group was a large platform which formed the entrance. On my approach the widow of the governor, who was sitting on this platform, suddenly rose and ran indoors, shutting herself up in the principal house and

How to find a governor.

bolting the door; but the other women, of whom there were about a dozen—concubines of the deceased chief—quietly continued their occupation of card-playing, while a group of children stood around as if mastering the elements of the favourite pastime. All the women were in mourning; dressed, that is, in snow-white calico, and with their heads clean-shaven. This gave them a most repulsive appearance, but would have afforded a good opportunity for a phrenologist to study their " bumps." They took little or no notice of me till Kao addressed them. Then they answered, one after the other, that they could do nothing; that the second governor [3] was in the forest with the men, and that till he returned I might wait or go away as I pleased.

Nothing that I could say could draw them out of their state of passive reserve, and I was meditating what step to take next when an obliging old Chinaman came forward, and undertook to go into the forest with one of my men, and hunt up the chief, and get him to come and see me.

In an open space, or compound, immediately adjoining the principal house, and placed on a lofty stand or pedestal, constructed of teak, was the coffin containing the remains of the deceased governor, awaiting the final ceremony of cremation, for which the priests were expecting orders from Bangkok. The body had already lain there seven months, and very little of it was probably left by this time, the coffin being as usual fitted with a bamboo pipe inserted in the bottom to convey the fluid product of decomposition to mother earth.

While awaiting the return of the second governor, I took a stroll in the neighbouring jungle, and found a number of shells, among which *vitrina* and *bulimus* were common, but came across nothing new. It was not till the next morning that the second governor returned, but he at once gave orders for a fresh crew to accompany me, so that I continued my journey without further delay.

---

[3] I may as well here distinguish the titles of the different officials one meets when travelling in Siam :—

Chow muang is a governor of a town or province, who is always a Phya.

Palat jai = chief of a large village.

Palat rong = chief of an ordinary village.

Kam nan jai = petty chief.

Kam nan rong = assistant chief (lowest grade).

The following afternoon Ban⁴ Den was reached. Here we had again to submit to another halt while a fresh crew was engaged, for the men would not go beyond the limit of their own district.

Large *unios* are very common here : the natives dive for the shells in the river, but are very much hindered by crocodiles, of which they are very much afraid. They sell the shells to the Chinese, who value them for their mother-of-pearl.

The governor of this place gave me a curiously-twisted portion of the branch or twig of a tree, tied completely into a figure-of-eight knot. Whether the knot was formed by an accident of nature, or, as is more probable, by artificially twisting the young shoot, I could not discover ; but I was assured that such things were· a valuable medicine or charm—a regular *panacea* for all sorts of ills, ghostly as well as bodily.

My possession of this charm did not assist me much ; perhaps because I had no faith in it ! On the other hand, I might have been tempted to attribute to its influence a succession of disasters which befell me soon afterwards. The first night after leaving Ban Den, we were nearly swamped by a terrific rain-storm Although it was the " dry season," Jupiter Pluvius was determined that his powers should not be forgotten, for the rain came down, not in " bucketfuls," but in what seemed to be an unbroken stream. Verily the floodgates of heaven were suddenly opened, and my boat was no ark to shelter its occupants. It became full of water, and sleep was out of the question. After incessant baling out, the cook tried to prepare some rice for an early breakfast, and only by dint of the greatest care in sheltering the few dry sticks he

⁴ *Ban* = village.

managed to secure, and closely screening his fireplace
with an umbrella all the time, did he succeed in his
task. But worse than this, the second boat, in which
two men were left in charge of the stock of provisions,
was carried away during the night, while the two men
were asleep, and the rest of the crew were ashore, as
usual, with their poles. It was not till the morning
that I heard of this disaster, and then discovered that
the boat, having been carried quietly down stream for
some distance, had got among the eddies before the two
sleepers awoke and saw their danger. Their cries did
not reach my ears, while the rest of the natives, if they
heard them at all, displayed their usual indifference to
the fate of their companions, and took no notice: at
least they made no effort to discover the missing men
and boat till I awoke in the morning. Fortunately
the boat had been carried against a log of wood fixed
in the river, to which the men held fast all night.
Beyond getting saturated and thoroughly frightened
—a warning against carelessly fastening up the boat
in future—they were none the worse, though they had
a very narrow escape; but a large tin-lined box containing rice, and another with dried fish sufficient to
last several months, were thrown out of the boat and
lost.

But more was to follow. In the course of the following
day the boat was found to be leaking fast; the salt-
bags were saturated, and the whole of the salt was
dissolved: not a grain was left; while the remaining
stock of dried fish was dry fish no longer. All
attempts to stop the leaks were fruitless, and I had
to send Kao on to the next village, Ban Krue, to get a
new boat and a fresh stock of eatables.

While waiting for Kao to return, the crew asked leave
to go and make offerings at the shrine known as San-

chow Taw Hok. Here, in an open space in the forest, close to some mighty trees on the left bank of the river, the Siamese had erected two small devotional chapels, very like the edifices of a similar nature to be seen in Italy and the Tyrol. One by one my men went up to pray for a safe journey, taking with them a cocoa-nut, or a few scented matches, which they lighted and stuck into little pots standing on the shabby-looking altar, already crowded with flags, rags, figures of Buddha, dolls, and other native offerings.

About noon we reached Ban Kem, where I only intended to stay for luncheon, and for the men to take their midday meal of rice; but my men, determined that their prayers at Sanchow Taw Hok should not be unanswered, and that no further danger should attend them on this particular journey, all deserted with the exception of two, and I had to apply to the Kam nan jai to supply me with substitutes. The head chief had gone to Kampheng, and his assistant showed his sense of responsibility in the matter by such extreme dilatoriness that it was night before I had collected a fresh crew.

The following day we arrived at Krong Krung, a place existing in little more than name, being only the temporary residence of a Burmese timber-merchant and of a few Siamese during the season for collecting resin in the forests. During the night my fresh crew deserted to a man, and as there was no possibility of finding substitutes where there was no population, I hired a light boat from the Siamese traders and sent Kao on to Kampheng Pet—two days' journey—with a request to the governor, backed by my official " passport," to supply me with a fresh crew. My first, and I may almost say, my last, experience of native promptitude must be duly recorded. Kao left on the 27th of

November, and returned with twelve men on the 2nd of
December, having experienced little difficulty in per-
suading the chief of Kampheng Pet to accede to my
request.   Two days later I reached this town, after a
journey of twenty-one days to compass the 100 geographical miles or so of river between it and Paknam Po,
owing to the delays, occasioned partly by the natural
swiftness of the current, and partly by the natural
slowness of the people.   The rapidity of the stream is
the more remarkable from the fact that the country on
either bank is a low stretch of flat land, covered, where
not inhabited, with patches of rank grass or a dense
growth of forest.   From Kampheng Pet, the mountains
of Raheng are visible, but below that point there is
little to relieve the monotony of the scene.   The
country appears to be but sparsely inhabited, though
the governor of Kampheng Pet assured me there were
sixty-eight villages between that town and Paknam Po.
At any rate there is little sign of enterprise among
the people, and, in the only two cases in which any
attempt is being made to utilize the vast teak-forests
which exist here, it is Burmese from Moulmein or
Rangoon who are at the bottom of the undertaking.

Immediately on arriving at Kampheng Pet, I called
upon the governor to express my thanks for his
prompt attention to my message—thanks mingled also
with some share of that kind of gratitude which has
been defined as a " keen appreciation of favours to
come," for I had to ask him to assist me in procuring
a night's lodging, and to furnish me with another set
of men to continue my journey on the morrow.

The governor very kindly sent an officer to point
out to me a Sala, or resting-house, in which I could
take up my abode.   Before leaving he invited me to
come and dine with him on the morrow; this was

followed by a message asking me if I could spare
my cook to help in preparing the dinner, and by
another (private) message to Kao, inquiring if I had
any champagne, as the governor wished to buy some
bottles. Although I had no champagne, I did not
enlighten the governor upon the subject, but sent
him over four bottles of zoedone with my compli-
ments.

The governor's dinner-party was limited to the
second governor and myself. Both the officials were
dressed in full Siamese court-suits, down to the white
stockings and buckled shoes, although the general surroundings were not of the most highly finished order.

The table was covered with a sheet of white calico,
which served as a table-cloth, and was spread in due
form with a fair array of " plate " and cutlery, old-
fashioned tumblers serving as wine glasses. The *menu*
was a good one, and the dinner was served in a style
that would have done credit to a first-class hotel. My
cook had had the assistance of Kao, himself an experienced *chef;* and the two had done credit to themselves,
their employer, and their master. First there was
chicken soup, followed by chicken cutlets, fowl *rissoles.*
roast pork, and stewed duck, with biscuits and Siamese
sweetmeats for dessert. The " champagne " was a
great success. As Kao broached the bottles of zoedone,
the liquid foamed right royally, and called forth the
remark of the two Siamese officials that it was " very
fine." Altogether the evening passed most pleasantly,
but was destined not to close so agreeably. Close upon
midnight, soon after I had returned from the hospitable
table of the governor, I was disturbed by the noise
of drums and gongs, accompanied by the desultory
discharge of firearms in all directions. Hastily getting
up, I crossed over to a temple which stood opposite

to my Sala, where I found the priests assembled in full force, surrounded by an excited multitude of natives gazing at the great dragon swallowing the moon, and endeavouring by dreadful clamour to avert the calamity. In other words there was an eclipse of the moon. Hence the sudden alarm which had brought to an untimely end my postprandial slumbers.

I left Kampheng Pet on the 7th of December, carrying away most pleasant recollections of my stay. A few hours' " poling " against a strong current brought us to a village called Ban Nonkling, near which are the ruins of a large wat, or temple—known as Wat Awat—said to have been built 400 years ago, when Kampheng was a kingdom and boasted of a king.

> " But kingdoms sink, and kings go down
> With all their pomp and pride,"

and " Ichabod " is written on this as on innumerable relics of former grandeur, more and more plainly, and apparently more and more indelibly, the farther north one gets. Until the tide of civilization turns backwards, or, sweeping on in its westward course, eventually reaches in full force its Eastern starting-point, these countries will remain the hidden memorials of departed glory of ages long since past. Until Western progress has galvanized into life the dead relics of that Oriental civilization which gave it birth, this part of the Asiatic continent will never develop its real capabilities, which are enormous.

I was anxious to see this ancient wat, this remnant of a dead age, but the natives placed all sorts of obstacles in my way, representing that it was far away in the forest, and inaccessible by reason of numberless pools of water. Still I determined to brave the supposed dangers of wood and water, and, by way of economizing my boots, prevailed upon one of the officials to lend me " a horse." But neither saddle nor bridle could I get; a horse was a horse, without such accessories. A bare-backed steed, however, was better than walking through the forest amid deep mud, and with occasional pools of water up to one's knees; and after two miles of such rough travelling, I found the ruined temple.

The area enclosed by the remaining walls attested the former great extent of the building: and its antiquity was shown in the character of the masonry, which consisted of blocks of a kind of coarse red-brown sandstone, eighteen inches long and six inches square. On each side of what appeared to be the main entrance were two sculptured Rachasees [5] —monstrous animals somewhat resembling lions, sacred in Buddhistic literature, and represented to be the most powerful creatures in the world. Within the outer walls were the remains of a great number of massive pillars, of which only short fragments remained intact; while scattered in all directions were bronze figures of Buddha, most of which had lost a head or an arm. I afterwards learned from the priests at Nonkling that the choice collection of Buddha figures which formerly rested here had been removed one by one by pious priests and pilgrims for presentation to different temples. The head priest kindly gave me permission to take away a few specimens, among which was a fine figure of Buddha, in regal attitude, with hands uplifted in the act of preaching. An engraving of this figure is given overleaf. For further particulars, see p. 284.

Among the ruins were several topes or phrachedees, themselves mostly in a very dilapidated state, but

[5] See p.165.

many of them representing a peculiarly characteristic
feature in the shape of the roof, which instead of being

Rare figure of "Buddha preaching."

surmounted by a spire, according to the usual custom,
was either rounded or flattened at the top, like a
Gothic roof with the apex cut off.

In every crevice of the masonry of these topes grew vegetation of some sort—ferns, grasses, creepers, in some cases large trees, which rose majestically above their summits, giving a most curious effect, as though nature, ashamed of the ruin she had wrought on the works of man, had done her best to hide the blemishes, and at the same time to show her superiority in her perennial power of recuperation, while man's best works were doomed to decay.

Whether or not the proximity of these ruins was the cause I know not, but the governor of Nonkling seemed particularly pious; sticking so closely to the letter, if not to the spirit, of Buddha's teaching, that the command, "Thou shalt not take life of any kind," impelled him to refuse to accede to a request which I made to him to be supplied with some fowls. He overcame his scruples at last by giving me permission to shoot any fowls I wanted, on condition that I paid the owners for them—a stipulation which to a European did not appear to be so unreasonable as it probably did to the Oriental mind.

CHAPTER XII.

On the 10th of December I arrived at Raheng, like Kampheng Pet the seat of two governors, and by far the most important town in Upper Siam, with a population of 9000. It is divided into three distinct "quarters," devoted respectively to the Siamese, Laosian, and Burmese inhabitants.

Situated on the left bank of the river, which is here over 400 feet wide, but obstructed by a number of sandbanks some distance below the town, Raheng is, like all Siamese towns, built without any regularity or order ; huts, wooden booths, and more ambitious houses being mixed together in delightful confusion, each located just where chance or the whim of the owner may have decided. There are no streets, properly so called, but narrow lanes, or rather passages between the houses, choked with filth of every description, and resembling in continuity the twists and turns and unexpected blocks and corners of a cunningly-planned maze. Dotted here and there are small booths or wooden sheds, wherein women sit all day, waiting till a customer calls to purchase or barter their provisions—a delightful assortment of dried fish in all stages of decay, fruits vying with them in rottenness, sweetmeats, rolls of calico, ironware, and various odds and ends. At intervals you will come across an arrack farm, where the native liquor, "sam shu," made of fermented rice, is manufactured and sold, "to be drunk on or off the premises." Next door, perhaps, is a gambling "hell," where the natives, men, women, and children, can satisfy to the full their craving for games of chance, and for wagering. The "streets" swarm with little children, roving and crawling about at their own sweet will, and it is no uncommon thing to see little creatures of seven or eight years old, supposed to be watching over the interests of the younger members of the family, joining, with all the zest imaginable, in "backing" the luck of older gamblers. It is "wheels within wheels." Dice-throwers stake their fortunes on the turning up of a high number, or a winning figure, and the lookers-on bet upon the luck of the dice-players.

John Chinaman turns this gambling propensity to his own profit. He provides all facilities, and, while he runs no risk of loss himself, makes a large profit out of those who patronize his appliances. A favourite game is to have a small board divided into eight squares, upon each of which is painted the figure of a different animal. The players then throw dice the faces of which bear figures corresponding with those on the board. If the dice fall with those faces uppermost which bear the same figure as the squares upon which they fall, the thrower wins; if not, he loses. But there are numberless variations of the game, and endless are the calculations which the "takers" and "layers of the odds" have to make upon the combinations of chances which may occur.

Card-playing, with the small, narrow Chinese cards, is also very popular among young and old alike.

Traffic, at all times difficult through the tortuous lanes, is often completely blocked by crowds of eager gamblers, who, starting, probably, on some errand having for its object the purchase of provisions, stop half-way, and, losing their money, have to go home empty-handed, or try their luck at fishing in the river to find the wherewithal to fill the pot.

The most commodious and pretentious edifice in the town is the new court of justice, in which the governor very kindly quartered me. The building was commenced some years ago ; but, as it appears to be the custom in Siam to begin and never finish, it was far from complete, and there seemed no sign of any disposition to continue the work. In the meantime, the officials held their councils in an open shed near by.

The outer walls of the court were of brick, white-washed, and the internal fittings of teak. The ceilings of the lofty rooms were supported by massive pillars of teak, many of them carved with the favourite and familiar allegorical figures to be seen everywhere, in all sorts of grotesque designs, in Siam and Lao.

With this exception the town boasts no buildings of any importance. Its temples are neither very old nor very fine, the Wat Doi Hoa Diet being perhaps the most noteworthy. A few miles outside the town are the ruins of a couple of temples, said to have been built only eighty years ago, and already in utter decay. The site is of importance from the fact that it is the burial-place of the governors of Raheng, whose charred bones are deposited here after cremation; and also from its contiguity to a curious natural cave, or rather recess in the side of a hill, which the people regard with superstitious veneration. The Siamese and Laosians alike hold in high estimation any freaks of nature, especially when they take the form of a cavern which may be utilized as a place of worship. Indeed, there is probably hardly a cave in the country which has not been turned into a temple, with its altar, and its images of Buddha all complete. In this instance the fall of some gigantic boulders from the cliff above has formed a curious recess, the floor of which consists of several stones, forming an almost even surface, while the roof is composed of a flat mass of rock, fixed at an angle of about 45°, one edge firmly embedded in the soil, while the other edge is projected upwards, somewhat like the upper jaw of the open mouth of a crocodile. In the cavity thus formed are strewn the usual miscellaneous assortment of native offerings, among which a profusion of Buddha figures predominate. The governor of Raheng, who accompanied me to the place, gave me permission to carry away two or three of the bronzes which I selected as presenting the most characteristic features.

Although in itself a town of no artificial attractiveness, the natural position of Raheng gives it great political importance, and many commercial advantages. Being near the frontiers of Burmah and Lao, it is regarded as an important military station, and the post of governor is a very responsible one.

While I was there, a Siamese official was sent by the minister for Northern Siam to mark the young men for the king's service. This is done by tattooing them on the inner side of the left arm—an operation to which all but the better classes, who can buy exemption, are, as I have already stated, liable.

Raheng is also a convict-station, a number of prisoners being employed here in sawing timber in

the forest, and preparing the logs to be sent down-
stream to Bangkok. With this exception the timber
trade here, as is generally the case elsewhere in the
country, is in the hands of British Burmese
subjects, who have obtained concessions to work the
forests, and who contribute, in the inland timber
tax, the principal share of the revenues of the district.
A tax of three ticals is levied upon each piece of
timber, irrespective of its size, so that there is every
inducement to the exporters to cut only the largest
trees. Six hundred elephants, ranging in value from
500 to 2000 rupees each, are employed in bringing the
timber from the forest to the river; where, after the
tax has been paid, and each log branded as a voucher,
the logs are tied together by means of rattan ropes,
into enormous rafts, which are then floated down to
Bangkok.

The purchasers of teak logs inland assume one
standard for the measurement of the length and thickness of the logs, but at Bangkok the measures vary
according to the whim of the purchaser. Usually each
log is supposed to have a specific value, called the
pikat nua (northern tariff), and when the logs reach
Bangkok the timber-speculator purchases the timber
from the rafter for a lump sum per raft, or for a
specified sum, greater than the " northern tariff,"
per log. But sometimes the sale is by measurement,
and when the bargain is made the Bangkok timber-
merchant produces a *mai-wah* stick with which he
insists the length of the logs shall be measured. This
mai-wah stick is first divided into two equal parts,
each of which is " saung sauk " (two sauk). Another
equal division is made, and each of these divisions
called a *sauk*. The sauk is again equally divided, and
each part called a *k'up*. The k'up is divided into

twelve equal parts, each of which is called a *niew*.
The niew is divided into four equal parts, each part of
which is called a *kabiet*. This is the basis of measurement for length not contemplating great distances.
When great distances are to be measured, the mai-wah
stick is the starting-point. Twenty wah make one
sen, 400 sen make one *yote*. The merchant also
produces a rattan string, with which he insists the
circumference of the logs shall be measured; and
every niew of the semi-circumference is called a
kam.

This statement enables us to make out the following
table :—

4	Kabiets make	1	Niew.
12	Niews ,,	1	K'up.
2	K'ups ,,	1	Sauk.
4	Sauk ,,	1	Wah.
20	Wah ,,	1	Sen.
400	Sen ,,	1	Yote.

The table is easily made out. But what of the
standard ? If you want to buy timber, you are at the
mercy of the log-merchant. Each merchant has his own
(short) mai-wah stick, which he compels you to accept
as his standard of measurement. If you refuse, he
refuses to sell to you. If you go to a Siamese or a
Chinese merchant offering to sell timber, he will place
before you a (long) wah and sauk stick and reduce
you to the alternative of measuring your stock with
his measuring-sticks or of having the timber left
on your hands. Endless are the wrongs growing out
of unequal measures and weights used in Siam. A
uniform system of measurement ought to be adopted,
and that uniformity ought to be supported by government enactment. Until this is done trade must be
hampered and fraud will be encouraged. During the

reign of H.M. Somdeth Phra-nang-klow, when foreign square-rigged vessels visited the port of Bangkok each vessel was required to pay a measurement duty, and the wah stick used to measure the beam of the vessel was notoriously rather short. Again, when the Siamese officials were sent to measure and fix the limits of land sold with government sanction, a sen measure was used containing twenty rattan links, each representing a wah, but the links were invariably larger than any wah stick that the timber-merchant would place at the disposal of his purchasers! Mr. Samuel Smith, from whom I have obtained these particulars, informs me that as long as he has been in the country—nearly fifty years —such has been the uncertainty attending the weights and measures as used among the common people. At the present time the Siamese Government rattan link is so near eighty English inches that a true wah may be reckoned at that length.[1]

During March and April the forests are liable to be devastated by great fires, in which, besides unfelled trees, thousands of sawn logs are often destroyed. To obviate such a disaster the Raheng merchants store

---

[1] Siamese liquid measure is very simple. A *k'anahn* is a cocoanut-shell supposed to be capable of holding 830 *met-makahn*, or tamarind-seeds. The government k'anahns do not vary in size. They all follow the standard given above. The *chank* is a small brass bowl four of which go to a k'anahn, and the *tang* is a wooden bucket containing twenty k'anahns.

The k'anahn is also used in dry measure, and is the starting-point, and the k'anahns used by the traders contain from a pint and a half to one quart, English measure. If the cocoanut-shell can hold 830 tamarind-seeds, the measure is a legal one. The following is the table of larger measures:—

25 k'anahns make	1 sat (usually the bamboo basket).
80 sats	,,	1 kwien (or cart).
Or—20 k'anahns	,,	1 tang (usually a wooden bucket).
100 tangs	,,	1 kwien.

their timber as much as possible in the creeks and shallow portions of the river, and at times, before the "lumbering" season arrives, the river may be lined for a considerable distance with enormous piles of timber, awaiting a sufficient volume of water to carry them down stream.

Besides teak, a considerable quantity of the sapan wood of commerce, called *mai fang* by the Siamese, is sent away, cut into short logs, and placed on board boats. A vast quantity of resin is also collected in this district, besides horns, skins, and beeswax.

So much for the exports. As to the imports, I noticed in the bazaars a quantity of English and German white calicoes and coloured prints, iron-ware, and "Birmingham" goods.

With its great natural advantages, even under the present *régime*, Raheng bears every evidence of present prosperity, and affords every facility for a career of future greatness. The agricultural resources of the district of which it is the centre and natural outlet are extremely rich. Its timber alone is sufficient to ensure prosperity, but it has further sources of wealth in the varied indigenous products of the country, and still more in the entirely undeveloped resources of its fertile soil. All that it wants is a railway to carry the produce of the country at all seasons, and without delay, to the markets of the world, and to enable it to receive the large imports which an increasing population would at once necessi-tate.

A railway from Bangkok to this point would offer no engineering difficulties. The whole country is one vast plain, presenting fewer obstacles than even the American prairie for the construction of a railway, which would have the advantage that it would pass

through a district thickly-studded with villages, each
of which would bring its quota to the traffic. The
river is the only existing highway, and necessarily an
important one; but it is not navigable for steamers
above Paknam Po, and the existence of numerous sand-
banks renders the navigation dangerous and uncertain.
The journey by boat from Bangkok to Raheng occu-
pies at the very best of times twelve days, while the
natives as a rule take much longer to do the voyage.
The journey down stream takes as long, and often
longer, for, relieved of the necessity of pulling against
the current, the natives cease rowing altogether, and
simply resign themselves and their merchandize to
the whims of the river-god.

A railway, on the other hand, would enable the
distance—about 300 miles—to be accomplished, at the
rate of only twenty miles an hour, in fifteen hours.
Even Oriental deliberation could hardly prevent a
traveller from breakfasting in Bangkok six a.m., and
dining at Raheng eight p.m.

The country would not only be enormously
developed by the construction of a railway, but I am
convinced that it would at once return a handsome
profit on the outlay. There are no "vested interests"
to buy up, no highly-priced properties to purchase.
Little more is wanted than to survey the route and
lay the rails. Neither embankments, nor cuttings,
nor tunnels, and scarcely a bridge, would be needed.

The country is in every sense worth opening up,
and, if a responsible company were to make overtures
for the concession, I have little doubt that the king
of Siam, with his enlightened ideas and his readiness
to make use of "the resources of civilization" for the
development of the country over which he rules, would
readily grant it. As already stated, his Majesty has

recently granted permission to French engineers to lay a telegraph-line across the country, to connect with the submarine cable at Saigon, so that before the end of the present year Siam will be in direct telegraphic communication with the Old World.

Judging from the marked favour which the king has shown to European enterprise in Siam, I have little hesitation in saying that a warm welcome would be accorded to any *bonâ fide* proposal to carry out so important a work as the construction of a railway from Bangkok to Raheng.

To show the probability of the commercial success of such an undertaking, it is only necessary to point out that the line would run through a much more densely populated district than that through which the railway in British Burmah passes. Yet that railway is paying a good dividend; and during the four or five years of its existence it is admitted to have done much towards the development of trade in all its branches.

Everything, therefore, augurs well for the success of a similar undertaking, performing the same service to Bangkok as the Burmese line does for Rangoon.

The only apparent obstacle to the prosecution of the work is the scarcity of labour; for though the population is abundant, the Siamese is no heaven-born navvy. Hard work is an abomination to him; the only labour he undertakes voluntarily is in the cultivation of his rice-fields, and in this he has the hearty co-operation of the women-kind; and the contractor who· had to depend on native labour for the completion of his work would require the insertion in his contract of a "time-clause" of unprecedented duration. Happily the ubiquitous Chinaman is ready at hand to fill the gap, to say nothing of coolie labour from India.

John Chinaman would do the work for very low wages, and with an energetic disregard for excessive hours of labour which would put to the blush the European workman whose watchword is—

> " Eight hours' work,
> Eight hours' play,
> Eight hours' sleep,
> And eight ' bob ' a day."

Besides, the Chinese would welcome such an opportunity of getting a footing in the country, where, when their work was done, they would settle down as agriculturists or traders. The Chinese have a wonderful aptitude for seeing opportunities to which other men are blind. Whenever there is the slightest indication of a demand for any particular form of service, not otherwise supplied, they will adapt themselves to circumstances, and, by almost imperceptibly meeting a small want, create a large one.

Altogether I am convinced that the opening-up of the country by the " iron horse" would result in large and immediate profits to all concerned, and, with the ready countenance which the present enlightened ruler of Siam gives to all projects for the advancement of the interests of his country, I think the day is not far distant when the railway train may be running between Bangkok and Raheng, bringing down the valuable products of Upper Siam, and taking back in exchange those English manufactures for which a large and increasing demand would readily be created, and thus opening up at once a market for the raw produce of that country, and for the manufactured products of this.

I left Raheng on the 18th of December, having been most courteously treated by the governor and his officials, and bearing away pleasant recollections of my stay there. The second governor was particularly obliging, and fully bore out the high opinion expressed among Siamese, Burmese, and Laosians alike, of his genial manner and kindness of heart. He seemed to be a general favourite among all classes. I entertained him to dinner one day, and was invited in return to dine with him and the governor and three of the next highest officials on the day before my departure. The zoedone did duty as champagne on each occasion with remarkable success.

Strange to say, Siamese coins cease to be current from Raheng northwards, although official calculations are made in ticals. The rupee of British Burmah is the current coin in the north, so I had to exchange my Siamese money for rupees before continuing my journey.

The standard coin in Siam is the *tical* or *baht*, equivalent to 2*s*. 6*d*. in English money. The royal *chang* or Siamese *catty* is eighty ticals, and weighs 2·675 lbs. avoirdupois. In commerce the Siamese and Chinese reckon large transactions in catties, but the actual coin is rarely seen. There are smaller silver coins, such as the *salung*, one-fourth of a tical; and the *fuang*, one-eighth of a tical. There are small copper coins known as the *at* and the *pie*, and in some parts of the country I have seen cowries, 1200 of which represent the value of a fuang. There are both old and new coins in circulation; the old silver tical is an irregular ball, with a deep cleavage on one side bearing the mint-marks. The new tical is a coin after the European model, about the size of a rupee, bearing on one side the king's head, and on the reverse the royal coat of arms. Gold coins are rarely seen; the value of the few that exist is calculated at sixteen times their weight in silver. They are reserved for distribution by the king on some grand occasion, such as a royal cremation, and now and then I have seen specimens kept as a curiosity.

In all parts of the country I found a number of porcelain coins of all shapes and sizes, bearing different Chinese characters and devices; these are issued by Chinamen holding monopolies, and are only current in their respective districts.

CHAPTER XIII.

DIVIDING my party into two sections, I sent Yang
and Cook in charge of the bulk of my luggage to
Chengmai in boats up the river—which, by the way,
above Raheng takes the name of Meping—while I proceeded overland in company with Kao and Kien,
intending to reach the same destination through the
Lao States.

The governor of Raheng accordingly supplied me
with six elephants and guides. Elephant-travelling
was a new experience to me, and, although I had a
commodious howdah, it was some time before I became
accustomed to the curious swinging motion of the
elephant's gait. The sensation is something like that
of being rocked—not too gently, and with a circular
movement—in a huge cradle. The pace is slow, and
this mode of locomotion altogether tedious, though,
when the country is open, there is an advantage in the
fine view to be had from a height of ten or eleven feet
or more from the ground. The elephants are decorated
with bells round the neck, with the object of giving

notice of their approach when meeting caravans coming
in an opposite direction.   As they tramp steadily along,
the huge beasts regale themselves with choice tufts of
grass, or with the tender shoots of the overhanging
branches of the trees, while but little effort is required
to twist off a branch which may chance to be in the
way of the howdah.   When crossing a stream they
generally take a trunkful of water, whether they want
to drink or not.   Fortunately the country is intersected
with innumerable watercourses, as it is essential to
camp for the night close to water, and there is always
at least a sufficient rivulet, even in the dry season—to
which overland travelling is confined—if not a considerable stream, within a short day's march from almost
any point.

From Raheng northwards, to the boundary of the
Ngiou and Lao States (in about 20° N. lat.), may be said
to be the centre of the supply of elephants in Siam, and,
while man's principal work in the country seems to
have been the erection of Temples, nature's supremest
effort, so far as the animal world is concerned, appears
to have been reserved for the multiplication of
Elephants.

Our road at first was through thin forest, with an
abundance of young teak promising in future years to
close up the gaps.   On the second day we came across
immense granite blocks scattered over the ground in
great abundance, while here and there the forest gave
place to open patches of country, in which the grass
grew to a height of from ten to fifteen feet, often
overtopping not only the backs of the elephants, but
even the roofs of the howdahs.   Nothing but an
elephant could have got through such country without
immense difficulty.   Here, unsheltered by the foliage
of the trees, the heat was intense during the day, and,

as a consequence of the radiation, the night-temperature was much lower. Heavy dews at night saturated everything, but in an hour or two the heat of the sun removed all traces of moisture. The average temperature in the early morning was 50° Fahr., while in the afternoon the thermometer marked 85°.

For five days we passed no habitation and met not a single soul ; but on the afternoon of the 22nd of December we crossed the River Menam Vang, a tributary of the Meping, and reached Muang Tunn, a town on the right bank of the river, of some 1000 inhabitants, exclusive of women and children, who are not thought of sufficient importance to take any place in the official numbering of the population !

Although situated within the borders of Siam, about sixty miles in a straight line from Raheng, this place is purely a Lao town, not a single Siamese living here.

A great deal of tobacco is grown in the neighbourhood, being cultivated on the banks of the river during the four dry months of the year.

After staying for the night here, and having procured fresh elephants and guides, I started next morning for Lakon, following the right bank of the River Menam Vang, and passing through undulating country covered with thick growths of bamboo.

Everywhere the effects of the absence of rain were visible in the withered and almost bleached appearance of the leaves, the vegetation all lacking the fresh green colour so characteristic of the foliage during the rainy season. The night-dews sometimes partially compensate for the absence of rain, and keep up the vitality of the trees, but here the country appeared to have suffered a serious drought. Here and there the course of a stream, now dwindled to a mere ditch, and half-hidden beneath the thick tangle of forest-undergrowth, but evidently capable of expanding in the wet season into a wide, deep, and impetuous torrent, could be traced for a considerable distance by the streak of bright foliage which fringed its grateful waters ; but, generally speaking, the forest was parched up.

As we got into higher ground the streams became more numerous and the vegetation looked more healthy, and the road was more and more rough.   On Christmas Day we reached our highest point, 1500 feet above sea-level, crossing the range of mountains by a deep pass through which flowed a considerable stream, the Me Tam, tributary to the Menam Vang. We were now well within the semi-independent Lao States.   Just before crossing the river we met a Burmese cattle-dealer, driving a herd of over 100 buffaloes which he had bought in the Chengmai district and was going to sell at Moulmein.   Close by, he informed me, was the village of Ban Chow Tam, in the district of Lakon. Camping on the banks of the stream after a long day's jolting on an elephant's back along an unusually steep and rough road, I made my " Christmas dinner" off a tin of preserved duck, with cocoa, as usual, for a beverage, and followed by some tinned pears, and a glass of brandy and water in which to toast distant friends in far-off Europe.

From this point the population became more and more dense.   All day we rode through village after village, all of them neat and clean in appearance, and presenting a marked contrast to those I had left behind me, and, as I afterwards found, to those I had yet to visit.   Numbers of elephants, and still larger herds of cattle, used as beasts of burden, were to be seen in every village.   Water was plentiful, deep wells being sunk at frequent intervals ; and altogether the people seemed quite well-to-do and progressive.   Large areas were planted with cotton-bush, the people doing a large trade in cotton, and in resins and gums collected in the forests.

On the 27th of December we arrived at Lakon, a place of some importance, and, like all Lao towns, surrounded by ramparts—here six or eight feet thick, built of thin bricks, but in a dilapidated condition. The Sala, or resting-house, was an old, neglected building, with a roof considerably damaged, and with overhanging eaves so wide that daylight was almost entirely excluded. Hoping to find more comfortable quarters than this, I called at the house of the Siamese Commissioner, but found he was, unfortunately, away, so I went to see the Chow Hluang. On my way I passed an open space in the middle of the town, where stood a quaint, old, teak building, which I took for another sala. Inquiring of some officials close by where the chief lived, I was very abruptly told that he was away looking after his rice-harvest, and that nobody was at home. So I made known my desire to find a lodging, pointing out that the first sala was almost in ruins, and, after some difficulty, induced the officials to let a guide take me to a house which, they added, was "new," and would " do very well for me."

This " new " house turned out to be the very sala I had already seen and had just complained of ; so I returned and requested that I might be furnished with some better accommodation. The officials, with an old Phya at their head, refused to help me any further, and, Kao confidentially informed me, spoke most insultingly of me, declaring that, as the Siamese Commissioner was away, they would not allow the *farang* to stay in their town. They were happy enough to be temporarily relieved of the presence of the Siamese, and they would not put up with another hateful foreigner.

Noticing that the building already referred to, which I took to be a sala, was vacant, with the exception of a small apartment at the back, I asked to be allowed to put up there. To this request I received no answer, so I went with Kao up to the old Phya, as the principal person present, and told him that if he did not assist me to find some better lodgings than the old sala, I should instal myself in the empty rooms of this building, supporting my request for assistance by offering him the official letter calling upon all the chiefs of the places through which I passed to give me accommodation. Still the old man turned a deaf ear to me, and stolidly sat without paying the slightest attention to what I said. So, to the evident astonishment of the lookers-on, who had come to stare at the white man, I ordered my men to deposit my luggage inside the building.

The Phya now commenced vociferating loudly to his companions, Kao interpreting his remarks to be of a most threatening character ; so I made a last appeal to him ; but whenever I spoke—or rather when Kao spoke for me—he at once became dumb. His behaviour so irritated me that, losing all patience, I gave him two strokes on the back with my stick. The effect was magical. I had no sooner struck him than I reflected that I might be bringing a hornet's nest about my ears, and I fully expected the bystanders to retaliate. Instead of this, however, the Phya's demeanour completely changed, not for the worse, but for the better. He became quite obsequious in his bearing. Reaching down from a shelf behind him a large, red-painted, wooden tray, he held it out for the letter which he had refused to look at before. When I told him to read it, he said he could not venture to do so, although it was open, but that he must wait till the chief came back.

"Besides," he added, "I could not understand a word. I cannot read modern Siamese characters;" though this, I felt sure, was only a pretence, and an excuse for his previous refusal to read the letter when offered to him.

I then hoisted the "white elephant" Siamese flag on a pole in front of the building, which in a very few minutes was surrounded by a throng of hundreds of men, women, and children, assembled to look at the *farang* who had come and—with what mixed feelings did I hear the statement!—beaten the Phya in the court of justice and taken up his lodging there!

Thus, then, ignorant of the nature of the building, and wilfully kept in the dark by the obstinate old Phya, I had, by somewhat summary proceedings, installed myself in the law courts. I consoled myself with the reflection that, if I had not administered the law, I had at least meted out justice, of a rough and ready sort, to its obstructive representative; and I was shortly afterwards comforted by a visit from the Radjaput, the late chief's eldest son—a by no means prepossessing individual, with an obliquity of vision which did not add to his personal charms—who apologized for the rudeness of his people in staring at me, and especially for the insolence of the old Phya. He then ordered some of his men to make a fireplace for me, for cooking purposes, and to see that I had everything I wanted.

I explained to him the object of my visit, and tendered him the letter which the Phya had treated, first with such disdain, and then with such pretended reverence. The Radjaput, too, seemed afraid to touch it, until I assured him that no harm would be done, as it was an open document intended for "all whom it might concern." So he took it aside and in a few moments I heard it being read by one of his attendants.

In the afternoon I returned the visit of this very obliging prince. He was most communicative, informing me, among other things, that he was about to be married to one of the chief's daughters, and inviting me then and there to be present at the ceremony. Of course I was delighted, for more reasons than one, to accept his offer, and assured him of my good wishes for his happiness.

On my return to my quarters I received a visit from a young man whom, as he shook hands with me, I took to be a Chow, or prince. Very few of the natives in Lao, I found, even among the higher officials and princes, had any idea of the European custom of shaking hands. Sometimes, when I proffered my hand, the act was responded to by a yellow palm, generally the left, with fingers wide open, being held up in return; but even this left-handed and awkward concession to foreign custom was practised only by the *crème de la crème* of Laosian society. The salutation to which I was most accustomed when I had occasion to call upon an official was a sort of grunt, "h'm! h'm!" reminding me of the sounds of contentment which emanate from a pig when wallowing in a more than usually unsavoury batch of filth, but, to show that no churlishness was intended by this inarticulate utterance, it was generally succeeded or accompanied by an invitation or a sign to be seated. I judged accordingly that my visitor was of "high degree," and Kao made private inquiries and found that my surmise was correct. He was a younger son of the chief. Opening the conversation by assuring me that he liked foreigners, and was anxious to be my friend, he at once asked me to come and spend the evening at his house, which he pointed out, only a few yards distant. So about five o'clock I found myself ascending a ladder leading to an outer platform which, after the Siamese style, formed the entrance to a large house, constructed entirely of teak, with several smaller buildings, containing the slaves' apartments, adjoining. The platform led to the principal room, and as I entered a couple of carpets were spread, each with a triangular cushion at one end, one for the Chow, the other for his guest. The Chow came forward and again shook hands—an accomplishment which, he explained, he had acquired in Bangkok—and motioned me to sit down. Immediately afterwards two women—one of whom the Chow told me was his sister—brought out two fine sets of betel-trays, with spittoons and all complete, one in solid gold, the other in silver. The former was placed at my side, the latter beside the Chow. Then two silver bowls of water were brought, accompanied each by a silver tankard, and followed very shortly afterwards by a huge silver tray, bearing glasses of native spirit. By this time we were pretty well surrounded by vessels of precious metal, in various shapes and sizes, sufficient to make a betel-chewer and arrack-drinker supremely happy. I did not indulge in the favourite stimulant, however, and was offered a buree, and, while the Chow chewed and I smoked, our conversation was somewhat as follows:—

" I am very glad to see you, and will always be your friend," said the Chow.

" I am very proud to be your friend," I replied, " and trust you will assist me in finding out all about your country. How many inhabitants are there in Lakon ? "

" We keep strict record of all the people, when they are born and when they die, but it would not be etiquette for me to answer my friend's question: the chief alone can answer it. But I am your friend, and my elephants, horses, and cattle are yours."

"You have many fine elephants," I replied. "Are there many horses in Lakon?"

"We know how many elephants and horses there are; every man has to give an account of them; but I cannot tell my friend: the chief alone can say."

"I am anxious to see the chief," said I, "but I know not where he is. Can I go to his rice-fields to find him?"

"I cannot say where the chief is, but he will be back soon."

And so, to every question I received the same answer; but, while the young chow could or would give me no information about the people or country, he was very inquisitive about my movements and intentions.

By-and-by tea was served. There was a teapot of native make, very well wrought in solid silver, and tea was poured into small cups, which were handed round without saucers. The Chow, however, preferred getting his tea as directly as possible from the source of supply, and sucked the spout of the teapot.

The Laosians are skilled in the manufacture of silverware, and some of the native work is really very well executed. There is a considerable demand for teapots, betelnut-services, and other articles, which are the symbols of rank among the Laosians as among the Siamese; and every village has one or more workers in the precious metals engaged in executing orders for the princes and better classes, betelnut-boxes called *app*, bowls, earrings, bangles, bracelets, hairpins, &c., being the articles most in request. The *modus operandi* is very primitive. If a box or bowl has to be made, it is first constructed of thin plain plates, and the inside filled with a composition of resin and wax. The design is then worked out entirely with a hammer, a style, and a sort of blunt chisel ; the ground-work is hammered down, the plastic material inside yielding to the blows, until the pattern, generally a medley of mythical figures of birds and animals, and of scroll-work, stands out in high relief. When the design is finished, the composition is taken out, and the vessel is finished. The work lacks finish, and will not always bear close examination, but the general result is bold and effective. There is a great want of variety in the designs, every man making it a point of honour not to deviate from his recollection—for they all work from memory, and not from any pattern or sketch—of the particular figures affected by his father and grandfather before him.

The value of such silver ornaments is always ascertained by the weight of pure metal employed, with an addition of fifty per cent. for the workmanship.

In opposition to the silversmith's craft is that of the makers of lacquer-ware. People who cannot afford silver " apps " have to put up with lacquer-work, and articles of this kind are in great demand. They are made of finely-woven strips of bamboo, and then coated several times over with the expensive native black varnish called " rack." When dry—and the varnish is by no means quickly dried, notwithstanding the heat of the climate—the surface is polished with husks of rice and water, which, even for polishing wood and metal, are the common substitute for sand-paper or the burnishing tool; a pattern of flowers or scroll-work is then engraved with a style, and the whole covered with a coat of red or brown paint. Betel-boxes in this ware are usually circular in shape, varying from four to eight inches in diameter, and from three-and-a-

half to five inches in height. They are invariably
made in three parts; first the betelnut-box itself, then
an outer cover or case for it, and a closely-fitting lid
covering the whole. A good large "app" of Lao
workmanship costs six rupees, while those usually
sold in the bazaars, which are of Burmese or Ngiou
make, and of inferior quality, can be had for from one
rupee upwards.

Drinking-cups, rice-bowls, and other articles of
domestic use are made in this way, and in most families
one or more members can be found at times making
useful utensils of this material.

CHAPTER XIV.

WHILE I was thus making friends with the younger
generation of Chows, the Phyas, taking advantage of
the chief's absence, and knowing there was no one to
whom I could appeal, were intent on tasting the sweets
of revenge, and on making me pay as dearly as they
could for my visit, and for having indulged in the
luxury of self-made justice in having, in a moment of
irritation, struck the old Phya who was the ringleader
of the obstructives.

Officials bearing the title of Phya, I may here say,
are exceedingly numerous throughout Lao, but of
course they do not rank as high as the Phyas to be met
with in Bangkok, where the office is one of great dignity,
accompanied with rich emoluments and handsome signs
of office. The Lao Phya receives merely a scroll of
thin silver, on which his name and title are engraved.

Chows or princes are equally, if not even still more
numerous, every relative of the rulers of the separate
provinces receiving this title. How many there are
may be gathered from the fact that the grandfather of
the present chief of Chengmai had 106 children, while

the late chief of Lampoon had ninety-five—all of whom were Chows or princes of different rank.

While on this subject, I may as well take the opportunity of putting together a few notes on the government of the Lao States, and the position of the different officials with whom I was brought in contact, and to whom I shall have to refer later on. There are six Lao states directly tributary to Siam, viz. Lakon, Lampoon, Chengmai, Muang Nan, Hluang Prabang, and Muang Prai. All are entirely independent of each other; but there are several minor states dependent upon these larger ones. The rulers of all the states, even the smaller ones, are autocratic in their authority. In the case of the six larger states two chiefs are appointed. The first of these is called Chow Hluang, and the second Chow Operat; but the second chief often overrules his principal, as I found to be the case both at Chengmai and at Kiang Hai. The offices are held for life, but are not hereditary, being filled nominally by the king of Siam, but really on the election and recommendation of the people, who send notice to Bangkok on the decease of a chief, with a private intimation of their views as to a successor. Each of the six Lao states is called upon to pay tribute to Siam. This is paid triennially, and takes the form of gold and silver betel-boxes, vases, and necklaces, each enriched with four rubies of the size of a lotus-seed, and a hundred of the size of a grain of Indian corn. Besides these are curious representations of trees in gold and silver, about eight feet high, each with four branches, from which again four twigs, with a single leaf at the end of each, depend. The gold trees are valued at 1080 ticals (135*l.*) each, and the silver ones at 120 ticals (15*l.*) each.

The whole of the land nominally belongs to the

chiefs, but in practice they grant certain districts or provinces to the numerous princes or Chows to " eat," as the Siamese and Laosians express it. These princes pay no taxes, but they take care not to let the people off. First comes a tax on rice, this is comparatively small in amount—about one per cent. on the average. Each farmer is called upon to pay one bucket of rice for every bucket planted, and as the yield is from sixty to three-hundred-fold, according to the quality of the soil, the supply of water, and other conditions, the tax is not a serious burden. As much as 400 buckets of rice have been gathered from a single bucket of seed, but the average yield may be put at a hundred-fold. There are also taxes, more or less heavy, on pork, opium, arrack, ironware, bamboo, betel-nuts, sticklac, fish, and—gambling! Officers are appointed in each village to gather the revenue, and they are responsible to the chiefs for its due collection. That they do not err on the side of leniency may be judged from the rapidity with which they accumulate wealth.

The princes and high officials are the money-lenders, the usurers, in Lao. Indeed it does not pay for any one but an official or a prince to make any profession of wealth, for if a farmer or trader has saved a little money, and injudiciously makes the fact known, he is sure to receive a visit from one of the " ruling class," who are adepts in the art of squeezing, by fair means or by foul, the uttermost farthing out of the common people. Complaint would be useless, so the unhappy possessor of wealth is driven to take refuge in secretly hoarding his money, often burying it in some secluded spot, where, perhaps, it lies hidden for ever. Thus the natural inclination of the people to miserly and secretive habits is intensified, and the country is kept poor and undeveloped.

To these princes and officials the greatest deference
is paid by the common people. When a member of
the Lao "upper ten" goes on a journey, or makes a
call, however short the distance, he is invariably
attended by a full retinue of servants, umbrella-bearer,
betel-box attendant, water-jar carrier, and slaves
bearing lances, swords, and other signs of authority
and rank. As the procession passes by the people " of

" How do you do ? "—a Lao salutation.

the meaner sort" show their humility by sitting down
on their haunches in the road, or even kneeling down,
and raising their hands to their face until the great
man has passed. The name of an official is never
uttered in conversation, but he is always called by his
title, and whenever an ordinary individual addresses
his betters he interlards every sentence with expressions of humility or homage, such as " Chow," and
" Khorab," (respect, or obedience), raising both hands
to the forehead each time, and bending the body
forward, keeping all the time at a respectful distance,
greater or less according to the rank of the personage
addressed. When leaving the presence of a superior,
the native Laosian shuffles out backwards, bending
low the whole time, sometimes even crouching down

on all fours and retreating in the most ludicrously
abject manner imaginable.

I have mentioned slaves. Great numbers of the
people are either slaves or "slave-debtors." As the
current rate of interest is thirty-six per cent. per annum,
it is not surprising that a good many debtors are
unable to pay so dear for the accommodation, and
much less to repay the capital. In such a case they
become "slave-debtors," *i.e.* they are under the obligation of rendering various services to the creditor, in
lieu of making money payments. Slave-debtors are
on a better footing than actual slaves, and are usually
treated well, and can approach and address their
master at any time. Besides these there are slaves
who have been taken captive in war, or the descendants of such captives. The legal price for war-slaves
is, for men, fifty-four rupees, and, for women, seventy-
two rupees each.

The current coin in Western Lao is the British-
Burmese rupee : no Siamese coin is ever seen there,
and it would not be accepted if tendered. Here and
there one may come across one of the old native pieces
of money, oval in shape, very thin, with a depression
on the reverse side, which is always varnished, and a
corresponding elevation on the obverse, giving the coin
a shrivelled appearance. Round the margin are stamped
different devices, representing the states from which
the coin originated, *e.g.* an elephant for Lakon, a horse
for Chengmai, &c.

The weight commonly adopted in trade is the
Chinese catty. The old native weights which are still
in use here and there for small quantities, are made of
brass in the form of the *hoong* or sacred goose (*henga*
in Burmese) or of an elephant.

Having said so much for the government of the Lao

States and their rulers, I must return to my friends the Chows at Lakon.

The Phyas and chiefs, in solemn conclave assembled, condemned me to pay a fine of fifteen rupees, and on my refusal to submit to this penalty they peremptorily declined to furnish me with elephants and guides, and intimated that I must consider myself a prisoner. Although not actually subjected to any indignity, I was placed under strict surveillance, and neither I nor my servants could go anywhere without being watched. My servants were in great alarm lest we should suffer bodily harm. I had not intended to stay at Lakon more than a couple of days, but there was no help for it. If I gave way to the pressure placed upon me by the Phyas, I might as well abandon the rest of my journey, for the news would be sure to precede me, and I should get no assistance anywhere. So I made a formal demand to see the Chow Hluang, but they refused to tell me where his rice-fields were, and entrenched themselves behind a stolid reserve which no attempts of mine succeeded in breaking. There was nothing for it but to make the best of my enforced detention—my personal liberty not being interfered with, although I was watched wherever I went—and to see as much as I could of the country and the people.

There was always something to be seen, indoors or out of doors, in the town or in the immediate neighbourhood. My residence in the temple of justice was favourably situated for seeing everything that passed in the town. It stood in an open space looking right up the principal street, in which were situated the gaol, the royal temple, the residences of the first and second chiefs, and the public stable or shed in which the elephants were kept. Opposite the court of justice this principal street divided into two branches, one passing to the right and the other to the left, and in one of these branches the public well was situated, so that there was a continuous stream of traffic past my windows. The court sat every day in the little chamber partitioned off in the back from the rest of the building, but the only case which was heard during my stay was that of one of two prisoners, who, lying in gaol under sentence of death for highway robbery, had managed to escape, but had been recaptured after having stolen fifty rupees. The gaoler had told me that the probability was that they would have been pardoned for the first offence if their relations would pay a sufficient sum as a "ransom," but the breaking gaol and the second offence required a second punishment, and the prisoner was sentenced to receive forty-five lashes. The sentence was carried into execution in front of the court, where there was an apparatus permanently fixed for facilitating the public flogging of criminals. This apparatus consisted of a bamboo cross about three feet high, firmly fixed into the ground, while in front of it, at a distance of about six feet, two wooden pegs were driven into the ground.

The culprit, with his feet chained so close together that he could scarcely walk, was brought out of gaol, in the presence of a dense crowd of people, the Chows and Phyas being accommodated with "reserved seats" in the court. He was then made to sit on the ground with his back to the cross and his feet close to the pegs already mentioned. Two bamboo poles were then placed, one over each shoulder, each being securely fastened, at one end to one of the pegs, and at the other to one arm of the cross. The man's arms were then tightly lashed to these poles so that he could not move backwards or forwards, his feet were secured to the lower end of them, and a line made fast between

M

his waist and the upright of the cross. The executioner was armed with a formidable instrument of torture, formed of a long stout rattan, split at one end into four "tails," and, after giving a preliminary flourish by whirling his " cat " in a circle round his head, on a signal from one of the princes carried out the sentence with exactitude. The first half-dozen strokes brought blood from the lacerated back of the unfortunate culprit, whose yells were painful to hear.

In the court of justice I saw a very ingenious contrivance for measuring the time. In a large brass bowl, filled with water, is placed a small brass basin with a tiny hole pierced in the bottom, through which, as it floats, the water slowly enters. It takes, of course, a fixed period for this vessel to become filled with water, when it sinks to the bottom. At that moment the guard strikes the gong, and, lifting the basin, empties it and replaces it to fill once more and mark the flight of another period. I found that the time which this bowl took to fill was exactly an hour.

Half an hour's walk from Lakon is a Phra Bat, or Buddha's foot-print, similar to those seen in Siam, measuring six feet one inch in length, and two feet three inches-and-a-half in width. It does not bear the least resemblance to a human foot-print, even in outline. The print of the toes, for instance, is represented by three rows of depressions, five in each row, and nearly all of the same size, intended to represent the triple joints of the toes of the very super-human foot of Buddha.

Close by the Phra Bat is a large temple, the Wat Hluang, which may be taken as a type of these edifices throughout Lao. As in Siam, a series of distinct buildings are included in the temple-grounds, the largest being known as the Wee-han, which answers to a Chris-

tian "church," being the place where the people meet
to worship and listen to the preaching of the priests.
It is an open structure, without walls, save one at the
back where the altar stands. The floor is of bricks
and plaster, and elevated a foot and a half above the
ground. From this floor spring massive pillars of
teak-wood, heavily lacquered and painted red, which
support the roof, or rather the roofs, the Wat being
divided into three sections, each somewhat higher than
the other, and each covered with a triple roof of small
tiles. The gables are elaborately carved into serpent-
like ornaments, heavily gilt and inlaid with an endless
number of bits of blue, green, red, and white glass, the
effect of which is most beautiful in bright sunlight.
The apex of each roof terminates in elegant spire-like
finials; the eaves above the entrance are elaborately
carved. To the right of the entrance is a screen,
whereon are painted frescoes illustrating the life of
Buddha. The temple has neither chairs nor seats, for
priests and congregation alike always sit on the floor.
At the farther end of the building, facing the entrance,
is the altar, in the centre of which is a large figure of
Buddha, in the usual sitting posture, built of brick
and mortar, heavily gilt, the eyes inlaid with mother-
of-pearl, a priest's cloth over his breast, and a big umbrella as a sign of dignity towering high above his head.
In front of this large idol is a varied collection of Buddha
figures, some in bronze, the majority of wood, but all
gilt. In front of this collection of idols are strewn
at random the invariable offerings of flowers, small
clay trays with parched rice, vessels for wax tapers
and incense, &c., &c. To the right of the altar are a
couple of " spirit-houses," inside one of which I saw
several choice bronze-gilt Buddhas, and one of ivory—
the offerings of the chief—while close by was a hand-

some litter of ivory and carved wood, whereon the late chief used to be carried, but which at his demise the present Chow thought proper to offer to the temple. To the left of the altar is the *tamat*, or pulpit, made of wood, on the model of a miniature pagoda, nicely carved with figures and scrolls, and gilt and inlaid with the never-failing bits of coloured glass. A loose ladder consisting of four steps leads up to the pulpit, which, however, is only used on special occasions, when another important adjunct to the temple is brought into requisition, viz. a painted and gilded four-wheeled car, with a canopy over it, not unlike a hearse, but much smaller, which stood close by. On great occasions this car is loaded with nicely embroidered pillows, a number of candles and wax ornaments, and a pyramid of beautiful flowers in the centre. Thus laden, and decorated all round with a number of staves or wands, with a golden scroll near the upper end, making them look very like gold battle-axes. This car [1] is drawn in procession by a number of men to the Wat, and its contents offered to the priests.

The main entrance to the Wec-han is guarded by a couple of huge figures, representing the upper portion of the body of the favourite monster, the Rachasee—a fabulous creature represented to be the greatest and most formidable of all animals, the king of beasts, whose origin was in the bear family. The legend connected with this monster is that his parents were bears, and he was born with a twin sister, who afterwards became his wife, and by whom he had Rachasee children. Immediately after birth he became as great and strong as a lion. The Rachasee and the lion are in fact synonymous terms among the Laosians. He

---

[1] In the temples at Chengmai there are quite a number of these " meritorious cars."

did not establish his kingship over all animals till
after repeated contests; the first king of the creation
was the owl, the second the crow, the third the
pheasant, and the fourth the peacock. To this last the
quadrupeds would not submit, and the animals held a
council for the selection of a king, and chose the
elephant, to which, however, the tiger refused allegi-

The Rachasee: king of beasts.

ance. The dispute continued until a trial of strength
which resulted in the Rachasee being invested with
royalty. Though born of bears, he was a sort of
divinity, hence his rising above his race and attaining
kingship of all animals, both great and small. The
throne or empire of the Rachasee and his queen was on
the top of a mountain cleft to the bottom, where deep
down flowed a crystal stream. His kingdom was the

forest or jungle-desert, called *Pha jai*, and his great
object was to keep all his subjects from going near to
men ; many of them, however, as the elephant, horse,
ox, pig, &c., disobeyed his order, and, wandering into
the haunts of man, were captured by him, and enslaved.
Nevertheless the Rachasee prided himself on being
the greatest, most powerful, and most beautiful of the
animal creation. The dog undertook to dethrone this
vain-glorious king, and enticed the Rachasee to the
edge of the precipice above the crystal stream, pretending he would show his majesty a king equal to
himself in every respect. The Rachasee went, and
looking down saw his image in the clear water.
Determined to struggle to the death with this shadow,
he leaped over the cliff, and was caught and crushed
between the rocks. The queen and royal children in
their grief and terror fled into the remote forest-
jungle, and remained hidden so closely that no mortal
eye has ever seen them since. Before the Rachasee's
death, he had delegated a part of his authority to the
albinoes, such as white elephants, &c., making each
albino a sub-king over its race. Thus a white elephant is the king of all elephants, and where there are
more than one of these animals the sovereignty is
shared between them. The skin of the dead Rachasee,
however, was secured by men, and whoever possessed
a portion of it was invested with authority. After a
time the Rachasee was born anew, and after many
transmigrations he became a god, and was worshipped
as such. His life as a deity was in an age previous to
that of the Buddhas ; hence in Buddhist worship his
image is put outside the temples, as indicating that the
age in which Rachasee was worshipped as a god is
past. The image is believed to exercise some charm
over the lives of the priests and the people of the

village, protecting them from danger, sickness, &c.
On the other hand those who travel in the jungle and
hear his voice have the drums of their ears broken,
and lose their lives at the same time.

The annexed woodcut of this dread beast is after a
native drawing made for me, in colours, by a native
artist at Chengmai (see p. 245). In the original drawing the figure is beautifully illuminated in red, blue,
and gold.

Outside the Wee-han, to the right, stands the Haw-
tam or library, where the sacred MSS. are preserved.
The building, which is of a most quaint and unique
style of architecture, stands on a brick-floor, raised
some two feet from the ground, on which are placed
eight square-hewn teak posts, some ten feet high,
which support a flat platform, from which projects a
verandah, protecting the lower platform or ground-
floor, whence a ladder leads up to the platform above.
Passing through a trap-door in this upper floor—the
door is always kept religiously bolted against in-
truders—we enter a room containing a number of
large chests, coloured red or black and decorated with
figures or scroll-work in gold-leaf, in which the sacred
palm-leaf MSS. are kept. Each "volume" is carefully wrapped in a gay-coloured cloth, and the chests
are kept closely locked.

The external appearance of this structure, mounted
on the top of an open shed with a wide verandah,
is very peculiar. The two side walls slope outwards, and support a double roof of wooden tiles,
the upper part of the roof overlapping the lower,
while from the finials on the ridge of the roof are
suspended small brass bells, which are kept perpetually tinkling whenever the wind blows. The
object of perching the library on the lofty posts

is to protect it from the attacks of rats and mice.

The Wee-han and the Haw-tam connected with the Wat Hluang at Lakon are shown in the accompanying sketch. In reducing my original drawing, however, the engraver has represented the library as too large in proportion to the temple.

On the lower platform of the Haw-tam is a large drum formed of the stem of a tree, with one end hollowed out and a skin stretched across. Behind the Wat is a belfry, with two or three melodious bells, for

Royal Wat and Sacred Library at Lakon.

the Laos deem it highly necessary that the music of bells and gongs should be sounded whenever a service takes place, while fireworks are let off at the same time in order to announce to Buddha that his presence is needed. In front of the Wat is a tall flagstaff, surmounted by a figure of a bird, representing the sacred goose. These flagstaves are to be seen in every temple-ground, with a number of streamers or flags (*tung*), and are often useful as landmarks for temples built near the rivers are often hidden from view by the thick forest, and the flagstaves are pur-

posely made very tall, for the purpose of directing the
traveller to the house of prayer.

To the left of the Wee-han is the Obosot, or most
sacred place (see p. 108), always kept locked by the
priests, in convenient juxtaposition with which is a
long, low, covered gallery or court, where the priests
can walk during their meditations; the walls are
ornamented with a series of frescoes representing
events in Buddha's life. Beyond this, again, is a Sala,
or resting-house, provided with a figure of Buddha before which the wanderer can offer his devotions: one of
these Salas is almost invariably erected in or close to
the temple-grounds: while close by is an open court
called the Sala-Bat, where the people come to listen to
the preaching of the priests. The last building to
be mentioned is that set apart as the dormitory, the
residence of the priests and students—at Lakon, as
elsewhere, the most neglected of all the edifices in the
temple-grounds, except, perhaps, the Sala.

CHAPTER XV.

A professor of tattooing—How the Laosians decorate their flesh—A
painful operation—The patterns and the instruments and colours
—Description of tattoo-marks—Mineral deposits near Lakon—
Abundance of elephants—Native carts—A dog-cart drawn by
men—Dinner with the Radjaput—At last I see the chief—The
Phya is " found out "—Smoked out—The interview closes
abruptly—The Radjaput's wedding—Preparing for the feast—
I join in the procession—" With all my worldly goods I thee
endow "—Feasting not wisely, but too well—Matrimonial agents
—Siamese and Laosian marriage ceremonies—Courtship and
betrothal—A characteristic Siamese proverb—The order of
matrimony—The festivities—Position of wives—Education
among Lao women.

WHEN visiting the Wat Hluang, I saw a native professor of tattooing engaged in decorating a young boy,
who lay stoically enduring an operation which must
have caused intense pain. The national habit is to
tattoo the body from a line or two above the navel to
below the knee-cap. Unlike their neighbours the
Burmese and the Ngious, the Laosians do not attribute any beneficial influence to the practice, but
adopt it partly for artistic effect and as a conservative
custom, and still more, perhaps, as a sign of manliness,
courage, and endurance on the part of those who submit to the voluntary infliction of pain. As the Dyak
women are tattooed to please their lovers, so the Laos
men undergo the ordeal for the sake of the women.
So general is the custom that it would be difficult to

find a man who was not more or less thoroughly tattooed in accordance with the local custom. The operation is necessarily a painful one, especially considering the sensitiveness of the skin in the parts operated upon. The parts tattooed swell up, and become highly inflamed, sometimes causing high fever, but I was informed, both at Lakon and at Chengmai, that not more than two per cent. die from the effects of the irritation so caused. I often noticed young boys continually scratching themselves, and on inquiry found that they were undergoing a course of being made " beautiful for ever."

Most persons submit to the operation while under the influence of opium, and have only a small portion done at a time. Yet I met several men who had gone through the whole process in two sittings.

The figures selected are much of the same character in all cases, though as only one colour—black—is used and as there are no special marks or signs to denote any particular rank—beggar and king being equal in the hands of the professional tattooer—the exact pattern is left to the individual choice of the patient or the skill of the operator. The pigment is made from the smoke of burning lard, the soot from which is collected in earthenware pots and mixed with the bile of the wild bull, bear, or pig, a little water being added to give it the proper consistency; once rubbed in the colour is indelible.

Two kinds of instruments are employed, one being a sharp, serrated plate, something resembling a grainer's " comb," and used for making the plain tracery, or " stippling," and the other a kind of style made of a solid piece of steel with a sharp point, and longitudinal grooves for holding the paint. With this instrument the various figures are pricked into the skin. The designs are invariably confined to animals, such as monkeys, bats, rats, vultures, pigeons, &c., or monsters, prominent among them being the fabulous Rachasee.

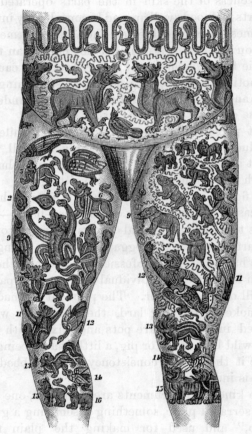

How a Laosian is tattooed.

With some little coaxing I induced the " professor " at Lakon to sketch the designs usually adopted by the Laosians for tattoo-marks. He produced a long rectangular piece of thin board, protected at each end by a frame, and coated on both sides with a thick layer of lacquer (*rack*) finely ground to a smooth surface and polished, which answered for a slate or drawing-board. On this he began to draw from memory in rapid succession different kinds of animals and emblematic figures of monsters, which I afterwards got him to reproduce on a piece of paper as shown in the opposite woodcut. His explanation of them is as follows :—The birds between the wavy lines round the waist are *nok jung*, or peacocks, the four large animals are Rachasees, beneath which is a *nok reng*, or vulture. The figures on the right leg are as follows :—

1. Noo (rat).

2. Mek, or lom (cloud).

3. Nok gatap (pigeon).

4, 9, and 14. Nok reng (vulture).

5, and 13. Mom, an ideal beast figured, before the Chinese came, in the frescoes in the Wats ; the animal is now mostly replaced by the Singto.

6, 15, and 16. Singto (lion).

7, and 11. A sort of bat (said to be an extinct species).

8. Then (a species of civet cat).

10. Rachasee.

12. Nok kapboa (species of heron).

On the left leg the figures are as follows :—

1, 2, 3, and 15. Mom.

4, and 13. Rachasee.

5, 6. Sua (tiger).

7, 11 and 14. Nok reng (vulture).

8. Singto (lion).

9. Chang (elephant).

10. Ling (monkey).

12. Hoalaman.

The artist told me that it took two sittings of a day

each to cover the entire surface as shown above. His *modus operandi* was to sketch in the outline of the figures first, in order to avoid mistakes, and then to puncture the pattern in, rubbing the pigment well in, afterwards filling up the interspaces with the wavy lines.

I should add that it is only the people of Western Lao that tattoo so large a portion of the body. Those Laosians whom I met in the Mekong districts had only an odd figure or two, either on the leg or the chest.

Karian boy from Lakon district.

The country round about Lakon is apparently rich, not only in timber, but in minerals. Near the town are some very rich iron mines, and I also saw a quantity of galena ore, of which I was assured that the mountains in the neighbourhood were full. Copper is also found in the district. The natives are skilled metalworkers, and make their own guns.

What struck me as much almost as anything was the enormous number of elephants. Wherever I went they were to be met, and the forests seemed as full of wild elephants as the town was of domesticated ones. The sight of them only made me the more indignant that I could not procure the service of a single one to continue my journey; but I lived in hope of the return of the Chow, who, I understood, would be sure to come to his daughter's wedding, the date fixed for which was drawing near, and for the advent of which I think I was more anxious than the Radjaput himself.

In the hills to the east of Lakon live a tribe of Karians, some of whom occasionally came into the city, so I took the opportunity of taking portraits of some of them, to compare with their exiled kindred in the Petchaburee district, from which they differ in some respects. The men, for instance (see woodcut), wear their topknot on the forehead, instead of at the side, and they do not keep the hair so long as their west coast relatives.

One day, while pondering what steps I should take to bring the Phyas to a sense of their responsibilities I was somewhat startled to hear the unaccustomed sound of wheels slowly rolling along the road and stop just outside my door. As elephants and bullocks are the beasts of burthen in Lao, carts of course are scarce. Occasionally, near the cities, an

Karian man from Lakon district.

unwieldy vehicle, on two wheels, each wheel being simply a huge solid wooden cylinder without spokes, which, never being oiled, make a harsh, squeaking noise that can be heard at a distance, may be seen being dragged along, not by horses or bullocks, but by a number of men. These rude carts are used for one purpose only, that of transporting the rice from the river-side to the princes' or government stores. I was therefore surprised to hear wheels outside my abode, and, on going forward to see what this strange phenomenon might be, I found a stylish-looking dog-cart, drawn, not by a horse, but by two slaves, and in it, dressed in a black suit of European cut, was seated my friend the Radjaput, who invited me to take a seat beside him, and to go at once and dine with him. So off we started, Kao following on foot behind.

The house was of the usual native character in design and construction, and calls for little detailed description. It was furnished, however, with a table and half a dozen chairs, while the floor was partly concealed by three pieces of Brussels carpet of different patterns and very inharmonious colours. The dinner, which consisted of little more than rice, fish, and boiled fowl, was served in anything but princely style. The first thing that attracted my attention was a bottle labelled " Best India Pale Ale "—a label which conjured up pleasant thoughts of a refreshing drink which would be doubly a treat for being served so unexpectedly. Great was my disappointment when a slave poured the contents into a tumbler, and the faint odour of the undrinkable native arrack saluted my nostrils. I did not need to see the colour of the beverage : to taste it was out of the question ; the sickly smell was enough.

At last, towards the close of the last day of the year, the Chow Hluang returned from his rice-fields ; and on New Year's Day I paid him a visit, accompanied by Kao and three native officials, all Phyas, among them being my old friend who was the cause of all my troubles, and who, though he had been outwardly civil and deferential since my untoward introduction to him on the day of my arrival, was, I felt sure, determined to do all he could to annoy me. He carried, on a big massive silver salver or vase, which he held high in the air as he walked, my official letter carefully deposited on a bunch of flowers.

The chief was reclining on raised pillows, placed on a carpet, in the centre of a kind of daïs, surrounded by emblems of his rank, a magnificent array of betel-boxes, spittoons, trays, &c., all of fine workmanship and in unalloyed gold. Below him, on another piece of carpet, lay the Second Chief. They did not rise as we entered, and, indeed, seemed to take very little notice of any of us as we entered the room, and, until Kao, speaking as my mouth-piece, addressed a few words to the chief, and pointed to the letter of introduction from Bangkok, which the old Phya still held, there was rather an embarrassing silence.

Now came the opportunity for the old Phya to make good his case against me, or for me to complain of him, before his face, to the chief. But an unexpected *dénouement* occurred. This very old Phya, who had refused to obey the directions contained in the letter, under pretence of being unable to read it, was at once called upon by the Chow to read it aloud; and read it aloud he did, though in a manner that to my mind did not indicate any sense of humiliation on his part at being "found out." The letter was all Greek to me, but I could gather that the name of Chow Fa Maha Mala, the Siamese minister for the North, frequently occurred, and every time it was mentioned the Chow raised his hand in token of respect.

Hardly had the reading of the letter concluded, when the room became full of a pungent smoke, caused by the women in the open space below roasting chillies. The sensation of suffocation was most irritating, and every one began to cough and sneeze violently; so that the meeting broke up abruptly.

I don't know whether I am right in my suspicion, but it struck me at the time, and the idea has since been strongly confirmed in my mind, that this was a little diversion suggested by the playful mind of my friend the Phya, in order that I might not have the opportunity, while the Siamese minister's letter was fresh in the Chow's mind, of requesting that his orders might be carried out, or of lodging a complaint against the Phya for his rudeness. Sometimes I have thought that it was not only the Phya who was at the bottom of the business, but that the Chow himself was in league with him, for he seemed not to be in a particularly amiable mood. While not liking the idea of assisting the *farang* he did not dare to actually refuse to obey the orders of his suzerain, and so he connived at the old Phya's expedient for bringing the interview to a speedy close. Whether designed or accidental, the occurrence certainly had the effect of breaking up the meeting, and of depriving me for the time being of the opportunity of coming to some understanding as to my future movements.

The next day was fixed for the Radjaput's wedding, and the town was astir early in anticipation of the event. All the morning I could see large quantities of provisions being carried into the Chow's palace—rice, curry, pork, buffalo meat, vegetables, roasted capsicums, and an endless supply of arrack. About midday a band of musicians passed through the town, discoursing music, anything but sweet, on tom-toms, gongs, and flutes, accompanied by a party of singers chanting a monotonous song that resembled a funeral-dirge rather than a wedding-march. Two dancing men followed— important personages, no doubt, but, like many of the crowd, already intoxicated. After them came servants and slaves carrying flowers arranged in different devices, some of them with great artistic taste and skill. The last floral device was a huge tower of flowers, carried on a bamboo litter, behind which came

the Radjaput's umbrella-bearer, with a big red umbrella
reared on a long silver shaft. More musicians preceded the prince's attendants, who came walking two
and two, some with gold- and silver-hilted swords
drawn, others with arms reversed—again, to Western
eyes, suggestive of a funeral rather than a marriage-
procession—and yet others, bearing the inevitable gold
or silver plate belonging to their master, such as tan-
kards, betel-boxes, spittoons, decanters, &c. Finally the
bridegroom himself, seated in a dog-cart, hauled, not
by his only pony, which was having a holiday to-day,
and was walking just in front fully harnessed in
European style, although drawing no vehicle, but by
a dozen men, who added to their labours by doing a
considerable amount of shouting. The bridegroom
himself, looking the picture of misery, and soothing
his nerves and seeking solace in a cigarette which he
smoked through a meerschaum holder, was dressed in
a blue silk jacket embroidered with gold, with a
violet *palai*, and a black velvet cap with a gold
band.

When he came opposite my house and saw me, he
beckoned me to take a seat alongside him in the dog-
cart. As I jumped into the vehicle the crowd burst
into a goodnatured laugh, whether of surprise at the
unusual invitation, or of merriment at the idea of a
stranger taking so prominent a part in the procession,
I cannot say, but I laughed heartily myself at thus unexpectedly acting " best man " to a Lao bridegroom.

Behind the Radjaput came another retinue of servants, two and two, each couple carrying between them
a box of hard cash, while a further instalment of the
family plate succeeded. Next came a body of lancers,
unmounted, followed by a fine display of nine large
elephants, all tuskers, the leader carrying a huge red

and gilt howdah, wherein were piled a quantity of gold-embroidered cushions of different shapes, and of mattresses, constructed to fold up like a lady's fan, or rather like a Siamese book, zigzag fashion; all destined to form the furniture of the future establishment of the happy pair.

On reaching the gates of the Chow Hluang's palace, the procession was stopped, and, at a signal from some official, every one sat down until the arrival of the Radjaput, of whom I took leave just before he entered the building, feeling that my presence would hardly add to the harmony of the proceedings. So I am unable to give an account of the actual wedding-ceremony, though I know that most of the guests who were feasted inside, and nearly all the populace who made holiday outside, became intoxicated long before evening, some of them being so perfectly incapable that they had to be carried home.

The Lao natives were shy of giving information about courtship and marriage. I ascertained, however, that the offering of a flower, or the request to be allowed to light a cigarette from that in the mouth of a fair lady, is regarded as a declaration of love, and the acceptance by the lady of the proffered tribute, or her acquiescence in the request, is a formal " engagement." In this and other similar signs the evidence of my own eyes was sufficient to show that human nature is human nature even in Lao, and that occasions for " flirting " and " making love " are no more despised by the Laosians than by more civilized people.

A wedding is generally an affair of importance and display, differing only in degree according to the rank and wealth of the parties immediately interested.

The details of the native wedding-ceremony, and of the preliminary step of " betrothal," are probably very similar to those prevailing among the Siamese, whose customs in other respects resemble very closely those of the Laosians. In matrimonial arrangements the Laosians and Siamese alike have adopted the custom, not altogether unknown in civilized countries, of intermediaries or go-betweens, who always make the formal arrangements as to dowry, &c., and who not infrequently save the marriageable youths and maidens the trouble of love-making.

So far as the Siamese are concerned, I can give the following particulars, kindly placed at my disposal by Capt. Ames, H.M. inspector of police.

The custom among the upper and more respectable classes of Siamese is for the parents, when they wish a son to marry, or when he has expressed a desire to enter into matrimony, to employ a *Maasu* (in English, a " go-between," literally, an " elderly woman "), who is well known to the parents of a suitable partner, or of the young girl with whom the son has fallen in love. The Maasu goes and talks the matter over with the parents. If no obstacles are apparent, the parents of the young man select several elderly persons, intimate friends of both the families, men as well as women, "endowed with discretion " and—this is important— " fluency of speech," and invite them to their house, for the purpose of having a consultation on the important subject. After due discussion, a resolution is unanimously arrived at in favour of the match, and the astrologers are asked to name a favourable day for these elders to visit the parents of the young woman in question. On the day appointed, the delegates proceed together to the home of the young woman, whose parents politely receive them, inviting them to be seated, according to their rank and age, and the first important formal ceremony takes place, namely the " betel ceremony," which consists in placing betel-nut, lime, sirih-leaf, and tobacco in gold or silver salvers before the visitors. While the members of the deputation are enjoying a good " chew," they broach the business on which they have come, taking particular care to address the parents of the young girl according to their rank. The parents having listened to, no doubt, a flowery speech, reply to the following effect :—

" Our daughter we love much, and the son of the parents whom you represent is a person whom we also much respect. An old Siamese proverb however says : ' Move slowly, and you will gain your object ; and a prolonged effort will be likely to result prosperously ;' hence we would first take counsel with our relatives and see what they think, and then we will give you an answer."

After a short time, when another favourable astrological day has come, the parents of the young man call upon the elders to go again and hear what decision the parents of the young girl have arrived at. A second visit is arranged, and, if the parents have come to the conclusion to entertain the proposal favourably, they reply as follows :—

" We have consulted with our relations concerning the proposed marriage, and find them unanimously of the opinion that, if the young man does truly feel that he can confide in our daughter to take care of him in sickness, and pay suitable attention to his body after death, his confidence should be planted and so cherished that it may grow and flourish."

But what about the ages of the parties ? Are the years, days of the week, and month suited to each other ? This question is raised in accordance with the superstition that persons born in certain years are incompatible with each other. As for instance, persons born in the year of the rat cannot agree with those born in the year of the dog, those in the year of the cow with those in the year of the tiger, or the year of the tiger with that of the rabbit, of the cock with the dog, or of the dog with the monkey. Such couples are regarded as unsuited to each other, for a husband born in any one of these years and a wife born in the other year of any one of these opposing pairs would have, as it were, the whole course of nature tempting them to quarrel, and to bite and devour each other. The parents therefore of both parties respectfully beg each from the other the favour of taking the ages of the young man and girl to some fortune-teller, and solicit his opinion on the point whether the years of their respective births, and the month and day of the week on which they were born, will allow of their living happily together as husband and wife. This request, mutually preferred, is of course mutually granted. If the astrologer finds no serious obstacle, the elders are again sent to the parents of the young girl, to make further arrangements about the marriage, and the bridegroom at once sets to work to seek timber for the future dwelling-house, the erection of which he superintends daily. It is always customary to erect this building near the home of the bride's father; hence a newly-married young man is scarcely ever to be found living with his own father, but with his father-in-law.

When the house is nearly ready, a priest is invited, according to ancient custom, to give his blessing to the abode.

The parents of the bride, with as little delay as possible, now apply to the astrologers to fix a suitable day for the wedding. This having been done, they make the day known to their relatives and neighbours, and the parents of both parties unite in appointing some four or more elders for each party, and a few other persons, to become bearers of the *Kong Toon* and the *Sinsawt*. The *Kong Toon* is equivalent to a dowry, and consists of a sum of money set aside for the purpose by the parents on both sides, " the lowest sum ever given to join their business amongst husband and wife," as my Siamese friend said to me in English, being twenty catties from the parents on both sides, or forty catties (400*l.*) altogether. The *Sinsawt* is a present given as a pledge that the parties are engaged : with it are two suits of white raiment, designed as an offering to the parents of the bride, together with the wedding-cakes, and trays of betel-nuts, &c. These articles are conveyed in quite a state procession, either by land or by water, with a band of musicians, performing, as my Siamese friend said, " airs suitable for wedding-ceremonies," to the new house, called in Siamese *Pua Mia*, to be presented to the bride ; for all presents given at a wedding afterwards belong to the wife, and the husband has no right to touch them. If a separation should take place, the husband can only claim what he himself put in.

The parents of the happy pair and their relations, together with the " delegates," being all assembled, seat themselves on mats on the floor, while the *Kong Toon* and *Sinsawt* are being exhibited ; the elders or delegates who have had the business all the time in hand see to it that the money brought by both parties is spread out and counted in their presence, that they may become legal witnesses of the transaction. They then mix the two sums together, and scatter sweet-scented oil, fragrant flowers, and a little paddy on the money, as a token of their wish that the happy couple may have rice, oil, and perfumery in abundance.

The elders then deliver the dowry over to the parents

of the bride, and then, after an hour or so spent in feasting, a company of priests, from five to six in number, previously invited by the bride or bridegroom, come upon the scene, and read a lesson from the Buddhist scriptures and invoke a blessing upon the intended new couple. All this time the bride, who has been conducted to her new house by a company of virgin attendants, remains with her suite hidden from view by a curtain stretched across the middle of the room.[1]

When the priests have finished their service, the curtain is lifted, and certain elders, especially chosen, proceed to administer the holy water of blessing. The bride and bridegroom are for this purpose conducted to a place prepared for the sprinkling, and are seated about eighteen inches apart from each other. The chief elder, taking up the vessel of holy water, pours a little first upon the head of the man, then upon that of the girl, pronouncing a blessing upon each.

The attendants of the bride then assist her in changing her wet apparel for a dry suit, more gorgeous than before. At the same time there appears at the door a boy, nicely dressed, bearing a silver platter, containing a new and elegant suit for the bridegroom, a present from the parents of the bride, called *Pa hawi-haw*, which he puts on. In the meantime the priests, in another apartment, rehearse prayers for the benefit of the new couple, and after they have been treated to tea, betel-nut, and yellow robes, every one returns home. It is then the turn of the family of the bride to give a feast, and in the evening of the third day the bride is at last conducted ceremoniously to her new abode to embrace her husband.

After two or three days the bridegroom takes his

[1] A similar custom prevails in Sumatra.

bride to visit his father's family, when she prostrates herself before them, and distributes among them a few small presents, in the form of flowers, cakes, &c. A few days later, the bride in turn is supposed to conduct her husband on a ceremonial visit to her parents, at whose feet he bows down.

At the time of the birth of their first child, the *Kong Toon*, which was committed to the care of the parents of the bride, is brought and delivered over to the young mother. Up to this time the newly-married couple have lived upon the parents of the bride; from this time onward it is arranged that they are left to take care of themselves.

It is a curious fact that that which gives the name to the whole wedding-ceremony is the betel-nut which is served on the occasion on a metal or plaited tray. This article in order to be complete must have three accompaniments, viz. a cake, called *Kanom-cheen;* a kind of mincemeat, highly seasoned, wrapped in plantain-leaves, and cooked by steaming; and, thirdly, the sirih-leaf and red lime. These are all termed *Kan mak*, literally, "a basin of betel-nut," and this is the common Siamese name for a wedding.

Monogamy is nominally practised by all the Laosians, who, like the Siamese, marry early. Among both people *the* wife, who has been married with all due pomp, takes rank with the husband, and has the management of the household; but the princes and officials who can afford to do so have a number of concubines, who can be sold or otherwise disposed of when they are tired of them.

The women in Lao, as well as in Siam, exercise a good deal of authority, and are by no means treated like the Malay women.

The wife of the late ex-regent was very powerful,

and if any one wanted a favour of the old ex-ruler, and could gain her voice, all would be serene with the Somdeth Chow. In Lao it is the same : the principal wife of a chief or prince always wields a large amount of power, not simply because she happens to be " under the shadow of the throne," but because a woman's naturally shrewd wit is recognized at its true value.

Of " education " properly speaking there is none for the female sex, and little more for the other. The women are not supposed to be taught anything in the way of " book-learning." Most of the boys, it is true, receive a small amount of tuition in reading and writing which it would be ridiculous to dignify with the name of education ; the priests are the teachers, and what they teach is confined to the precepts of Buddha and the legends connected with his life, but it is a most exceptional thing to meet with a woman, even among the " princesses," who can read or write.

CHAPTER XVI.

Liberty at last—Princes as cicerones—Elephants sliding down-hill
—Ngiou traders—A bullock caravan—Mules in masquerade—
A dangerous road—Native pottery-works and brick-fields—
How they make pots and pans—A curious oven—The city of
Lampoon—Ancient records—A famous Wat and Phrachedee—
Buried relics—Ransacking the Phrachedees—Treasure trove—
Keeping away the spirits—Merit-making—Steps unto heaven
—Lao notion of the universe—The different celestial chambers
—The highest heaven.

EARLY in the morning on the day after the wedding,
the Chow Hluang went away again to his rice-fields,
leaving me once more to the tender mercies of the
Phyas, who, being relieved from the fear of any inter-
ference on the part of their chief, were able to annoy
me to their hearts' content.   That the Chow was privy
to this arrangement I have not the slightest doubt,
though I believe that he gave instructions that, after
they had "baited" me a little longer, I was to be
allowed to go on my way.   For, at last, on the 7th of
January, the officials, apparently convinced of the fu-
tility of keeping me any longer in durance vile, suddenly informed me that I might go.   Having arranged
for elephants and guides, I entered a formal protest
against my prolonged detention, in the shape of a claim
for damages against the chiefs and people of Lakon,
and then shook the dust of the place off my feet, starting about midday with two guides for Chengmai.

I noticed that my two guides were dressed more

neatly than usual, and on making inquiries Kao learnt that they were Chows. At first I began to think that they must have assumed the character of guides in order to keep a watch on my movements ; but it turned out that they had an eye to business of another kind. Princes, it seems, are so common a commodity in Lao that the authorities can afford to give them as guides, and so poor are they that they do not think it *infra dig.* to undertake the duty for the sake of the small gratuities attached to the office.

The road lay alternately through rice-fields and brushwood, till six p.m., when we crossed the river Metan, another tributary of the Menam Vang. Here we found a Sala, at which we put up for the night.

Next day we entered a fine forest, and the travelling became very rough. We crossed the Metan, I should think, twenty times in the course of the day, and in the alternate ascents and descents I had ample opportunity of noting the sureness of foot of the elephants, which seemed quite to enjoy the excitement of climbing and descending the steep acclivities, mounting rugged slopes where a goat would seem hardly to find a foot-hold, and sliding down-hill on their bellies, with their forelegs spread straight out in front, and their hind-legs behind, with an ease and self-command which a mule, using all his legs, might have envied. During the latter part of the day, we travelled literally along the bed of the river, gradually ascending till, at night, we encamped at an altitude of 1100 feet above sea-level. The air was cold and damp at night, the thermometer falling as low as 50° Fahr. in the early morning.

On the following day we met several caravans of Ngiou traders, with oxen laden with betel-nuts, chillies,

and capsicums, which they were taking to Lakon to
sell. These Ngiou (or Shan) traders from the north
do as large a trade with Lao and Siam as the Yunnanese on the east. Their caravans are always entirely
composed of oxen, while those of the Yunnanese com-
prise small horses or ponies, and mules. Neither
people employ elephants, which are scarce beyond the
borders of Lao, and a dozen oxen, valued at from fifteen

Yunnan trader and mule (*front view*).

to twenty-five rupees apiece, are to a Ngiou what an
elephant is to a Laosian. It is a very common thing
to meet long processions of cattle, to the number of
perhaps two or three hundred, passing in single file
along the narrow tracks that do duty for roads, each
carrying a pair of pack-saddles, hung crosswise over
the back, laden with the produce of their own country,
or taking back that of Lao or Siam. The driver of an

elephant meeting such a train of cattle makes way for it by "backing" into an opening in the forest, or making a "siding" if in the open country; and, to give warning of their approach, each bullock carries a number of small brass bells, which make a musical sound, the effect of which is very pretty as it is borne through the forest-glades, or echoed from a steep mountainside. Sometimes, instead of brass bells, some of the oxen will have hung over their heads a huge wooden bell, *i.e.* a bell-shaped piece of wood, hewn out and

Side view of leader of Yunnan caravan.

shaped with infinite labour, and fitted with a clapper, which plays a drum-like accompaniment to the music of the metal bells.

These bells are useful also in enabling the herdsman to find his cattle when grazing during a halt. To prevent delays the beasts are not allowed to graze *en route*, being provided with a rattan muzzle, under the preventive influence of which they plod quietly forward till a halt is called. In this respect they are not so well off as the elephants of Lao and Siam, which are able to eat as they go along.

Like the cattle of the Ngious, the mules and ponies of the Yunnanese are muzzled, but the most curious feature in these Yunnan mule caravans is the extraordinary way in which the leader of the drove is decorated. The head of the animal is covered with a mask made of small cowrie shells, beads, or seeds, with two openings for the eyes, and surmounted by a high tuft of feathers from the tail of a peacock or an Argus pheasant, while an additional supply of bells is hung round the neck and shoulders and also round the hind quarters of the beast, and one tuft of hair is suspended beneath the tail, and another on the left side of the neck. The annexed woodcuts represent the front and side views of a mule thus strangely caparisoned. The object of all these trappings is to protect the caravan from the assaults of evil spirits.

Our road was still upwards amid magnificent scenery: here along the edge of precipices some two hundred feet deep, down which a single false step on the part of our trusty elephants would have precipitated us into a tangled waste of trees, creepers, and great boulders; there through thick vegetable growth which any other quadruped could hardly have penetrated, till at midday we found ourselves 500 feet higher than on starting in the morning. Then for three hours we gradually descended till the Lampoon River was reached. Crossing this, we entered a thin forest of young teak-trees, still passing through rugged and undulating country, till we suddenly emerged on to an immense arid plain, with here a rice-field, and there a brick-field, where the natives were busy moulding clay vessels or their peculiar thin bricks, and leaving them to "bake" in the sun.

Scattered at intervals all over the country may be seen these brick-fields and pottery-works, where the domestic water-jars and other vessels and the curious native ovens are made. The ware is of a very porous and brittle description, and the natives have not yet learnt the art of glazing it. The ordinary kitchen utensils are of very inferior make, but more attention is paid to the manufacture of the decanters or water-bottles, by which the natives set great store. These

Laosians steaming rice.

vary in shape from that of an ordinary wine decanter or *carafe* to that of a really well-designed and artistically-worked goblet or tureen. The larger and better kinds are furnished with a silver or gold cup, which is kept inverted over the mouth of the decanter. The best water-vessels, however, are of Ngiou make. These are either of a black or slate colour, and bear a polish. The earthenware ovens are strange little affairs, somewhat in the shape of a boot. In the opening at the

o

top, through which the foot would be inserted, is placed the pot containing the food to be cooked. Suppose the leather, covering the lower part of the foot, to be removed from the boot—as a gouty patient would cut it away to relieve the pressure on his toes—leaving only the sole and the side part of the upper covering, and suppose the boot then filled with fuel, and you have a good idea of a Lao oven or cooking-stove ; the only fuel used is wood. This oven is a very convenient contrivance, handy to carry about, and easily replaced at the cost of only a few pence if broken.

At noon on the 10th of January we reached Lampoon, the capital of the Lao state of the same name, situated on both sides of the river Me Kuang, an affluent of the Meping.

Lampoon was at one time a flourishing city, as the following extract from the earliest state records preserved in the library of the chief of Chengmai will show. It is recorded that when Muang Rai, who was ruler of Kiang Tsen in the thirteenth century, heard of the greatness of Lampoon he desired to conquer the city ; so he despatched an agent whose name was Ai Fah, with instructions to use intrigue and to get into favour with Phya Nye Bah, the ruler of Lampoon. Ai Fah was soon appointed by the chief to collect taxes, and eventually was given absolute control over the entire province of Lampoon. In the beginning he acted with wisdom and justice ; but after a couple of years he oppressed the population in every respect. This he did in order to make the people dissatisfied with their ruler. Among other things he had a canal dug to connect the river Meping with the city. The canal began twenty miles south of Chengmai ; traces of it are still to be seen. The work was of no benefit to the Lampoon people, but was simply undertaken in

order to overwork them. After five years his plans
were ready, and he sent word to Muang Rai at Kiang
Tsen to come with an army and invade the country.
Muang Rai came with a great army, and Ai Fah got
himself appointed as generalissimo over Phya Nye
Bah's army to operate against Muang Rai. He
marched out to meet the "enemy," and sent back
word for reinforcements. After he had got all the
Lampoon troops together, he treacherously surrendered
the army to Muang Rai, who became chief of the
country in the year A.D. 1281.

The record adds that Muang Rai was at that time
forty-three years of age, and that, previously to this,
twenty-five sovereigns had reigned over Lampoon.

The people of Lampoon had, no doubt, heard of my
treatment at Lakon, for immediately on arrival I was
requested to take up my abode in the Sala, a fairly
comfortable building just outside the city-walls. On
going to pay a visit to the chiefs, I found they were
not in town. The Phyas, however, informed me that
they were in the rice-fields, looking after their harvest,
adding that it was very necessary that they should do
so, or else buckets of paddy would get stolen.

Having obtained a promise that I should be provided
on the morrow with elephants and fresh guides, I went
at once to see the chief glory of Lampoon, its famous
Wat Pratat.

Just entering the grounds, stand two Rachasees in
their usual attitude, with jaws wide open, and tongue
rolling out. These figures, which are made of bricks
and mortar, painted red and then partly gilt and ornamented with bits of inlaid coloured glass, are netted
over with wirework, apparently to preserve them from
decay, and sheltered beneath wooden pavilions. To
the left of the entrance stands a house, in which is a

gigantic Buddha " in repose," just newly gilt and
generally repaired—I have no doubt all free of charge !

Facing the main entrance is the principal temple, a
new building in an unfinished state, which a good many
priestly hands were yet busily engaged in painting
and varnishing and gilding, both outside and inside,
and inlaying the outer carvings of the gables with
bits of different coloured glass. The temple is built
entirely of wood, with the single exception of the
floor, which is of stone, and from which massive teak
pillars spring to support the lofty roof. The altar is
studded with bronze figures of Buddha in all sorts of
positions. To the left of the main temple stands a
small brick building, wherein is preserved the sacred
literature.

In the temple-grounds is a very fine phrachedee—
certainly the finest and most interesting structure of
the kind I have seen outside the walls of Bangkok, and
visited annually by thousands of pilgrims. It is of the
usual conical shape, composed of a succession of graduating rings, ending in a pinnacle of, I should say, some
eighty feet in height, built of stone, having an outer
casing of brass. The entire structure from top to
bottom is heavily gilt. On the top of this pinnacle are
five bronze-gilt umbrellas, placed in tiers one above the
other, and diminishing in size from bottom to top.
These umbrellas indicate that the structure contains
something " Phra," or sacred. Round the upper portion of the phrachedee are hung a number of small bells,
fastened with wire in such a way that when the wind
blows the bells are set tinkling. The whole structure
is surrounded by a double brass railing, at each corner
of which is a small temple, with a stone figure seated
inside : these are the guardian angels, before each of
which, again, stands an immense gilt umbrella,

decorated all round with fringes. Round the outer railing are eight small brass-gilt models of temples, serving as lamps. One of these models is in the shape of a Chinese junk, and the inscription on it says that it is 1200 years old.

The priests say that formerly there stood on the spot where the present phrachedee is built, a solid gold temple in the shape of a Chinese junk, of which the model just mentioned is a copy, but that it is now buried underneath the phrachedee. No doubt the phrachedee marks the site where some sacred treasure once lay buried, and, as the building is in a good state of repair, the treasure may possibly remain there still, though the majority of these relic-shrines, especially the ancient ones, have undoubtedly been rifled of everything valuable that they ever possessed. This has been done by the Laosians themselves; sometimes, perhaps, by the Ngious with whom they have frequently been at war; and yet, as will be seen later on, they raised the cry of " desecrating our sacred places," when I searched some of the old neglected ruins, because it suited them to find a special cause of complaint against me.

There is little doubt that the treasure hidden beneath many of these ancient phrachedees is, or was, very large. To build a phrachedee is one of the principal religious exercises of Laosians and Siamese alike, who, whenever they wish to perform a work of unusual merit in the eyes of Buddha, devote a little time, labour, and money to the multiplication of these sacred shrines, under one corner of which it is the invariable practice to deposit either a figure of Buddha, or some coins, or a gold or silver ornament, together with a record of the name of the builder and the date, written on a silver leaf. In an old phrachedee, on the top of the mountain near Chengmai, Dr. Cheek, the head of the American Mission there, found a small crystal figure of Buddha with three small crystal ornaments, two of them round and one pear-shaped, the former of which, the natives said, represented the kidneys, and the last the heart, of Buddha.

Some of the phrachedees, even in Lao, though not so fine as those in Siam, are really imposing structures, sometimes as much as from 50 to 200 feet high. They are mostly built of sun-dried bricks, and always coated over with a white plaster; but here and there I have noticed a phrachedee made simply of earth, or mud, as if the earthly means of the pious builder had fallen short of his celestial aspirations.

The double object which the natives have in view in the erection of this interminable array of phrachedees is to keep at arm's length the evil spirits, and to secure the favour of Buddha and the good spirits. The desire to propitiate the good spirits and to exorcize the bad ones is the prevailing influence upon the life of a Laosian. With " Phees " to right of him, to left of him, in front of him, behind him, all round him, his mind is haunted with a perpetual desire to make terms with them, and to ensure the assistance of the great Buddha, so that he may preserve both body and soul from the hands of the spirits, and, by making merit either in almsgiving, in feeding the priests, in building temples or phrachedees, and making therein his offerings to the founder of his religion, may ultimately attain supreme happiness in the seventh or rather eighth heaven, or " Nirwana."

In the steps unto heaven the erection of phrachedees and the performance of other good works are only the preliminary stages. After death several transmigrations through successive heavenly states have to be accomplished before Nirwana (called by the Siamese Nipphan) itself is reached.

According to the Laosian idea, the centre of the world is Mount Zinnalo (called in Siamese Mount Meru), which is half under water, and half above. The sub-aqueous part of the mount is a solid rock which has three root-like rocks protruding from the water into the air below. Round this mountain is coiled a large fish, called "Pla anun," of such leviathan dimensions that it can embrace and move the mountain : when it sleeps the earth is quiet, but when it moves it produces earthquakes. In the accompanying engraving, taken from a drawing given to me by a native of Lao, the roots of Mount Zinnalo, emerging into the air, are marked x x x.[1]

Mount Zinnalo is full of caves, which under the water are inhabited by dragons called "Naks," while those above are the home of angels, or "Thewedas." Above the earth and around this great mountain is the firmament, with the sun, the moon, and the stars. These are looked upon as the ornaments of the heavenly temples. It is recorded that one of Buddha's disciples once interrupted him in his lecture, and asked the master what was beyond the firmament, when the great sage simply told him to " shut up."

Above the water is the inhabited earth, and on each of the four sides of Mount Zinnalo are seven hills rising in equal gradations one above the other, which are the first ascents the departed has to make. If he is wanting in " merit," he cannot get to the top ; but, having got to the summit, he now comes to the different chambers in heaven.

[1] I must give Mr. Cooper, the engraver, the credit of having " invested with artistic merit " the original drawing, which was very crude, and devoid of the realistic appearance of the earth, water, and sky which he has imparted.

The first heavenly space, immediately on the summit of Mount Zinnalo, is *T'ja to maha la chee ka taua,*

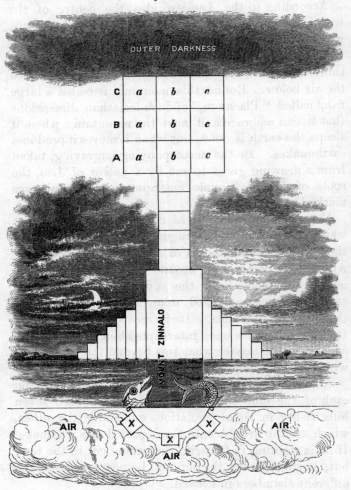

Lao notion of the universe.

which is the abode of good spirits, and where also resides a king or chief called Phya Wett So'wan.

A step higher up is *Tawah tingsah nang tewa nang*, here live the persons who when on earth built *Salas*, and houses for the priests, and to each of them is allowed 16,000 wives. Phya In is the chief of the company here, and he receives his orders from above.

The next chamber of heaven is *Tut sida tewa*. The folks residing here are those who when on earth wore white clothing, and passed the time in saying prayers, and each of these pious individuals has 30,000 wives.

Chamber No. 4 is the *Yama tewa*, inhabited by both sexes, who when on earth performed works of great merit.

The fifth heaven is *Nimma nalatee*, also an abode for good persons. Each man has 600,000 wives.

Heaven No. 6 is *Para min mitta*, a home where the people have perfect peace; they spend their time in singing and dancing, and one hundred and five millions of wives are allotted to each gentleman.

Beyond this is a heaven divided into three chambers or kingdoms (marked A B and C), each of which is subdivided again into three compartments (*a b* and *c*) as follows :—

A *a*. *Poma tewa* is for both sexes, who have more merit than " Indra."

A *b*. *Maha pom ma*, also for men and women of the highest order; here reside the four regents of heaven.

A *c*. *Poma palo pitta*, likewise for people of both sexes, whose business is to take care of heaven.

In B are the three places, or highest heavens, reserved for those who have made great merit to enjoy for a season " felicity " and " glory " before going to Nirwana—*a* is for gentlemen, *b* for priests, and *c* for ladies.

In C reside the three orders of angels :—

C *a.* *Theweda newa sunja,* only for females.

C *b.* *Tewa butt utang,* for men only, who are the most perfect angels and reside here before becoming gods, and ruling over men, like Buddha.

C *c.* Those who have merit enough to attain this point become mothers of gods.

Above all is Outer Darkness or " Nirwana," which Buddha is said to have compared to the disappearance of gunpowder [2] when lighted in your hand. By some the word Nirwana is accordingly interpreted to mean " non-existence," but I doubt if this is the correct interpretation.

According to Mr. Alabaster, who is without a doubt the highest authority on Siamese Buddhism, it is " a place of comfort where there is no care : lovely is the glorious realm of Nirwana ;" and I agree with Mr. Alabaster that it is a place of perfect happiness. On ancient figures of Buddha [3] inscriptions are often found in which the maker of the image implores the aid of Buddha in reaching the " highest heaven." If the inferior heavens are the places of enjoyment described above, there would be no object in praying for removal thence to a place of non-existence or unconsciousness.

[2] A proof of the antiquity of gunpowder.
[3] See p. 279.

CHAPTER XVII.

Buddhism in Lao—The degrees of the priesthood—Acolytes—
"Children of the crystal bottle"—Heavenly theatricals—
Entering the priesthood—Prince-priests—The ordination
ceremony—Priests gathering alms—Daily round of temple-
life—Resemblance between Romish and Buddhist ritual—
The government of the priesthood—The abode of the priests—
The service of the temple—The sacred Bo-tree—Occupation of
the priests—Trial for breach of vow of chastity—The religious
feeling of the Laosians—Priests *versus* Laity—European opinion
on Buddha and Buddhism.

THERE are several points in which the religious customs of the Laosians differ from those of the Siamese.
The Laosian priests have a different code of laws from
that prevailing in Siam proper. The service of the
church, *i.e.* "priesthood," in Siam is like military
service on the continent; it is compulsory, although,
as I have previously stated, the admission to the
priesthood is in many cases a mere formality. In Lao,
however, the admission to the priesthood is optional,
though, as a general rule, one member of the family
takes "holy orders." Further, the Laosian priests
are allowed the privilege—if that be any advantage
to them—of possessing worldly goods; in fact many
of them are quite rich, and own, not only goods and
chattels, but a number of slaves. Unlike the Siamese
priests, again, the Laosian priesthood have no regular
hours for meals.

There are three degrees in the Lao priesthood.

The first stage is called *Look sit* (*look* is " disciple," or " child :" *sit* is " graduate ").

The second stage is called *Phra,* (which means " lord ").

The third stage is called *Too* (*i.e.* a graduate, or one who has more learning).

When the *Too* has become chief priest, he may attain still further five degrees :—

1. *Too noi* (little graduate).
2. *Too jai* (big graduate).
3. *Kroo bah* (one who is accustomed to teach).
4. *Oopasai* (vice-president).
5. *Radjakoo* (president).

In every wat are always a number of boys, varying in age from five to twelve years. These are novices, who go into the temple without any change of clothing, and merely shave the head. A boy is generally taken to some head priest by his parents, who beg him to prepare the boy for religious instruction ; the parents on such an occasion never fail to take the indispensable offering of flowers, wax tapers, and parched rice. The boy then passes under the priests' entire control ; he performs the menial services for them, such as carrying water, sweeping clean the temples and grounds, &c., in return for which he is fed, and taught to read and write and say his prayers. He must leave his home and sleep in the monastery. If he rebels against authority, and flees to his parents, the priest can come to their house, bind the boy, whip him, and carry him back to the temple. If the boy is obedient and docile, as soon as he can read and write, and has learned the code of prayers, he can be introduced into the novitiate of the priesthood. When this period arrives, the parents secure priest's clothing, and make offerings to the priests of the temple, and the boy is now inducted

into the priesthood, and becomes a disciple or *Look
sit.*

The first step in the induction appears anything but
a solemn ceremony. The disciple is dressed in the
gayest attire his friends can find for him, and a crown
is placed on his head. This is done to remind him of
Kotamah (the Lao word for Gaudama) in his regal
state. Thus attired he is called *Look kaaow,* or "child
of the crystal bottle "—a name which has its origin in
the following peculiar legend. Once upon a time a
great merry-making was being held by a prince and
his wife, on the occasion of one of their children
entering the priesthood. Theatricals of all sorts were
being held, and, as the prince and his children were
sitting watching the performance, the inhabitants of
the upper world came to see what was going on.
They appreciated the proceedings so much that they
went and reported them to Phya In (or Indra, the
ruler of heaven), who himself came to have a peep at the
show. So pleased was he that when leaving he stole
three of the sons of the prince, who were sitting as
spectators, and took them with him to heaven for the
purpose of assisting him in establishing theatrical performances in the celestial regions. He accomplished
his purpose in three days, and then brought each of
the princely boys back in a large crystal bottle, and
set them down in the place from whence he had
snatched them.

The *Look kaaow,* dressed in these royal robes, and
riding on a richly-caparisoned horse, if one is to be had
—if not, carried upon the shoulders of his friends—
has a grand procession, in which drums and tambourines
are pitted against each other, and boys with flutes vie
with boys without flutes to see who can make the most
hideous noises. The *Look kaaow* is about to leave

behind him the frivolities of the world, and his last day is marked by the most outrageous extravagances.

The time usually appointed for entering the priesthood is either in the second, fourth, sixth, eighth, or occasionally the tenth month, and, if the parents of the candidate for ecclesiastical honours have the means, great preparations are made for the event, a grand festival entertainment with theatricals being given, especially if it is a prince who is about to enter the priesthood.

When the day for the entertainment is fixed, the parents take a nice brass or silver salver—it may be borrowed for the occasion—on which they put the yellow robes which their son is to wear in the temple, and on the top of these clothes are placed the inevitable waxen tapers, parched rice, and flowers. They then carry the salver round to each of their friends and neighbours—if in " high life," they go to the chief and his nobles—as an intimation that each person so honoured is invited to come to the *poy*, or entertainment. Those thus invited must respond by an offering of wax tapers, rice, flowers, and so on, which they deposit on the tray; with perhaps an offering of a pillow or mat, or some other article likely to be needed by the new priest after his inauguration. Others are perhaps disposed to make an offering of money. Those friends who are prevented from going will pay their tribute just the same, and lay it down on the cloth, while those who prefer doing so reserve their gift to be offered personally on the day of the entertainment. The money thus collected, which varies in amount according to circumstances from 5 to 100 rupees, is given to the young ecclesiastic to use as he thinks proper. If he is of an economical turn, he keeps it to assist him to enter married life, after he has graduated at the temple. The majority who enter the priesthood remain from one to two years in "holy orders;" but I stayed with a prince at Kiang Hai who had been thirteen years a priest—till he got tired and thought it was time to marry.

Formerly the merriment was kept up seven days; but now one day is deemed sufficient, and when the procession is over the party returns to the temple, where the *Look kaaow* doffs the regal paraphernalia and dons the priestly robes, first giving his ordinary clothing—which certainly does not represent much in value—to his parents. On entering the temple he prostrates himself first before the image of Buddha, next before the sacred books in the library, and then before the priests—who are seated on the floor to receive him—and at the same time begs their permission to enter the religious service of the temple. This request is, I hear, never refused, however bad the moral character of the man or boy may be. Permission being formally granted, the parents present the priests with the yellow robes to be worn by the newly-inducted *Look sit*, and, while they robe him, he in return makes offerings of wax tapers, flowers, and parched rice to the priests. The *Look sit*, having been duly robed, is conducted to a head priest, to whom is assigned the duty of asking him "Will you observe the ordinances of Buddha?" &c., &c., repeating each of them in succession; to each question, as a matter of course, the answer "Yes" is given, and the head priest then states the rules of the temple service, and gives his blessing to the *Look sit*. At the end a bountiful feast is offered to the officiating priests. As for the young priest himself, if he wishes to be very religious, he eats only once during the day for three days after induction.

At the age of twenty, or, if he exceeded that age on entering, after certain formalities have been gone through, the *Look sit* is permitted to enter upon the second degree of holy orders—and becomes a *Phra*, or lord. The ceremonies observed are similar to those followed on entering upon the first stage. The priest is now permitted, and indeed required, to go round in the morning to receive rice and other food from the people; though in small villages or lonely settlements I frequently found the priests did not go their rounds for food, which was brought to them as regularly as clockwork by the natives: but a procession of three or four yellow-robed men, preceded by a chief priest, carrying a large jar in his hand, and followed by four or five juvenile pupils bearing the rice-pot, in which to receive the alms of the people, is one of the characteristic incidents of every-day life throughout the country. I have often been in native houses when the priests have called for their food. It is always ready for them, and the natives appear glad to give their share, which they offer with an air of respectful request, as much as to say, "Do me the favour to accept this food." Occasionally flowers, which are abundant all the year round, or a bundle of wax tapers, are given as a sort of special offering.

The first two or three hours of every day are devoted to the recitation of the Pali formulæ, from the sacred books—long narrow strips of palm-leaves, strung together on a piece of string passed through the centre, on which the characters are engraved with an iron *stylus*. Offerings are then made to Buddha, and the younger brethren are taught to read and write, priests and boys chanting in chorus, or alternately, verses from the scriptures.

Then comes the daily round in search of alms, and

during the middle of the day priests and pupils take a long siesta. Towards sunset they again proceed to the temple, recite their formulæ, and make fresh offerings. On entering the temple the worshipper first lights a taper, which, together with a tray of parched rice or flowers, he carefully deposits in front of the figure of Buddha, on which he occasionally places a piece of yellow cloth. Then he calmly sits down on the floor before the altar, with a lighted taper in his folded hands, and pours out a string of formal prayers.

The daily offerings to Buddha, and the general style of ritual, reminded me very much of that of the Roman Catholic priests. Instead of the figures of the Virgin there are figures of Buddha. The tall candles of the Roman Catholic Churches are replaced by the wax tapers[1] which the priest or suppliant places reverently before the image, or in a receptacle provided for the purpose. Incense is as freely used in a Buddhist Wat as in a Catholic cathedral, and fast-days are common to both religions. The Latin prayers which the Romish priests recite before the crucifix may be likened to the Pali liturgy which the Buddhist priest mutters before the figure of Buddha—both alike being in a dead language. Even in the ornamentation of the places of worship there is a parallel, the beautiful frescoes illustrative of the life of Christ being replaced by rude frescoes representing events in the life of Buddha, which ornament the walls of every Wat; while the entrancing music of the Italian churches has a distant analogy in the dull gongs and drums of the Buddhist temple.

[1] The quantity of wax burnt in the worship of Buddha is enormous. In some temples tapers are kept constantly burning. The supply of the native forests is not sufficient for local use, and large quantities of wax are imported from Yunnan.

On the subject of the devotional offerings made to the figures of Buddha, it is interesting to note that, according to Captain Forbes' "British Burma," the Burmese, the neighbours of the Laosians, do not worship Gaudama, while the Lao people say that Buddha left word that, when they worshipped these figures, they worshipped him. When they pray, the Laosians pray to the spirits of their ancestors, beginning with *Mung Hai,* who lived about 600 years ago. Now the Burmese, according to Captain Forbes, say that Gaudama has ceased to be: "he hears no prayer, sees no one, can afford no help," and that it is solely out of gratitude that they revere him who, "by preaching the law, has been to men a saviour, in showing the way open for escape from the endless miseries of ever-changing existence."

In India Buddha is looked upon as the Reformer of the laws, whereas the Laosians regard him as the Inventor.

There is a head priest in every temple, and over the fraternity of head priests is a high priest, whose position is invested with as much honour as that of the chief ruler of the country, and who is almost looked upon as a living Buddha.[2] Higher than this most high priest is the hermit, whose home is in the desert jungle, or the dark cave. I made many inquiries about hermits, but was always assured that, in all the kingdoms of Lao, there are none at present.

From what I have seen and heard in my travels in Lao—and the remark practically applies equally to Siam —it is the priests, and the priests only, who honestly and conscientiously endeavour to keep strictly to, at least, the five principal commandments as laid down by

[2] The Thibetans have living Buddhas, called *Gogen,* men without blemish and reproach, and learned in the Buddhistic scriptures.

the pious and virtuous founder of their religion ; in most cases their lives are a quiet round of peaceful asceticism.

Their food is of the plainest description, rice and chillies, with a little fish, and tea to drink when they can get it : but they smoke a great number of burees, and chew betel and sirih.

They never touch any spirit, of which the Laosians generally are so fond. Their domiciles—long low buildings, sometimes of brick, but mostly of wood, and even, in out-of-the-way places, constructed of bamboo— are miserable, uncomfortable, and dirty to a degree.

Sunlight hardly ever enters into these dark and dusty abodes, where many a priest spends his whole lifetime. The best quarters for a head priest that I saw in Lao were those attached to the Wat Hluang at Lakon, and even these would compare unfavourably with an average " house " in Seven Dials. Of furniture there was of course none, only mats to sit on, and a good selection of pillows to recline on. In front of the spot where the head priest generally lay were two big jars filled with water, which, for the want of tumblers, was drunk out of spoons made of cocoa-nut-shells with a wooden handle, while by the side was always the sirih and betelnut-box, with a tray of flowers ready at hand as offerings to Buddha. On the walls hung a number of small baskets used for keeping the rice in. Near the cushion were piled bundles of sacred MSS., while in the corners were deposited the state umbrellas and a number of trays, mostly of wood, and heaps of English and American illustrated newspapers, which managed to find a place amid these strange surroundings. Over all lay a layer of dust, dark and dense, and apparently more sacred than anything else, for it was never disturbed.

The priests, who also are the medical practitioners of the country, have always in stock a great number of medicinal plants.[3]

A tree to be found in the grounds of every temple is the Bo-tree (*Ficus religiosa*), held sacred by all Buddhists, because under it, so the legend runs, Gaudama, while on earth, found a pleasant shade to rest his weary limbs as he toiled up the inaccessible mountain of good works, on his way to storm the citadel of Nipan in the spirit-world, where, having succeeded in his assault, he now sleeps in utter unconsciousness of existence. The seeds from this tree are often carried by birds and dropped on walls, trees, &c., where, being covered with a glutinous substance, they adhere and quickly germinate. Besides the Bo-tree, the priests always cultivate a stock of flowering plants, especially lilies, orchids, and trees producing a jasmine-like flower, which they use as offerings to Buddha.

If the Wat is near the river, the priests build their own boats, and all of them spend their leisure time in painting and decorating the temples, while during the dry seasons they perform pilgrimages to caves and temples of hallowed memories, such as the famous limestone cavern of Tam tap tau, the temple Doi sua tape at Chengmai, or the Wat Phra Bat near Lakon, with its footprint of Buddha.

In the government of the fraternity of the priests there are some curious customs. When, for instance, a priest is charged with unchastity, the case is tried in a very odd way. The accused parties, priest and woman, are compelled to take a mouthful of beaten rice, uncooked, and to chew and swallow it. The one who can eat the rice and swallow it without difficulty is "innocent," but the one whose mouth fails of saliva, and

[3] Lunatics generally find their home in a Wat.

who asks for water, is "guilty." That is to say, if the priest swallows the rice, and the woman fails to do so, she is adjudged guilty of making a false accusation, and is punished. On the other hand, if the priest fails, he is adjudged guilty of unchastity, and meets with his reward.

Some thirty years ago in Western Lao another custom prevailed in the trial of charges of adultery, but it is now only practised in rare instances. The accused parties are brought before the chief priests. The accused priest first takes the water of the oath, which is done in the following way: he takes two of the metal rice-pots used by the order in receiving alms; one of these he hangs down by his side with a sling passed over the right shoulder, when it is filled with water, and has a cover placed on it. The other is also filled with water, but is without a cover, and he has to hold this to his breast in the left arm. If he can walk a few yards without spilling any water, he is adjudged innocent of the charge brought against him; if he spills, he is guilty. Next comes the woman, who holds one pot to her breast with both arms and walks. If she does not spill any water, her word is taken. So the result is arrived at this way: priest spills the water, woman does not, a clear case against him. Priest spills and woman also spills, a minor punishment is inflicted on the priest, but the woman gets nothing. Priest does not spill and woman does, he is free, but the woman is heavily fined. Neither priest nor woman spills, the case is one of false accusation; the priest goes free, and a small punishment is inflicted on the woman.

The Siamese assert that the Lao form of Buddhism is corrupted from the original purity of the code established by Buddha. Whether this is so or not, I leave for those to decide who have studied the remarkable faith of Buddhism, merely stating the foregoing facts to speak for themselves. In outward evidences of the depth of their faith there is nothing to choose between Siam and Lao. In both countries alike the traveller cannot fail to be impressed by the endless succession of temples and phrachedees that meet the eye on every side, showing how deep is the influence of their faith on the minds of the people. I do not think that their *hearts* are deeply impressed with the devotion by which their acts would seem to show that they are animated, but I believe the whole religious instinct of the people has no deeper root than in their *minds*. Certainly the Laosian laity leave it to the priests to act up to the standard of morality laid down by Gaudama, and limit their participation in the fulfilment of his laws to the occasional erection of a phrachedee, to the frequent offering of gifts to Buddha, and to seeking periodical consolation and absolution at the hands of the priest.

So far as the tenets of the religion are concerned, there are among Buddhist theologians no differences of opinion similar to those which light such fires of dissent and *odium* among the Christian clergy. The creed unites the whole mass alike of the priesthood and laity, and moulds the minds of the people to implicit obedience to their spiritual and temporal " pastors and masters."

The moral code of Buddha is excellent, and, if carried into practice by the mass of the people instead of being limited to the priests, would elevate and refine them. The Right Rev. Bishop Bigandet, in his work on the " Life and Legends of Gaudama," gives credit in this respect to the remarkable religion whose moral precepts bear so strong a resemblance to those prescribed in the Bible; and M. Barthelemy St. Hilaire, though he thinks it has a deteriorating influence on civilization, says in eloquent language :—

"I do not hesitate to add that, save the Christ alone, there is not among the founders of religion a figure more pure, more touching, than that of Buddha. His life is without blemish, his constant heroism equals his conviction, and, if the theory he extols is false, the personal examples he affords are irreproachable. He is the accomplished model of all the virtues he preaches ; his abnegation, his charity, his unalterable sweetness, never belie themselves. At the age of twenty-nine, he retires from the court of the king his father, to become a devotee and beggar. He silently prepares his doctrine by six years of seclusion and meditation. He propagates it, by the unaided power of speech and persuasion, for more than half a century, and, when he dies in the arms of his disciples, it is with the serenity of a sage who has practised goodness all his life, and knows that he has truth."

CHAPTER XVIII.

Arrival at Chengmai—Pra Udon, the second Siamese Commissioner
—A "floating house"—Introduction of carriages into Lao—A
projected cab-stand—Dr. Cheek and the American Mission—
Work and prospects of the mission—Influence on the natives
—An opening for missionary ladies—A visit to the Chow
Hluang—How to carry a flower—Ear-piercing, and ear-orna-
ments—Long ears and long life—Two kings on one throne—A
Chow's promise, and his performances—History of Chengmai—
Temples, old and new—The market at Chengmai—Yunnan
trading caravans—Spurious coins—"Cruelty to animals"—
How the pack-saddles are loaded—Camping for the night—
Tigers—Haw watch-dogs.

On the 11th of January I left Lampoon for Chengmai,
which is distant only four hours' ride by elephant, or,
as Paddy would say, half that distance on horseback.
On entering the town I at once inquired for Phya
Radjasena, the Siamese Commissioner, but no one
seemed to know where he was until I had passed
through the walled city and entered the suburbs on the
side near the river. Here I met a Siamese who had, as
Kao expressed it, the "look of an official," and who
pointed out as the residence of Radjasena a large
white-washed brick building, before which floated a
streamer at the extremity of a long bamboo pole, which
bent and swayed backwards and forwards with every
breath of wind.

Our volunteer guide turned out to be the son of
Pra Udon, the second Siamese Commissioner, and as
soon as I made myself known to him he very

kindly took me at once to his father's house. Hardly had I entered, when Pra Udón himself made his appearance—a short, well-built Ceylonese, with a pleasant smile ever playing round his jovial mouth, and a merry twinkle in his eye, dressed in a gorgeous, loose, flowing gown of grey and green silk, richly embroidered, and with a good allowance left for his increasing corpulency.

Pra Udon's skin was so much darker than that of the natives that they called him "black," and there seemed to be some little jealousy of him, particularly among the Siamese, although his pleasant, jovial ways made him generally popular. He had come out to Siam from Ceylon as a priest many years ago, when the late King of Siam sent for a number of ecclesiastics well versed in Buddhism and Pali. I do not know what particular part was assigned to Pra Udon in this galaxy of learning—he would have made a better jester, I should have thought, than priest—but he attracted the king's attention by his pleasant ways, ready wit, and undoubted ability, and, after receiving many marks of favour at the hands of the late sovereign, was appointed by the present king to the post of Assistant-Commissioner in Lao, under Phya Radjasena, with whom, by the way, he did not quite " hit it," and who was decidedly no favourite with the Laosians.[1]

Pra Udon spoke a few words of English, and at once made me welcome, explaining that the house which he

[1] Since my return I have heard from Bangkok that his Majesty has recalled Phya Radjasena, owing to the many complaints made against him by the people, especially as to his loose administration of justice. While I was at Chengmai, not only the Laosians, but the Burmese also, used to come to me, and give vent to their grievances against the Siamese Commissioner, always finishing up with the expression of a hope that a British Consul would be appointed.

placed at my disposal was what he called in English his " floating house," where he hoped I should be comfortable. The house was of the ordinary native style, built on posts, and the only claim which it had to the appellation of " floating " was that it was built so close to the river that in times of flood the water often surrounded it, reaching up to the floor of the verandah. I have no doubt that if it were not substantially built the strong current would soon convert a figurative expression into a reality, and that the house would " float " bodily away. The two rooms of which the house consisted were luxuriously furnished, containing, among other signs of civilization unusual in this part of the world, half a dozen chairs and a table, which made up in strength what they lacked in finish.

" Me made them Chengmai," said Pra Udon, standing in his favourite attitude when conversing, with his hands spread before him, the tips of the fingers just meeting, and alternately bending and straightening the fingers, in order to show off to advantage a splendid cat's eye ring on one hand and an equally fine diamond hoop on the other. " Me made them Chengmai. You no think good ? "

I assured him I admired the result of his energy in introducing civilized notions among the Laosians ; whereupon he exclaimed with evident enthusiasm :—

" Me brought carriages Chengmai. Elephants not good. Horse carriages very good."

His energy overcoming, or rather prompted by, his natural love of *otium cum dignitate* had led the easy-going Pra Udon to introduce European carriages into this Land of Elephants, and he pointed with pride to a couple of bamboo sheds across the road, which he said were his stables and coach-house, where he already had several horses and two carriages, to which he intended to add others. When he first brought them from Bangkok the people were so much interested in these vehicles that Pra Udon was actually tempted to think of trying to establish a " cab-stand " in Chengmai, where he thought it would prove very popular, and be a financial success. I doubt, however, if, when the novelty of the thing died away, the people would care to adopt this mode of locomotion in preference to elephant-riding, especially if they had to pay anything for the privilege of travelling in a wheeled carriage drawn by horses. Even then, roads would have to be constructed for this purpose and the Laosian is not yet educated up to that high pitch of civilization.

When I told my chatty host of the difficulties I had encountered at Lakon, he expressed his opinion of the natives there in the laconic utterance " great rascals Lakon : d—d rascals, Lakon," and laughed heartily at the idea of my having chastised the old Phya; afterwards adding that when he was first appointed Assistant-Commissioner he had a large residence at Lakon, which, indeed, was still at his service, but that the Lakon princes and officials made themselves so obnoxious that he could not remain there.

While I was talking with Pra Udon, Dr. Cheek, the medical head of the American Mission at Chengmai, came in, and while thanking me for bringing "the mail" —I had brought on a few letters for the missionaries from Bangkok, a service which it was a great pleasure to me to have had the opportunity of rendering, for this earnest body of Christian workers in a dark land were dependent on chance opportunities of receiving news from " home "—gave me a hearty welcome on behalf of himself and his coadjutors.

A word as to the position and objects of the American Mission, of which Dr. Cheek is the able and respected

medical head.   Established sixteen or seventeen years
ago, the mission has aimed not so much at proselytiz-
ing the natives as at instructing them and inducing
them to apply themselves to industries of a nature
to elevate their minds, and to improve their general tone.   After sixteen years' labour, the mission
claimed at the time of my visit only some seventy or
eighty living converts to Christianity.   Many of these
had embraced Christianity for the sake of temporal
rather than spiritual benefits, being desirous of being
redeemed out of slavery, or of getting paid for the
employment which the mission afforded them.   The
success of the mission must not, therefore, be measured by the number of converts, but by the influence
it has had upon the habits of the people in the district.
The religion which the people profess has such an influence upon them, and harmonizes so peculiarly with
their natural habit of mind, that it is not surprising
that so few proselytes to Christianity have been made.
But if they have not succeeded in penetrating the
darkness of superstition with the bright beams of
Christianity, the missionaries have shed upon the
country a ray of the light of civilization.

Dr. Cheek, as medical director of the mission, has
relieved the sufferings and saved the lives of hundreds
of natives, and has thereby earned their warm gratitude.   His name is a synonym of all that is good and
kind throughout the Chengmai district.   Adjoining his
house he has erected a long bamboo shed, subdivided
into a number of small apartments, which serve as
the wards of a hospital.   Here he has performed hundreds of operations, with such skill and with such
success that even the superstitious Laosians come
from long distances to be cured by him when suffering
from painful diseases or from severe wounds.   Con-

tiguous to the hospital is a dispensary, where he finds
a ready sale for the simpler drugs of the English and
American pharmacopœia, and where those who cannot afford to buy are sure to get advice and medicine
gratuitously. The chiefs and princes often send for
him when their reliance upon the superstitious rites
of the native "faculty" begins to fail them, and
though, in such cases, his advice has often only been
asked when the patients have been *in extremis*, and the
average of successful cases has therefore been small,
he has the reputation among all classes of being both
clever and kind. Two or three years ago he saved the
life of the chief's wife, when all the drugs and incantations of several native medicos had been called into
requisition in vain. For this service he received no
direct acknowledgment, but the chief has shown his
gratitude by affording the doctor every facility in
travelling from place to place within his district, and in
other ways.

In addition to his medical skill, Dr. Cheek has earned
the gratitude of the natives by establishing a boat-
building yard, where he gives employment to large
numbers of men, and where he has introduced improved
models of boats and better modes of construction.
Many slaves are now in this boat-building yard, working out, in accordance with the customs of the country,
their own redemption from slavery, by making boats
for their masters ; and many others have in this way
become owners of boats of their own construction, and
are now engaged in trade. American tools have been
introduced, and are gradually superseding the primitive
adzes and saws of the natives.

Upon the senior missionary, Mr. Wilson, falls the
actual missionary work of visiting the natives in their
homes, preaching to and teaching them, a work in

which he mutually assists, and is assisted by, Dr.
Cheek's practical labours as a doctor. The lady-mis-
sionaries, Mrs. Cheek and Miss Coole, have a commodious schoolroom, where the girls are taught the ordinary subjects of study, besides receiving practical
instruction in needlework, household duties, &c., with
lessons in music and singing as a recreation. The
Ladies' Board of the Society in New York frequently
send out sums of money with which Lao girls are redeemed from slavery and taken into the school. At the
time of my visit there were seven or eight girls, ranging
from thirteen to twenty years of age, bright, intelligent
creatures, perfectly content with their lot, apt at learning, and quick and cheerful in their habits—very different from their sisters in the Laosian world outside.

A yearly report of their proceedings is made by this
devoted band, who are supported and encouraged by
the liberality of friends in the United States, who do
not fail to study their welfare. A comfortable house,
neatly furnished with every convenience and modern appliance, including a good harmonium, and surrounded
with a nice garden in which bloom the lovely
flowers of the tropics, with occasional exotics from
America, introduced for "auld lang syne," has been
provided for them, and the natives who have received
favours at their hands are always ready to help in
keeping the garden in order, or in assisting in any
other work that may be beyond the capacity of those
in their immediate care and employ. So far as material
comforts go, these ladies and gentlemen are probably
as well supplied as the most fortunate of their fellow-
creatures; but no one will envy them their lot—cut off
as they are from the companionship of relations and
friends, and the society to which, in former years, they
were accustomed. Supported by the knowledge of the

good they are doing and trying to do, and by the gratitude of those whom they are benefiting, their greatest
joy is when a mail arrives now and then from America,
through the intervention of trading-boats, or of Siamese
officials and others on a tour through the country.

Since my return to Europe I have received letters
from Bangkok stating that reinforcements had arrived
there, *en route* for the missionary station at Chengmai
—a considerable number of missionaries, ladies and
gentlemen, having decided to throw in their lot with
that of Dr. and Mrs. Cheek, Mr. Wilson, and Miss
Coole, and to endeavour to civilize the natives of Upper
Siam. This accession of new members will revolu-
tionize the conditions of missionary life in Lao ; and for
ladies with whom, for instance, the course of love has
not run smooth, and who are willing to seek solace in
devoting themselves to a good work far away from the
scene of their disappointments, or who have a taste
for adventure, coupled with a desire to help in a
praiseworthy cause, I do not know any opening that
offers better opportunities than that of the now rapidly
expanding American Mission at Chengmai.

I cannot omit here to publicly express my gratitude,
collectively and individually, to the four members of
the American Mission at Chengmai, whose names I
have mentioned above, for their hospitality and great
kindness to me during my stay in this city.

On the day after my arrival at Chengmai I paid a
visit in company with Pra Udon to Phya Radjasena,
and afterwards to the Chow Hluang, whose house and
grounds, situated in the middle of the city, were surrounded by a high wall, a symbol of the rank and
authority of the chief of this populous province.

On alighting from Pra Udon's carriage and pair,
and entering the compound, we were informed that the

chief was taking a bath, and so in the interval of waiting I had ample opportunity of examining the house. The building was a mixture of Chinese and Lao architecture; along the whole front extended a long, open room, partially furnished with European furniture, the only article of native workmanship I saw being a large gilt state chair or throne, which Pra Udon said was reserved for the use of the head priest when he came to visit the Chow. In one corner of the room an old Chinaman tailor was busy making a coat of light blue cloth for the Chow, who himself shortly appeared, an old man, tall of stature, but slightly stooping beneath his load of sixty-four years, dressed in a black jacket with gold buttons, and a *palai*, but barefooted. He was smoking a buree, which went out as soon as he left off " pulling " in order to speak to us, as these native cigars always do ; upon which the slave who followed him took it from him, placed it between his own lips to relight it, and handed it back to his master. When I presented my letter from Bangkok, the Chow called in one of his secretaries to read it aloud, whereupon he said the natives were forbidden to shoot birds, but he would see if an exception could be made in my case, and sent for six Phyas, to consult with them on the point. The country, he said, was rich in flowers, especially orchids, many of which were scented, and especially reserved for the princes' use. One mountain, a few days' journey distant, was noted for certain varieties, which could be found nowhere else. Picking up a couple of specimens, he handed them to me ; they were a species of scented *Dendrobium*. As I held them in my hand, the Chow told me to follow the Lao custom, and stick them in my ears ; and when I pointed out that my ears were not pierced, he took one, and showed me how to make up for this deficiency by fixing it after the fashion of a quill in a clerk's ear.

The fashion of piercing the ears is universal among both sexes of all ages in Lao. The ears are bored when very young, and a wooden peg inserted, the hole being gradually enlarged by being stretched with pieces of wood, ivory, or metal, or with a leaf rolled up, or any other article that may be at hand, till it is capable of receiving the full-sized *lan*, or ear-ornament. This consists of a plate of unalloyed gold, a little over an inch wide, lightly twisted up until it forms a roll of cylindrical shape, about half an inch in diameter, which is simply held together by tying a string round it, and inserted into the enlarged ear-lobe. The poorest girls content themselves with a hollow cylinder formed of a single coil of plate, the cavity of which is filled up with lead, while the wealthy classes have a many-coiled roll, the edges of which are ornamented with diamonds or rubies. When a gold ear-ornament is not forthcoming, a flower takes its place. The men seldom wear ear-ornaments, but invariably carry a flower in the ear, or use the hole as a convenient receptacle for a buree.

This fashion of stretching the ear-lobes and the practice of carrying flowers, cigars, and other articles on the top of the ear, causing the upper part of the ear to project from the side of the head, makes the naturally large ears of the natives look still larger. But large ears are regarded as a sign of longevity, and are appreciated accordingly. The chief of Chengmai is especially remarkable for the large development of his aural appendages. The Siamese commissioner once remarked to him that he ought to live to a green old age, if the size of his ears was to be regarded as a sign, and the simple old chief seemed quite flattered by the remark.

Q

As I explained to the Chow my intention of passing through Lao into Ngiou, and asked for his assistance, he listened very quietly—generally with his mouth wide open—nodding assent, but declining to commit himself by words. He looked—as he had the reputation of being—a kindly-disposed man, but weak. He was, it appeared, quite overruled by his wife, who seemed to be quite a sufficiently strong-minded individual to make up for his weakness. She was his third wife, and when he married her she compelled him not only to enter the priesthood, but to put away all his concubines. He did not wear the yellow cloth long—only seven days—but that was considered long enough to cleanse him.

What to me was a much more serious matter was the fact that he was also under the thumb of the Chow Operat or second chief, who, having secured the allegiance of a much larger number of armed adherents than the titular first chief, was able to set his orders at defiance, and actually to countermand them. How far this was the case I had occasion to discover to my loss later on in my journey, as will be related in due course, but the following instance will serve to show how the first chief is at the mercy of the second, and will illustrate the anything but harmonious relations often existing between the two. Certain villages or communities in Chengmai are exempt from the performance of the ordinary work on behalf of the government of the chief, their service being limited to the care of the temples, which they have to keep clean and in repair, and to the building of new ones as required. Hence they are called *ka wat*, or slaves of the temple. While I was staying at Chengmai the Chow Hluang summoned a number of ka wats from Tjamtong, a small village near by, to assist in completing the large new temple which he was building in the capital. The people, however, did not feel inclined to do any work, so they went to the Chow Operat with a present, and requested to be relieved of the necessity of obeying the chief's orders. Without further ceremony the Chow Operat gave them the required dispensation, and ordered them to return to their homes in peace ! And the Chow Hluang was powerless to enforce obedience to his orders. As at Brentford in the play, so here in reality,

> " United yet divided, twain at once,
> So sit two kings of *Chengmai* on one throne."

But to return to my interview with this first chief, who was thus obliged to play second fiddle to his coadjutor. By-and-by the Phyas came in, and the letter was read again for their information, when it was agreed that facilities might, as an exceptional favour, be granted to me, and that natives should be instructed to help me in collecting birds and animals. My subsequent experience, however, proved that the Psalmist's advice about putting trust in princes applied with especial force to Lao Chows. The Chow Hluang might promise, but he could do no more, even if he would. I give him the credit of believing that he was really sincere in his promise to help me : but I did not then realize how far it remained with the Chow Operat to permit or prevent the fulfilment of those promises, though I knew that, however well-disposed the chiefs might be, there was the *vis inertiæ* of native apathy to overcome, and that it was well if that passive force did not develop into an active antagonism. But although I could pretty well foreshadow the part the people and subordinate officers were likely to play, and though I had my suspicions of the good faith of even the ruling chiefs, I was unsophisticated enough to think that

there was a fair prospect of my plans being at least
countenanced, if not actually furthered, by the chief
of Chengmai, if only I could get his written authority
to carry out my enterprise, and explicit orders to his
people to assist me in it, little dreaming that there was
the Nemesis of the Chow Operat to reckon with.

Although Chengmai is now the most powerful of all the
Lao states, and practically supreme over all its neighbours, its history has been somewhat checkered. When
it was founded, 600 years ago, Muang Fang was the
principal city. After being several times conquered
and sacked, first by Burmese, and then by Ngious, it
remained quite deserted for twenty years, till, seventy
years ago, several princes, all brothers, came over
from Lakon, founded the present dynasty, and raised
Chengmai to its present importance.

There are said to be upwards of eighty temples in
the city, but I think this is somewhat an exaggeration.
The Wat Hluang, or royal temple, was in course of
construction while I was there, on the site of the old
temple, the ruins of which were still to be seen. On
the ground there was collected a vast number of old
figures ready to be received under shelter as soon as
the new temple should be completed and dedicated,
which was expected to take place at the end of the
year 1883.

Close by is another old temple, the Wat Presing,
built, some seventy years ago, by the then Chow Radjawong.[2] Outside the steps of the main temple is a
tablet of stone, recording particulars of the amount of
gold, silver, *rack*, and other materials expended on
the building, but there is nothing striking about the
building except its gloom, light being admitted only
through the door. The priests were at prayer when I

[2] See Appendix on position of princes in Siam.

visited it, and after service I called upon the head priest, an old man, sixty-nine years of age, and said to be the most learned man in the country. The cloisters, like the temple, were both dirty and dark, but the grounds were kept and swept very clean, and planted with some beautiful lilies. A woman came in while I was there, and made some offerings of flowers to the priest, so I came away leaving her to pour out her grievances to him, and to seek consolation at his feet.

Just outside the city-walls is a third temple, the Wat Kaotu, now deserted, but once an important place, judging from a very fine phrachedee adjoining, under which a large quantity of silver was said to have been buried, but which was fast falling into decay. When perfect it must have been a magnificent tope, second only to the " glory of Lampoon."

Among the daily sights worth seeing in Chengmai is the market, which is held every morning from eight to eleven a.m. Along the main streets, on both sides, is one long file of women, who have come from the suburbs or neighbouring villages to sell their produce. As in the island of Bali, the women do all the selling.[3] They all sit on the ground, with a basket on each side of them, sometimes with the contents emptied out and spread on a couple of plantain-leaves. The principal articles offered for sale are provisions, fruits and vege-tables; tobacco, betel-nuts, and lime; fish, dried, salted, and stewed, but always all more or less stinking; buf-falo-meat, and pieces of buffalo-hide, also eaten and con-sidered good; roasted *mankap*, a large aquatic insect belonging to the order of *Hemiptera*, and probably the same as the Petchaburee delicacy, *mangda-na*, only under another name; mushrooms, of which the Laosians are

[3] The pork-stalls alone are kept by men, but they always seem to have more dogs round them than customers.

very fond; wax and cotton; earthenware pots, jars, and
jugs, so brittle that they almost break at a touch; and
always a good stock of flowers that would be the envy
of a Parisian. Behind this line of women are fixed
sheds or bazaars, where a few Chinese and a good
sprinkling of Burmese sit and sell cotton goods, calico
prints, *palais*, brass and wooden trays, and a varied
assortment of Burmese lacquer-ware.

Occasionly a caravan of Haw or Yunnan traders
brings a fresh supply of merchandize into the city,
principally wax; opium, a great quantity of which
they smuggle under their wide coats and trowsers;

Trading pack-saddle.

scissors and ironware
of various sorts, brass
bells, skin jackets,
silk cloth, numbers of
their characteristic huge
straw hats, and a small
quantity of adulterated
musk. The articles that
they buy up in exchange
most eagerly are young

deer-horns, for which they will give fabulous prices.
While I was there I saw forty-five rupees paid for
one catty (1¾ lb. Eng.) of them. The Chengmai
people were very careful to "ring" every rupee they
received from the Haws, for at Muang Prai, a village
to the north of Chengmai, spurious rupees are
manufactured wholesale.

The Yunnan traders generally halt outside the
city-walls, unloading their overworked mules and
ponies, and depositing the pack-saddles in a row along
the road, to be guarded by their savage dogs, while
the unfortunate beasts of burden are allowed to stray
in search of their supper. From the above illustration

it will be seen that the pack-saddle [4] is by no means calculated to be an easy burden to bear, and few of the horses and mules, which are generally little more than skin and bone, have even a sound skin left. One caravan had lost eleven horses on the road—killed by tigers, the men said, but I should doubt if any sensible tiger would choose such fleshless victims. If a " Cruelty to Animals " Act existed in Lao and Yunnan, these deaths would not have occurred.

Yunnan trader on his pony.

When a start is to be made in the morning, the animals answer readily to the curious " Hoi! hoi! hoi! " cry of the men, knowing that they will receive their scanty meal of rice before starting, muzzled, on their day's journey.

I bought one of the Haw dogs, " Tali " by name, as a protection against thieves, and he fully justified the confidence which the traders place in these animals

[4] The horn shown in the sketch is an indispensable adjunct to the trader's outfit, being used to carry the supply of lard for cooking and lighting purposes.

as good watch-dogs, with a ready bark rendering them faithful friends, and a tenacious bite that made them very undesirable foes. The Yunnan traders represented that it would not be difficult to get as far as Kiang Hung with elephants, but that beyond that point there was a broad table-land to be crossed, which they always made a point of reaching on the return journey, soon after the setting in of the rainy season, so as to make the most of the scanty vegetation which it afforded.

CHAPTER XIX.

Curious legal ceremony—An appeal to the " Water-God "—Betting
on the result—A test of endurance—The " verdict "—Justice
in Chengmai—A prince sentenced to death—His execution—
The native execution-block—Pardoning a criminal—Qualms of
conscience—Releasing the slaves—An invitation to dine with
the Chow Hluang—Native substitute for paper—An eye-
witness of the Delhi Durbar—Dinner and theatricals—A native
artist—How they paint in Lao—Wood-carvings—Presents to
royalty—Native partiality for strong drink—Tea-drinkers.

ON the morning of the 14th of January my friend Pra
Udon informed me that an appeal in a law-suit of some
importance was about to be tried between two Phyas,
who both claimed the ownership of a number of slaves.
The defendant in the case said he had lost the "title
deed" to the "property" in question, the document
having, according to his statement, been burnt during
an attack on his house by Ngiou raiders. The judges
before whom the case was first tried had been unable
to agree upon the evidence brought before them, and
"granted a case" for a superior court, in which the
Water-Spirit was the presiding genius! In other
words the disputants were ordered to settle their case
by what in former times in this country would have been
called the " ordeal of water;" that is to say, they were
to dive into the river, and whoever remained under
water the longest would be adjudged the winner of
the cause. This, I was told, was a very ancient custom
in Lao, but it was not often that this mode of settling

a dispute was resorted to, and great importance was consequently attached to it. The present trial derived additional significance from the position of the two litigants, and from the value of the stake at issue; for each party, before appealing to the Water-God, was obliged to deposit the sum of 2000 rupees, which would go, together with the slaves, to the winner; while the defeated suitor, besides losing the slaves and this considerable forfeit-money, would himself become a slave for life.

The people consequently turned out in force on the day appointed for the " hearing " to witness the trial, the scene of which was the Meping River. Early in the morning both banks of the stream were lined with thousands of spectators. Among the crowd were all the numerous Chows and officials of every grade, the more important of whom were easily distinguishable by their great state umbrellas—large canopies of red, yellow, or blue silk or cotton cloth, supported on bamboo handles encased in silver, and towering often as high as six or eight feet in the air. From the amount of wagering that went on on all sides, I am afraid that, had the scene been England instead of Lao, many of these gorgeous umbrellas would have been seized by the police as illegal " betting-places." Besides their umbrella-bearers, the most important personages were attended by numbers of slaves, bearing the usual array of gold or silver betel-boxes, teapots, spittoons, decanters, and other " insignia of office," some single pieces of which were worth perhaps 6000 or 7000 rupees.

There was no pushing or apparent excitement among the crowd, but every one seemed to take a deep interest in the proceedings, an interest which was increased by the frequent giving and taking of " the odds." I was invited to stake a few rupees on one or other of the litigants, but preferred to keep myself free from partisanship.

In the thick of the leading members of the company stood the two Phyas most directly interested in this novel trial; but, as time went on and they made no sign of divesting themselves of their robes and of preparing for the dive, I inquired whether they would— in sporting parlance—don "the buff" or dive in full dress. The reply was that the diving would be done by proxy, each Phya having provided himself with a "champion," who would do his best to prove his master in the right. At that moment there was a stir amid the umbrellas, and two natives came forward with an offering of flowers which they laid before the Chow and his council of Phyas, each making an oath at the same time that he firmly believed in the justice of the side which he represented. The two men then walked into the river, each with a rope round his waist, which was held by a third man, to prevent them from being carried away by the swift current. Each man bore some flowers on his head, and a string of leaves round his neck, as a sort of mute appeal for the favour of the Water-Spirit.

Amid a breathless silence the two swarthy figures stood awaiting the word to dive; then a splash, and they were lost to view. I carefully timed the duration of the dive, and sixty seconds, that seemed like an age, so still was the vast crowd, passed without a sign of either of them. One minute and a half! Two minutes! Surely the swift current of the river must have carried them beyond our sight, and, while we were watching the point at which they had entered the water, vainly expecting to see them emerge, they were being whirled away down stream! A few moments

later and a great shout greeted the reappearance of a
dark, round object above the water, and the trial was
over. It was the head of the losing diver, who had
remained under water exactly two minutes fifteen
seconds. The man who held the ropes then gave the
signal to the other competitor to come up : but he made
no sign, and the cry ran round that he was dead !
No, at last he emerges from the water, evidently exhausted, but with a "record" several seconds better
than his opponent. A general rush took place to see
if the "right man" had won—the right man being, of
course, he upon whose staying powers each individual
in the crowd had staked his money !

But as in horse-racing the first horse sometimes
turns out not to be the winner, the judge's verdict
being reversed on an objection lodged with the stewards,
or, to take a more appropriate parallel, just as the
verdict of the "twelve good men and true" is apt
sometimes in the home of trial by jury to be upset by
a "demurrer," an "application for a new trial," an
"appeal," or some other incident calculated to add to
the glorious uncertainty of the law—so here the jubi-
lations of those who had backed the possessor of the
strongest lungs, and of his fortunate employer, were
destined to be cut short. The umpires came to the
conclusion that one of the divers had entered the water
a moment before the other, and so the appeal was
fruitless, and the matter would have to be remitted to
the "court for the consideration of Crown cases
reserved"—otherwise to the chief himself as the
fountain of justice.

What sort of a fountain of justice the Chow Hluang
of Chengmai was, may be gathered from what happened
a few days afterwards. I have already said that Phya
Radjasena, the Siamese commissioner, has been re-

called from his post at Chengmai because of the complaints of the people about his mode of administering
the law. It is not for me to defend any more than it
is for me to blame Phya Radjasena, but the following
narrative will show either that the notions of the
people as to the due ordering of justice must be rather
confused, or that some one else besides Phya Radjasena is worthy of degradation on the same plea. But
tastes differ.

It appears that one evening, while the third Siamese
commissioner was riding through the city of Lampoon
after dusk, the elephant on which he was seated was
stabbed by some person and seriously injured. Now
it so happened that, just previously to this, a brother
of the chief of Lampoon, while gambling in a native
" hell " in that city, had had a quarrel with the followers
of this commissioner, who at once attributed the deed
to the prince in question. The Chow was generally
credited with being a scapegrace—though, if he was
worse than his brethren and fellow Chows, he must have
been bad indeed!—so he was denounced to the Phya
Radjasena and to the Chow of Chengmai, whose
anger was aroused by the fact that the injured elephant
belonged to himself: so the young prince was selected
to pay the extreme penalty of the law, first for offering
an indignity to the Siamese representative; second, for
injuring the Chow's elephant; third, for his general
bad character; and fourth, because a scapegoat was
wanted on whom injured justice could avenge itself for
the wrongs inflicted by others equally worthy of
punishment, but against whom no suitable pretext
could be found. The Chow of Lampoon made inquiry
into the matter before allowing his own brother to be
executed, and succeeded in establishing his innocence
of this particular crime; but the Chow of Chengmai

was inexorable, and the young prince was condemned to die, his brother making the stipulation that he should not be " disgraced " by having the condemned man's body brought back to Lampoon, but that he should be buried at the place of execution near the temple of Tawangtang, outside the city walls.

Early on the morning of the 17th of January, I heard that the execution was to take place that day, and at once started for the scene of the dreadful ceremony. The town was already half deserted, nearly every one having gone to witness the tragic spectacle, for, although executions are common enough in Chengmai, it is not every day that a prince is beheaded; so I hastened to walk across the rice-fields to the scene of execution. It was only an hour's walk, but before I had got half-way I met an unusually large train of elephants—some fifteen or twenty beasts, all fine tuskers—besides several hundred men on foot, and a few on horseback, who were returning from the scene, the execution having already taken place. I did not turn back, however, and on arriving at this Laosian Aceldama I found two natives just digging a shallow grave, by the side of which lay the headless trunk—most beautifully tattooed —of a fine-built youth, who but a few minutes before had been in the full enjoyment of health, and whose corpse a few minutes later would be rolled ignominiously into a shallow trench, surrounded by many similar graves of dishonour. On examining the body I found the executioner had missed his first stroke, and left a deep gash in the left shoulder. The head, which lay face downwards close by, was that of a really handsome youth of about two and twenty years of age. The face bore a calm expression, with no trace of the agony which the first blow of the executioner's axe must have occasioned.

The execution-ground was full of graves—not the long, narrow mounds to which the eye is accustomed in Europe, but—a series of shallow depressions, which in the rainy season would be filled with water, each marking the last resting-place of some "criminal," whose body, hastily covered beneath a few inches of earth, had returned to its original dust, leaving the soil to fall in as it crumbled away, or when, as perhaps was more likely, it was filched by vultures.

Scattered around in all directions were a number of logs of wood which, roughly shaped, as they were, somewhat in the shape of a cross, might at first sight almost have been mistaken for gravestones—many of them uprooted, but a few still standing—in a desecrated Christian churchyard. They were, however, rather in the shape of the letter Y than of a cross; and a pool of blood, in which stood one of these forked crosses, close by the dead Chow's body, plainly indicated that they were the execution-blocks upon which the doomed man lays his head to enable the executioner to do his bloody work.

The victim is made to walk to the field of execution with these worse-than-Caudine forks attached to his neck by ropes, led by the gaoler, who, when the fatal spot is reached, stretches him prone on the earth in such a manner that his head is lifted from the ground and firmly held between the projecting arms of the *crux*.

How many graves represented the spilling of innocent blood—blood, that is, innocent of the particular crime for which the Laosian goddess of justice had exacted retribution—it would be hard to say. Judging from this last addition to the roll of decapitated victims, I should say the percentage of really just sentences carried into execution would be very small indeed.

I might give other examples of the way in which the law is administered in Lao; but one more will suffice. We have just seen how a prince could be put to death at the wish of his chief, ostensibly for an offence which he had never committed; and the following instance will show how, on the other hand, a guilty man may be spared when the caprice of the Chow so ordains it. Only a short time before the events above narrated, a Lampoon man had entered a house in Chengmai in order to violate a young girl who he knew was alone. The girl's screams attracted the attention of a man, who, on coming to the rescue, was stabbed to death by the offender. Next day the murderer was caught and identified by the girl, and condemned to death, but, being in favour with the chief of Lampoon, he was not only pardoned, but set at liberty, the consent of the chief of Chengmai being purchased by the payment of a "fine" of six rupees.

Sometimes, however, it would seem that the conscience of the native administrators of the law is touched, and atonement is made, not only by offerings to Buddha, but in a more practical way.

A few days after the execution of the Lampoon prince, I was invited by the Chow Hluang to dine with him and the principal chiefs and officials of Chengmai. Among the first topics of conversation was the probable result of the appeal from the undecided trial by ordeal in the recent Water-Spirit case. The Chow was quick to tell me that neither of the Phyas interested in the slaves in dispute would be able to make good his title to them, since he had liberated them all. This, I thought, was a novel mode of cutting the Gordian knot, and I complimented the chief on his astuteness. But he added that he had liberated not only these particular slaves, but all the other slaves in

Chengmai, and had paid the value of them, amounting to several thousand rupees, to their owners—an act, I was assured, utterly unparalleled in the history of Chengmai. This I was quite prepared to believe: and the whole proceeding seemed so completely out of harmony with the ordinary course of Laosian traditions that I felt sure there must have been some unseen motive at work. Then I thought of the dead body of the Lampoon prince, and wondered whether all this generosity might not have been prompted by a desire to make amends in some way for a manifest miscarriage of justice. So I delicately broached the subject, to see if I could find any indication in his manner or his words of the chief's feelings on the point. He was evidently unwilling that the matter should be mentioned, and resolutely kept the manumission of the slaves in the forefront of the conversation.

Some days afterwards I was assured by one of the Phyas that the liberation of the slaves was really, as I had suspected, an act of contrition for what the chief felt to be a flagrant breach of Buddha's laws, and a desire to make atonement for the spilling of innocent blood.

But I am neglecting my dinner for the sake of the conversation. The banquet itself was not a very sumptuous affair, but was a notable event, if for no other reason, from the fact that the invitation which I received was a formal written document, instead of a personal request. Throughout Lao the material almost invariably used for written documents is a strip of palm-leaf (*Borassus flabelliformis*), called *Tala* in Sanskrit—which is to the Siamese what papyrus was to the ancient Egyptians—on which the words are scratched or engraved with a style. These leaves are

almost imperishable, being tough and entirely un-
affected by water, and in this respect are so much superior to paper that the natives often laughed at me
when they saw me making my notes on paper. When
the writing becomes indistinct, it is easily made legible
by wetting the finger and rubbing it over the leaf,
which has the effect of cleaning the smooth surface and
filling the scratches with a film of dirt. But in this
instance the chief's invitation was not engraved on
this native substitute for paper, but was written in ink
on a piece of veritable paper, a small scrap, it is true,
and not particularly clean, but still paper; what was
more, it was duly enclosed in a paper envelope, and
delivered at my house in formal European style, very
different from my experience of invitations to dinner
elsewhere in the country.

Pra Udon came to fetch me in his carriage about six
p.m., and took the opportunity of asking me to send
my three boys to wait at table, and, above all, to take
some bottles of wine, as the chief's cellar was very low.
The Chow, he added, had a great partiality for
effervescing drinks, so I complied with his request by
taking a dozen bottles of my *pseudo*-champagne, zoedone. The company consisted of the Radjaput, the
eldest son of the chief, and two other princes of the
first rank ; the Chow Operat of Chengmai, and the
Chow Operat of Kiang Hai ; the three Siamese officials ;
the two American missionaries, Messrs. Wilson and
Cheek; and last, but not least, a rich Burmese from
Moulmein, who had come over here hoping to win a
law-suit, having previously distributed presents to
the value of 12,000 rupees among the Chows and
princes, which they all gladly accepted, and then forgot
all about his case. He had now come to see the
cause of the "law's delay," and found that, at whatever

speed the rest of the world may travel, the Laosians
are never in a hurry.

This Burmese gentleman was one of the deputation
sent to the Durbar at Delhi, when the Queen was
proclaimed Empress of India, and had a good deal to
say about that imposing ceremony. The dining-room
was an open hall adjoining the Chow's theatre, so that
while dining one could also enjoy the sight of the
lakon, or theatrical performance. At the end of the
hall was a platform where the ladies of rank sat
on mats as spectators, surrounded by their silver
sirih-baskets, and big water-jugs with golden goblets,
and with their slaves behind. Then there was a
large mixed audience all round the hall, in the centre
of which two tables were laid. One was a small
round table, at the " head " of which the chief sat,
with the Siamese commissioner to his right, and the
Chow Operat and the Chow Buree, one of the principal
Chows in Chengmai, on his left ; the other was a long
narrow table adjoining the round one, as if forming a
part of it, but unmistakably distinct, in so far that it
was several inches lower. My seat was next to that of
the chief Siamese commissioner, with Dr. Cheek on
my right.

As he had deferred to European customs in the
form his invitation to dinner had taken, so the Chow
now did his best to conform to civilized habits by
using a knife and fork to eat with. But he was
manifestly uncomfortable, and the effort at last
became so irksome that he cast aside these unaccustomed implements, and fell back on his fingers
and thumbs. The dishes were mostly Chinese, and
call for no special comment. One item in the bill of
fare, however, reminded me of home, viz. potatoes—
which had been introduced along with other vegetables

into this country by the American missionaries, and which the Chow ate with great relish, helping himself to them *sans cérémonie*, in the good old-fashioned country-peasant style, and blowing his fingers to keep them cool.

The rattle of the dishes was drowned beneath the much louder clapping noise of the wooden sticks with which the musicians in the theatre emphasized the music in the lakon.

The acting or dancing was fair, but the dresses of the girls—all Laosians, trained by Siamese—were really very fine, superior to any I have ever seen in Bangkok. The music was, as usual, monotonous, but it appeared to exercise its usual " charm " in " soothing the savage breast," for the old Chow Hluang was particularly gay, and even the Chow Operat forgot his jealousies for the time, and gave a languid assent to the Chow Hluang's profuse promises of help in the collection of animals, birds, and plants. The Chow Hluang even offered to give me a model of a Lao boat, but with all these promises I had to take a good deal of salt, and the salt was all that remained, save in one instance. Our talk presently ran upon art, of which the Chow Hluang professed himself a great lover. He had, he said, one of the best artists in all Lao in his special employment; would I like some specimens of his art? I not only replied affirmatively to this question, but added that I would willingly pay for some, and to this fact I am ungracious enough to attribute the appearance, on the following morning, at the door of my house of Noi Meta, the artist in question, armed with the paraphernalia of his art.

Noi Meta was a Ngiou who had been employed by the chief of Chengmai for the last twenty years as his " artist in ordinary," and was not permitted to work

A THEWEDA OR ANGEL

(facsimile of a native drawing)

for any one else except " by command." His materials
were all home-made; the brushes, of civet-cat hair,
or bristles, were particularly bad, being thin, and very
long. His paper, again, was of very poor quality.
My sketching-blocks he was particularly pleased with,
remarking very quickly that the paper was better than
any he had ever used, or even seen. His colours
were of native make. One he called " Krang "
was a rich carmine. A bright yellow was obtained
from some bulbous roots, while red and yellow ochre,
and indigo, were to be had nearly everywhere. Only
one colour, as far as I could make out, was of foreign
origin, and that was a cinnabar red, which I believe
came from Germany.

In the annexed plate will be found an exact representation of one specimen of Noi Meta's art—representing a Theweda, or angel—which is not without merit,
particularly in the blending of the colours. The delicate
finish and enamel-like surface of the original painting
are very remarkable, particularly when the wretched
quality of the brushes is taken into account. He also
drew me a representation of the Hoalaman and of the
Rachasee, both equally well finished, of which woodcuts
are given on pp. 69 and 165.

I asked Noi Meta why the native artists always
made caricatures instead of exact representations
of their subjects, and particularly of the elephant, of
which they had plenty of examples to copy from. He
replied that they were not allowed to make a true
picture of the elephant: that was left to the *farang*
to do.

While on the subject of the fine arts I may as well
here mention that I came across several really good
artists—using the word in its mechanical sense—among
the Laosians, particularly among the priests, who

amuse their leisure hours by painting frescoes, or by the elaborate gilding of most intricate designs on the walls of the temples, or on the altars, door-panels, "pulpits," and the chests containing the sacred books or MSS. The drawings are always devoid of perspective, and for this reason the fantastic geometrical and arabesque designs, and quasi-heraldic drawings of mythological beasts, which are often as skilfully executed as they are weirdly imagined, are, to European eyes, always the most pleasing—the method of treatment being usually grotesque, and partaking rather of the nature of caricature. Where colours are used, however, they are always harmoniously blended, and the effect is pleasing.

Wood-carving, again, is a favourite occupation, in which some technical artistic skill is displayed, and the native chiefs and some of the princes constantly employ a number of men to make ornaments, though I fear the remuneration is not always adequate to the skill and time occupied. Carved scroll-work for doors, posts, household articles, &c., &c., is in much request. The wood-carvers have a quaint taste for inlaying their work with odd bits of coloured glass, tinsel, or other bright material: such work will not bear close inspection, but it has a remarkably striking effect when the sun shines on these glittering objects.

Soon after Noi Meta's departure, his master drove up in Pra Udon's open carriage and pair, followed by a dozen—only a dozen, as the visit was a private one—attendants, carrying as emblems of his dignity a solid gold and blue-enamelled betel-box, with teapot, goblet, and spittoon to match, all of which he informed me were presents from his Majesty the King of Siam.

The chief had been very kind in sending me

occasional presents, such as a pig—of which he had enough and to spare from the "pig-farming" monopoly held by a Chinaman—or a bucketful of rice,[1] or a fowl or two, and I tried to think of some article that I could give him in exchange; but these splendid tokens of wealth and power made me fear lest I might insult him in offering him anything out of my slender stock of goods. He soon relieved me from my difficulty, however, by admiring a coil of Manilla rope, and saying he should like to have some. So I gave him half the piece, which he carefully measured after me, to see that I had fairly divided it! I then offered him a glass of brandy, as a sort of compensation for the innocent deception I had practised upon him on the occasion of his dinner, by passing off zoedone as champagne. He took two or three glasses of it neat, with all the ease of a confirmed dram-drinker. I finally comforted him by giving him a bottle to take away with him, and he left me with renewed protestations of his eternal friendship.

There is no Blue Ribbon Army among the Laosians. The first thing a prince will ask for is brandy or beer, for both of which they have a decided preference over *samshu*, the native drink of the country, which is made of fermented rice, and, somewhat resembles the bhang of Hindostan. To my taste it is a most nauseous liquor, but the natives are as fond of it as any Irishman is of his "potheen," and many are the illicit stills at work in secluded spots, though the manufacture of samshu by unlicensed persons involves a heavy fine. The usual run of the liquor is as weak as it is nauseous, and the average Laosian can put

---

[1] Rice was very cheap in Chengmai while I was there. Five buckets (equal to one picul) could be bought for one rupee. From four to six fowls, again, could be had for one rupee.

away a considerable quantity of it, as is evidenced by the fact that I have often met men and women returning from market, or from a visit in the evening, whose unsteady gait proclaimed that they loved, ' not wisely, but too well," the attractions of the native grog-shop.

The princes, who, I have said, are particularly partial to brandy and beer, have also a liking for tea, in which they indulge after dinner. They never think of gratifying their taste by purchasing this beverage, but depend for their supplies of it upon the goodwill of the Chinese traders, just as they look to the Burmese timber-merchants as an unfailing resource for replenishing their stock of cheroots.

CHAPTER XX.

Preparing to leave Chengmai—I receive my passports—Sealing a native document—An important omission—Insulting the foreigner—Good-bye—The road to Muang Pau—A narrow escape from drowning—Betel-chewers—Women smokers—My quarters at Muang Pau—Laosian furniture—A comfortable cradle—Lao customs in relation to childbirth—Propitiating the spirits—A fiery ordeal—Naming the child—Death-ceremonies—Cremation not universal—Fighting mourners—*En route* to heaven.

IT was not till the 21st of January that Yang and Cook arrived with the rest of my luggage, which they were bringing up by water from Raheng, having been thirty-four days on the way. Yang said the delay was caused principally by the captain of the boat and Cook having been continually drunk. I had been most anxiously awaiting their arrival, and now began to chafe still more under the various little occasions for delay that were seized upon by the Chow Hluang before he made up his mind to give me the promised written authority to travel through the northern Lao States, and to shoot birds on the way. One fine morning I found that he had quietly gone off to look after his rice-fields. These visits to the rice-fields seem to afford the chiefs a very convenient pretext for evading their engagements, especially towards foreigners. However, this gave me an admirable opportunity of appealing to the Chow Operat, to whom—although, as already stated, he was really *the* chief of Chengmai, his name being respected and dreaded throughout all the neigh-

bouring states—it would not have been etiquette for
me to have applied while his superior was " on duty :"
and I accordingly, after a day or two's delay to save
appearances, went to him and asked him to supply me
with the needful authority. Still the watchword was
procrastination ; and it was only on the morning of the
2nd of February that I received from the Chow Operat's
secretary two official " passports "—curious documents
consisting of long, narrow strips of palm-leaf, about an
inch and a half wide, and coiled up into a ring, fastened
with threads of fibre.   At the end of each strip was an
embossed stamp—the official seal at which every native
official looks before he begins to read one of these
documents, graduating his obedience according to the
rank of the person represented by the seal.   If it is a
great Chow's seal, the letter will be read with attention
and its injunctions obeyed with a certain amount of
strictness.   If it is an inferior Chow's seal, the orders
may take their chance of being obeyed or disregarded
at the whim of the reader.   If it is a mere secretary's
seal, the writer runs great risk of being insulted
behind his back by having his letter spat upon.   The
leaves, I may explain, are stamped or sealed by being
placed on a piece of hard wood, when the actual seal
—in steel or iron—is placed upon it, and struck a sharp
blow with a mallet, when the impression stands out in
slight relief.

The Chow's secretary assured me, as he handed me
the " papers," that they contained strongly-worded
orders to the chiefs of the other Lao States to afford
me every facility in my journey through their territories.   But as they were written in the Lao character
and dialect, and were utterly beyond my comprehension,
I took them to Dr. Cheek, and asked him to show me
the interpretation thereof.   He, with his usual courtesy

and kindness, read them through in English, when I found that, although they contained most explicit and peremptory directions to the chiefs on every other point, one of the principal objects was left out, viz. that I should be supplied with hunters and be allowed to shoot all kinds of animals. Dr. Cheek then offered to accompany me to the residence of the Chow Operat, to try and get this omission rectified. The chief listened to what Dr. Cheek had to say on my behalf, but repeated that the shooting of birds was forbidden by a general law throughout his country. I urged that I would gladly pay for the hunters' services, and for any birds they might bring to me, and at last, with Dr. Cheek's powerful advocacy, the " almighty dollar " prevailed over the chief's scruples, and the secretary was ordered to add to the letter a direction that I was to be supplied with five hunters, and with hunting elephants, and to be allowed to make war on the furred and feathered tribes, on condition that I paid for whatever I caught or killed.

This point being so far satisfactorily settled, I had another delicate subject to broach. The natives who had been been instructed to furnish me with elephants for my journey had provided six of these animals, all of which, however, with the exception of one, were females ; and this one was too young to be of much use as a beast of burden, and was quite useless for hunting purposes. Now to offer any one, especially a stranger, a female elephant to ride, is regarded among both Siamese and Laosians as a great insult, and I felt that the object was to expose me to ridicule and contempt, should I unsuspectingly employ these animals, and, above all, ride one of them. Dr. Cheek had informed me that the Laosians delighted thus to insult foreigners, and that even the Siamese representative had once been subjected to the indignity of being offered a she-elephant to ride when visiting Chengmai. So I mentioned the fact to the chief, and reminding him that I had come with the authority of the king of Siam, inquired whether it was done by his direction or with his knowledge. He coolly replied that he knew nothing of it, that the elephants had been drafted in the villages, and that possibly no others were available. Dr. Cheek smiled, and whispered to me something about the " ready tongue " of the Laosians, but finding that no offer of reparation was made, and fearing further detention, I preferred not to insist on the point, and left the Chow Operat with an expression of thanks for his services, determining to make the best of a bad bargain. My subsequent experience, however, showed that I was unwise in coming to this conclusion.

The natives, in many out of the way places especially, offered me insults, and placed impediments in my way, which they would never have dared to do if I had ridden a "tusker." A she-elephant, indeed, holds much the same place in the estimation of the Siamese and Laosians as a donkey does in England, and a gentleman riding down Rotten Row mounted on the humble ass would hardly be exposed to greater ridicule, certainly not to so much unsuspected " obstruction," as a foreigner in Lao riding a female elephant.

After leaving the chief, we called upon the Chow Operat of Kiang Hai, who was still staying in Chengmai, to bid him good-bye. He was good enough to give me a letter of introduction to the Chow Hluang of his state, and another to his son-in-law ; and after lunching with my kind friend Dr. Cheek, I made final preparations for my departure.

The loading of the elephants, and the duty of seeing the baggage divided equally among the twenty coolies allotted to me, was no easy task. There were the invariable complaints on the part of each man that he had more to carry than any of his comrades—complaints familiar to every one who has travelled in the East ; but at last everything was settled, and at four o'clock I started, crossing the river and taking a N.N.E. direction with the ultimate intention of passing through Lao, then into the Ngiou States, and eventually reaching Yunnan.

Not the least important member of the caravan was my dog "Tali." He was my constant companion throughout my journey, proving himself a good and faithful watch-dog, and rendering signal service on more than one occasion.

For the first two days we passed over ground divided into small sections devoted alternately to rice-growing and cattle-grazing. Villages were plentiful, and on the evening of the second day we stopped at one of considerable size, called Ban Hun Hluang, where we took fresh supplies of rice and curry. Arrived here, however, my men pretended not to know the way any further, so I prevailed upon the head man of the village to grant me half a dozen men as guides, and under their direction started next day, about nine a.m., for Muang Pau, or, as it is sometimes called, Muang Prau. Our course was direct north for three hours, when we turned due west, arriving at Muang Kenn about two o'clock in the afternoon. Here we halted for the rest of the day, the road beyond being represented as rough, and without any shelter for at least a day's journey, and my followers showing great objection to camping out so long as they could get a roof to sleep under.

Next morning an early start, in a westerly direction again, brought us into very wild mountain-scenery, the hill-sides being clothed to the top with trees, the shade of which was grateful to both man and beast. The road was very difficult and steep, and before noon we had ascended over 1000 feet above the sea-level, along a pass through which flows, in a south-westerly direction, the River Mengap, till it unites its waters with those of the Meping. We crossed and recrossed this stream several times, the elephants quietly wading through. At one point, where a sudden bend of the river caused a rapid eddy, the " baby " elephant which formed part of our caravan was washed away, and only saved himself by cleverly catching the overhanging branch of a tree with his trunk.

At another place, in crossing a ravine, the slope was so steep that every man dismounted, while the elephants, lying with their bellies on the ground, with hind legs thrown back, and fore feet spread out in front, slid in their peculiar characteristic manner down hill, with their backs at an angle of something like forty-five degrees. For nearly twelve hours we saw no sign of human habitation, till, about six p.m., we crossed some rice-fields, and fifteen minutes later entered a small village called Me Pang. Here we rested for the night, reaching Muang Pau, after a six-hours ride to the N.N.E., on the 6th of February.

Muang Pau is a small and poor-looking settlement, with an adult male population of about 700, situated on a vast plateau, about 1050 feet above sea-level, and entirely hemmed in by mountains.

I made at once for the chief's house, to show him my " passport," which Kao read aloud to him in the presence of his wife and a few slaves, who sat around, all chewing betel.

Like the Siamese, the Laosians are perpetually chewing. Whether they are busy or idle, they chew : whether they sit or walk, they chew. Teeth or no teeth, every Laosian, from almost infancy to old age, chews betel. The toothless old folks assist nature by placing the betel-nut with the accompanying ingredients into a small mortar—a sort of hybrid between a child's pop-gun and a syringe, which they always carry with them; a few strokes of the rod suffice to crush the nuts and reduce them to a pulpy mass warranted not to hurt the softest gums.

This perpetual cramming of the mouth with betel is not conducive to ease in conversation, and the Laosians seem to seize on every occasion for conversation as an opportunity for replenishing the mouth. The habit is very unpleasant, owing to the blackness which it imparts to the teeth as much as to the incessant spitting it gives rise to, and to the necessity for ever and anon removing the remains of the " quid " from the mouth. It is said to assist digestion : but it seems to me to corrode and rot the teeth.

Tobacco is smoked, not only by men, but by women and children. How the men find time to smoke between the intervals of betel-chewing, and how they find time to chew between the intervals of smoking, it is hard to say. The women especially are hardly ever seen with-out a *buree*, or native cigarette, in the mouth. The finest *burees* are made of tobacco rolled up and encased in the thin white *liber*, or inner coating of the bark of the betel-tree, but those usually offered for sale in the markets are rolled in plantain or maize-leaves. The native tobacco is inferior to that grown in Siam. A few women smoke pipes, but these are not so popular among either men or women as cigarettes. The pipes are made of wood, with a bent bamboo stem.

On the conclusion of the reading of my letter, the chief remarked that it was " very strong," and that he had a very great respect for the Chow Operat of Cheng-mai, who would order a head to be cut off for a very trifling offence. His wife, I observed, without waiting for any instructions, quietly spoke to two of the servants, who at once set to work to prepare a bed for me in a corner of the room. This was neither a long nor a costly operation; a couple of mats, with pillows, were laid on the floor, and a cotton curtain hung

Lao girl smoking.

round as a screen, and I was, without ceremony, informed that my sleeping-quarters were already at my service.

It will be seen that the furniture of the house was not of a very elaborate description; indeed, an ordinary Lao householder thinks his dwelling well-appointed if he has a few plaited rattan or bamboo mats and cushions ready to spread upon the floor, for, when not actually in use, they are kept piled up in a heap in some con-

venient corner. The best mats are edged with a red
border, and the cushions, which are either oblong or
three-sided, have their ends embroidered in silk or
gold. When a visitor enters, a mat is spread on the
floor, with a cushion either behind to lean against, or
at the side as a support to the arm—the quality of the
cushions and mats selected depending entirely upon
the rank of the visitor. The Chows have, as a rule, a
table and a few chairs, but seldom use the latter except
when visited by "distinguished strangers," when they
look very uncomfortable as they sit cross-legged on the
seat. Of bedsteads there are none, the people sleeping on home-made mattresses stuffed with cotton
wool, and surrounded by a mosquito-curtain

Of utensils there are only a few of the native earthenware pots and pans, and occasionally one or two
immense iron pans, imported from Yunnan, almost as
fragile as the native pottery, with a few wooden or
cocoanut-shell spoons. Lamps to burn petroleum, and
even clocks and looking-glasses, are always to be found
in a princely house, but no such signs of civilization
are to be met with in an ordinary dwelling, where
damar (resin) torches and a vessel of pork-fat or oil,
with a cotton wick, are the only artificial illuminants.
A few guns and swords may occasionally be seen placed
on a rack in the room, and sometimes the sporting
instincts of the owner are evidenced by a pair of stag-
horns hung against the wall.

As children are rarely wanting in any house, a
primitive cradle is sure to be seen in a corner of the
sleeping apartment, consisting of an oval or oblong
basket with shallow sides, and with a small mattress,
or a roll or two of cloth, at the bottom. It is suspended
by long cords from a beam in the roof, and the mother
or one of the "rising generation" may be seen swing-

s

ing, rather than rocking, the infant to sleep. This cradle, though serviceable, is not nearly so neat and practical as that used by the Siamese, which has been adopted by many European ladies even out of Siam, and which consists of what looks like a simple oblong basket with flat sides, suspended from the ceiling by a cord at each corner.

In the bottom of this basket a mattress is placed, and the child can lie down or stand up at will, without any danger of falling out. Instead of being " rocked," it forms a " swing." The four sides are so fitted that when out of use they fall down flat on the bottom of the cradle, which can then be stowed away in any corner, without taking up any room.

The mention of children reminds me of some curious customs prevalent among the Laosians in regard to childbirth. The natives believe that an infant is the child, not of its parents, but of the spirits, and in this belief they go through the following formalities.

As soon as an infant is born it is bathed and dressed, laid upon a rice-sieve, and placed—by the grandmother if present, if not, by the next near female relative—at the head of the stairs or of the ladder leading to the house. The person performing this duty calls out in a loud tone to the spirits to come and take the child away to-day, or for ever after to let it alone; at the same moment she stamps violently on the floor to frighten the child, or give it a jerk, and make it cry. If it does not cry this is regarded as an evil omen. If, on the other hand, it follows the ordinary laws of nature and begins to exercise its vocal organs, it is supposed to have a happy and prosperous life before it. Sometimes the spirits do come and take the infant away, *i.e.* it dies before it is twenty-four hours old, but, to prevent such a calamity, strings are tied round its wrists on the first night after its birth, and if it sickens or is feeble the spirit-doctors [1] are called in to prescribe certain offerings to be made to keep away the very spirits who, only a few hours previously, were ceremoniously called upon to come and carry the child off. On the day after its birth the child is regarded as being the property no longer of the spirits, who could have taken it if they had wanted it, but of the parents, who forthwith sell it to some relation for a nominal sum—an eighth or a quarter of a rupee perhaps. This again is a further guarantee against molestation by the spirits, who apparently are regarded as honest folk that would not stoop to take what has been bought and paid for.

While such precautions are taken for the welfare of the child, the mother is subjected to a very different mode of treatment. As soon as the woman is safely delivered of the child, a couple of old women cut some stems from the banana-tree into lengths of from three to four feet, split them, and lay them round the woman as she lies upon the bed. These are covered with twigs of the same tree, and the whole is then set on fire, so that the poor woman is literally half-baked.

This cruel ceremony, the object of which is to hasten her recovery, is, I am informed, repeated for several days. The statement will hardly be credited, but I am in a position to vouch for its correctness, for I was an eye-witness on one occasion of the whole scene, when a woman was confined in the house in which I happened to be staying at Krong Krung, and I took a mean advantage of the cracks in the wall to spy out the proceedings ; for I could hardly believe that such inhuman rites could be tolerated. In this case the child was

[1] See p. 338.

still-born, and, according to rule, it was placed in a jar and thrown into the river.

A curious custom is always to bury the *placenta* under the door-step, or rather at the foot of the ladder leading up to the door.

The lying-in period lasts a month, and then comes the ceremony of naming the child. Here again the spirits have to be appeased, and for this purpose the most unattractive name that can be thought of is given to the infant, in order that the spirits shall not take a fancy to the child on account of its pretty name! Such names as *Kee mu* (pig-dung) and *Kee han* (goose-dung) are not at all uncommon. I once met a prince who bore the latter appellation without any sense of shame or discomfort, and with no notion of giving notice in the *Times* of his intention to change his name. Later on, when the child enters upon manhood or womanhood, the first names are discarded for others somewhat less repulsive; but even then the improvement is often only slight, for toad, rat, rabbit, &c., are common names in the country.

Infants are generally suckled for three years, though at three or four months their rations are increased by an occasional mess of soft-boiled rice and bananas.

Many of the foregoing customs obtaining among the Laosians are practised also by the Siamese. In the case of a first-born child the " baking process " is continued for at least a month, but afterwards the period is reduced to twenty days. The patient at the same time washes herself every day for a week with salt and water, being kept all the time on a low diet of boiled rice and plantains. The child is fed on honey, and is not allowed to take the breast for three days, but, among all but the very rich, it is compensated for this deprivation by being suckled till it is two or three years old. Indeed it is not an uncommon thing to see a child, after taking the breast, having a small cigarette handed to it to smoke.

Children go naked up to six or seven years of age, and, in the country districts, and in Lao, even longer. Those of the better classes in Siam wear a small silver leaf or heart-shaped plate hung by a string round the waist.

Before concluding this chapter I may as well, having described the ceremonies attending the entry of the new-born Laosian into the world, give an outline of the rites connected with " the last scene of all in the strange eventful history " of a Laosian, so far as they differ from those practised by the Siamese.

When a person dies, the eyes and mouth are closed by some one, who gently invites the spirit to quit its abode, leaving behind every anxiety, every care about friends and worldly affairs. A small piece of money, or a precious stone, is sometimes slipped into the mouth of the corpse, to pay the spirit-fine in the next world, the natives believing that the future state cannot be entered without payment.

Afterwards the body is cremated, with ceremonies similar to those in vogue among the Siamese. People, however, who die under the age of fifteen are believed to have been taken by their former parents who are now in the spirit-world, and are buried instead of being cremated, the bodies being simply wrapped up in mats, and interred without the privilege of a coffin. If the young person or child dies with its jacket on, the garment is slit at the sides, and the front turned to the back, a way of saying to the spirit of the dead child, " Don't come back again."

Persons dying suddenly, or from the effects of an accident or of a malignant disease, or women dying in childbirth, are also not considered worthy of cremation. The fact of an accident having happened to cause death is a sure sign that a certain kind of evil spirit has come to take the spirit of the person away to be its fellow in the spirit-world. The bodies of women dying in childbirth, or within a month afterwards, are not even taken out of the house in the ordinary way by the door, but are let down through the floor.

When a Lao chief dies, men are hired to engage in pugilistic encounters, being paid, victors and vanquished alike, from four to twenty rupees apiece for the honour and privilege of getting a black eye or losing their front teeth *in memoriam.*

Men, when buried or cremated, are laid with their faces downwards, and women on their backs. This distinction is explained by the native belief that women have never seen heaven, but came orginally from the infernal regions. Thus, when they die, they look up for the first time; while the men, who came from above, and who are anxious to have the women with them in the happy spirit-world, are able to look downwards without fear, and to seek for their ascending female relatives and friends.

CHAPTER XXI.

A chatty Chow—Bravery of the Muang Pau people—No elephants !
—My Lord Tiger, the tiger-hunter—Rack-gathering—A menda-
cious Chow—Cheap poultry—Talios or charms—A tiger shot—
Sharing the booty—The road to Muang Fang—A prince's
hunting expedition—Native hunters—Decoying the wild fowl—
A modern settlement on an ancient site—Hiring a house—An
Augean stable—Seeing spirits through the telescope—Clearing
the forest—Threatened with famine.

THE Chow was in a communicative mood, and entertained me with an account of his people and State.
Four years ago, he said, a force of 600 Ngious invaded
his province, not in a mere predatory raid, but with
the object of conquering the country. The Muang
Pau people, however, defeated the enemy in a fight
which lasted the whole day, capturing the Ngiou chief's
golden umbrella, which the Chow sent to the king of
Chengmai, and killing sixty of the Ngious, while they
themselves did not lose a single man !

Other information, probably equally authentic, he
gave me about his people; but when I came to ask to
be supplied with a fresh lot of elephants, he changed
his tone, assuring me that elephants were scarce. On
my pressing the point, and insisting that I must have
eight elephants in the next three days, three of
which must be tuskers, he coolly said that there were
no male elephants in the district, as a Chengmai
prince, who had gone to Muang Fang a few days
previously, had taken all there were, viz. four.

"Surely," I said, "so powerful a prince and so rich and brave a people must have more than four elephants in their country. The Chow will not like the *farang* to go to the enemy's country and say that the people of Muang Pau are slaves, that even the Chow rides on female elephants, while a prince from Chengmai comes and carries off all his tuskers."

Thus challenged, he lost his self-control for a moment, and apologized by saying he was only trying how far I was prepared to insist on my demands, that not even a prince of Chengmai should have his elephants simply for the asking, and that, out of respect for, but not obedience to, the Chow Operat of Chengmai, he would let me have two tuskers.

"See," he said, "how already I have done my best to pay honour to you. Yesterday Mau Sua the hunter left Muang Pau on a tusker, to shoot animals for you at Muang Fang."

Mau Sua was a celebrated hunter whom the chief of Chengmai had ordered to place himself at my disposal. He lived in a hut on a piece of land granted to him by the chief of Chengmai, with whom he was a special favourite, and who had at the same time conferred upon him the title of " Mau Sua," or " Lord Tiger," in recognition of his services as a tiger-hunter. From all accounts he was a very human tiger in his love for, and success in, hunting all the larger game.

But I could plainly see that there was very little sincerity in these forced protestations of goodwill, and other incidents occurred to confirm the statement of Dr. Cheek that the only way to secure the performance of any promise, or even to obtain a direct answer to a simple question, was by a judicious mixture of diplomacy, cross-examination, and bribery.

Having heard that the country round Muang Pau

was celebrated for its supplies of the valuable black lacquer called *rack*, I asked the chief for a sample. He denied all knowledge of its existence. " But," he added, " I will inquire for my friend among my people." When I replied that I did not wish to receive any rack as a present, but that I would buy some, he at once went to the adjoining room, and fetched two long bamboos filled with the lacquer, one of which I bought for a rupee.

The rack is collected by the natives by making a hole in the trunk of a particular species of tree and inserting in it a bamboo, into which the substance slowly runs. It takes about a week for a large tree to fill a piece of bamboo two feet long and four inches in diameter, from a single " tapping."

The collection of this resin is a monopoly in the Lao country ; very little is exported, the bulk of the produce being used in preparing the temples and religious images for receiving their coat of paint or gold leaf. It dries to a perfectly smooth, hard surface. The people keep the priests supplied with it by their offerings.

On the second day, when making preparations to start on the morrow, I asked the Chow to let me have covered howdahs for the elephants, but he said he had none. " Then I shall keep those I brought with me from Chengmai," I replied, whereupon the wily old diplomatist looked grave, said something about getting into trouble with the Chow Operat, went out into the yard, and returned in a few minutes, followed by a number of men with the requisite number of howdahs.

My last negotiation with this excellent ruler was of a somewhat more pleasant nature. I wanted a supply of fowls to take to Muang Fang, where nothing of the kind was to be had, and asked the Chow to let

me have a score or so each of fowls and ducks.
Poultry is wonderfully plentiful and cheap here—
about fourpence a bird—so, although it would have
been customary, and in accordance with the instructions in my letters of introduction, for the Chow to
have supplied me with provisions without charge, I
greased the old man's itching palm with the magnificent sum of seven rupees. The alacrity with which he
supplied me, in return, with twenty fowls and twenty-
two ducks, was quite a treat to see. But even now
the obstructive tactics were not finally abandoned, and
I found only six out of the eight elephants had been

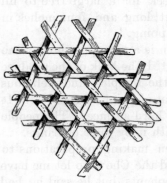

got ready for me. While
waiting for the tale to be
completed, news arrived
that a tiger had been shot
during the night in a small
village close by, whither
the Chow sent a dozen
men to fetch it to Muang
Pau. All the village
turned out to give the
dead beast a welcome, as
it was carried in triumph
on a stretcher. It was

Talio, or charm.

a full-grown male, measuring five feet six inches from
the head to the root of the tail, and two feet nine
inches from root to tip of tail. On its head was
hung one of the peculiar native *talios*, or charms to
keep away the evil spirits which the people believe to
exist everywhere, and of which the tiger is supposed
to be a particularly malignant representative. These
talios are made of rattan or bamboo, plaited together
like an open piece of lattice-work, and may be seen
hung in front of a house, or suspended from sticks

in the rice-fields, or by the roadside; in fact, turn where you will, you see one of these wonderful charms.

The Chow would not allow the beast to be brought inside the walls—I suppose because he had more fear of the spirits than faith in the talio—so it was deposited in a field just outside the town. It is the custom when a tiger is killed to take the skin to the chief at Chengmai, who gives the fortunate hunter a gratuity of eighteen rupees, or rather he allows him to collect this amount in small sums from the people, who dare not refuse to contribute a few "cents," till the full amount is made up.

The skin was, therefore, first carefully removed, and then there were applicants enough for almost every particle of the body. Some wanted the flesh, which was roasted and eaten at a feast the same evening; the Laos love to partake of this dish, from the notion that it will make them strong. Others asked for the bones to sell to the Chinese, to be powdered and made into a medicine. The intestines were also in request for a similar purpose. The gall-bladder, which is also used to make a highly-prized and expensive Chinese drug, was hurriedly snatched by my Chinese cook. For the claws and skull I put in a modest claim myself, at the same time giving the hunter a few rupees for them. Lastly the bullets were carefully extracted and treasured by the hunter as souvenirs of his feat.

This tiger episode relieved the monotony of another day of waiting, and at last, on the following morning, I left Muang Pau with more than the stipulated number of elephants. To the eight for which I had bargained —three of which were tuskers—a ninth was added, to carry an additional quantity of rice, and two baby-elephants helped to swell the cavalcade.

Our direction was N.N.W. all day. The road was
very steep and difficult—through a mountain-pass at
a maximum altitude of 1900 feet, with numerous
ravines to cross, along the edge of high precipices,
or following a narrow track hardly discernible amid
the tangled forest-undergrowth. About midday we
crossed the Mengap River again, and towards evening
arrived at a deserted camp, where the coolies quickly
made three fresh huts. The night was cold, the thermometer registering 45° Fahr., and we were not sorry
to have the warmth of the fires, which were lighted as
a matter of course as a protection against beasts of
prey.

Next day we started at 8.10 a.m., still taking a
N.N.W. or northerly direction. I walked all day,
following the unmistakable, deep, round footprints of
the elephants, and wading through small streams, with
which the mountain-slopes were intersected. At four
p.m. we crossed the Me Fang River—here only twenty
feet wide—and presently came to a large caravan of
Ngiou traders, just preparing to encamp for the night.
A long array of pack-saddles, laden principally with
chillies and cotton, were standing in a line on the
ground, while the jingling sound of bells in the forest
told that the cattle were grazing close at hand.

We pitched our camp close by, parting company at
eight the next morning. The road, still about 1700
feet above sea-level, got better, and it was very pleasant walking under the shade of the forest. We met
several more parties of Ngiou traders, driving along, in
single file, hundreds of oxen laden with the inevitable
chillies, capsicums, and cotton, on the road to Chengmai.

At noon we reached a small sandy plateau, with a
patch of fine, tall pine-trees. This was on the verge of

the forest, on emerging from which we entered an immense plain covered with high grass, and dotted here and there with an occasional clump of trees. While crossing this plain, we met a Chengmai prince returning home from a hunting expedition in Muang Fang, with a train of a dozen magnificent tuskers, all experienced hunting-elephants, laden with the spoil of his trip, among the trophies being one old elephant, a buffalo, and a few deer. Not only the skins, hoofs, and horns of the buffalo, and the tusks, teeth, and hoofs of the elephant, but even the bones were being carried away, to be sold eventually to Chinese traders, these articles forming a considerable item in the trade of the Lao States.

Two or three times a year, grand hunting expeditions are organized by the principal Chows, who reserve to themselves the sole right to hunt the elephant and rhinoceros. When one of these expeditions leaves or returns to a town, the scene is one of great animation and some splendour, as a dozen or more splendid tuskers, destined to decoy or do battle with their wild brethren, and bring them into captivity, head the procession. Except when pressed into the service of the chiefs to do duty in an elephant-hunt, the bulk of the people do not indulge much in the pleasures and perils of the chase. Not being dependent upon their skill as hunters for any of the ordinary supplies of food, they take to hunting only as a pastime. There are a few noted hunters who make a profession of hunting tigers; but, with these exceptions, the people confine their attentions to the smaller game, occasionally aspiring so high as to hunt—if their mode of circumventing these animals can be dignified with the name of hunting—the deer. Their general practice is to lie in ambush near a favourite feeding-ground, or

watering-place frequented by these animals, and
attract them within range by imitating their cry.

But their principal attentions are reserved for the
native wild fowl, which are so abundant throughout the
country. Whenever they go into the jungle or on a
short journey, the Laosians take with them one of their
domestic cocks, to serve as a decoy. Selecting a suitable spot, they tether the decoy by a string round the
leg to a stone or a peg stuck in the ground, and lay
all round it a number of looped strings, or snares, in
which the wild birds, attracted by the cry of the captive chanticleer, are entangled.

All the next day the road lay across this grassy
plain, till, at four p.m., we entered the ruined gates of
Muang Fang, a city now only in name.

This is the site of the ancient great capital of
Western Lao, of which all that now remains are fragments of the city walls, with here and there the ruins
of temples and phrachedees. All the rest is buried
beneath a dense growth of grass, jungle, and thin
forest, which the present inhabitants, who, at the time
of my visit, had only been settled there a twelvemonth,
were busily engaged—men, women, and children
—in clearing. There were no houses, merely a few
temporary huts and sheds, and no paths or roads whatever. I had some difficulty in finding the governor
of the place, an illiterate old Phya who could not
decipher the letter from Chengmai which I presented
to him, and had to get a clerk to read it for him. He,
however, was unusually prompt in making arrangements for my accommodation, taking me to a lively
little old man who readily turned his few goods and
chattels out of his hut to make room for me and my
baggage. As an acknowledgment of his cheerful
complaisance, and a sort of " compensation for dis-

turbance," I put ten rupees into the old man's hand, which to my surprise he seemed reluctant to accept. On my asking why he did not take my money, he said the hut was worth twice as much, and that he could not sell it at any price. I told Kao to explain to him that the money was intended as a present, or rather as an equivalent for the use of his hut, which I had no desire to appropriate, even temporarily, without a

My hut at Muang Fang.

quid pro quo, and so the old man went on his way rejoicing.

It did not take long to unpack my baggage, but the house itself was out of repair, and, although I had not taken the premises on a "repairing lease," I had at once to take steps to get the roof patched up. The presence of the cattle under the building at night—for my landlord still maintained his right to give them shelter there as usual—brought into prominence

another matter which proved the unsoundness of the
bamboo floor, even more than the manner in which it
bent and creaked under the weight of its five occupants
—for my four servants (to say nothing of Tali the
dog) were all quartered in the same room with myself.
The odour which arose from the stable below was
truly Augean, and on the following morning I had to
perform—fortunately by deputy—the task of Hercules,
in clearing out the thick deposit of filth that looked as
if it must have lain there undisturbed for ages.

This task had hardly been accomplished, when the
governor paid me a visit, accompanied by a retinue of
several petty chiefs and slaves.　Their arrival was the
signal to Tali to give a prolonged barking, which
alarmed them not a little.　"Ma! ma!" (dog! dog!)
was the cry as the party stood irresolute at the foot
of the ladder, two or three of them preparing to fly
precipitately.　But Tali was securely chained to my
heaviest trunk; and when I assured my visitors that
they ran no risk, they entered my room and ranged
themselves close to the door, casting furtive glances
on the dog, who would only be pacified when he saw
me offering my guests Burmese cheroots and tea.　The
former they did not smoke, but stowed them carefully
away in their bags—indispensable articles carried by
every Laosian—while over the latter they soon opened
quite a fire of questions about every article belonging
to me that they saw ranged round the hut.　My guns
they examined carefully, and with longing eyes; and
they were especially amused to look through my telescope.

"Can you see the spirits through it?" asked one of
their number.

I assured him that, if the Phees of which they had so
much fear really existed, I had no doubt they could

be seen through it. "But," I added, "see how you can keep the spirits away. If you look through the telescope this way (reversing it) you will see everything goes a long way off, instead of coming nearer. That is the way to keep the Phees away." And they were still more delighted when they found this instrument had the power of making things large or small, near or far off, at the will of the owner.

They were all most profuse in their promises to comply with my request to be supplied with birds and animals, insects and reptiles, of every rare kind ; and I gave them a small quantity of powder and shot to start with. Every able-bodied man in the country has one or more guns, old " blunderbusses " of George III. pattern, brought from Moulmein, or primitive imitations, of native manufacture. The chiefs in some cases had, however, a few breechloaders, in the use of which some of them were fairly proficient.

As much to my surprise as to my gratification they really began well; the first specimen brought to me consisted of some grey flying-squirrels, which one of the petty chiefs found in a hole while felling a tree. He called them " bang," but this seems to be the generic name for squirrels of every kind. Among other specimens were a few hornbills and monkeys, but nothing very rare, and after the novelty of the thing had passed off all pretence of collecting specimens for me ceased.

The people were more intent on clearing the forest of trees than on attempting to diminish its stock of birds and animals, and for once in my experience I found them really hard at work in a systematic manner. Every half-hour the crash of a big tree was heard, as it fell to the industrious axes of the natives. And, as the ground was gradually cleared, gangs of men and

T

women went over it to clean it, and prepare it for the cultivation of rice, cotton, tobacco, chillies, or capsicums. The soil hereabouts is very fertile and capable of producing large crops, but just then the supply of provisions was scanty, and I had not been here three days before my men complained that they were short of rice. This I felt sure was only a device on the part of the Muang Pau men to get back home again, for I had distinctly warned them to lay in a plentiful supply, and an additional elephant had been engaged for the express purpose of bringing an extra quantity to guard against the possibility of famine.

But this elephant had been brought, to eat its own head off, with a sham load of rice, while several of the others had carried only half their full loads; and, as my stock of fish had long since been exhausted by the accidents on the river, there was nothing to do but to send back to Muang Pau for a fresh supply of rice; so I induced the governor, by a bribe of four rupees, to instruct his clerk to write to the Chow there for eighty baskets of rice, which I promised to pay for.

This letter I sent by special messengers with elephants, but my position was by no means a pleasant one. Seeing that I was in difficulties, the natives refused to do anything for me. Even the Phya's clerk, to whom I gave a rupee for his trouble in writing the letter, refused a modest request which Kao made for a few fish from the river, where they were abundant. He certainly did relent so far as to send up two small fishes, but the transaction savoured rather of a desire to show that we were pretty well at the mercy of the people than of a wish to oblige.

CHAPTER XXII.

IT was more than a fortnight before my elephants
returned from Muang Pau, bringing with them only a
portion of the rice that had been requisitioned. In the
meantime, with my men threatened with famine, and
the people the very reverse of hospitable, I was
seized with an attack of fever, which, in spite of
quinine, clung to me for nearly a week. I tried, as
an experiment appropriate to my sojourn in the midst
of a superstitious people, a box of " Dr. Sutton's Magic
Pills," which a friend had put into my hand just before
leaving Bangkok, but the pellets proved as devoid of
magic as of any other property, and I pinned my faith
to quinine and patience. For five days I subsisted on
a little chicken-broth and tamarind-water, and was
getting very weak, when one night I was startled by
Tali and another dog in the camp barking most
furiously. Every one in camp seemed to be aroused,
but as it was very dark it was difficult to make out
what was the cause of the disturbance. At last some
one cried out " Sua ! sua ! " (tiger), pointing to the hut
opposite mine, round which a huge tiger was stealthily

creeping, but before any one could get a shot at the
brute it had vanished.

A little later, in the same night, or rather early on
the following morning, the sound of five shots in succession again aroused the camp, and half an hour
afterwards the body of a large female tiger was brought
in.

This little excitement seemed to do me more good
than all the medicine, and next day my appetite returned and I was able to partake of solid food again.
But, still unequal to much exertion, I wandered about
in the forest, stumbling, at almost every step, over
ruins, from beneath which here and there peeped the
head or arm of an ancient figure of Buddha. The
ground in some places, especially where the *débris* of
brickwork and masonry indicated the site of a former
tope or temple, was thickly strewn with these discarded and almost forgotten relics of former grandeur
and religious fervour. Seeing that the natives paid no
heed to the presence of these once sacred figures, I
determined to make a selection of a few of the finest,
and spent several days in examining the ground, and
partially excavating some of the heaps of ruins, and
was fortunate enough to find some very fine specimens
of ancient workmanship. They were all of bronze,
mixed in many cases with a large proportion of silver,
so that they had withstood the ravages of time and
weather, and were in a very good state of preserva-
tion.

One day I found buried beneath the ruins of a
temple quite a heap of figures of Buddha, some of
them of gigantic size, but nearly all in the well-known
meditating attitude. Two moderate-sized ones I selected, and had no difficulty in getting some natives—
they took four men each to lift—to deposit them, on

payment of a few rupees, in front of my temporary residence, where they stood for some time, the admiration of every one that passed by. Hitherto my proceedings had been watched with curiosity by the natives, who, however, offered no actual opposition to them, and even, as occasion required, and a rupee or two tempted them, lent me a hand in searching for relics. As time went on, however, I found myself more and more closely watched, and one day a couple of priests, who had arrived from Chengmai about the same time as myself to settle at Muang Fang, suddenly proclaimed their intention of building a temple, in which to collect the scattered figures of Buddha. Upon this I thought it best to announce openly that I had received permission to collect some of the figures, and that I intended to remove such of them as I might select. I added—what was the fact—that I had been specially advised by the princes and others at Chengmai to come to Muang Fang for that express purpose, as the figures lying on the ground here were not within the sanctuary of a temple.

So I extended the range of my search—in quite a different direction from that in which the other figures had been found—and crawled up the crumbling sides of a couple of large phrachedees. The ruined brickwork was overgrown with trees and other vegetation, which afforded a slight foothold ; but as I made my way up, now clinging to the branch or root of a tree, now by the help of a projecting brick or stone, masses of rubbish would roll down, half smothering me in dust, and often nearly carrying me down with them, much to the amusement of the group of natives who always followed me about to spy out my movements. At last I reached the recesses of what remained of the spire, and was rewarded by finding some

very fine figures, two of them choice Buddhas
bearing an inscription.

Annexed is an engraving of the larger of the two,

Figure of Buddha from Muang Fang.

and the following is a translation of the inscription,
made for me on my return to Chengmai by a couple of
intelligent Laosians in the service of Dr. Cheek, who very

kindly gave me all the assistance in his power. This was a task of several days' duration, as the characters were in the Fakkam language, the extinct dialect of Lao, which they had some difficulty in deciphering.

The inscription runs as follows :—

"In the year Paksi (*i.e.* 930 [1]), that is, the great dragon, in the third of the waxing of the fifth moon, on Wednesday, the eight following persons, husband, wife, and children, and mother, [2] Tam Matjula, [3] Nangta, [4] Ponai, Kata, Malikali, Maha vichai, Munla, [5] and Oina, [6] cast this image. They pray to reach the highest heaven."

In the centre of the pedestal, with the inscription on each side of it, is a geometrical design representing the signs of the zodiac, to which the following is a key :—

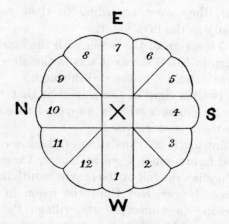

In the centre, at X, is Mount Zinnalo, the centre of the universe: at N, E, S, and W, are the four corners of the earth, the intermediate spaces being the oceans.

---

[1] That is, A.D. 1568, which would make the figure 315 years old.
[2] Probably of the husband.   [3] Husband's name.
[4] Wife's name.   [5] The children's names.   [6] Mother's name.

Round the mount are the twelve signs of the zodiac, which revolve from right to left, the sun rising in one sign of the zodiac for thirty days, thus making 360 days in the year.[7] Each of the spaces numbered one to twelve represents a month, and is also taken to signify one of the twelve "watches" of two hours into which the day is divided.

According to the signs made in these spaces, the star from which the day took its name on which the casting of this image occurred was Venus, as shown in the third space.

The sun (shown in space No. 4), was in the fifth month, and was in conjunction with a star called Dow angkan (which is the same word as for Tuesday). Although the sun is here placed in the fourth sign of the zodiac, they were, according to their reckoning, then already in the fifth month.

In No. 5 is a sign of the moon with the star Jupiter.

The sign in No. 8 shows it was in the afternoon the casting was done, *i.e.* in the eighth watch.

In the twelfth sign of the zodiac at that time was the Rahoo, a monster who is supposed to eat up the sun when there is an eclipse !

The following is a translation of the inscription on the second figure which I got at Muang Fang :—

" On Tuesday the full of the fourth month in the year 902,[8] name of year, Kot Chi ; the moon in Cancer, Nang Heeang (a woman) of the village Pa Mahooa, cast an image of Phra Sikkhee, coated with gold, as an offering to Wat Pa Hoa, that she may obtain great merit. May the giver be blessed with abundance, and obtain mercy and grace of Phra Sikkhee.

" Tumapanja, the son of Nang Heeang, and Nang Boon Too [perhaps the wife of Tumapanja] pray to

[7] See Appendix.   [8] A.D. 1540.

Phra Sikkhee that we may meet and serve thee, doing works of merit in every transmigration. Let us never be separated until we shall reach heaven and pass into Nirwana. Grant thy help, gracious Phra Sikkhee; let not thy servant be like Nang Witsaka,[9] but let thy servant reach the abode of those that are free from sin."

The images of Buddha, as generally cast or carved in Lao, may be divided into three classes, (1) seated, (2) standing, and (3) recumbent.

The most common model, seen in every temple, is the one shown in the foregoing woodcut, representing the lord Buddha in his usual crossed-legged position. It was while so sitting under the banyan-tree, deep in meditation, that the great Master attained omniscience. These idols are generally beautifully modelled and well proportioned, except the ears, which are always very long and furrowed. It appears as if Buddha had his ears pierced, for in some cases I have seen him represented with cylindrical earrings of the same pattern as those to this day worn by the Lao women. His tapering skull is covered with large curls of hair, each curl being twisted separately from left to right, and very much resembling the apex of a snail-shell. On the top of the head is a sign of glory, which spreads up like a flame.

The figure is usually seated on a pedestal, ornamented with a scroll of the lotus-flower, which is as sacred and favourite amongst Buddhists as it was amongst the old Egyptians, who saw in it the emblem of the great generative and conceptive powers of the world. In the large Buddha described and figured above, which I obtained at Muang Fang, it will be seen that the

[9] Nang Witsaka prayed that she might not be hurried off to Nipan; she desired to live through a thousand transmigrations, and to have husbands in abundance.

right hand hangs loose over the knee, while the left hand lies in the lap with the palm turned upwards. This figure of Buddha is by the Laosians called " Phra sing," and is more highly esteemed amongst them and the Siamese than any other representation of the deity.

The pedestal represents the crystal throne on which Buddha sat when he was in the forest and became endowed with infinite wisdom and omnipotence. He had gone out and become a priest under the banyan-tree ;[1] when he met " Sote nya palm," [2] who brought some long grass or thatch as an offering, which, when Buddha sat on it, became a crystal throne. It was while sitting on this splendid throne, his hands folded in peaceful meditation, that the lord exclaimed, " I will never rise from this throne until I have attained the omniscience of Buddhahood." Mara, the prince of devils, then came with myriads of his followers and attacked Buddha, in order to take his throne from him, besieging him with arrows of fire, boiling water, and all the diabolical ingenuities that he had any command over. Buddha, startled by the hissing of the boiling water that Satan was pouring over him, moved his right hand, when Nang taw rani (mother of the earth, or protecting goddess of the earth) came out and chid him for being frightened, saying she had absolute control over these devils ; so she took down her hair and wrung the knot, or braid, and water came out of her hair, and flooded the devils, so that they had to run off in great confusion.

[1] The banyan-tree is the *Ficus indica* (or *Vuta* in Sanscrit), a tree found in most parts of India and the Malay Archipelago. It attains great dimensions, covering with its multiplication of trunks and branches a space large enough to hold a market or meeting under, as I have seen in Sumatra. This sacred tree is called *Mai Seli* in Lao.

[2] " Sote nya palm " (*Sotiya* in Siamese) was a Brahmin.

The Buddhists regard Gaudama's mental agonies at this moment as the most important event in his career. Hence the general desire to perpetuate this incident in the figure seated with one hand on the knee.

Mr. Alabaster, in his "Wheel of the Law," gives a different version of the story of the moving of Buddha's hand. After King Mara had hurled all his forces against him in vain, he says, "the grand being reflected, 'Truly here is no man to bear me witness, but I will call on the earth itself, though it has neither spirit nor understanding, and it shall be my witness.' *Stretching forth his hand*, he thus invoked the earth : ' O holy earth ! I who have attained the thirty powers of virtue, and performed the five great alms, each time that I have performed a great act have not failed to pour water upon thee. Now that I have no other witness, I call upon thee to give thy testimony. If this throne was created by my merits, let the earth quake and show it, and if not, let the earth be still ! ' "

After the devils had fled, Phya In (*i.e.* Indra) came with angels and ministered unto Buddha, and worshipped him, as he still continued to sit on his throne under the banyan-tree. After that, Phya Nakh (Naga in Siamese) came from the bowels of the earth, and crept round Buddha's throne of crystal. Phya nakh was a great spirit in the shape of a three, five, or seven-headed monster, who could go up the skies and descend again and so forth, and he put his head over Buddha like an umbrella, to protect him from all external influences, such as heat, cold, wind, rain, &c.[3]

---

[3] In the sacred books it is related that Buddha was completely hidden from view (from profane eyes) by this Phya nakh, but it would tax all the ingenuity of the native artists to represent an

From this legend of the many-headed monster springs the use of the umbrella as an offering to Buddha; and to it also is due a variation in the form of the figures of the " sitting " Buddha, which sometimes represent him as covered with a crown bearing a distant resemblance to a three, five, or seven-headed monster, instead of the usual pointed or flame-shaped " glory." I obtained a specimen of the Buddha with the five-headed serpent coiled round him at a ruined temple near Kiang Tsen.

The next favourite representation of Buddha, less common than the first, is the reclining figure of the great Master as he died—resting on his right side and supporting his head on his hand. These recumbent figures are always surrounded by a number of others representing his disciples, some holding fans.

A still rarer model represents Gaudama with both hands elevated in the act of preaching or giving benediction to mankind, and ornamented with a crown and chains, and several rings on his fingers. The Lao people call this figure Phra Sikkhee. It was one of these that I obtained at Kampheng Pet; it is shown in the woodcut at p. 128.

The figures of Buddha vary in size from six inches to about ten feet in height; the larger ones being generally made of bricks and mortar, then lacquered over and heavily gilt.

In Lao the ancient well-executed bronze figures are seldom made, the average Laosian contenting himself with roughly carving a clumsy wooden model. In all of them, however, the features of the lord Buddha are well defined and handsome, but, I always think, some-

invisible statue, and, for the sake of the worshippers, whose faith needs to be fostered by sight, the invisible god is represented in the material form above described.

what feminine. The eyes are formed of black stones, the white of the eye being as a rule inlaid with mother-of-pearl. I have heard of rubies and other gems being put in for eyes, but never saw any. But, whatever the material, age, or size of the figures, the same expression, calm, meditating, and benignant, is preserved in them all. Just as in the Christian Church painters and sculptors have vied with each other in pencil and chisel to hand down to posterity the features of our Saviour and the Virgin, so in the statues of Buddha, in different poses, and in a variety of material, his worshippers have kept intact the handsome and regular countenance of their saint.

Besides desiring to make merit with their deity in the multiplication of his images, the Laosians believe that when the proper number of figures have been built and established—but they don't pretend to fix the number—Buddha will come again and preach for seven days.

CHAPTER XXIII.

A scapegoat for the ravages of the tigers—Curious mode of herding cattle—Tiger-bait—A visit to the cave of Tam tap tau—An ancient shrine—A gigantic Buddha—A thunder-storm—I receive a deputation—Arguing with the Phyas—A dilemma—Rhinoceros-blood as a medicine—Cheating a Chinaman—Mau Sua's hunting-box—At Tatong—Spurious gems—A Ngiou village—Customs of the people.

I PAID somewhat dearly for my success in Buddha-collecting. The natives, instigated by the priests, and, as I afterwards learned, by a secret message from the Chow Operat of Chengmai, made my researches the pretext for openly displaying their hatred of the *farang* which they had so long been nursing in their breasts, but had repressed for fear of the very chief who, having encouraged me to my face, was now scheming against me behind my back.

In the ravages of the tigers with which the forest abounded, they found a ready cause of complaint against me. The large herds of cattle which the people had brought with them to this wilderness had naturally attracted the attention of these beasts, and hardly a night passed without two or three head of cattle being either wounded or carried off by these marauders.[1] One night a bullock was actually killed under the very

[1] The new settlers had brought plenty of cattle with them, which of course tempted the tigers. The natives had a curious method of herding their cattle. The herdsmen were armed with a bow and a number of clay pellets, about half an inch in diameter, and whenever

hut I was occupying. For all these depredations the
people blamed me, saying that the spirit was angry
because I had defiled the images of their lord; and, on
the afternoon of the 5th of March, the Phyas held a
council to consider what should be done; as a result
of which two Taus, or petty officials, came to me and
earnestly begged me to return at least the largest of
the figures I had removed, in order to appease the
anger of the spirits. I replied that, spirits or no
spirits, the removal or return of the figures could have
no effect on the appetite of a tiger, and that, where
there were hundreds of head of cattle, the tigers would
be sure to take advantage of the opportunity. I even
tried to turn this visit to account by urging that greater
encouragement should be given to me and my hunters
to collect natural history specimens. The men whom
I had engaged to shoot brought me nothing, although
they had taken my powder and shot, and although I
had promised to pay them well; and I urged that, if
the Phyas would give me facilities in carrying out my
object, I would do my best to assist them by taking
every opportunity, and by encouraging others to
neglect no chance, of hunting and killing the tigers.
But it was all of no avail. The deputation that waited
upon me was no more to be persuaded to my view
than I was to theirs, and we parted with mutual com-
pliments on our lips, but renewed distrust of each other
in our hearts.

After this my attempts at hunting relics and hunting wild animals were equally vain. I tried to get
some natives to dig round the corners of the ruined
phrachedees in search of relics; but no bribe would in-

the oxen began to roam too far away they would circumvent them,
and drive them back by discharging two or three of these pellets at
them from the bow.

duce them to help me, and even my own attendants
were afraid to assist, so I was reluctantly compelled
to relinquish my design.

Mau Sua, my principal hunter, was away at his
"hunting-box" on the Ngiou frontier, and pending
his return the monotony of enforced idleness was
broken only by the mild excitement of long caravans
of Ngiou traders passing through Muang Fang for
Chengmai, or by a group of pilgrims from the Ngiou
country, always accompanied by a yellow-robed priest
or two, on their way to the famous cave of Tam tap
tau, there to offer their devotions and gifts to the great
Buddha.

This seemed a favourable opportunity to visit the
celebrated shrine, so I gave notice to Kao to have three
elephants and half a dozen men ready, as I should
start for the place in a couple of days. We started,
accordingly, on the 11th of March, under the leader-
ship of a guide whom the governor recommended to
me.

The road lay all day across the plain surrounding
Muang Fang, sometimes through thin forest and
bamboo-groves, but mostly through long, rank jungle-
grass which the Laosians cut for roofing their huts.
At several places the grass had taken fire, through the
intense heat of the last few days, and at one spot the
flames were so fierce and the smoke so dense that we
had to make a *détour* through the forest, the elephants
being afraid of fire. Here we came to a camp of
twenty-five or thirty Ngious, men, women, and children,
returning from a visit to Tam tap tau, where they had
offered their gifts of cloth, wax tapers, and gold leaves.
We camped close by, and left again early next morning, arriving at the cavern about noon.

The entrance to the cave itself is between seventy

and eighty feet up the steep side of a limestone hill some 300 feet high, rising suddenly from the plateau, which is itself 600 feet above sea-level. The footway up the hill is very difficult to traverse, starting at first in water, and gradually rising along the sharp edges of fractured rock, which neither time nor weather nor the traffic of centuries of pilgrimages has smoothed away, till it leads at last along the top of a precipice down which one false step would throw the traveller to certain death among huge boulders, tree-trunks, and pools of water.

On the entrance to the cavern some human labour had, in times gone by, been bestowed. Bricks and plaster had been shaped to form a rude archway, while above the portal were some carved sandstone figures of the Hoalaman, and of a bird evidently intended for a peacock, which I took for a pretty certain sign that the cave formerly belonged to the Burmese, or more probably the Ngious, as this bird is a distinctive feature in the heraldry of both peoples. The cave, I was subsequently informed, is mostly venerated by the Ngious. To the left of the entrance was a narrow niche or recess in which was a broken figure of Buddha, at whose feet the pious pilgrims had laid a collection of the characteristic clay decanters or water-jugs, pots, and jars of the country. The cavern itself was of interesting formation, the roof being a fantastic array of stalactites of various forms.

High up in the centre of the roof, which was probably sixty feet in height, was a natural skylight, through which a dusky beam of light fell on the head of a gigantic recumbent figure of Buddha, in, as the legend runs, his " dying attitude," lying on an elevated platform in the centre of the cave : but this light from above only made the rest of the great cave appear darker by comparison, so I lighted my lamp in order thoroughly to explore the interior.

The great Buddha is made of brick-work, covered with a coating of thick varnish, and once heavily gilt, but now in a dilapidated condition, like the great Buddha at Wat Po in Bangkok, the varnish and gilt peeling off like a serpent shedding its coat. As soon as we entered, my followers, including my two Chinese servants, sat down on their haunches and made obeisance to Buddha, bowing two or three times to the ground, and I left them to their devotions, while I examined the surroundings.

All around the central god was an assemblage of figures, half life-size, of the same material as the great Buddha, representing disciples of the great Master, sitting and praying or listening, with uplifted folded hands. Every one of these smaller figures was covered with a great number of yellow rags and skull-caps on their heads, left by the priests as tokens of their devotion. At the feet of the gigantic idol lay another heap of clay pots and jars, with rice-trays containing rice, small wooden and stone figures of Buddha, brought all the way from the Ngiou States, and deposited there by worshippers; while heaped upon an adjacent altar was an immense collection of representations of Buddha, together with a curious assortment of priests' clothing, water-jars, streamers, tufts of hair, spittoons, and other odds and ends.

At the further end of the cave, some thirty feet above the floor, was a smaller figure of Buddha, posed in the act of giving blessing, with a bamboo ladder, very shaky in structure, and almost vertically placed, leading up to it. Before this figure was another altar, on which a miscellaneous assemblage of old mattresses, pillows, and mats, swarming with cockroaches and

other insects, were deposited, in accordance with the
native idea that such offerings would be credited to
the donors for righteousness. When I came back to
the great figure, I found Kao and the cook offering
their mite to the lord Buddha, placing a dozen or
more wax tapers at intervals round the figure. Near
his head Kao had put two small trays with parched rice
and flowers, while on the altar he had deposited two
gorgeously coloured photographs of a Chinaman and
his wife.

We only got back to Muang Fang in time to
get shelter from a most terrific thunderstorm, the
prelude to the break-up of the dry season. The thermometer was standing at 75° Fahr., when suddenly it
fell to 65°; a stiff northerly wind sprang up, rapidly
developing strength till it blew quite a hurricane,
shaking my hut to the foundation, and threatening every
moment to send it bodily away in pursuit of several
other similar structures that were blown completely
down. As it was, the grass roofing was torn off,
leaving a fine opening for the clouds of hail-stones,
ranging in size from the diameter of a sixpence to that
of a large strawberry, which fell in incessant volleys
as of shot from " heaven's artillery," the roar of
which made the woods ring again ; while the brief
intervals between the brilliant flashes of lightning,
the duration and rapid succession of which had the
effect of a continuous fire, only threw into deeper contrast the intense blue-black of the overladen clouds.
For almost half an hour the roaring of the wind, the
louder voice of the thunder, and the musketry-like rattle
of the falling hail kept up a din which might well be
compared to the noise of a battle-field during the most
hotly contested portion of the fight. Then the forces
of nature seemed spent; the commotion ceased, and a

refreshing rain fell, as if in atonement for the fury with which the wet season had set in.

Had I been superstitious, I might have regarded this storm as a presage of personal evil, for on the following day the Second Governor of the place, accompanied by a Phya from Muang Pau and two followers, waited upon me, and began reading one of their curious palmleaf letters addressed to the Chow from the Chow Operat of Chengmai, giving orders that I was not to be furnished with men or elephants, and that I was not to be allowed to remove the Buddha figures which had been the cause of so many serious manifestations of ill.

Against all this I protested with as much vehemence as I could, with the disadvantage of having to speak through an interpreter who could not always be trusted to repeat my language, and whose delinquencies I had no means of checking. I again told the deputation that the Chow Operat of Chengmai had actually advised me to come here to get the figures which he now prevented me from taking away.

The old Phya replied that his people had made constant complaints about me, saying that I had disturbed their peace, that I had angered the spirits, and that it was entirely due to my presence, and particularly to my excavations among the ruins, that the tigers had come to destroy their cattle. So long as I retained the figures, he added, the spirits would be angry and send tigers among them. For twelve months, he concluded, the settlement had been very prosperous, and nothing had befallen them till the *farang* came to anger the spirits.

For a long time I tried to reason with them, but at last, in my vexation, I plainly told them that the idea about the spirits was all nonsense, that they could not

make me believe that the tigers had never been tempted
to dine off their fat cattle before I came. Kao, however, himself as strong a believer in the spirits as
any of them, hesitated to translate my remarks in dis-
paragement of them, but I insisted on his repeating what
I told him. Whether he really said what I told him, I
know not, but at once the old Phya, with a look on his
face that showed me his thoughts as clearly as if he
were speaking in English, turned to his companions,
plainly using what was said, as the police reports have
it, "as evidence against me." Seeing that matters
were not mending, I tried to turn the tables on them
by referring to the damage the storm last night
had done to their dwellings. "Why was this?" I
said.

"Because the spirits were angry with the *farang*."

"No," I replied, "but because the spirits were angry
that the Chow's messengers should be brought here
upon a false mission."

"You know," I continued, "how often you yourselves, and your neighbours the Ngious, have ransacked
the ruins here, not only for the images, but for the
coins and gold and silver articles deposited beneath the
pradchedees. How is it that these figures," and I pointed
to the images before the entrance to my hut, "have no
eyes? Because your people have knocked out the
rubies and other precious stones with which they and
many others were ornamented; and now you want to
prevent me from collecting a few of the figures you
yourselves have damaged. Your people melted the
silver images for the sake of the precious metal; but
I shall preserve those I have collected, and they will
be taken care of for ever."

Here the old Phya explained that they did not so
much mind my having the smaller figures, but that the

two large ones were specially prized, as no doubt they were—because I had selected them.

" Besides," I continued, " you have not assisted me and my men to collect natural history specimens, but have put every obstacle in my way, although I offered to kill tigers for you. No wonder your spirits are angry when you disobey the Chow's orders, and insult the stranger whom he sent to you to help."

Here the subject dropped and the deputation withdrew, Tali not forgetting to give a good growl at them and to hasten their departure by barking loudly as they descended the rickety ladder.

I was now in a " fix." I did not want to enter into a correspondence with the Chow Operat at Chengmai, nor did I desire to excite the further animosity of the natives here. The best thing to do was probably to take my departure. I had been here a month; I had seen all I wanted to see of the neighbourhood, and could not expect to add anything to my scanty natural history collection or to my archæological booty. Indeed, it was questionable whether I should be able to carry off the principal portion of the latter at all. I tried to induce some of the people who had accompanied me from Muang Pau to help me take them away on the promise of good payment, but they were afraid of being punished if it ever came to the Chow's ears.

At the same time Mau Sua was still away with some of my followers, and I had nothing to do but to impatiently await his return and meanwhile devise some scheme for getting away with my figures, without further ado.

On the 16th of March a party of Ngious came to the settlement, offering for sale some dried rhinoceros-blood, which the Laosians, like the Chinese, value for its supposed medicinal properties. In Lao it fetches its weight in silver. It is done up in rolls like sausages, in the intestines of the rhinoceros. Kao invested six rupees in the purchase of half a dozen large sausages, but to his chagrin afterwards discovered that it was not the real article. It is difficult to cheat a Chinaman, but it would puzzle a good many men to tell the difference between bullock's blood and rhinoceros-blood, especially when the former is carefully preserved in the " genuine " covering. Kao did not forget this robbery for some time, for he had calculated on making a little profit out of his purchase when he should return to Chengmai—though I do not think he was a Chinaman if he allowed his discovery to stand in the way of the fulfilment of this purchase.

At last on the 17th of March, Mau Sua returned, bringing a few hornbills and lizards, a tortoise or two, and one of the *Ngao-pa,* or wild buffaloes, which are by no means rare in the forests on the mountains. I retained the skull and skeleton, and left him the more profitable part, the flesh, which he disposed of among the natives. I was, of course, much disappointed too, that this great hunter had done so little. So I determined to return with him to his mountain-retreat on the Ngiou frontier, and see how far it was feasible to carry out my intention of proceeding across the Ngiou States. Here, I thought, I might possibly engage men to return with me to Muang Fang and carry away my images ; and if the worst came to the worst I could go on to Kiang Hai with my letter of introduction to the chief there, and endeavour to get him to allow me the services of some of his men for the purpose.

To make quite sure of my ground, I sent a letter to Dr. Cheek, at Chengmai, telling him exactly how I was situated, and begging him to get a letter from the Chow there, with instructions to the Chow of

Muang Fang, to give me any assistance I might require in removing the figures and the rest of my
luggage.

So, leaving Yang and Cook to keep house, and Tali to
take care of them during my absence, I started on the
19th of March for Tatong, a Ngiou village, just on the
border, close to which Mau Sua's " hunting-box" was
situated, on the banks of the Me San, tributary of the
Me Fang, about twenty miles N.N.E. of Muang Fang.
Mau Sua himself I found quite a hardy and intelligent
mountaineer and huntsman, leading a typical hunter's
life, in solitude amid the deer, wild buffaloes, and
tigers of the forest-clad mountains, and spending the
intervals between his hunting expeditions in fishing
in the river, or in collecting bees'-wax, and honey in
the forest.

He was the least superstitious of all the Laosians
I ever met, and seemed as little afraid of the spirits
as he was of either man or beast.

The road to Tatong lay through a somewhat open
forest, with a high mountain-chain, running north
and south, rising abruptly to our left. The trees
about here were literally covered with orchids, which
were just past their prime, the dry season being the
time for flowering. Many other varieties of flowers,
of most gorgeous colours, and often of gigantic size,
flourished in the open patches between the trees. I
do not remember to have seen anywhere such a profusion of flowers as when travelling through Lao, and
in this particular district they seemed more abundant
than ever.

On every side could be heard the crowing of cocks
in the forest, alternating with the weird, shrill cry of
the peacock. We subsisted largely on these and
other wild birds, but found them remarkably tough.

Tatong itself is a small village, or rather a collection of little more than a dozen huts, scattered on both banks of the River Mekok, which is here very shallow, and, at least at this season, not more than 150 feet wide, and hemmed in on all sides by mountains of gneiss and granite. It was the first purely Ngiou village I had entered, the people being, however, under the protection of the king of Burmah.

I unloaded my baggage on the banks of the river, and my men soon made a hut for the night. Early on the following morning the natives crowded round me, offering to sell " precious stones " at three rupees apiece. Their gems turned out, however, to be small crystals, worth perhaps a penny each, opaque rubies, garnets, and others of equally small value. Evidently they thought to make the most of a stranger's visit, for when I applied to the chief for a boat to take me down the river to Kiang Hai, he asked the moderate sum of sixty rupees, although he admitted that it only took a boat two days to get there, simply drifting with the current. After some bargaining he consented to take twenty rupees, though I afterwards found that half that sum would have been considered good pay by the natives, who are accustomed to visit Kiang Hai as a market for their cotton and other produce.

The Ngious are decidedly of the same race as the Burmese. I have had opportunities of seeing hundreds of both countries, and of closely watching their features and build. The Ngious wear the hair in a top-knot in the same way as the Burmese, but they are easily distinguished by their tattooing, which is much more elaborate. They are as a rule tattooed right down to the ankle from the neck, or from immediately under the arm—from the arm-pit very often. Besides tattooing themselves, they make a number of incisions in the arm, in which they insert bits of precious stones, or small lumps of silver or gold, with the object of making themselves strong, and of protecting themselves against the spirits.

These strange amulets can easily be felt in the flesh, and wherever they are inserted they leave a small black lump, as may be seen in the sketch.

The Ngiou dress is very characteristic, consisting generally of only a pair of wide trousers, reaching two

Ngiou man.

or three inches above the ankle, and always very dirty; for, although cotton is very cheap here, it is very seldom that a pair of really white trousers is to be seen. The garments have all been that colour once, but constant use without washing has generally converted them into an elegant mud-colour. Like the Burmese, the Ngious wear a coloured silk handkerchief on the head to cover up the hair; but when they are on the move in the forest, or on board their boats,

they replace the handkerchief by the favourite huge
straw hats, imported from Yunnan, which are a very
excellent protection against the sun, as shown in the
accompanying sketch. Across the shoulder they carry
a large bag—an indispensable travelling-companion—
containing tobacco and betel-nut, while from the other
shoulder is slung a sword of native make. On festive
occasions they wear a tight-fitting jacket; but ordi-
narily the upper part of the body is bare.

CHAPTER XXIV.

Down the River Mekok—Another cave-temple at Kiang Hai—The
Chow Radjasee—Lao architecture—A typical habitation—A
Laosian princess at the toilet—A Lao garden—A visit from the
Mussus—Arrow-poison—Spirit-worship—Customs of the Mus-
sus—A social system based on borrowing—Marketing—A Lao
family-dinner—A princess crockery-dealer—Chignons for sale.

AT Tatong I tried to induce some of the natives to
return to Muang Fang, and carry my figures across
country to the River Meping; but I found the shrewd
old Phya had actually forestalled me, and had sent
word to the people not to help me. So next day I
started for Kiang Hai in the chief's canoe, a small
open craft, without a cabin or any kind of shelter,
in company with another Ngiou trading-canoe. Two
hours of barely more than drifting with the stream
brought us to the junction of the Me Fang River
with the Mekok, at the boundary between the Lao and
the Ngiou States.

The River Mekok itself is little more than a mountain-stream, filled with huge stones, between which
the water eddies with a gurgling sound, making the
navigation difficult for the shallow canoes. The
scenery along the banks is very beautiful, hills of
from 400 to 500 feet high rising abruptly from the
water, thickly clad with trees and other vegetation.
During the day I saw more wild animal-life than I
had hitherto seen in any consecutive twenty-four

hours since I had been in Lao. Birds were numerous :
peacocks, some sitting on the branch of a tree ; snake-
darters, old acquaintances in Borneo; cormorants ;
herons ; hornbills, beating the air with their loud
flapping wings ; jungle-fowls, continually crowing ;
lovely-coloured king-fishers, plovers, and many other
kinds.

Gambolling among the branches of the trees, were
numbers of the black *hylobates*, while here and there
the natives pointed out the great foot-prints of wild
elephants, where they had come down to the river
in the early morning to drink and bathe.

As we glided rapidly down stream the country began
to get less and less hilly, and the river became wider
and deeper. Towards evening of the second day we
came to a cave called Tam Pa, on the left bank of the
river. Steps, roughly cut out of the side of the steep
limestone hill, led to the mouth of the cavern, which
was evidently well frequented by pilgrims, though not
in sufficient numbers to frighten away the bats and
swallows that swarmed in the lofty roof. The area of
the cave was small, which made its height seem perhaps
greater than it really was, though I should judge the
roof to be at least seventy or eighty feet above the
floor. The floor was strewn with the usual assortment
of miscellaneous articles offered to the hundreds of
figures of Buddha deposited in the cavern; and the
whole place, with its contents, was covered with
perhaps more than the usual amount of dust and dirt.
Among the rubbish I found a curious piece of pottery,
which the natives said was of great antiquity, but of
the use of which they were ignorant.

It was already dark before we reached Kiang Hai,
—sometimes also called Kiang Rai—and we found
our course blocked by a number of fishing-stakes

placed across the river.   Judging from the number of
lights moving about on shore, the people were evidently
engaged in fishing ; so, in order not to interfere with
them, I had the boat hauled up the bank a short distance above the town, and here we slept for the night.

On awaking in the morning, the view that lay before
me struck me as being so exceedingly pretty and
characteristic, that I made a sketch of it, which is

View near Kiang Hai.

shown in the accompanying illustration.   Right in front,
rising from a plain in the foreground, was a hill, on
the summit of which were a temple and phrachedee, the
gilt spires of which glistened in the rosy beams of the
rising sun ; while another temple, with a phrachedee
contiguous, stood close to the river, partially surrounded
by trees.

Presently I went into the village, and called upon
the Chow Hluang, who said the only accommodation

he had for me was a small Sala, which, being out of repair, I declined. I then went, with the letter of introduction which the Chow Operat had given me, to his son-in-law, the Chow Radjasee, who very kindly offered me hospitality in his own house.

My host and hostess, who warmly shook hands with me, seemed friendly disposed, and were greatly delighted when I presented them with sixteen yards of blue silk cloth, interwoven with gold thread, and it was not long before they returned the compliment with the usual gift of rice and eggs, fruits and fowls.

My host was a man of about forty-five years of age, who, after being eighteen years in the priesthood, had married, two years previously, the Chow Operat's daughter, a very plain woman with a terrible squint, but a very good heart withal. They lived in a good-sized house, built in the ordinary style of teak and bamboo, where they did everything to make me comfortable.

As I have not yet fully described a Lao house, I give here a picture of the residence of the Chow Radjasee, not because it is of the most elaborate design, but because it will serve as a type of Lao architecture and domestic arrangements. There are no fine houses or palaces in the country; the houses of prince and peasant are the same in general plan and in mode of construction, the only difference being in the size and in the quality of material and workmanship. A few bits of extra carving on the gables, and the fact that it is constructed throughout of teak, may distinguish a prince's house from that of any ordinary person; but, beyond a difference in size, that is all. The roof of the house is usually of thatch, which is cheap and easily replaced. The better houses are sometimes roofed with "tiles" made of teak, which are of course more durable, but do not keep the rain out any better than a well-repaired thatch.

The houses are never more than one story high, and always built on posts, with the floor at an elevation of from five to eight feet above the ground. In this space under the floor the elephant-howdahs or oxen-pack-saddles are piled; while the fowls and ducks congregate here, and even the cattle themselves are very commonly sheltered for the night.

Going up some three or four rude steps in front of the house, one comes to a platform or balcony,

Lao architecture: the Chow Radjasee's house at Kiang Hai.

running right round the house. The flooring is commonly made of split bamboo, laid across the main rafters supported by the posts on which the house is erected; but in the case of the wealthier classes the flooring is sometimes made entirely of teak. These balconies are always very slippery, and, what is worse, are often out of repair. I have a painful recollection of the dilapidated state into which this part of the house is often allowed to fall, for while staying at Kiang Hai I had several narrow escapes of falling, and one evening my foot slipped into one of the holes, and I sprained my ankle so severely that my kind host, though he could not mend my foot, did his best to prevent a repetition of the accident by setting his slaves to work next day to lay down a new bamboo flooring.

At one end of this platform is invariably erected a small covered shelf, or shed, called *han nam*, made of a few boards raised on posts, with a thatch-roof over the top. Here stand several large unglazed water-jars, which are daily filled with water for ordinary domestic purposes. By the side of these water-vessels lies a spoon, made of the half of a cocoanut-shell, with a wooden handle, with which, in dirty weather, any person entering the house ladles out some water from the jar, and pours it over his feet, to cleanse them.

Every morning and evening, the prince and princess would go out in turn on this platform to have a bath ; it was too far for them to walk three or four minutes to the river. Their ablutions consisted merely in pouring water over themselves from the big water-jars with a large spoon or cup. Sometimes the lady would finish up by having a huge silver basin brought, containing a mixture of tamarind-water and lime-juice, with which she would wash her hair. I took the liberty of making the accompanying sketch of the princess during this operation.

This entrance-platform is generally ornamented by pots of orchids or other flowering plants.

The floor of the house proper is raised about a foot above this platform, the entrance to the room or rooms being through a passage with a covered apartment on each side, one for domestics and slaves, the other for members of the family. Each of these apartments is divided by walls of planks or plaited bamboo into two separate rooms, one used as a sleeping-chamber, and the other as a general living-room. The room appropriated to the members of the family is often subdivided again, either by a wall or a series of posts, into two sections, the innermost of which is raised above the level of the rest, and set apart for purely private purposes, or for the reception of " distinguished visitors."

Behind the servants' room is the kitchen, which generally extends along the whole length of the back of the house. On the kitchen-floor is a mound of earth

Laosian princess at the toilet.

or clay, several inches high, which serves as a fireplace, hemmed in all round with boards, and with a tripod in the centre, formed of three stones, on which the fire and oven are placed.

The house is surrounded by a garden, enclosed with a tall bamboo fence, spiked at the top. The entrance to this compound is guarded by a sliding door, made of teak, fitted at the bottom with a wheel which enables it to be easily opened and closed.

It is always fastened at dark, to keep out thieves, both biped and quadruped; for tigers are numerous in some parts, and very aggressive. As an additional guard several pariah dogs are kept, but, though they bark at the slightest alarm, they seldom bite, for they are very timid, and easily frightened away with a stick or stone, and are not nearly such good watch-dogs as the trained dogs from Yunnan, which the better classes of Laosians keep, and which it is dangerous for a stranger to approach.

In the gardens are grown, in wild confusion, cocoa-palms, betelnut-palms, capsicums, and a few "vege-tables."

Before I had been long in the house, several of my host's relatives and a number of slaves crowded the platform to look at the *farang.* Among the visitors were some women, whose handsome regular features and erect gait proclaimed them to belong to quite a distinct race of people. A portrait of one is given on the following page. They were exchanging chillies for rice with my hostess, who informed me that they were Mussus, of whom there are several tribes scattered about the mountains in the Ngiou States. They are a nomadic race, never staying long in one place, subsisting largely on what the forest yields, shooting all sorts of animals with bows and poisoned arrows, and exchanging the flesh, horns, and hides, for rice and salt, with the people of Kiang Hai and other towns.

The women wore their hair *à la* Burmese, in a top-knot. On their heads they wore a covering of white and black cotton cloth, the ends of which hung down loose behind. Their dress consisted of a short black jacket, embroidered round the edges with bits of red or blue cloth, and a petticoat to match. On state oc-casions this jacket is replaced by a long sort of mantle, with silver buttons and a more extensive border of the same bits of blue or red cloth. The whole of the material is of their own manufacture.

For ornaments they wear a number of necklaces made of silver or grass and rattan, which are very becoming on the brown skin, especially those made of grass, which, when fresh, have a beautiful golden hue.

I was much struck with their large silver earrings, and endeavoured to bargain with one of them for a pair; but, like dutiful wives, they refused to part with them without the consent of their husbands.

Mussu woman.

Later in the afternoon the men came, headed by their chief, a good-looking man, with a tiny moustache carefully waxed at the ends! Their dress consisted of a short, tight-fitting jacket of black cloth, similar to that worn by the women, and wide short trousers of the same material. They were not tattooed as a rule, but one or two of them had a small representation of an animal on the thighs. They said they had never before seen a *farang*, and were as much interested in me as I in them, putting all sorts of curious questions to me, but, as the Mussu language is entirely distinct from that of the Laosians, the conversation had to be carried on through the double intermediation of the Chow and of Kao, and it consequently lost much of its effect. I gave them each a small silver coin—a British Burmese sixpence—which delighted them very much, and bought specimens of their necklaces and large earrings.

I asked to see their bows and arrows, but they said they never brought them to the towns, always leaving them " with the spirits," in some tree, and that they did not much care to part with them. However, the chief promised to bring me a bow and a couple of arrows, as, he said, he should be returning to Kiang Hai in a few days.

The poison with which they prepare their arrows is said to be so potent that a big animal like a rhinoceros will die half an hour after being wounded, if a large quantity is used, and that even a small dose is fatal within twenty-four hours.

The Mussus profess to be entirely devoid of fear, saying that their spirits protect them against tigers and other wild beasts. How useful one of these people might have been at Muang Fang, at the time of my difficulty with the old Phya there ! In proof of their fearlessness, the Chow told me that they were the only people who dared to travel through the woods at night, sleeping, often quite alone, in the thickest parts of the forest. Their faith is entirely in spirits, which they believe to be located everywhere, in trees, stones, &c. They have no idols, but once or twice a year they have a " spirit-dance," at which they offer the blood of fowls and beasts to the spirits. Both men and women were very quiet and well-behaved, the women being particularly shy.

A few days afterwards, another batch of Mussus came down, expressly to see the *farang* who, they said, they had heard was so liberal ; and so to maintain my reputation I had to treat them to a sixpence apiece, and to make a few small purchases. The chief, true to his word, brought me the bow and arrows, for which I gave him a gift of tobacco and a piece of cloth.

With the help of the Chow Radjasee I was enabled to obtain a few more particulars concerning the customs of these people.

When any one dies, the body is dressed in white cloth, and the whole tribe is summoned, men, women, and children, to mourn round the corpse—no crocodile's tears, the people are bound to weep.

"But what about those who cannot summon tears?" I interrupted. Artificial means are resorted to ; a quantity of chillies—which the Mussus grow largely— are held under the nose, or in the mouth, and that will make the eyes water.

When any one wants to marry, offerings are made to the spirit, and a general feast given to the people. I asked the chief if any one had ever seen a spirit; whereupon he gave a very quick answer. "They are like the wind," he said, "one cannot see them."

I had not been here more than two or three days when I discovered that, although I was supposed to be the guest of the Chow Radjasee, I was practically living at the expense of the community at large; for the slaves of my host were sent round every morning to the people, collecting fowls, eggs, fruit, and other comestibles, which the common folk did not dare to refuse to deliver on demand. The whole social system here, indeed, seems to be based on a recognized round of begging or borrowing, so that the borrower of a fowl to-day is asked to lend a few eggs to-morrow, and so on, right round the circle. For myself, I endeavoured to set a good example by promptly paying for everything that I wanted, but I was continually

besieged by applicants for needles, candles, skeins of
thread, bottles of scent, and other articles, of which I
had brought a small stock to give away, but any of
which could be bought at Chengmai, and most of which
I even found on sale in the small market here. I was
a frequent visitor to the market, for, as soon as I discovered the conditions on which the Chow Radjasee
supplied me with my "board," I did not allow the system
to continue, and went out every morning to lay in a daily
stock of food. The young girls and old women do all
the provisioning of the place, sitting half the day with
their baskets of rice, fowls, and eggs, before them. There
is very little downright buying and selling; hardly any
money changes hands, everything being done by
"exchange and barter."

Neither guest nor host, I think, regretted my determination to take into my own hands my commis-
sariat arrangements. The chief's *menu* comprised rice,
chillies, and dried putrid fish, diversified occasionally
with an egg more or less nearly approaching a state
of rottenness. I asked him one day if he did not eat
poultry or fresh eggs, which were very cheap, fifteen
eggs costing a "fuang," or one-eighth of a rupee, and
eight fowls a rupee. He laughed, and replied "Sometimes"—"once a month," I believe he added. This
abstemiousness was purely the result of the native
meanness of character, for, although the Chow had
many fowls brought to the house as the result of the
requisitioning expeditions of his slaves, he preferred to
sell them whenever a buyer offered. He could, however, enjoy a dinner of roast chicken as much as any-
body, and as I always passed on to my host and
hostess whatever remained from my meals, after I had
taken to provisioning myself, this accommodation was
mutually advantageous, and the chief and his wife

visibly improved in appearance under the more
generous diet.

The Laosians take their meals twice daily, at about
seven in the morning and towards sunset. They sit
in a circle on the floor, or on mats, with a lacquer or
brazen tray before them, on which are placed a number of saucers or small bowls containing dried or boiled
fish, bits of buffalo-meat stewed, a salted egg, or a
piece of the favourite pork: all these meats are
invariably served with rice and curry. For vegetables
they eat stewed bamboo shoots—not at all a bad substitute for asparagus—beans, plantains, tamarinds, and
powdered capsicums. Pervading everything is the
inevitable fishy flavour, which, like the garlic among
the Spaniards, is never absent. This is imparted by
adding to the dishes a small quantity of rotten fish—
the *ngapee* of the Burmese—the preparation of which is
as much an art among Laosians and Siamese, Burmese
and Malays, as the anxious endeavour on the part of
the European housewife to keep her fish fresh. The
rice, simply boiled or steamed, is served separately to
each person in a small basket; and coarse salt is also
provided separately; many persons, indeed, carrying
about a supply of salt with them. From the basket
of dry rice a small quantity is taken with the fingers
and rolled between the hands into a ball, which is then
dipped into one or more of the various curries and
flavouring dishes. Plates are as little known as knives
and forks, and that is not at all. Among the very
poor a plantain-leaf, always at hand, and easily thrown
away, involving neither cost nor trouble in " washing
up," takes the place of the bowls or saucers which the
better classes use. Strict silence is observed at meal-
times, and when the repast is finished a small quantity
of water is drunk from the heavy clay decanters or

goblets, which are passed round, each person rinsing out his or her mouth, and ejecting the contents into a spittoon, or, if this convenient receptacle be wanting, through an equally convenient hole in the floor.

The princess, my hostess, was in the crockery trade, and dealt in china cups, among other things. One day she sold fourteen cups of the commonest Chinese make to a visitor for two rupees, and tried to induce me to invest in some of a slightly better quality at a considerably higher price. Failing in this, she pressed me—with a quiet persuasiveness and importunity which would have made her fortune as a saleswoman in a Paris *boutique*—to purchase some hair, warranted human, and cut from the living head. This is a common article of trade, and is eagerly bought by Chinese and Burmese; the former to add to the length of their pigtails, the latter to increase the bulk of their topknots. When I explained that I indulged neither in the distinction of a pigtail nor in the luxury of a topknot, the commercial instincts of my distinguished hostess were not at all abashed, and she replied that I could easily sell the hair again when I got back to Bangkok. It certainly did not cost much to make a grand display of pigtail, for she offered me a thick tuft of hair over two feet long for a rupee.

CHAPTER XXV.

THE town of Kiang Hai is a small place, not a
shadow of the important city it is represented to have
been 400 years ago. It has a population of about
3500 men, and the province of which it is the capital
numbers 2000 men more. Of these the Chow Operat,
who, like the Chow Operat of Chengmai is, *de facto*,
supreme chief, claims the allegiance of 1500 men, the
rest adhering to the Chow Hluang and minor chiefs.

In front of the court of justice I noticed an "instrument of torture " precisely similar to the " stocks "
which were formerly used in this country as a means
of punishing certain classes of offenders—two large
planks fixed between uprights, with circular holes cut
through just where the edges of the two boards meet.
The upper board being raised, the prisoner's feet are
passed through the holes, from which, when the plank
is closed down, they cannot be removed. I never saw
these " stocks " in use, but near the " town-hall," *i.e.*
the house at which all official business is transacted, I

saw half a dozen prisoners chained together by the feet, awaiting trial for having kidnapped slaves and sold them at Hluang Prabang. The Chow told me that for a robbery of over a thousand rupees, or for killing or stealing an elephant, the punishment of death is inflicted.

There are several temples in the town, but all of them in a miserably dilapidated and dirty condition, with priests who, if they are devout, certainly do not exemplify the adage that cleanliness is next to godliness. It was in one of these temples that the famous Emerald Buddha, now at Bangkok, was discovered 400 years ago.

In all respects the people are on a par with the town they live in : of all Laosians those living in the extreme north are the most backward ; and from what has already been said, it will be gathered that the instincts of the people generally are not of a very high order.

They are mean to a degree ; liberality and generosity are words they do not understand ; they are devoid of ordinary human sympathy, being eaten up by an absorbing desire to keep themselves—each man for himself—out of the clutches of the spirits. Their highest earthly ambition is to hoard up money, vessels and ornaments of gold and silver, and anything else of value ; as to the means adopted for obtaining which they are not over scrupulous.

They are extremely untruthful, and wonderfully apt at making excuses ; and think no more of being discovered in a lie than of being seen smoking. I give them the credit, however, of being, generally speaking, moral in their domestic relations.

If a man's face is an index to his feelings, then the Laosians must be bereft of all capacity to appreciate any variety of mental emotions. It is the rarest phenomenon to see any change in their countenance or deportment, except—there is always one exception to every rule—when they are aroused to anger. This statement is more particularly true of the men, but even the women—demonstrative as the sex usually are—are seldom moved to either laughter or tears. Whatever news a Laosian may receive, whether of disaster or of joy, he hears it with a philosophic indifference depicted on his calm stoical countenance that a European diplomatist would give a fortune to be able to imitate. But when any sudden feeling of anger or any latent resentment is aroused, then the passion begins to display itself, if not in any great change of facial expression, at any rate in general demeanour, and in quick restless movements of impatience and irritation.

This natural stoical indifference to their surroundings is fostered by the influence of their religious belief, and by the general state of ignorance in which the people are kept, as well as by their isolation from the rest of the world. They are naturally lazy, and, with a fertile soil which provides them with all the necessaries of life without any appreciable effort on their part, their indolence is encouraged. In their opinion a man is an animal with a certain capacity to eat and drink, with certain duties to perform in order to keep body and soul together, and with the liability to pay a certain amount annually for the support of his chiefs. As to improving his own material or social position, he has no idea of such a possibility, except by indulging in the favourite vice of avariciously hoarding up all the money and other valuables he can lay his hands upon.

Their lives are consequently monotonous, and, to a

European, intolerably dull. Throughout the country, and particularly in the remoter districts, stagnation reigns over everything but Nature—man himself not excepted.

The women do all the really hard work which falls to the lot of the Laosians. They plant the rice, they gather the harvest, they husk and clean it, they cook it and they help to eat it, and this is one of the few things they do on an equality with the men.

The men certainly make a great show of helping their " better halves " during the planting season, but they are present rather as spectators than as workers, and allow the women to monopolize the honour and privilege of doing all the hard labour. If a man is making love to a girl, he will so far condescend as to take advantage of the opportunity for a *tête-à-tête* which the process of husking the paddy offers.

The primitive apparatus with which this is done consists of a beam of wood through which, at about a fourth of its length, a pivot is passed, each end of which rests in a groove in a small block of wood just high enough to raise the beam from the ground; at the extremity of the longest end of this beam is fixed a wooden head which is raised by pressing on the shorter end of the beam, and then allowed to fall upon the rice, which is placed in a wooden vessel on the ground. This work affords capital exercise, some considerable amount of exertion being required to raise the heavy beam, and the young women, who perform this duty night and morning, do not object to the proffered assistance of their lovers.

When the paddy has undergone a sufficient thrashing under the blows of the heavy " pestle," a lighter one is brought into requisition to give the finishing touches. It is then placed in a circular flat basket, and winnowed by the simple expedient of throwing it into the air.

The granaries in which the paddy is stored are huge, plaited-bamboo, barrel-shaped baskets, large enough to hold several hundredweights of rice apiece. In order to keep rats and insects out, these baskets are plastered with buffalo-dung, and dried in the sun.

While the women are engaged in these duties, or the similar ones of drying fish, weaving, and making clothes, the men now and then go into the forest with their cattle and elephants, cut wood, collect bamboo, or gather grass for roofing, never forgetting before going to work to make their offerings in the nearest temple.

Such is a sketch of the every-day occupations of the people. Their life is a dreary round of listless existence. Of amusements they have few.

Like the Siamese, the Laosians are fond of music, but they seem to have, besides their gongs and drums, nothing but a sort of reed organ which may be occasionally heard played by a group of children or young men. Their outdoor sports are made subservient to the necessity for providing the means of subsistence. The only pastime in which men and women equally engage is that of fishing, in which they are adepts, and here it is not the sport, but the prospect of getting the food, that is the attraction.

The people are hardy, and stand their variable climate well, sleeping on the ground at night with a fire round them, with the double object of keeping them warm and frightening away wild beasts, but with nothing but a cotton blanket round them, although the dew falls heavily, and, during the dry (and cool) season, which lasts from November to May, the temperature early in the morning varies from 40° to 50° Fahr. It is true they complain of cold, and suffer occasionally from dysentery and fever, but they will endure a considerable amount of exposure.

At the dry season the climate is somewhat similar to that of the spring in this country : but not a drop of rain falls during that period ; the trees and grass look withered and dead, and the whole course of vegetation seems interrupted ; only the orchids, which flourish in great numbers and in beautiful variety, showing any signs of life. But in May a sudden vigour seems to be imparted to everything. The rice-planting begins with the first fall of rain, which is often heralded by violent hurricanes and hail-storms, and in a few days the new leaves begin to shoot forth rapidly, and the whole face of nature assumes its most beauteous and smiling aspect. With the rainy season intense heat prevails, and before the end of May the thermometer registers 95° to 100° in the shade in the afternoon.

The primitive Laosians, as I term those living in or near the forests in small villages or hamlets, are very dirty in their habits. I noticed, not once, but over and over again throughout the country, that when they prepare fish or a piece of meat they never wash it clean first—this they say would spoil it—but they leave all the dirt on, and simply roast it over the fire, or boil it in a kettle made of a thick cylinder of bamboo. The same with the rice they eat ; it contains some ten per cent. of dirt.

Like the Siamese, the Lao people are, in all probability, of a common origin with the Malay race, dating back to that remote period when Sumatra and Borneo were connected with the mainland. Unlike the Siamese, however, as well as the Malays inhabiting the mainland, who are both much intermixed with Chinese, Cambodians, Peguans, and other peoples, the Laosians keep themselves distinct, and are consequently of a much purer type. I never saw, nor did I ever hear of, a single Lao man who had married a Siamese woman, although the Laosian women are, from their superior physique and better features, as well as from their fairer skin, often sought for in marriage by the richer Siamese.

The colour of the Laosians is much lighter than that of the Siamese : for greater accuracy of comparison I may refer those curious in such matters to Nos. 29, 30, and 37, of Professor Broca's colour-types (in " Anthropological Notes and Queries "); No. 30 bears perhaps the most exact resemblance to the Lao colour, except that it wants a slight red tint.

In Chengmai I saw two albinoes, both with a light reddish skin, white hair, resembling a very pale glossy hemp, and pink eyes, which they were in the habit of blinking much in the daytime, being unable without difficulty to bear the strong light. These albinoes were sisters, with a difference of four years between their ages.

Besides these *lusus naturæ*, I · heard of several hermaphrodites.

The women are always paler in complexion than the men, with rather an olive tint, closely approaching to No. 44 of Broca's types. The hair is coarse and straight, and of a glossy black, with occasionally a brown tinge.

In facial expression the Laosians are better-looking than the Malays, having good high foreheads, and the men particularly having regular and well-shaped noses, with nostrils not so wide as those of their neighbours. The lips, however, and more especially the upper lip, are somewhat protruding ; the eyes are slightly oblique. The women when young, often have fat moon-shaped faces, and are frequently disfigured by large wens.

A peculiar accomplishment of the women, and one which the men sometimes imitate, is to bend the elbow-joint the wrong way, so that the arm is not merely straightened, but bent backwards, the inner side of the arm being bent outwards like the elbow. · The wrist-joint is similarly distorted, so that the hand can be bent over till the back of it touches the arm. The chief of Chengmai, who has acquired both these elegant accomplishments, and can do the backward bend of arm and wrist to perfection, told me that in order to be able to accomplish this feat—which is also a fashionable trick throughout Siam—the girls have to begin to practise it when quite young, and that force is often resorted to in order to distort nature's handiwork.

What the natives sadly want is a better outlet for their trade than they at present enjoy. If they had better means of sending their produce to market, and if they could adopt more enlightened and liberal ideas of what is expected of a trading community, they might exchange their present state of poverty for one of average prosperity. Whether their meanness is a cause or a result of their practical isolation from the rest of the world, it is hard to say. They have fine timber in abundance; they grow, or could grow, cotton in plenty; their cattle are numerous; their forests are well stocked with deer and elephants, and the rivers teem with fish; but their trade is limited to a small exchange of dried fish, cotton, deer-horns, and a few tusks of ivory, for the scanty merchandize brought by the Yunnan and Ngiou traders, who make Kiang Hai a centre from which they radiate in different directions to Chengmai, Hluang Prabang, and Muang Nan. One curious article of trade which deserves mention is found in the skins of the scaly ant-eaters. These animals abound near

Y

Kiang Hai, and their skins are valuable as medicine.

One day the Chow Operat's son returned from a
hunting expedition, bringing back a trophy in the
shape of a female rhinoceros. Here was an opportunity for Kao to recoup himself for his bad bargain
in rhinoceros-blood at Muang Fang, so he bought
several pieces of the hoof and hide of the beast, in
order to prove to his future customers at Bangkok
that the bullock's blood which he had on his hands
was the "real article." He also purchased a small
quantity of the genuine blood for his personal use, and
at the same time secured a few chips of the horn.
Rhinoceros-horns are worth, according to size, from
10*l.* to 50*l.* apiece, for medicinal purposes. "It
strengthens the body," Kao said. All Chinese drugs
seem to have the same property !

I gave the Chow a breechloader and a few cartridges
in return for the skull of the pachyderm.

The flesh and the thick hide were reserved as deli-
cacies for the natives, who greatly relish this kind of
"game." They eat almost anything, from buffalo to
tiger, monkey, and rhinoceros—hide as well as flesh.

I often paid a visit to the Chow Operat's wife, a kind
and obliging old lady, who used to send me presents
of rice and plantains, in return for which I gave her a
bottle of scent, and a needle-case, with which she was
extremely delighted. She lived in a large, roomy,
teak-built house, and was always busy making silken
garments, while one of her slaves worked at the loom
spinning silk thread. The Chow Operat, as rumour
has it, is very rich, having a good deal of cash, besides
some sixty elephants ; but even a wealthy princess is
not exempt from the necessity for making the silken
garments which are the symbol of her rank, any more

than the poorer women can do without weaving their cotton clothes. Many of the "upper classes" are also skilled in embroidering the cushions or pillows which take the place of chairs. Much of the women's time

Laosian on a journey.

again, whether rich or poor, is taken up in making clothing for the priests.

The principal garment of a Lao man is the *patoi*, which corresponds to the Siamese *pa-nung* or *palai*, and consists simply of a piece of cotton cloth, or silk, about two or two and a half yards long, and from two to three feet wide. This simple garment is as simply worn ; neither string nor button is used, and no seam is needed to make it adapt its shape to the figure of the wearer. Passed round the body and hanging from the waist downwards, the two ends are held together in front, and then rolled or twisted up till they meet the body. The end of the roll, which often reaches to the ground, is picked up, passed between the legs, and tucked into the upper edge of the cloth at the back. Thus fixed, the *patoi* will keep itself in position ; but the better classes generally use a belt, often of European manufacture, and ornamented, in the case of the princes and wealthier people, with a buckle inlaid with precious stones.

When the ordinary Laosian goes boating, or into the fields or forests to labour, he tucks up the lower edge of his *patoi* for convenience-sake, thus displaying to advantage the charms of his tattooed thighs. Stuck in this *patoi*, at the back, he carries his hatchet or knife.

These garments are generally home-spun, nearly every house having, either in one of the rooms or in the space under the house, a native loom. Cotton is very plentiful in Lao, and very cheap. Some of the princes go in for silk [1] with a few stripes of gold thread introduced. The colours mostly chosen are either dark blue—the most popular of all—orange yellow, maroon, or chocolate. One colour is generally thought sufficient, but in Lakon, where the people are less dis-

---

[1] The cocoons of the wild silkworm are collected, and employed in the manufacture of native silk fabrics. The quality is coarse, and the supply insufficient for the home demand, considerable quantities of silk being bought from the Yunnan traders in exchange for the Lao cotton, of which far more than enough for local consumption is grown.

ciples of the "æsthetic" school than their neighbours, a check pattern of blue, yellow, and red is very fashionable.

During the cold season, when the thermometer marks as low as 45° Fahr., both men and women wear a large thick cotton shawl, nearly always in red and white stripes; besides this, they have a long scarf of cotton, or, on state occasions, of silk, either yellow, white, or pink. This is worn round the waist, not round the neck, or thrown across one shoulder. The princes and nobles wear a tight-fitting jacket of cotton or silk.

Laosian with the thermometer at 50°.

At this time, too, the men wear sandals, simply made of two pieces of buffalo-hide sewn together round the edges by a thread made of sinews.

Of head-coverings there is quite a variety; every district seeming to have its own peculiar local fashion in the matter. The most common kind is made of strips of palm-leaves, partly overlapping each other and sewn together; the shape is somewhat that of the typical "planter's hat," without, however, a definite crown, the broad brim gradually curving inwards and upwards to the top, which is flat. In the far north, the huge but very practical and useful Yunnan straw hats, which serve equally as a shelter from the sun and from the rain, are to be bought at a price of from four to eight rupees apiece. The palm hat of the Ngious is also frequently worn, as well as a stitched cotton skull-cap, padded with cotton wool. This cap is a favourite head-gear of the priests.

So much for the men's fashions. I will now describe the very becoming costume worn by the women. The principal garment, which answers the same purpose as the European petticoat, corresponds with the *patoi* worn by the men, with the important difference that it is composed of three distinct pieces, generally of different colours and materials, sewn together. The main portion of the garment, or that part which covers the body from about the breast to the knees, is made, for ordinary wear, of cotton, and, for gala purposes, of silk. It measures from twenty to twenty-two inches in breadth from top to bottom. It is always of a striped pattern, the usual colours being yellow, blue, and red; the stripes, though made lengthwise in the material, being worn horizontally round the body. Above this, just reaching to the breast, is a narrow strip of black, dark-brown, or white cotton stuff, while below hangs a cotton border, about a foot deep, in dark red or dark brown. When the " body " is made of silk, this border is made of the same material, often beautifully interwoven with gold and silver threads. These rich borders sometimes cost as much as sixty rupees apiece, while the whole garment, when made entirely of cotton, strong and durable as it is, does not cost more than from one and a half to two rupees. The garment thus complete is called a *sĭn*.[2] It is worn by

[2] Pronounced short. When used with the *i* pronounced long the word signifies " keeping the sacred day."

being passed round the body, with the ends overlapping and tucked in at the waist behind.

Above the *sin*, and partially covering the breast is worn a calico shawl or scarf, called a *pahtong*, either white, yellow, or light pink, the last-named being the favourite colour. This is worn in various ways according to individual taste; either thrown across one shoulder, passing across the breast, under the opposite arm and round the back, till the end reaches over the shoulder again from which it started, when the end hangs down in front, or simply tied firmly round the breast under the arms.

A few Lao women are beginning to wear tight-fitting jackets, cut to the shape of the figure, with equally tight sleeves, something after the style of the "ladies' jerseys" recently so fashionable in Paris and London, and involving no small amount of labour to get on and off, being made, not of elastic knitted work, but of unyielding cotton or silk. But this innovation spoils the pleasing appearance of the women in their ordinary dress. No women in the East wear so simple and at the same time so becoming an attire as the *sin* and *pahtong* of the Laosians. When the colours are nicely blended—and to do the ladies justice they generally are—the effect is very pleasing, the garments showing off to advantage the erect and well-balanced bodies of the women, and not hampering their naturally free and graceful movements. Nor is their appearance disfigured by any unbecoming head-gear. The women allow the hair to grow long, and, after plentifully smothering it with grease, they tie it up in a neat knot at the back of the head, never without a wreath of flowers encircling it. Sometimes a bunch of flowers or an orchid is also stuck in at the side, or fastened above the ear. Both men and women are passionately fond of flowers, and nature has given them the means of indulging their tastes to the full, for the forests teem with flowers, among them being the most lovely orchids, many of them scented.

Sometimes the hair is fastened, or rather ornamented, with a gold hair-pin, the head of which is usually in the shape of a pyramid of small plain or chased beads or knobs.

Gold or silver bracelets are worn on state occasions, either plain, or in a twisted pattern like a rope, or formed of a series of small rings or links.

The men wear their hair in a peculiar fashion, the head being cut closely or shaved all round with only a tuft left growing on the crown, where it is trimmed off evenly like a brush.

Like the Malays and Dyaks, the Laos are devoid of that facial ornament a beard, and any stray hairs which appear, as they sometimes do, on the lip or chin are remorselessly plucked out. Once a Lao man with a pair of whiskers was pointed out to me as a curiosity.

In publishing these notes, and the other information scattered through the pages of this book, on the people of Western Lao, the so-called " black-bellied" Laosians, I must ask the indulgence of the reader for the meagreness of the details given on certain points, on the ground of the great difficulty which is designedly placed in the way of all strangers seeking information about them or their country. What I have written, however, may at least be regarded as trustworthy, being either—and chiefly—from personal observation, or from the particulars kindly furnished to me by the two able missionaries, Dr. Cheek and Mr. John Wilson, who from their long residence in Lao have been able to collect information not otherwise obtainable.

CHAPTER XXVI.

The Chow Hluang of Kiang Hai—Hostilities with the Ngious—A
travelled Lao prince—Anecdotes of Kiang Tung—Troubles
threatening—Starting for the Ngiou States—A cyclone—Displaying the Siamese standard—An unmannerly Chow—Rumours
of war—Phee-ka, the spirit-complaint—Exiles—More ruined
topes and Buddha figures—Beautiful scenery—Return to Kiang
Hai—The Chow's baby is ill—Native doctor's prescription—
Diseases and doctors—Spirit-doctors—A royal spirit-medium—
Spirit-dances and dancers—Tjang-too : a miraculous power.

In the evening of the 21st of March I paid a visit
to the Chow Hluang, an old man between sixty and
seventy years of age, who lived in a miserable house
worthy of his miserable capital. I asked him about
continuing my journey through Kiang Tung into
Yunnan, but he said it could not be done. He could
not risk his elephants across the frontier, for the
people were not friendly with the Ngious, who were
suspected of a design to come to Kiang Tsen with the
object of recapturing the town.

This piece of information received unexpected corro-
boration, in the following manner. One afternoon I
called upon the Radjawong, a prince who takes rank
next after the Chow Operat. He was very chatty,
and, among other things, told me he had been as far
as Kiang Tung, where he had remained five months.
He related some curious customs prevalent there. For
example, when a man steals a horse, his arms and legs

are secured, and he is fastened by a rope to a horse, which is made to gallop and drag him to death. If a pig is stolen, the thief is bound, the skin of a pig is put round him, which is set on fire, and thus he is tortured to death. Notwithstanding these punishments, he said, many robberies were committed, especially on strangers, and he strongly advised me not to enter the Ngiou country. Besides, Kiang Tung was in a disorganized state; the chief was constantly praying in the Wats, or getting drunk: at seven in the evening he would begin drinking, and go on right through the night, sleeping only in the morning, and never to be seen except at noon. This conduct had so incensed the king of Burmah, that he had given the reins of government to the Chow Fa of Kiang Keng. During the summer at Kiang Tung, the Chow added, the heat was so great in the daytime that the natives could not lie on the mats without first damping them with water. While all these amusing stories were being told, a messenger came in and read a letter from the chief of Kiang Tsen to say that the Ngious there were making powder and bullets, in expectation of the arrival of a neighbouring Ngiou chief, who was coming to claim half the province of Kiang Tsen.

Still I determined to see for myself if it were not possible to accomplish my design, and on the 25th of March—Lady Day—I surrendered my temporary tenancy of the apartments in the residence of the Chow, and continued my journey down the Mekok to Kiang Tsen in a large boat kindly lent to me by the chief of Kiang Hai. I started at seven a.m., followed by an old Phya and his suite, bent on watching my movements and reporting them, as I afterwards found out, at Muang Fang. The river was full of sand-banks, and the navigation was precarious, until, in the afternoon of the second day, we entered the Mekong—a glorious stream, twice as wide here, a thousand miles from its mouth, as the Menam at Bangkok, deep and with a rapid current, for the country, which had hitherto been comparatively flat, now began to get hilly.

Just as we debouched into the main stream, the sky suddenly darkened, and a chill wind burst upon us. In the distance, in a westerly direction, was a thick cloud, only a few feet above the surface of the river, which rapidly swooped down upon us—a whirling mass of dust, chips, leaves, grass, and twigs of trees. The cyclone made straight for us, with a roaring sound, lashing the water into foam, till it resembled quite a little sea. Fortunately we were close to the shore, and were able to make the boat fast to the bank with three stout rattan ropes, just before the eye of the storm reached us. Even so we were very nearly swamped, and what the wind did not accomplish the rain effected pretty completely. Amid a volley of thunder, and a perfect blaze of almost incessant lightning-flashes, the rain came down, as it can come down only in the tropics, in a deluge, and found its way through the grass roofing of the boat, till the vessel was half full of water. Some of the men, who were shivering, and complaining *Nau! Nau!* (cold), squeezed themselves into the cabin for shelter, while the rest hid themselves in the thick jungle on shore. By the time the first violence of the storm was over, everything was soaking wet; it was impossible to sleep, either in the boat or ashore, but the men were unwilling to move, and preferred the misery of a damp bed to the alternative of a little extra labour. Finding they showed no inclination to do as I told them, and row up the river towards Kiang Tsen, I cut the rattan ropes by which we were

moored to the shore, and the boat began to drift rapidly
down stream. In a moment they sprang to the oars,
and a few minutes later we fortunately came in sight
of two boats fastened to the shore. From this I knew
there must be a habitation near at hand, and, following
a narrow path leading from the water's edge into
the forest, I came upon a couple of miserable huts.
The inhabitants were amazed to see a white man, but
very soon agreed to give me and my men a night's
shelter. The accommodation was not of the first class,
but even a leaky roof was better than no shelter at all,
and " sleep, gentle sleep, nature's soft nurse," soon
" steeped my senses in forgetfulness " of all my surroundings.

Kiang Tsen, I learnt next morning, was distant only
an hour by water from here, so, before starting, I fixed
a pole in the stern of the boat, from which I displayed
the Siamese royal standard—the handsome and characteristic white-elephant flag—in order that I might
enter this the most northerly town in the dominions
under the rule of the king of Siam, with as much *éclat*
as possible. An hour's " poling " against a stiff current,
in a due westerly direction, brought us to Kiang
Tsen, where our arrival created some little stir among
the sleepy inhabitants. I was installed in a neat little
hut, recently occupied by a Chengmai prince, and
improved the occasion by hoisting the royal banner on
a staff directly in front of my temporary residence.

The inhabitants, mostly Laosians, had only been here
about three years, the town having been captured from
the Ngious by the Chengmai people; and they had
never before seen the royal standard of the sovereign
to whom they owed allegiance displayed here.

Almost immediately after landing, I paid a visit of
respect to the Chow—a Lampoon prince whose chief

characteristic seemed to be a desire to make himself
as disobliging as possible. Fortunately, although he
might be very disagreeable, he could not do me any
material harm, for his authority was of very limited
extent; so much so that, as I had been informed at
Chengmai, I did not need a special letter of introduction to him, that to the chief of Kiang Hai covering
the chief of Kiang Tsen as well.

I asked his chiefship to let me have some men to
hunt in the surrounding forests, where, judging from
their size, and from the fact that the population hereabouts was sparser than ever, I hoped to get some
zoological specimens. His curt reply was that he had
no men. I should have thought, from the long array
of titled officers in the place—ranging from Chow
Hluang and Chow Operat to Radjawong and Radjaput
—and of plain Chows innumerable, that there were not
only men but officials enough to run a first-class
empire, as the Americans would say. But the Chow
was neither to be reasoned, nor—what was " passing
strange "—even to be bribed, into being courteous, and
still refused when I made it clear to him that I would
not only pay the men, and supply them with powder and
shot, but would give him a present into the bargain.

So I tried to make friends with the people, but the
times were not propitious. Men's minds were unsettled
by a rumour that a force of 2000 Burmese had joined
the Ngious, and had settled in the mountains a few
miles off, where they were busy making powder and
bullets, with the intention of making a swoop down on
Kiang Tsen, and recapturing it—a rumour which
entirely confirmed what the Chow Hluang at Kiang
Hai had told me.

This expectation of imminent hostilities completely
precluded all possibility of entering the Ngiou States.

The Chow absolutely refused to allow any of his people to go, either by land or by water, across the frontier, and, even if he had ordered them to do so, I doubt if they would have obeyed him. They were altogether about as churlish a community, as a whole, as I have ever come across, though, perhaps, some excuse may be found for them in the fact that they were nearly all exiles, having been banished from their homes and sent to this distant spot on suspicion of being affected with " Phee-ka."

Phee-ka is an evil spirit through whose supposed presence hundreds of people are annually driven from their homes. The method adopted to discover if any one is possessed of this devil is as follows: when a native is in a high fever, the spirit-doctor, who does duty in Lao for the medical man, is called in, and proceeds to tie cords tightly round the upper arm of the patient, and then runs his finger down the course of the veins, causing them to swell till they stand out in great knots, which look ready to burst, and in which Phee-ka is supposed to be located. The patient is then cudgelled, both mentally and physically, being tormented with questions, on the one hand, and his swollen veins beaten or pricked with sharp-pointed pieces of iron, on the other, until he gives an affirmative reply to the inquiry whether he is under the spell of any particular person whose name is mentioned. If he answers that he is, or in his delirium calls out the name of any other individual, the person so named—and not the patient—is accused of being Phee-ka, and accordingly denounced and sentenced to exile. His dwelling is burnt, his trees are cut down, his rice-fields seized, and he is driven from his home with all his family, to make a fresh start in life elsewhere—always in a different province from that which originally claimed him as a citizen. Before leaving Chengmai I noticed a considerable stir in the town one day, and observed a number of families, men, women, and children, hurriedly preparing to leave their homes. On inquiring the cause of this sudden emigration, I was told that the unfortunate people were to be banished to this very place, Kiang Tsen, because they were afflicted with Phee-ka.

The town itself, situated on the left bank of the river, at an altitude of about 870 feet above the level of the sea, was in a generally uncomfortable state, but bore traces, in the ruins of numerous temples, of having been of some importance in former times. Disappointed in my intention of collecting birds and animals, I carefully examined many of the ruins, which showed signs of quaint architectural design, and of much better workmanship than any other similar structure I had seen further south. Some of the topes had been profusely decorated with carvings and other ornamental work, both inside and out, but they had every one been desecrated and destroyed by the invading Laosians, who had removed everything of intrinsic value.

The ground was covered with numberless bronze figures of Buddha, some of them of gigantic size. To these the neighbouring Ngious still came at regular intervals to make their offerings of flowers, rice, and gold-leaf, with the last of which they gilded the figures ; and this fact seemed to give some colour to the rumour that they would not be content till they had had their revenge on the invaders.

I went inside several of the ruined phrachedees, in one of which I found a figure of Buddha, sitting under a canopy, with the five-headed serpent coiled round him. In securing this figure I was nearly suffocated, for the air inside the tope was so fœtid that I had to go outside two or three times to breathe. The natives told me that the figure was a very rare representation of Buddha ;[1] indeed, I have not seen more than half a dozen of the same pattern in all the Siamese and Laosian temples I have entered.

The country round the settlement was most beautiful —the most charming, I think, that I met with in my travels in Indo-China. The river flows along its deep channel some fifteen feet below the edge of its banks. On the right side, stretching behind the town, far into the Ngiou country, the mountains rise terrace above terrace, range above range ; while, in the opposite direction, in the country known as Komaw, on the left side of the Mekong and extending to the borders of Tongking, lie a series of hills and valleys, clothed with magnificent forests of teak, and endless varieties of gum-yielding trees, which would, if properly worked, be a source of enormous wealth. A careful survey of the country to the east should be made, to discover, if possible, a water-route, shorter than that down the Mekong, along which the timber could be floated to the coast. The climate of this region is much more temperate than that of Siam, owing to the height of the land, which gradually rises from 700 feet at Chengmai to 1200 feet at Muang Fang, but diminishes again to 1150 feet at Kiang Hai, and 870 feet at Kiang Tsen. I frequently found the temperature here as low as 50° at eight o'clock in the morning.

After a short stay at Kiang Tsen I returned to Kiang Hai, and again took up my abode with my former host, who, as soon as he noticed the image which I had brought from the ruins at Kiang Tsen,

[1] See p. 284.

objected to its being carried indoors, on the ground that it would cause spirits to visit his house, and ordered the figure to be taken to the temple opposite, where it could remain till I left.

I am afraid the goodnatured but superstitious Chow must have thought that either I or my idol, or both, really did bring illness and ill-luck to his house, for his baby, who was just recovering from an attack of fever, had a relapse, and became much worse soon after my return. Thereupon one of the slaves set to work to make a couple of clay figures, bearing some faint resemblance to a buffalo, and placed them, along with some rice, curry, and fish, on a tray made of bits of the stem of the plantain, under the verandah. The whole thing looked very much like a bird-trap, but I suppressed any desire to make irreverent comparisons, and, on inquiring what was the object of this operation, was informed that it was to drive away the offended spirits. I fancy I detected a sly glance towards myself of anything but goodwill in the slave's eye when this answer was given, as if I were held to be the incarnation of the evil spirits ; but I drove away the thought, and heartily wished the baby might recover.

An hour later the " doctor " came ; a tall, well-built, middle-aged man, carrying a silver bowl containing some mixture which I innocently took to be medicine. The infant was brought out by the father, who held it in his lap while the " member of the faculty " recited some prayers or incantations, and wound up by smashing a couple of boiled eggs—Ugh ! the odour, they were rotten !—an act which, instead of soothing the child, had the effect of startling it and making it redouble its screams. He then tied a piece of string round the baby's wrists and took his departure, supported, no

z

doubt, by the strongest belief in his skill, and completely satisfied with the manner in which he had practised the healing art.

On the following day, I was informed, if the child did not get better, medicine would be brought into requisition. " But if it dies in the meantime," I thought, " I shall be charged with having been the original cause of its illness and death ! " I was delighted to find, however, that the little creature, being safeguarded by the bits of string and the rotten eggs against the machinations of the evil spirits, did get better, and did not even require any of the learned man's medicine. So the doctor took his fee, a few yards of white calico, with which, to judge by the string of " chow, chows," that he uttered, and the number of obeisances he made, he was highly delighted.

This gentleman was a " distinguished member of the medical profession" in Lao—a type of the " duly-qualified practitioners " who combine psychological with physiological practice, and try to carry out bodily cures through a " spiritual" medium. As a matter of course, while everybody is steeped in superstitious fear of the spirits, attributing every evil to their influence, there are the knowing ones who set up as " spirit-doctors," and prey upon the fears of others by pretending to drive away the evil spirits, to cure spirit-diseases, or, if need be, to bring neighbours and enemies under their influence. Professional spirit-doctors are to be found in every village, and their services are called into requisition in all cases of sickness, real or supposed. The common diseases of the country are malarial fevers, which are very prevalent, dysentery, and small-pox. At Lampoon I found many people suffering from stone ; and leprosy is also a very common complaint. Persons afflicted with this loathsome disease are not allowed to live in the towns, but are relegated to a special leper village.

When sickness occurs in a family, the first thing done is to propitiate the spirits. Offerings of rice and flowers are made, and tapers are kept burning near the patient for at least a day before medicines can be given.

What the medicines consist of I had great difficulty in finding out, and I only discovered the ingredients in one case. While I was at Muang Fang, my landlord's little girl was sadly troubled with boils. A woman was sent for who brought some dark-looking ointment in a saucer, and put it round the parts where the matter was, as she expressed it, "in bloom," and in a few minutes she said the boil would burst. Shortly after this application, with, I have no doubt, the assistance of a little pressure with her finger, the boil did burst, and a copious flow of discharge took place. What was this potent medecine composed of? I asked. Burnt plantain-skins, mixed with woman's milk, and a small quantity of the lime used in betel-chewing.

Besides depending on the paid services of professional advisers, nearly every family has its private "medium," and the new "Society of Psychical Research" might turn its attention to this new ground, where it would find ample field for investigation among a people fully imbued with a belief in the existence of a spiritual world with which they are in constant communion. For instance, in the family of the Chow Hluang of Chengmai the "medium" was the Princess Oobon Lawana, the sister of the chief's wife, a homely but eccentric lady, with whom I established such friendly relations during my stay in that town that I often spoke to her on the subject of her relations with the spirit-world. It was very difficult, however, to extract any information, and Dr. Cheek, who often tried to help me, was not much more successful in his efforts to " draw " the princess. She admitted, however, that she was called upon to question the spirits whenever any difficulty occurred either in public or private affairs. At such times she works herself into a state of great excitement, surrounding herself with a number of dancers, whom she occasionally joins in " tripping the light fantastic toe," every now and then ejaculating short sentences, which are regarded as the utterances of the spirits. My private opinion is that at such times the " medium " is indeed under the influence of spirits, but of a different kind from those with which she professes to be in communion ; material and not invisible; alcoholic and not ethereal. Certainly, if the princess herself does not partake too freely of samshu, the professional dancers engaged to assist her always manage to retire in a state of intoxication.

I have several times seen these spirit-dancers at work. On one occasion, while I was at Chengmai, the chief's wife was seized with illness, and Chow Oobon was called upon to ask the spirits the cause of this visitation. After a great deal of terpsichorean exercise, and the pouring out of the needful libations, the spirit was pleased to utter, through the medium of the princess, the following portentous warning : " The spirit forbids the whisky monopoly ! " There can be no doubt that spirits were at the bottom of that utterance, though its connexion with the illness of the chief's wife is not so clear !

On another occasion I saw a public exhibition of a " spirit-dance " in the streets of Chengmai. While strolling through the city, I heard in a narrow lane a great noise of shouting and rough " music," and found

a crowd of people with tom-toms and flutes encouraging
the frantic movements of a couple of elderly women,
who were dancing wildly about, pulling their hair, and
shouting at the top of their voice. These were professional spirit-dancers, who had been hired to drive
the spirits away from a neighbouring house.

These extraordinary superstitions of the people make
it very difficult for a foreigner to associate with them,
even when they are disposed to be friendly. If anything goes amiss—if it rains too much or too little,
if any one dies or is taken ill, if the tigers make a
night-raid, or somebody's buffalo or elephant strays
—the *farang* is at the bottom of it; his presence is
distasteful to the spirits, who show their anger by
causing a catastrophe, and acting in a generally disagreeable manner. The natives are then only too ready
to take the hint and make a scapegoat—or rather a
sacrifice—of the unfortunate *farang*. If the spirits
are anything like as unpleasantly-disposed beings as
the native Laosians believe them to be, I am not
surprised at their general hatred and fear of them.

The following narrative, the authenticity of which
was vouched for by one of the missionaries at Chengmai, will illustrate the extraordinary hold which
their superstitions have upon the people of Lao. It
sometimes happens that when a body is cremated the
whole corpse is not reduced to ashes, a certain
portion (probably part of the intestines) being found
in a solidified form, and only partially charred, instead
of being wholly calcined. The Laosians say that this
phenomenon is caused by the presence of pieces of
buffalo-hide, stones, bits of wood, or other similarly
uncomfortable objects which an enemy had, by super-
natural agency, caused to enter into the body of the
deceased person at some period of his life. The power

to do this unneighbourly act is known as " Tjang-too," and persons possessed of this faculty are supposed to be in the habit every seven days of burning the skins, bones, or horns of different animals, out of the ashes of which a peculiar insect is evolved. This insect then touches the body of the person whom it is desired to injure, carrying with it some hard substance, and causes his death, with the strange result that, upon cremation, this " foreign substance " remains unconsumed. A short time before my arrival, it appears that two Karians had gone to a certain man wishing to buy a musical instrument, which he refused to part with. Two days afterwards, this man died, and when, a fortnight later, his body was cremated, there was found among the ashes a peculiar substance which the natives declared to be the head of the very musical instrument which the Karians had wished to buy! This was quite sufficient evidence that the musical amateurs were possessed of the power of Tjang-too, and they were accordingly beheaded. The Siamese have a mortal fear of Tjang-too, and are very much afraid of the Laosians and Karians exercising this power.

CHAPTER XXVII.

A prevaricating Chow—An unexpected ally—Forcing the rapids—
Fresh disappointments—At Muang Fang again—New Year's
festivities—Fishing—The silver key—Carrying off my trophies
—Tribute to the priests—Homage to Buddha—Swearing
allegiance—Purification of the priests—More delays—An
appeal to Chengmai.

I WAS now anxious to get back to Chengmai, and
went to the chief to ask him to let me have thirty men
to go to Muang Fang, and carry away my luggage and
collection of figures. The chief raised the usual string
of objections and excuses. Like the famous story about
Queen Elizabeth and the bell-ringers, where the thirteenth
good reason for not ringing the bells on the occasion
of her most gracious Majesty's visit was that there
were no bells to ring—but differing from that veracious
chronicle to the extent that the last reason was not the
best, but the worst, of all, being simply untrue—the
list of reasons, good, bad, and indifferent, which the
Chow urged against compliance with my request, closed
with the barefaced statement that he had no men.
After much debate, he saw that the only way of escape
from my importunities was to stave me off with a
promise; and he undertook to let me have the thirty
men in a week's time. Now the Laosians are not
skilled in the art of making pies, but they make up
for any deficiency in this respect by fabricating an
overplus of promises, to which the proverb which couples

these two things together in the common fate of being broken applies with full force. I knew, therefore, very well that this particular promise, like every other, was a broken reed to lean on, and I was not surprised when my kind host informed me, a day or two later, that the Chow did not intend to keep to his bargain; but matters looked still less hopeful when he added that the Radjawong and Radjaput were scheming against me, and using their influence to confirm the chief in his resolution to break his word. So I sent a message to remind the Chow that the week's interval was drawing to a close and that I was anxious to make all my arrangements to bid him farewell. A messenger came back with the reply that I must be satisfied with fifteen men. To this I resolutely refused to consent, and I sent word back that I must have thirty coolies and two boats, or there would be trouble in store for somebody.

Thereupon the great gong was sounded, and the chiefs were summoned together to decide whether the Chow should go back from his plighted word. His two sons, I heard, were strongly of opinion that this would be the proper thing for their parent and ruler to do; but he proposed to compromise the matter by again offering to let half the number of men go with me, and to save his dignity by promising that the other half should *follow* me to Tatong. But I was rather too experienced a hand to be caught napping thus, and held the chief to his original bargain. Negotiations might have gone on thus indefinitely, but fortunately the Chow Operat, or rather, let me say to her honour, his wife, had, with a woman's wit, cut the Gordian knot by offering to supply me with the necessary tale of men herself, and so render me independent of the aid of the enlightened Chow Hluang and his obstructive sons. With a promptitude that deserves the fullest recognition, and which earned my lasting gratitude, the Chow Operat had four boats, manned by thirty men, ready on the following morning, April 7th, to start for Tatong; the Chow Operat's wife increasing the obligation under which I lay, by giving me a letter to the keeper of her plantain plantation at Ban Mejau, a small village a few miles up the river, with instructions to supply me with a quantity of this luscious fruit.

It was noon before our leave-taking was accomplished, and we started under a broiling sun, pulling against the current, which, owing to recent rains, was running strong. At five p.m. we halted at Ban Mejau, where we passed the night—a wet one unfortunately, for we were now just below a series of rapids, and every inch of rain that fell meant a large addition to the force of the current which we had to stem. The river here ran between almost perpendicular walls of rock, so that there was no chance of taking the boats or their freight overland, and there was nothing for it but to force the boats by the laborious exertion of "poling" by sheer strength of arms and legs up through the seething water. Every now and then, the crew, with an amount of courage with which I could hardly have credited them, would wade in the foaming torrent, amid jagged rocks where a stumble seemed to promise certain death, and, by means of rattan ropes, haul the boats up the rapids—their voices, as they urged each other to sturdier efforts, rising above even the din of the boiling mass of water as it rushed between or leaped over the impeding rocks. Twice my boat " shipped," in nautical parlance," a sea," and was nearly capsized. At one point, where there was a considerable fall, every bit of luggage had to be taken out of the boats, which were hauled up the face of the cataract amid a chorus of frantic cries, while the freight was carried round a narrow ledge of dry rock. For three days, more or less continuously, this kind of work had to be repeated, while we could find no suitable camping-place on which to land, and had to moor at night to the edge of the river. At last we reached a sand-bank, where the camp-fires could be lit and a comfortable meal cooked.

On the fourth day Tatong was reached. Here I left three men to look after the boats, while I took the others overland to Muang Fang, calling *en route* at Mau Sua's hut, where another disappointment awaited me; for during the whole time I had been away he had shot absolutely nothing. When I remonstrated with him, he said he had had orders from Chengmai not to shoot, adding that instructions had been sent everywhere to the people to place every obstacle in my way. He actually produced a letter from the Chow Operat at Chengmai, stating that the orders of the Chow Hluang were to be ignored.

At Muang Fang I found letters awaiting me from my good friend Dr. Cheek, saying that he had sent by a trusty messenger a document from the chief of Chengmai, calling upon the officials here, as well as at Muang Pau, to furnish me with elephants and men. I at once sent for the old Phya, who was not a little surprised, and still more annoyed, to find I had succeeded in bringing such a number of men with me from Kiang Hai. Unfortunately, the Chow's letter had been delivered at Muang Pau first, and had not yet come on from there; and as soon as the old Phya heard this he at once set to work to checkmate me. No sooner had he left me than I heard that sound of evil omen, the striking of the gong summoning a council to consider what should be done with the " troublesome foreigner." It was very soon decided to wait and see if any assistance came to me from Muang Pau, and to do nothing till the Chow's letter arrived. As I felt sure I could expect no help from Muang Pau, I was in a somewhat desperate strait, with twenty-seven extra men to feed in a hostile camp where rice was scarce and every one was bent on thwarting me. The very beasts of the forest were again unpropitious, for on the first night after my arrival a tiger killed a dog under the hut adjoining mine, and I was of course credited with being the cause of this mischance. Fortunately the people managed to shoot the marauder, but the incident was not in my favour.

But the populace soon had something to divert their attention. Next day, the 12th of April, was the first day of the Laosian and Siamese New Year, and on this and the following day the people were busily engaged in making cakes of rice and sugar, and various offerings for the priests, and in preparing for a general festival to be held on the third day of the year, in prospect of which the priesthood was reinforced by a number of holy men from the neighbouring villages.

The late rains had put the water in good condition for fishing, and the banks of the river were lined with people armed with nets, intent on laying in a stock of fish for the coming festivities. The net generally used is a kind of casting-net, or dip-net, suspended from the ends of two cross pieces of bamboo, which, again, are held at the end of a long pole by the fisherman, who wades out into the water, and casts his net into a likely hole, raising it from time to time, and taking out the fish, of which some are pretty sure to be intercepted every time. The fish caught in the morning are cured in the afternoon, being beheaded and gutted, split open, laid upon bamboo sticks, and smoked over a wood fire.

I hoped to take advantage of the general interest in the new year's festivities to get my men to carry away the bulk of my luggage, and especially the collection of idols which had been such a stumbling-block in the way of my peaceful departure; so I ordered every one to be in readiness to get overland to Muang Nai, the nearest village on the Meping River, there to make a raft and float down to Chengmai, whither I would follow them with the rest of my *impedimenta*. The old Phya got wind of my intentions somehow, and sending for the head man from Kiang Hai gave him strict injunctions on no account to let his men take away the two large figures, which still stood as sentinels outside my hut. Accordingly, when I gave the word for the start, the leader of the band stood sullenly by, and refused to give any orders to his men. A crowd gradually collected round my hut, many of them highly delighted at my predicament, but, I must say, showing no ill-feeling, and treating the matter as a huge joke at the expense of the *farang*. Argument was of no avail. The head man stood firm to the orders of the Phya; not that he cared one button for him or for the figures, but that he thought it best to be on the stronger side. Remembering at this juncture a pithy piece of advice given to me by a witty American a couple of years before at Buitenzorg in Java, " The silver key fits every lock in the East," I took the recalcitrant foreman by the arm, and, beckoning Kao to follow me, led him up into the hut, where I made him a present of a fine gold-embroidered silk waist-cloth and a few rupees. This had the desired effect. I could see that his heart, if not altogether " in the right place," was located somewhere between the palm of his hand and his loins, and that I had gained his temporary affections. Without a word he went out, made a short harangue to his men, to the effect that they had nothing to do with the Phya here, but were under orders from Kiang Hai, and quietly told them to shoulder their burdens and be off. By eight o'clock I had the satisfaction of seeing my treasures fairly on their way out of the village. Accompanying the party a short distance on their journey, I gave them the comforting assurance that in certain packages they would find rice and tobacco for their own use, and promised them a gratuity in money when they should return from the fulfilment of their mission. Leaving Yang to supervise them, I returned to the village to " assist " at the festivities.

About ten o'clock every one in the place, men, women, and children, babies in arms excepted, repaired to the Wat—or rather to the temporary structure of bamboo, with a thatch-roof so low that one could not stand erect inside, which did duty for the sacred edifice—to make their offerings of rice, trays of flowers, pieces of cloth, water-jars, fireworks, and cakes neatly wrapped in a leaf, to their deity. These offerings were placed on the ground in front of the Wat, where a goodly array of miscellaneous articles, resembling somewhat the motley contributions tendered for the service of the semi-religious function known as a " bazaar " in England, was collected so rapidly that the priests were unable to keep pace with them, and could not gather them up fast enough to deposit them in the Wat. Indeed, this modest edifice soon became literally full to overflowing, and a pile of offerings was necessarily left on the ground.

As the people filed past and deposited their tribute, they ranged themselves in a semicircle in front of the

Wat, in four separate masses—a group of women on
each wing, and two groups of men in the centre. Between the latter and the front of the Wat was a covered
place, open all round, where the Chow and officials
were accommodated, a prince from Chengmai being a
conspicuous figure, reclining on a many-coloured carpet,
on which was placed a gorgeously-embroidered triangular cushion or pillow. Behind the semicircle was a
third group of men, who did not appear to be regular
worshippers, or were possibly slaves and men of
inferior degree, for they did not carry the tray of
flowers and wax tapers with which every member of
the congregation proper seemed to be provided.

As soon as all the offerings had been duly deposited
before the Wat, the principal priest came forward and
intoned a long sermon, hiding his face from the people
all the time behind a large fan. Then my landlord,
Nan Inta, went forward, sat down in front of the Chow
and officials, with his face towards the Wat, and recited
a long prayer, during which he and the entire congregation, always excepting the outsiders in the rear,
held their hands tightly pressed together with a flower
(which had to do duty for the sacred lotus, of which
there were none growing at Muang Fang) clasped between the palms. This over, a small gilt figure of
Buddha, wrapped in a yellow cloth, was brought on a
tray out of the Wat by the priests, and placed under
the canopy which sheltered the Chow and officials. At
this moment the majority of the congregation turned
round and looked deliberately at me, as I stood, a
little apart from the congregation, between a group of
men on one side and of women on the other. The
recollection of the morning's work with the old figures
of Buddha, which I had succeeded in carrying away on
the very day of their great annual religious festival,

after they had opposed me so long, was too fresh in their minds for the coincidence not to strike every one present. I could not refrain from laughing, only too glad to feel that, whatever the old Phya might think, the people were not very sorely exercised about the departure of their relics.

The cloth was removed from the figure, and the men and women, each in turn, went forward with a bowl of water which they poured over its head, till the figure had received such a thorough ablution that the water ran down in a stream to the door of the Wat. The Buddha was then carefully dried, robed by the priests, and carried back to the Wat. Another sermon followed, of which the congregation took advantage to hold a general conversation, or to bring their betel-boxes into requisition. A long narrow strip of white calico was next hoisted on a flagstaff adjoining the Wat; Nan Inta offered another prayer, and then the tapers on the trays carried by the congregation were lit all round, each person sitting with a tray in one hand and a flower in the other, while another sermon was delivered by the priest. Last of all, some fireworks, the object of which had excited my curiosity, were brought into play. There was quite a lively display, which, had it only been night instead of day, would no doubt have been very effective. Every time a rocket went off a gong was struck to call the attention, as I was informed, of the spirits, who were supposed to be especially gratified by this form of homage.

This closed the day's proceedings. On the following morning the two ceremonies of confirming the allegiance of the people to the governor, and of purifying the priests, took place. In both of these, water played a prominent part, and, as if in keeping with the arrangements, the day was ushered in with a violent storm of rain, with vivid flashes of lightning, and terrific thunder-claps. Several large trees in the immediate neighbourhood of the town were struck by the lightning, three of them falling in different directions with a tremendous crash, within a few minutes of each other.

In the ceremony of confirming the allegiance of the people to the chief, all the men of the Muang Fang district were supposed to take part. They were prepared for the occasion by having the head shaved, with the exception of a small tuft on the crown, and again came laden with presents, intended, on this occasion, for their temporal and not their spiritual governors. Each man was expected to bring some gift, however trifling, as a proof of his loyalty, and no one who failed to do so could expect to receive advice or assistance from the authorities for the rest of the year. As they passed in procession before the assembled Chows and Phyas, depositing at their feet the tokens of their fealty, each man stooped down while the Phya or his assistant poured water over his head. The men then returned the compliment by sprinkling water on the head of the officiating priests, each of whom had not only his head, but his whole face, eyebrows included, clean shaven for the occasion.

This double ceremony concluded the New Year solemnities, and the people began to settle down again to their daily avocations. That same evening Yang and my Kiang Hai porters returned from Muang Nai, having safely deposited my Buddha figures and the rest of my *impedimenta* there, ready for me to pick them up on my return to Chengmai. Having discharged my liability towards them, and sent them on their way rejoicing back to Kiang Hai, it became necessary for me to make another decided move towards getting away myself.

Only one elephant had turned up from Muang Pau, and this was a female, and sick into the bargain. But, worse than all, the letter on which I had grounded my hope of being able to confuse the machinations of my secret enemies here turned out to have been written by, and to bear the seal, not of the Chow Operat of Chengmai, but only of his secretary.

When I sent it on by Kao to the Phya, he not only openly ridiculed the notion of paying any attention to such a document, unauthenticated by the Chow's seal, but actually spat upon the letter in Kao's presence, and directed him to take it back to me, with an insulting message to the effect that I had not told the truth, and that I might get away on the sick she-elephant, if I liked, for he would not help me. I was in a pretty fix, with neither elephants nor men, and a considerable amount of heavy baggage still to take away. If I lowered myself again so far as to ride a she-elephant, I should expose myself to fresh insults. If I walked, I must leave my luggage behind, and should no doubt be preceded by scouts who would inflame the country round about against me. Every day that I stayed here I was getting more and more into the power of the old Phya. Kao and Yang were becoming alarmed, and made sure we should all be massacred. There was nothing to be done but to send another letter to Dr. Cheek, telling him the serious state of affairs, how his last endeavour to help me had landed me in worse straits, because the orders issued for my assistance were not authenticated by the chief's seal, and begging him to get the Chow Operat of Chengmai to send me a strongly-worded letter, duly sealed, that would enforce compliance on the part of the Muang Fang chiefs.

CHAPTER XXVIII.

An untoward incident—My landlord Nan Inta—Release at last—
  Leaving Muang Fang—The sources of the River Meping—
  Back to Chengmai—Complaining to the Chow—An unlucky
  investment—Mischievous coolies—A claim for damages—A
  lengthy indictment—Gaining the day—An offer of reconciliation
  —A picnic at Doi sua tape—Fireworks for the spirits—Work-
  ing the teak-forests—Philosophic labourers—A much-tattooed
  Burmese—A princess's intrigues.

WHILE awaiting the issue of this last appeal to
Chengmai, we passed several sleepless nights. Tali,
I knew, would do his duty, and would not allow any
one to enter my hut without good warning; but the
demeanour of the people changed for the worse; I
met with scant civility, and sometimes with downright
rudeness, at the hands even of those whom I paid for
their services: and very little was needed to raise up
a whirlwind of open hostility against me. One night an
untoward circumstance occurred to turn even my
landlord against me. Although old Nan Inta was superstitious to a degree, and often reproached me quietly
for having excited the anger of the spirits by inter-
fering with the Buddhas, and although I knew he was
anxious to curry favour with the Phyas, I always had
a sneaking liking for the old man. He could at times
be quite demonstrative in his sociability, and many
times got up a dance at the house in honour of my
presence. Besides, he seemed always too much occupied with his basket-making, his religious duties, and

his rice-culture, to be able to nurse any unfriendly feelings towards me.

He was the busiest specimen of a Laosian I ever met, always having something to do. The first thing in the morning he would go and gather a few flowers, put them on a tray, with rice or fish, and make his daily offering to the priests. I never knew him to miss

Nan Inta, or " Arai," my landlord at Muang Fang.

this duty once, and always watched for his return from the Wat, with a self-satisfied half-smile on his complacent Mephistophelean visage. His portrait, which is given above, is a perfect likeness of him, representing him in his favourite attitude, as he used to come into my room when I called him, with an inquiring " *Arai?* " (What is it ?)—a characteristic expression which I

A a 2

adopted as a nickname for him. His type of face is not an uncommon one among old men of the better class of Laosians. After his first meal, he would go into the forest, and cut bamboos or young trees, and collect materials for making baskets, at which work he would often sit at home half the day ; then he had his rice-fields to cultivate, his cattle to look after, and his religious duties to attend to.

But with all his virtues he allowed himself to be carried with the tide of popular favour, and, when he found the general feeling setting strongly against me, he seized the first opportunity of letting his gradually in-creasing coolness of manner suddenly develop into open hostility. This opportunity occurred when one night a tiger managed to kill a dog and a bullock belonging to him. Here, to his superstitious mind, was conclusive evidence of my guilt ; whatever may have been the case when other people's live stock was attacked, the fact of a tiger seizing a bullock—his bullock—under the very house—his house—in which I was staying, was convincing proof that I was at the bottom of the mischief. So from that time he was included in the list of my active enemies. His influence seemed to have increased as the New Year grew, and when I endeavoured to make a private bargain with a few natives, through the influence of Kao's persuasiveness and of a distribution of *backsheesh*, I found Nan Inta's name linked with those of the Chow and the Phya as authorities whose strict orders to refuse me all aid the people dared not disobey.

There was nothing for it but to live on hope—not a very generous diet with a scarcity of rice and in the absence of almost every other kind of provisions— and to trust to a speedy relief from Chengmai. One of those little rolls of palm-leaves, bearing the talis-

manic seal of the Chow, would avail more than all my
remonstrances, more than all Tali's growls, more than
all Kao's eloquence, more than even *backsheesh*. At
last, on the first day of May, the hour of deliverance
came. After seventeen days of weary waiting, to say
nothing of dangers impending, I received the long-
looked-for letter from Dr. Cheek, enclosing a strongly-
worded, and, what was more important, a duly-sealed,
letter from the Chow Operat of Chengmai, ordering
the Muang Fang chiefs and people to supply me with
ten elephants and men, and to see my luggage delivered
at Chengmai within seven days of my departure.
The Chow and the Phya were bound to act upon these
instructions, and on the following day seven elephants
were already waiting for me. After seeing Yang and
the coolies start off with the baggage, to pick up that
portion which had already gone on to Muang Nai,
and directing them to proceed to Chengmai, I had
the satisfaction, in the early afternoon, of shaking
the dust of Muang Fang off my feet, and, after
taking what I hoped might be a long farewell of
my persecutors, of striking out to the westward, with
the object of finding, if possible, the sources of the
Meping.

Our route was through a mountain-pass over 2000
feet high, along a narrow track full of loose stones,
and most difficult for the elephants to traverse, as
they often seemed to slip back, in going up steep
places, two paces for every one they took forward.
At the end of the third day we reached the River
Meping, here a mountain-torrent only twenty feet
wide and barely a foot deep. The natives said its
winding course could be followed for several days
although its source was in Lao, and not, as generally
supposed, in the Ngiou States. But they said pro-

visions were scarce, and, as we were only provided for
a seven-days' journey to Chengmai, I reluctantly turned
about and followed the downward course of the
stream, in a south-west and south-south-west direction,
crossing and recrossing it several times for two days,
till we reached Muang Shandau, a small village apparently the highest on the river. After passing Ban
Pau—not to be confounded with Muang Pau—and
Muang Kenn, we reached Chengmai on the afternoon
of the 7th of May. As we crossed the bridge, Dr.
Cheek came out to meet me, and gave me a warm
welcome, most kindly offering me hospitality and
placing at my disposal the house which he had recently
occupied, and which he had left for more convenient
premises on the opposite side of the river. One of
the first things I did was to call upon the Chow in
company with Dr. Cheek, who was kind enough to act
as my interpreter.

The word "interpreter," by the way, is rendered in
the Lao tongue, *cha kra pien*, literally "one who
changes words." I had no fear that Dr. Cheek would
illustrate one sense which these words might be made
to bear, although I had a strong belief that many of my
difficulties, on other occasions, were due to the perver-
sion, either ignorantly or wilfully, of words which were
changed, not only in language, but in meaning as well,
while passing through the channel of the interpreter's
mouth.

The chief was not in his palace, but in his boat-yard,
whither we followed him, and where we found him
sitting under a shed, superintending the construction
of several fine boats in preparation for his intended
journey to Bangkok, on a visit to the king of Siam.

In one corner of the yard I noticed a Chinaman in
chains. It appeared that formerly he had had the

gambling-monopoly in Chengmai, *i.e.* he paid the chief so much a year for the sole right to provide the where-withal for gamblers to indulge in their all-absorbing pastime. I confess I don't quite understand how the thing worked, since it would have been absolutely impossible for the Chinaman to prevent all the inhabitants from giving way, without his permission, to their besetting vice. Anyhow, one night a rich Chinaman lost 8000 rupees, which he either could not or would not pay, but for which he gave the gambling-farmer an I.O.U. When the time arrived for the gambling-monopolist to pay to the state the price of his mono-poly, he had not sufficient money for the purpose, having run his " farm " at a loss; so, as his defaulting countryman did not take up his I.O.U., he asked the chief to accept it in part payment, and to collect the account from the debtor. The chief's wife, however, who evidently looked after her husband's exchequer, and with whom the Chinese debtor was in high favour, was very indignant at such a proposal, and not only deprived the poor Chinaman of his monopoly, but ordered him into chains into the bargain, and left the defaulting debtor at large.

I gave the chief a pretty full account of the obstacles that had been placed in my way, particularly at Muang Fang and Muang Pau. He listened quietly, open-mouthed, to all Dr. Cheek said on my behalf, but said nothing, and the subject would probably have dropped but for the fact that when, a few days later, my baggage arrived from Muang Fang, I found that the coolies, in order to lighten their burden, had emptied out all the spirit from the tins containing my natural history specimens, which were completely dried up and spoiled. With bare-faced effrontery they said it had " done itself." I wonder they did not say it was the immaterial spirits who had been playing tricks with the material spirits; but there was ample evidence that the packages had been wilfully injured, and, on the advice of Dr. Cheek, I at once sent in to the Chow of Chengmai a claim for damages; first, for my detention at Muang Fang, and for the hindrances placed in the way of my making a collection of animals and birds; and next for the destruction of the few specimens I had with much difficulty succeeded in getting together.

This claim naturally brought up the whole question of my collection of the Buddha figures, and of the action of the Phyas at Muang Pau and Muang Fang. A general meeting of Siamese and Lao officials was summoned, before whom I myself and the messengers who had brought my luggage were summoned. The Muang Fang folk made out a pretty strong indictment against me of how I had brought the tigers to the settlement, how the tigers had ceased from troubling when I was away up the country, how they came back directly I returned, and so on *ad lib.* In reply, I asked if they were authorized to make any demand for the restoration of the figures, and was answered, No. I pointed out that if I was in league with the evil spirits I should have brought tigers, or worse, with me to Chengmai, and asked if Dr. Cheek would be likely to be friendly with any one who would do harm to the people. When I related how the Chow at Muang Pau had insulted me by sending me a sick female elephant to ride upon, and how the Phya at Muang Fang had insulted the chief of Chengmai by spitting on the letter his secretary had sent on my behalf, I fairly won the day.

Neither the Chow nor the Siamese Commissioner, Pra Udon, would allow their dignity, nor that of a foreigner whom they had taken under their protection, to be compromised in this way; and they at once decided that the question could not be allowed to rest there, but that there should be a general reprimand all round. The negotiations for a settlement of my claim and the inquiry into the mutual recriminations between myself and these Chows lasted nearly three weeks. The Siamese Commissioner was assisted by Phya Nai, one of the chief's secretaries, and Chow Radjasampan, the most intelligent of the Laosian princes, a very straightforward individual, who admitted that the Phya who had spat upon the chief's letter was his own brother, and, although he endeavoured to make fraternal excuses for him, stated that he was a " great rascal," who had had to be punished more than once before.

At last the Chow offered to settle the whole business by inviting me to what the Laosians call a *Pook Quan* —a feast at which all the princes in the district would be present, and where I should undergo a ceremony in which the tying of strings round my wrists as a means of reconciliation with the offended spirits, and the offer of a pyramid of flowers with a few of the old Lao silver coins, called Nan tok,[1] as a sign of the amity of the people, would form the principal features. I understood that it would take some days, and perhaps weeks, before all the arrangements for this ceremony could be completed, for all the chiefs in the district would be summoned to attend, and as I was pretty well wearied out with the prolonged negotiations, and was anxious to get back to Bangkok, I declined the offer.

I very much regret, however, that, at whatever cost of time, I did not accept this mode of settling the matter; for it would have been interesting to witness,

[1] Worth about 6s. each.

and to take part in, a *Pook Quan*, while it would have pleased the Chows. I should for ever, as I afterwards learned, have closed the mouths of the people who looked upon me as an enemy, instead of which their false complaints against me followed me even to Bangkok.

While the negotiations were proceeding, a very pleasant break was occasioned by the occurrence of a Lao religious festival, which my missionary hosts and I devoted to the Western feast known as a " picnic." Immediately behind the city of Chengmai rises the mountain called Doi sua tape, on the slope of which, some 2700 feet above sea-level, is a famous temple. This spot we determined to visit, and, the missionary ladies having provided a substantial luncheon, I asked the chief to oblige us with seven elephants. Dr. Cheek had given me a valuable hint—which I wish I had received earlier in my travels in Lao—always to ask for more elephants or coolies than you really require, as the native custom is to take a large discount off your orders. Instead of seven elephants, only five turned up—just the number we required—so we started off at sunrise, in glorious weather, in the wake of a large procession of natives, both men and women, priests and laymen, whose destination was the same as ours, viz. the temple of Doi sua tape.

It took us fully three hours to scale the steep acclivity and reach the temple, and there we found a large assemblage—I should think over a thousand— already engaged in making peace-offerings to the spirits, and sending their pious remembrances to Buddha. The women were laden with flowers, which they arranged on the altar in all sorts of tasteful designs, and with cakes and rice, as if the numerous figures of Buddha, with which the temple was thronged, were in want of food. The men offered wax tapers, which they lighted and placed before the figures, while they clothed them with yellow garments, or offered bits of gold leaf, with which the priests would presently enrich the largest figure.

In the centre of the temple-grounds, towering above the tree-tops, was a tall pradchedee, heavily gilt, like the temple itself, and glistening in the brilliant sunlight against the dark background of the surrounding forest, while *tungs* or flags innumerable floated gaily from flagstaves placed at every few yards, and from every projection on the sacred edifices from which it was possible to suspend them. A continuous round of services was proceeding inside and outside the temple, while beyond the immediate temple-grounds quite a fair was being held. Rockets were going off every moment, which delighted the younger portion of the assemblage with the hissing sound of their upward flight and the aerial detonation, but of which little or nothing could be seen, as the full blaze of the midday sun put to shame every lesser light, while the adult lookers-on were satisfied to regard every rocket that went off as another offering to the spirits.

From the plateau on which the temple was situated, a most magnificent panorama of the plain of Chengmai, hemmed in by distant mountains, could be obtained.

Before leaving Chengmai I went to see the operation of cutting timber in the teak-forests, the best of which are situate at Mi Long Gui, west of Chengmai, and are leased out to the timber-merchants by the princes who have a monopoly of the right to cut them.

The labourers mostly employed are men belonging to a hill-tribe called Komaws, living to the eastward beyond the Mekong river. They are darker in colour than the Laosians, short of stature, but very muscular, and with particularly big legs. They do not believe in a supreme being, but worship the spirits of their ancestors. These men are hired as a rule for a period of three years, and receive as wages the magnificent sum of about eighty rupees a year in return for their arduous labour. Even so, I am sorry to say that they are often cheated by the lower class of employers. For every Komaw hired on the three-years system the employer has to get a permit from the Chow Radja-sampan, for which he has to pay twelve rupees, and, as a set-off against this, the unfortunate labourer is mulct in a portion of his hard-earned money. These primitive mountaineers do not take away their money, when returning to their hill-retreats, but invest in one of the much-prized gongs made by the red Karians. " If," they philosophically argue, " we take the money back to our country it gets less every day, till at last it is all gone; whereas the gong we can keep, and hear its beautiful sound daily."

The forests are leased almost exclusively by British Burmese subjects, and there is quite a Burmese colony in Chengmai. Of one of the number who was very elaborately tattooed I took the annexed sketch. It will be seen that this pattern is very similar to that affected by the Laosians, but that some of the figures are scattered on the upper part of the body.

At the time of my visit the members of the Burmese colony were in great trepidation lest any of them should suffer the fate of one of their number, who had recently been murdered. There was, however, little fear of that, unless they followed the example of their fellow-subject, who met his fate because he had paid too intimate attention to a Lao princess. This was no other than the Chow Oobon Lawana, of spirit-notoriety.

She had had many husbands and lovers at different times, and had dispensed with them at her pleasure : first a Siamese official, then a Ngiou who was tutor to her children, next a Lao prince, then a Burmese,

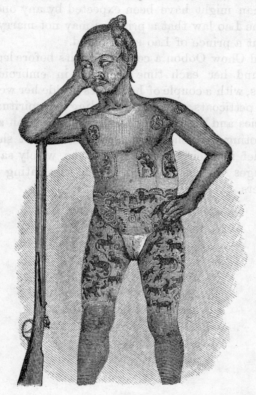

A tattooed Burmese.

whom they did not murder, but whom the Laosian authorities politely escorted over the frontier, with an intimation that he need never return. She seemed to have a liking for the Burmese, for her last paramour was a Burmese who farmed one of the timber-forests.

The chief's wife, however—Chow Oobon's own sister
—and his son, became so annoyed this time at her conduct that they laid a scheme to murder him, which was
accomplished without much difficulty, and was nothing
more than might have been expected by any one who
knew the Lao law that a princess may not marry any-
body but a prince of Lao royal blood.

I paid Chow Oobon a couple of visits before leaving,
and found her each time occupied in embroidering
cushions, with a couple of her slaves beside her weaving
silk for petticoats. Notwithstanding her spiritualistic
tendencies and her amatory failings, she was on a very
good footing with the missionaries : not that she had
any belief in their doctrines, but she wisely saw the
advantages to be derived from associating with
foreigners.

CHAPTER XXIX.

Departure from Chengmai—Down the Meping—Ingenious irriga-
tion-system—A leper village—Through a deep gorge—Preparing for a plunge—A queer ingredient in gunpowder—Strange
water-worn rocks—Shooting the rapids—The build of native
boats—Raheng again—Characteristic native indifference—
Siamese landing-places—Kampheng—Xainat—Ayuthia—Bangkok *en fête*—The origin of the city—History of the present
Siamese dynasty—The " bone-relic " ceremonies.

On the 28th of May I left Chengmai, Dr. Cheek
adding to his many other kindnesses the parting one
of placing at my disposal a most comfortable boat, built
in his yard; so that I had an opportunity of appre-
ciating the improvements which he has effected in the
native build of boat ; while the chief provided me with
letters to enable me to pass through his territory,
and to get pilots to take me through the rapids at
Mutka.

The river for a long distance below Chengmai is
lined with villages, and with the never-ending paddy-
fields, and betel-nut and cocoa-palm plantations, which
are irrigated by means of curious revolving water-
wheels, built of bamboo, and fitted with short pieces of
thick bamboo which both serve as paddles and at the
same time as " lifts " for the water. Every time they
dip into the river they raise a small quantity of water,
which, in descending, they empty into a conduit of
bamboo which conveys it to the plantation. The
contrivance is ingenious and simple, and is, of course,

self-working, so long as there is sufficient water in the river for the paddle to reach an inch or two below the surface.

Alternating with the water-wheels were native fishing-weirs or stakes, similar in construction to those on the coast, and often a serious obstacle to navigation.

On the second day we reached · the leper village Ban Tapee, a living graveyard, inhabited by five or six hundred wretched diseased and crippled creatures, whose appearance was sickening and painful to see, with the glazed look of approaching death in their eyes, and with features, hands, and feet rotting away under the loathsome disease with which they were afflicted.

Another day's journey brought us to Muang Hawt, a village famous for its six-toed fowls, and a halting-station on the road to Moulmein. The banks of the river are here hemmed in with limestone mountains, which stand out like silhouettes against the bright blue sky, studded to the top with trees and vegetation growing in bewildering but enchanting confusion. The whole face of the cliffs was alive with bats and swallows, flitting about their nests, scooped out in the soft stone. But we had not time to examine the beauties of the course of the river through this gorge. Already the current was becoming more and more rapid, necessitating the greatest care in steering our boats between the treacherous rocks, as we were impelled irresistibly towards a series of rapids, thirty-two in all, which would make the strongest claim upon our undivided attention. We arrived at Mutka about three in the afternoon, and I at once sought out the Phya, to present my " passport," and get arrangements made for shooting the rapids on the morrow. The boats had to be specially prepared for the purpose, a double bulwark being placed round the bows, to prevent the ingress of water while plunging through the seething surf. The Phya was very attentive, and was very grateful for the small "tip" of five rupees which I offered him, for, as he said, "money was very scarce."

Early the next morning we continued the journey down stream, having taken on board a steersman and two pilots for each boat. In the river were several dead buffaloes, on some of which vultures were feeding as they floated rapidly down towards the sea. The natives said a plague had carried off many hundreds of cattle, entailing heavy loss on some of the villages. Monkeys were numerous in the trees on the banks, and we passed adjutants and other wading birds in abundance. About three miles below Mutka broken water was reached—the first "kong" or rapid— immediately below which is a small native village called Ban Kau, the inhabitants of which get their living by collecting bats' dung in the numerous caves in the neighbourhood, which they use in the manufacture of gunpowder.

Two or three hours' "drifting" below this, the river runs between perpendicular walls of limestone rocks, the strata of which are distorted in a remarkable manner, sometimes lying almost at right angles with each other. Where the strata are horizontal, near the water's edge, the action of the stream has eaten out deep, narrow fissures, giving the rock the appearance of a huge series of neatly-wrought shelves. We put up for the night at Keng Soi, named after, or giving its name to, one of the rapids. Near here, on the top of a high hill on the right bank of the river, are a Wat and a phrachedee, both of them visible for many miles above and below.

So long as the hill was in sight, I noticed my steersman, every time a rapid was passed, bow reverently in its direction, with hands pressed tightly together and held close to the forehead.

Below Keng Soi the scenery on the banks became more rugged, an indication of our approach to still rougher water. The view was very impressive; at every bend of the river, which takes sharp curves just here, the landscape seems to change, not only in effect, but in character, according as the softness of the distance, or the rugged grandeur of the foreground, predominates. The edges of the stream are dotted with huge boulders, borne down with irresistible force in times of flood from the distant hills, and we are swiftly nearing Doi Omlo, the heaviest and most dangerous of the rapids. It needs strength as well as skill to avoid the sunken rocks, for the river takes so sharp a bend that it requires the united force of several men to keep the rudder in place. In sweeping round the curve my boat swerved broadside on, being twisted round by the constant eddies, and narrowly escaped collision with a rock, but, by dint of great shouting and exertion on the part of the crew, some of whom stood in the bow with their long poles, ready for such an emergency — though, had we struck, the force of the collision would have made matchwood of the stoutest bamboo — the boat was made obedient to the enormous rudder, and the danger was avoided. The second boat, however, was carried too near the shore, and the over-arching branches caught the attap roofing of the cabin, and stripped it off, while, more disastrous still, one of the pilots fell into the roaring current. How he escaped drowning is a miracle; but fortunately he was near the shore, and was able to reach *terra firma*, and, following us along the shore for some two miles, was subsequently taken on board with a sound, if a wet, skin. When we were safely through the danger, the steersmen offered a short thanksgiving to the mountain-spirit.

The ordinary native boats, from thirty to sixty feet long, employed in the navigation of these rapids are singularly well adapted for the work. They are flat-bottomed craft without keels, the lower part of the hull being constructed of a solid log[1] of teak cut from a single tree, which is scooped out with the adze, —a long and tedious piece of work. A number of wooden beams are then placed across the hollow trunk inside, like thick thwarts reaching from gunwale to gunwale, and the hull is then placed on logs, raised a foot or two from the ground, and fires lighted underneath its whole length. This has the effect of causing the sides to expand, giving greater beam to the boat, and the crosspieces are then replaced by longer ones, to give the boat stiffness and keep it in shape. A long bamboo or board " house," open at the ends, but closed at the sides, is then built amidships to a height of four or five feet above the gunwale; a high, projecting stern is then added, through which an enormous oar, which is used as a rudder, protrudes. At the stern of the boat a second house, somewhat higher than the other, is built for the use of the steersman, who is provided with a three-legged chair, perched on which he can keep a look-out ahead over the roof of the main house.

These boats are well adapted for the rough work they have to go through. When a recent Atlantic

[1] The boat-builders are entitled to go into the forests and cut trees for boats, on condition of paying a fee of one trunk out of every five that they use themselves. They are also called upon to supply the princes with boats free of expense whenever required.

steamship went ashore and broke up at short notice, the builder replied to the expressions of surprise which her sudden collapse called forth by saying that the vessel was built to sail on the water and not on dry land. The Laosian boats, on the other hand, are specially constructed with this object. The upper reaches of the river are full of rocks and shoals, and these stout, solid, flat-bottomed boats are peculiarly well adapted for passing over such obstacles without sustaining serious injury. They are never fitted with sails, but float with the stream, or are propelled against it by oars.

When they go aground, or get into a maze of rocks, the oars are laid aside for long bamboo poles, fitted at one end with a small iron fork to give a hold on the rocks, or river-bed or banks, and with these the native boatmen laboriously but skilfully propel and pilot their craft through any such difficulty, standing in the bows, and needing all their strength to keep the head of the boat in the desired direction. Only long practice and great natural " knack " can enable these men to seize the fleeting opportunities offered by the rocks, past which the boat whirls with terrific speed.

At Mutka, before passing through the rapids, the boats are specially fitted with doubly high bulwarks, to meet the plunge through the broken water, and to prevent them from " shipping a sea," which they certainly would do if not so prepared.

Dr. Cheek's boat, with such an increased freeboard, went through the ordeal of " shooting the rapids " most successfully, and brought me safely to Raheng. Here I changed this excellent craft for the larger boat sent me by Prince Devan, in which I had come up from Bangkok, and which, while I went overland to Chengmai, I had left in charge of the Governor, who had promised to take care of it, and see it properly housed during my absence. But the Governor, who had gone to Bangkok to take part in the festivities in celebration of the centenary of the city, had forgotten all about the boat, and promises unfulfilled had not availed to do the needful work. There I found the boat lying on the very sand-bank on which I had landed from it, and where, left high and dry, and exposed to the scorching sun all through the dry season, its seaworthy qualities had by no means been improved. When it was set afloat, it was found to leak so fast that it took half a dozen men two days to caulk and paint it, and generally to put it into decent trim.

Nowhere in Siam—saving, of course, in the city of Bangkok itself—is there such a thing as a proper landing-place, although in the upper portion of the country the river is the principal and in some cases the only highway. When almost every one, from the highest officials to the meanest coolie, has a boat, which is as much part of the establishment of a native as his house, it is strange that no one should have conceived the happy idea of constructing a landing-stage, or, at least, of maintaining a gangway or path of some kind between the place where his boat lies and his house. Occasionally a ricketty bamboo ladder, more often than not so unserviceable as to be a stumbling-block rather than a help, is placed to assist one in climbing the steep sides of the river in the dry season; but as a rule it is a "hands-and-knees" business to crawl up the bank—no pleasant task in wet weather when the mud is several inches deep. In the dry season it is almost as bad, if not in some respects even worse; for the natives trust to Jupiter Pluvius as the universal scavenger. When he discharges torrential rains from his clouds, there is a chance of the mud being washed away; but when he holds his hands the natives prepare a goodly share of work in readiness for his next visit, by strewing the ground with every imaginable kind of garbage; so that to go ashore anywhere is to scramble through filth of one kind or another, wet or fine. Even at so important a place as Raheng there was no " wharf " accommodation; the river had gradually receded from the convenient sand-bank on which Prince Devan's boat had been run ashore to land me, and so it had been left alone as the easiest thing to do with it.

The rainy season had now, however, set in in earnest, and there was plenty of water in the Menam, which was rising rapidly to flood-level, so that we sped merrily downwards to Bangkok, past Kampheng, Xainat, and Ayuthia. Thousands of birds—darters, herons, pelicans, adjutants, cranes, and others—were busily at work among the shoals of migratory fish now about to spawn.

At Kampheng, as at Raheng, I found the governor was absent on a visit to Bangkok. His house was turned into a temporary dancing-saloon and theatre, and, when I called, I saw in the large open hall a dozen young girls rehearsing a theatrical performance, in preparation for the festivities in which they were to take part later on.

At Xainat all boats arriving from the interior have to be examined, and pay "inland" duties, an old Chinaman being entrusted with the duty of collecting the taxes.

At Ayuthia I stayed only long enough to pay a visit to the deaf old governor, an obliging gentleman, seventy-nine years of age; and reached Bangkok on the 14th of June, to find the city *en fête* in celebration of its hundredth birthday.

It was in the reign of King Phra Puttha Yot Fa Chulalok, the founder of the present dynasty, that, Ayuthia, the former capital, having been partially destroyed during the troublous period of the preceding reigns, Bangkok became the capital of Siam, under the following circumstances.

"The king," according to Siamese records, "mounted on a royal elephant, having surveyed the ruins of Ayuthia, became filled with pity, and meditated the rebuilding of the city, and placing it again upon its former basis. Gathering together the citizens of the realm, the priests, and teachers, he proposed to establish a royal rule and a succession of sovereigns to rule the realm; to build up and resuscitate Krung Tape Maha Nakaun Sri Ayuthia, which had been demolished, so that it should be again, as before, the capital of the kingdom. One night he dreamed that the former sovereigns drove him away and would not allow him to remain. Early next morning the king related his dream for the information of his noblemen, and remarked : ' Noticing that the city has become an overgrown waste, it has been my wish to rebuild and resuscitate it, and place it upon its former prosperous footing. As the former owners of the city still jealously cling to it, let us mutually stimulate each other to build up the town Tonaburee.'

"Having made known his dream and his determination, he gave orders to disband the army, gather together the people, the priests, and the descendants of the former royal families that remained. Heading these, he returned and located himself and them in the town Tonaburee. He then sent messengers to hunt up and find his scattered relatives. These were collected together at Lopaburee, and were brought from thence to Tonaburee, where the king constructed for himself a palace, adequate to the necessity of the times."

On the 21st day of April in the year 1144 (A.D. 1782) King Chulalok declared the site of the future capital. Since then the city now known as Bangkok—or, to give it its full Siamese designation, "Krung Tep Maha Nakhon Amaratna Kosindr Mahindr Ayuthia"— has grown till it numbers at present, according to estimate, about a million inhabitants. The ancient palace has long since become in-"adequate to the necessity of the times," and the present king has just completed the new royal residence already described : but his improvements have not ended here, and the celebration of the centenary of the city was marked by the inauguration of many reforms, many of which are personified in the public buildings then commenced or already erected for their administration.

The importance which the Siamese attached to the celebration of the centenary of Bangkok may be gathered from the following extracts from an address presented to the king by all the princes :—

"Judging by the history of Siam when its sovereigns reigned at Ayuthia—but omitting all the fabulous part, which is but a collection of stories without date or credibility, and taking only the credible part—there never was any time that Siam enjoyed the prosperity it has enjoyed as under this dynasty.

" Of the five dynasties which ruled at Ayuthia, the Cheng Rai dynasty alone endured for any long period. The six reigns of that dynasty extended over a period of ninety-five years, a less time than your Majesty's dynasty has already ruled.

" Every sovereign of this dynasty has been more good-hearted than the sovereigns of former dynasties, and more full of compassion and kindness to all people. No king of this dynasty has made his own comfort his principal care, but each has earnestly sought to do right and justice.

"And the members of this family have honestly endeavoured to serve their sovereign; the greatest of them have not considered that their greatness makes all they may do right, the lesser of them have not attempted to exaggerate their importance: and now there is unity among us; we rise together and sit together, no longer separated as in former days, when each prince held himself apart. It is therefore an incomparable pleasure to us to reflect on former times and to set forth, on this great festive gathering, recollections of the good acts of sovereigns of this dynasty, ruling in succession up to this day.

"The first sovereign of this dynasty, Phrabat Somdeth Phra Puttha Yot Fa Chulalok, came to the throne by conquest, having overcome the thorns, the enemies of the state, who had brought confusion into the land of Tonaburee, so that the people were greatly afflicted, and their hamlets were broken up, and rebels surrounded the palace and deposed the king of Tonaburee. Having established himself on the thone by wisdom and valour, the Burmese four times invaded Siam with even greater armies than those with which they conquered Ayuthia, but they were defeated by his Majesty's power. His Majesty applied his wisdom to the internal administration of the kingdom, founded Wat Phra Sri Ratana Satsadaram, appointed officers of government in every department, selecting these according to their deserts, and assembled the monks of Buddha—such an assembly as had never been held in the days of Ayuthia—acting as upholder of the Buddhist faith, and making it flourish. He had the laws examined and collected into standard copies to show the way of justice, which in the time of Ayuthia was only once done. The people lived in peace, quiet, and happiness, without oppression, and those who had by the oppressions of former days been forced to run away from their villages returned, and they and we have enjoyed the benefit of the royal might and grace, which have protected and held together the kingdom from that time forth.

" The second sovereign of the dynasty, His Majesty Phra Puttha Lot La Nophalai, maintained the same virtuous purposes. The Burmese were defeated in several attacks on Western Siam. The capital was improved, and Nakhon ku'an kan built, and the fame of his Majesty's happy rule spread far and wide, so that Laos and Burmese left their own countries to live in Siam.

" His Majesty King Phra Nang Klao, third of the dynasty, engaged in great religious works, and built and dedicated many splendid temples, and encouraged Pali scholarship, so that learned men became numerous, and to remove the oppression of the people he instituted the custom of striking the great bell and appealing to his Majesty in person—a plan for the benefit of the people of which the history of Siam gives no previous indication.

" The fourth sovereign was His Majesty King Phra Chom Klao, most virtuous, wise, and learned in all kinds of knowledge. He protected the land with mercy and boldness. He opened commercial relations with all nations and abolished the old restrictions on trade, and thereby greatly increased the wealth of the country. He made many new laws and amended old laws for the maintenance of justice. He went forth among the people, and with his own hands received from them appeals and their complaints against oppressive officials, that those whose complaints were true feared no one, but had the opportunity of being heard by the king. In that reign no one tried to do evil to the kingdom nor to the king, a reign unparalleled, and of unprecedented peace and happiness.

" During the fourteen years this present reign has already lasted, the good royal customs of previous kings have not been departed from, and your Majesty's unceasing care has been for the increase of the happiness and benefit of your people.

" Your Majesty, by providing for the emancipation of slaves by years of age, effected the freedom of all as they reached manhood, without any trouble or inconvenience to any one—a remarkable act, and differing much from the results of abolition of slavery in other countries. Also the uncomfortable and unbecoming position formerly obligatory in the presence of the king was by your Majesty's kindness changed to that of standing.

" Also your Majesty has been pleased to permit us and other officers of government to submit to your Majesty our written opinions on all points which we think proper, a practice formerly forbidden. The people have increased in happiness daily. Foreign relations have been established on a still better footing than before by your Majesty's wisdom.

" Also Wat Phra Sri Ratana Satsadaram, which had been so long building that no one believed in its ever being finished, has now been perfectly finished by your Majesty's grace taking it under your own management —a great glory of your Majesty's reign for the wonder of all people.

" We, dependent on your Majesty's grace and protection, having lived till now in so much peace and happiness, are grateful to your Majesty for your goodness beyond measure. In all your Majesty's further plans for the protection of the people, and for the firm establishment of this dynasty, continuously to reign by justice, we beg to offer up our bodies and our lives in your Majesty's service, faithfully and truly to accomplish all your Majesty may ask of us.

"In conclusion, in the midst of our joy at this great festival, we pray the three holy jewels and the great gods, who are most mighty in the universe, may keep and protect your Majesty, with long life to reign over this kingdom, with all blessings, happiness and glory and renown throughout all quarters of the world and to all time.

"May every one of your Majesty's desires be easily accomplished, and may your Majesty be the support and protector of ourselves and all people."

I was fortunate enough to arrive at Bangkok from my journey in the Lao country just at the commencement of the ceremony of removing from the Wat Phra Kao the bone-relics of the past four sovereigns of the dynasty, whose merits are set forth in the above address to his Majesty, and depositing them in the Amarindra Winichai, or throne-hall. For seven days the gold urns containing the ashes of the king's predecessors were carried from court to court, and hall to hall, before they reached their final resting-place, where, after an oration eulogistic of the virtues of the deceased had been pronounced by the prince-high-priest of Siam, H.R.H. Krom Phra Pawaratsawariyalongkaun, uncle of the king, the urns were deposited on gold stands, amid the firing of salutes from the batteries outside, and the devotional chants of the priests within the building.

In the mean time the populace had their share in the "bone-relic" ceremonies by being treated to sports of every kind, with illuminations and fireworks; while presents concealed in fruit were daily scattered among them.

During the festivities upwards of a hundred leading priests were daily fed at the palace, besides being supplied with new robes and laden with presents. In return they had a laborious round of ceremonial and religious duties to perform, which occupied them daily from sunrise till a late hour of the night, preaching, praying, singing devotional chants, uttering panegyrics on the piety and virtues of the past and present kings, and invoking blessings on the head of His Majesty King Chulalonkorn.

CHAPTER XXX.

The king and the furtherance of justice—The new law courts—
Educational advancement—Postal facilities—The great Wat
Phra Kao—A hundred years in building—Division of labour—
Completion and centennial celebration—The Emerald Buddha
—The king's speech.

WHATEVER may be the case with the dead, it cannot be
questioned that, so far as the present ruler of Siam is
concerned, the foregoing eulogy of the princes is well
merited. Leaving for later consideration the great work
of completing the great temple, let us glance at the other
achievements the completion or the inception of which
will always be identified with the celebration of the
centenary festival of Bangkok. Of the public buildings
which will always be the monuments of the king's
wisdom and energy, perhaps the most important is the
new Court of Justice, which will be to Siam what the
Royal Courts of Justice in London are to England, for,
as the Kalahome or prime minister expressed it
in his address to the king on the occasion of the
laying of the foundation-stone: "Your Majesty's
glorious ancestor, having won his throne by his
victories, and being crowned as a conquering king,
ruled over the people, arranged the laws in good
order, and established a royal court to relieve the
distresses of his people throughout the land by means
of justice, which is the highest source of a nation's
happiness and prosperity, the greatest cause of quiet

and peace and of the development of trade and commerce; your Majesty now, considering that the completion of this centennial period should be marked by the further development of the ideas of the founder of the dynasty, and that the administration of justice might be promoted and made permanent, and the people therein find happiness, has directed the erection of a royal court of justice, where all the present courts might be united, and all the judges be present in one building, so as to facilitate the speedy trial of cases."

The king's reply was worthy of the Queen of England herself.

"I have had great pleasure," said his Majesty, "in listening to the address of the Samuha Phra Kalahome, proving to me that my plan for promoting the happiness of the people has been approved by you all. I will now lay the first stone, and beg to name the building *Sala sathit Yutithan* (the abode of justice). May the continuance of the work be prosperous and without difficulties, and may my object in building it— the maintenance of justice and the relief of the people's griefs—be accomplished fully, and established firmly as long as earth and sky shall last ! "

The building is to be, according to the Kalahome's statement, twenty-four fathoms high, fifty-six fathoms long; with two roofs, one eleven fathoms, one sok, one kub wide, and the other five fathoms, two sok, one kub wide; and is to cost 2427 catties and 4 tamlungs.

Besides a new era in the administration of law, the centenary of Bangkok marks a fresh advance in the education of the people. A splendid college—quite a palace in appearance, and with every modern appliance —has been built at the public expense in Bangkok, and will shortly be opened. The king's enlightened views on the subject of education have already been referred to; but I may take the opportunity of adding that, besides directing the foundation of this college, the king has given several grants of money and land to the American Mission, besides a special donation of a thousand dollars towards the mission-school building at Petchaburee. These schools are for boys only, but it is to be hoped that before long similar institutions for women will be multiplied in the land, for the Siamese women are, as is the case with the females of all oriental races, sadly neglected, and almost entirely without means of education. There is, I believe, only one school for girls in Bangkok, and that is under the charge of, and entirely conducted by, two devoted American ladies, the Misses Hartwell and Olmstead, supported by the American Mission.

Postal and telegraphic facilities, again, are among the blessings which Siam will owe to the foresight of its present ruler. A fine building has just been erected as the " St. Martin's-le-Grand " of Bangkok, and to facilitate the work of the post-office all the houses in the city have been numbered; but here the administrative faculties of the officials have fallen short of the intelligent intentions of their king, for the clumsy method has been adopted of painting the numbers in Siamese characters on small boards, one of which is affixed to each house. Postage-stamps have been ordered from England, and, when I left, a batch of twenty telegraph clerks had been installed, ready for the completion of the lines from Saigon to Bang-kok, and arrangements were practically complete for adopting the European postal and telegraphic system. At the head of this department is Prince Krom Hluang Banupantawongse, one of the king's full brothers.

But the work which, in popular estimation at least, will make his Majesty's reign most memorable in Siam, is the completion and dedication of the great royal temple, Phra Sri Ratana Satsadaram, or, as it is usually called, Wat Phra Kao. The erection of this magnificent pile of buildings was commenced by King Phra Puttha Yot Fa Chulalok, " as a temple for the Emerald Buddha, the palladium of the capital, for the glory of the king, and as an especial work of royal piety." This temple was inaugurated with a grand religious festival in the year Maseng, 7th of cycle,[1] 1147, (A.D. 1785), but, having been very hastily got ready for the celebration of the third anniversary of the foundation of the capital, it was incomplete, only the church and library being finished. Various additions were made from time to time, but the Wat remained in an unfinished state until the present king came to the throne. The vow to complete the works was made on Tuesday, the 23rd of December, 1879. The works were commenced during the next month and completed on Monday, the 17th of April, 1882, a period of two years, three months, and twenty days. Thus it was reserved for King Chulalonkorn, at an enormous outlay, entirely defrayed out of his private purse, and by dint of great exertions on the part of those to whom the work was immediately entrusted, to complete this structure, and, on the hundredth anniversary of the capital of Siam, to give the city its crowning glory.

The work was placed under the direct superintendence of the king's brothers, each of whom had a particular part of the work allotted to him. One, for instance, relaid the marble pavement, and decorated the Obosot with pictures of the sacred elephant;

[1] For Siamese mode of reckoning time, see Appendix.

while a second renewed the stone inscriptions inside the Obosot; a third laid down a brass pavement in the Obosot; a fourth undertook to restore all the inlaid pearl work; another undertook the work of repairing the ceiling, paving, and wall-decoration, and made three stands for the seals of the kingdom; another changed the decayed roof-beams; another covered the great phrachedee with gold tiles—the effect of which in the brilliant sunlight is marvellously beautiful—and repaired and gilded all the small phrachedees; another renewed and repaired and re-decorated all the stone ornaments and flower-pots in the temple-grounds, and made the copper-plated and gilt figures of demons, and purchased many marble statues; two princes divided between them the repairs of the cloisters, renewing the roof where required, painting, gilding, paving with stone, and completing the capitals of columns, and so on. Thus, by division of labour, under the stimulus of devotion to the religion of the country, and of brotherly loyalty to the king, the great work was at length completed, after having been exactly 100 years in course of con-struction. On the 21st of April, 1882, the ceremony of final dedication was performed, with the greatest pomp, and amid general rejoicings.

Under the name "Wat Phra Kao" are included various buildings covering a large area of ground, which is surrounded by walls decorated with elaborate frescoes. In the centre is a temple, called the Phra Marodop, built in the form of a cross, where on festive occasions the king goes to hear a sermon from the prince-high-priest. The walls of this building are richly decorated with inlaid work, and the ceiling painted with a chaste design in blue and gold. The most striking feature, however, is the beautiful work

in the ebony doors, which are elaborately inlaid with
mother-of-pearl figures representing Thewedas, bor-
dered by a rich scroll. Behind this chapel-royal is the
great phrachedee, called the Sri Ratana Phrachedee,
entirely covered with gilt tiles, which were specially
made for the purpose in Germany to the order of
H.R.H. Krom Mun Aditson Udom Det.

There are several other large buildings in the
temple-grounds, but the structure in which the interest of the place centres is the Obosot, which shelters
the famous " Emerald Buddha," a green jade figure
of matchless beauty, which was found at Kiang Hai
in A.D. 1436, and, after various vicissitudes of fortune,
was at last placed in safety in the royal temple at
Bangkok. This image is, according to the season of
the year, differently attired in gold ornaments and
robes. The Emerald Buddha is raised so high up,
at the very summit of a high altar, that it is somewhat
difficult to see it, especially as light is not over plentiful, the windows being generally kept closely shut-
tered. For the convenience of visitors, however, the
attendants will for a small fee open one or two of the
heavy shutters, which are decorated on the outside
with gilt figures of Thewedas in contorted attitudes.
When at last the sun's rays are admitted through the
" dim religious light," and the beam of brightness
shines on the resplendent figure—enthroned above a
gorgeous array of coloured vases, with real flowers
and their waxen imitations, of gold, silver, and bronze
representations of Buddha, of Bohemian glassware,
lamps, and candlesticks, with here and there a
flickering taper still burning, and surrounded with a
profusion of many-storied umbrellas, emblems of the
esteem in which the gem is held—the scene is remarkably beautiful, and well calculated to have a lasting

effect on the minds of those who are brought up to
see in the calm, solemn, and dignified form of Buddha
the representation of all that is good here, and the
symbol of all happiness hereafter. The floor of the
Obosot is of tesselated brass, and the walls are
decorated with the usual perspectiveless frescoes,
representing scenes in Siamese or Buddhist history.

It is in this Obosot that the semi-annual ceremony
of *Tunam,* or drinking the water of allegiance, takes
place, when the subjects of Siam, through their representatives, and the princes and high officers of state
renew or confirm their oath of allegiance. The ceremony consists of drinking water sanctified by the
priests, and occurs twice a year—on the third day of
the waxing of the Siamese fifth month (*i.e.* the 1st of
April), and on the thirteenth day of the waning of the
Siamese tenth month (*i.e.* the 21st of September).

The foregoing description gives but a faint idea of
this sacred and historic edifice, which will henceforth
be regarded as a symbol of the rule of the present
Siamese dynasty, and the completion of which will
mark an epoch in Siamese history. On the morning
of the great day of dedication, all the princes assembled together, and recited before the king a full
account of the progress of the work, and of the share
taken in its completion by each of their number. His
Majesty's speech in reply is so characteristic that I
venture to reproduce it *in extenso :*—

"Princes of my family, and all who have assisted in
completing this temple Phra Ratana Satsadaram, who
have now come before me and given me the great
pleasure of hearing from you that this temple is finished
as I had desired! I rejoice as I thank you!

"This work of completing Wat Sri Ratana Satsadaram was undertaken in pious and grateful memory

of King Phra Puttha Yot Fa Chulalok, the first king of
this dynasty, who built this temple as a work of
royal merit, and the chief beauty and glory of this
capital, and of his successors, sovereigns of Siam, who
have worshipped in, and added to, this temple without
ceasing, down to our father, who took even a greater
interest than his predecessors in this great jewel
Buddha, but the completion of the temple according
to his Majesty's desires was interrupted by his prema-
ture decease. Hereafter, although the works continued
under various superintendents, the intricacy and costliness of the work precluded any satisfactory progress,
until, by division of the labour of superintendence and
the provision of ample funds, the temple has been
finished.

" When I reflected on the four sovereigns, my predecessors, adding to this temple and worshipping here,
and earnestly caring with deep devotion for this
jewel Buddha, I was moved by the strongest desire to
see this holy place completed and perfected in time
for the celebration of the centenary of the planting of
the palladium of this capital, Krung Ratana Kosindra,
as the temple and the capital were founded in the same
year and it would be the centenary of both ; but at
first almost all of you were really of opinion that so
great a work could not be completed within the time
desired.

" I also felt the greatest doubt as to the possibility of
completing the work ; but, for the two reasons already
mentioned, I was emboldened to worship and offer a
prayer before the jewel Buddha that, if I were to
continue long to reign over Siam, this temple might be
finished within the period I desired. Having thus
prayed, I assembled you, princes of my family, and
explained to you the two reasons for my wish as above

stated, namely that when our royal father died we were all very young, and there was no one able to show gratitude and love for him, and, having grown up, we were now of full age to do that great work on which our deceased father had set his heart as a work of merit and honour, but which was still unfinished, and that we ought to use all our efforts to finish it as he desired. Thus we should perform an afterwork of gratitude, and that not to the honour of His Majesty King Phra Bat Somdeth Pora Chom Klao only, but also to the enduring honour of His Majesty King Phra Bat Somdeth Phra Puttha Yot Fa Chulalok, founder of the dynasty.

" Secondly, I desired that the work should be finished in time for the centenary festival. I depended on you, my brothers, whom I have affectionately supported, helped, and brought up from childhood, and who have never had any single occasion of ill-will towards me, but have invariably shown your love for me, and I felt assured that this vow that I had made would have the effect of inspiring you to the utmost efforts to complete the work quickly, as you would surely desire the continuation of my life. As for the funds requisite, if they had to be paid from the public treasury, there would have arisen difficulties. After paying the ordinary public disbursements the balance would have been insufficient for the temple-works. Therefore I used money from the royal private treasury, left by King Phra Nang Klao, which just before his decease his Majesty devoted to temple-building, and my own private funds. The temple has been completed by funds from these two sources only.

" These my desires have been fulfilled, and now it is manifest that my wishes and my thoughts were correct and true. The completion of this temple makes my heart expand with joyfulness, for by it I have shown my gratitude to his Majesty the founder of my dynasty, and his Majesty my father and benefactor. And I have seen the ability, industry, and affection of you, my brothers, a significant token that you will with one accord help me to protect and to increase the prosperity of Siam by your fidelity, firmness, courage, energy, and perseverance, and—what is the most important of all—your unity and concord, in promoting continued prosperity. Also I am rejoiced by the fulfilment of this great work of piety in the religion of the Lord Buddha as I had designed, and I believe that the joy I feel will for the reasons given be also felt by you, my family.

"Princes of my family, I pray for blessings on you. May you enjoy long life, gladdened by high happiness. honour, wealth, and wisdom, to the advantage of the government of this country and its enduring prosperity, even as I have already told you of my desire! All of you have helped in completing this temple, some by the labour of your minds, some by the work of your hands; all have shown your affection to me. You have brought this work to a conclusion in accordance with my desires, and I thank you and invoke blessings on you.

"Princes and officers of all degrees, priests and laymen of all orders, all ye who, moved by pious regard for the three jewels, have assembled here, I invite you to join in our rejoicing, and may you obtain a share of the reward of merit, the happiness that each desires! I beg to make this offering of merit on behalf of the founder of my dynasty, long since passed away, and all his family. Angels in every place and every part of this realm join in praise and rejoicing at the completion of this eminent work of merit according to our desire!"

CHAPTER XXXI.

A national Siamese exhibition—Costly display of gems—Native
jewellery—National costumes—Fine arts—Inlaid mother-of-
pearl work and lacquer-ware—Bamboo and its uses—Agricultural
and forest produce—Fisheries—Minerals and precious stones—
Antiquities—Manufacture of Buddha images—The future of
Siam.

A VERY interesting feature of the centenary festivities was the Siamese National Exhibition—the first
ever held—for which a special building, consisting of
a series of bamboo pavilions, with a bamboo railing
round, was erected on an open plot of ground opposite
the royal palace. The exhibition was guarded by companies of soldiers—a very necessary precaution, not only
on account of the immense value of costly and unique
articles stored there, but from the fact that just before
the opening of the exhibition an attempt was made by
some miscreant to set fire to the buildings, a carefully-
prepared bundle of inflammable materials being discovered on fire against the railing, fortunately in time
for the soldiers on guard to extinguish it before any
serious damage was done. The exhibition embraced
in all some sixty sections, to each of which a separate
room was devoted. The attraction of the exhibition
was undoubtedly section nine, where a great number
of glass cases were arranged, displaying an endless
variety of beautiful and costly jewellery, most of it
the property of his Majesty, who constantly employs

a great number of jewellers and silversmiths. There were some lovely gold boxes, enamelled and inlaid with precious gems, the king's initials, the royal arms, &c.; heavy gold chains, bangles, gold and silver goblets, a great variety of gold and silver betel-boxes and spittoons, cigar-cases, and other articles, such as are from time to time given away as marks of the sovereign's favour.

Prominent among this array was a large glass case, in the centre of the room, containing a raised stand, in four tiers, the whole of which, from top to bottom, glittered with gems, mounted and unmounted, some of large size—especially diamonds and rubies—set in snuff-boxes, bracelets, vases, and rings, of all shapes and sizes. It was said that there were no less than 10,000 finger-rings, some of which were of huge size, and that the contents of the whole case were worth a million sterling.

In the room adjoining a great assortment of silver dishes, bowls, cups, and goblets were exhibited.

The manufacture of gold and silver jewellery, which is carried on to a large extent in Bangkok, is entirely in the hands of the Chinese. I have been into many workshops, and seen the workmen chiselling and hammering away at the *repoussé* work, melting the precious metals, gilding the silver-ware, but failed to find a single Siamese workman; they were all Chinese: and I was informed that of the numerous goldsmiths employed by his Majesty and the princes—all of whom have one or more gold and silversmiths always at work—not one was a Siamese. The natives, besides being unskilled in this branch of industry, lack the habits of industry and perseverance which are so characteristic of the Chinese.

The work is always done to order. There are no

elaborate displays in the shop-windows, and little to indicate the nature of the trade except a strip of red paper with black characters in China pasted on the wall, or a white board with black characters in Siamese hung outside the door. Sometimes the men sit in the windows, or in the doorway, to get the light, oblivious of the interest which the stranger to the city takes in their operations. Give a jeweller so much gold or silver, and you will receive it back in the shape of the object ordered, with a bill varying from half the weight to the full weight of the metal, according to the workmanship. The work is wanting in delicacy and finish, but is well suited for large objects, such as vases, open goblets, &c.

There is made in Bangkok one very effective kind of jewellery in silver, with patterns in gold embossed; the designs are original to Siam, but not the method of working them, for the work is a copy of the Indian Niello work, and reminded me of the celebrated Tula ware I have seen in Russia, though the Russian knows how to give a touch and finish to his work which the Oriental craftsman cannot imitate.

In another court at the exhibition were some interesting figures representing the Siamese officials in their state-costumes, and ladies from the royal harem in court-dress; the national costume was represented in a great variety of silk panungs, belts, sashes, jackets, and clothing of all kinds in use among prince and peasant; while cushions, triangular and square, and embroidered beautifully at each end in silk and gold, and mats of all shapes and sizes, represented the ordinary " furniture " of a house.

Fine art was not wanting. There was a room full of sketches, watercolour drawings, and oil-paintings, the subjects were mostly elephants, Rachasees, and

Hanumans. There were a few portraits, the work, I believe, of one artist, limner to his Majesty; and candour compels me to say that they were dreadful daubs. The artist was very polite, showing me his pictures, and explaining them, and saying that his Majesty had been pleased to buy a great number of him. He added that he was thinking of sending some of his works to "the Academy" in London, as he had a friend who could make interest for him, but I endeavoured to dissuade him from doing so, urging that the subjects and style were not suited to European tastes, for I felt sure he would only be disappointed.

If they have no painters, the Siamese can boast of a few sculptors, as I have remarked elsewhere; and in another section, the sculpture-gallery, were shown a number of well-modelled elephants and rhinoceroses, anatomically correct in design, beautifully finished, and altogether marvellously well executed. There were also some cleverly-executed models, in wood, of the principal temples and palaces.

Section fifty-two was devoted to specimens of the beautiful inlaid mother-of-pearl and lacquer-work, containing a number of trays and fruit-baskets, book-cases and panels of doors, most effectively inlaid with thousands of bits of mother-of-pearl in patterns representing angels, elephants, and other objects. This inlaid mother-of-pearl work is very popular among the Siamese, and gives employment to numbers of people. The effect of the iridescent nacre on the dark woods or lacquered ware is very fine, and now that the artistic and æsthetic caprice of fashion in Europe and the States is to decorate houses with china-ware and bronzes from Japan, crystal and jade carvings from China, Benares brass and silver-ware and other *bric-à-brac*, I think the Siamese should contribute their share

of ornamentation to the drawing and dining-rooms in
the West. I am sure their inlaid mother-of-pearl ware
would find a ready sale, and, besides being a source of
great profit to them, these effective works of art would
serve to relieve the dulness of the dirty yellow and sulky
grey ornaments that now reign supreme on our mantle-
pieces and sideboards. His Majesty exhibited a magnificent collection of works of this kind, two of which, large
inlaid mother-of-pearl pictures, one of the royal arms,
the other of the " Adoration of Buddha by Thewedas,"
attracted special attention. The latter was an exqui-
sitely-finished and effective specimen of this quaint
art, the colours, caused by the refraction of the rays of
light by the nacre, and dependent therefore upon the
selection of the pieces and upon the manner in which
they were inserted, being wonderfully well arranged.

Besides these were two large cabinets destined to
contain the sacred manuscripts in some temple-library,
also inlaid with thousands upon thousands of carefully-
cut bits of pearl-shell ; and a number of *talum muk*—the
trays given by the princes and nobles to high priests
when they make offerings of garments.

The use of these trays, which are very expensive, is
practically confined to the high priests, as they are as
expensive as silver-ware, and the priests are not allowed
to possess any articles of either gold or silver or their
equivalents. The trays made for the use of the
ordinary priests are manufactured in a peculiar manner. Although firm and apparently solid, as if made
of wood, they are made of strips of bamboo woven
together, upon which a paste, made of a mixture of
rack lacquer, oil, and ashes, is run. The pattern in
mother-of-pearl is then stuck on, and the intervening
spaces filled up with rack to the level of the surface of
the mother-of-pearl.

Of ordinary wicker-work or bamboo-plait articles, unlacquered, there was (in section thirty-three) an instructive collection. What bamboo is *not* used for, it is difficult to say, and the array of mats, baskets, water-buckets, paddy-bins, &c., used by the Siamese, large as it was, might have been indefinitely enlarged if the exhibition had been open to foreign nations, and if the value of the bamboo were everywhere as fully appreciated as it is in Siam.

Very characteristic of this Land of Elephants was a small room full of a grand and probably matchless variety of elephant-tusks, with a few rhinoceros-horns. There were seven grades of ivory exhibited, the finest of which would sell in Bangkok for $360 the picul. Rhinoceros-horn, used as medicine, is worth as much as $22 for 1⅓ lbs.

Of planters' (cultivated) and forest (wild) produce I have only space to mention *en bloc* a great many varieties of rice and tobacco, which no doubt deserved careful attention; cardamoms—the true variety—of which there are large plantations in the Chantaboon and Singora districts, and which sell in Bangkok for $150 per picul, whereas the bastard cardamoms (also exhibited from Matabaung, Siamrahp, &c.) realize only $18 per picul; golden gamboge from Chantaburee, which sells in Bangkok at $78 per picul, while inferior gamboge only realizes $24 per picul; teak-wood, sapan-wood, eagle-wood, and rose-wood; sugar; pepper; sticklac; birds'-nests; buffalo, deer, elephant, and rhinoceros-hides; cotton; mangrove-bark; gum Benjamin; Lukrabow seed; resins; and bees-wax. This last I have already mentioned as being largely used in the service of the temples throughout Siam and Lao, but it deserves special reference here, on account of the great skill the Siamese display in making not only wax candles, but wax flowers, figures, models of buildings, and other objects, often beautifully coloured, all of which go to the temples to be burned, being offered to the priests at certain festivals.

The fishing industry was also represented in the well-known *pla-tu*, *pla-heng*, and *pla-salit*, in holothuria, dried mussels and prawns, echinoderms, ray-skins and shark-fins, and tortoise-shells.

The section devoted to minerals and precious stones in their natural state was very interesting, Siam being very rich in ores. Gold[1] is found in several parts of the kingdom, principally at Kabin,[2] about 100 miles E.N.E. of Bangkok, where vast amounts of money of late years have been expended in machinery. Kabin is, I am told, connected by a railway with Pachin, twenty-five miles to the W.N.W. Copper is found in large quantities, especially rich ores existing in Korat. Iron also of excellent quality is plentiful; argentiferous lead is abundant in the north-eastern provinces, but tin is the most abundant ore of all, and an important article of export. It is found in the Siamese provinces of Xalang, Xaija, Xumphon, and Pak Phrëk, and also throughout the Malay Peninsula. As in the island of Banca, and Billiton, the mines are worked by Chinese Kongsees, or companies.

Precious stones are collected in many parts, especially sapphires, rubies, zircons, garnets, and cat's-eyes near the mountains round Chantaboon.

Of antiquities and curiosities, there was a fine col-

---

[1] The Siamese distinguish six qualities of gold : (1) Nopakun kow nam; (2) Nua paat; (3) Nua chet; (4) Nua hok; (5) Nua ha; (6) Nua see. These six grades date from olden times—as early as 1347—when gold was plentiful in Chieng Saan. Gold of the first two grades realizes in value from sixteen to eighteen times its weight in silver.

[2] See Appendix for geographical sketch of Siam.

lection of weapons and arms from hill-tribes scattered throughout Siam and Lao, and an equally interesting show of ancient coins, some flat and some spherical, solid bars of silver or gold with a stamp at one end, side by side with old paper currency, lead, crockery, and porcelain tokens, and cowries.

An industry which was not represented at the exhibition, but which in this sketch of the industries of the Land of Temples deserves brief mention here, is the manufacture of figures of Buddha. In the main road just outside the city-wall are three or four establishments for the manufacture and sale of these idols, which must be one of the most profitable industries in Bangkok. The sale is constant and increasing, and the mere work of gilding and regilding the more expensive figures never ceases. The models vary in quality and price to suit every pocket, from the rudely-moulded resin figures covered with a thin sheathing of silver, to the more elaborately-wrought carved figures of wood, ornamented with bits of glass or bright metal inlaid, and so on to the carefully-wrought bronze castings, which are, however, becoming more and more rare. Artistic taste in this respect in modern Siam does not equal the skill which produced the old bronze figures such as those which I unearthed in Lao.

The exhibition was a decided success, and fitly proved one of the features of the centennial festivities of Bangkok by bringing into one general view the resources of the country, and suggesting future possibilities of the expansion of its trade. The natural resources of the country are very great, and, with the "awakening" which the progressive policy of the present king has brought about, Siam has a prosperous future in store.

CHAPTER XXXII.

A farewell interview with the king—A royal art-critic—Visit to the
royal harem—The "chapel royal"—A crystal Buddha—The
royal monastery—Good-bye to Siam—Return to Europe.

SUCH claims were made upon the time and attention
of the king by the various ceremonies in connexion
with the celebration of the hundredth birthday of his
capital, that it was the middle of July before his
Majesty was able to fix a day on which I was to have
the honour of an audience, which I solicited in order to
thank his Majesty for the gracious and generous aid
he had afforded me in the prosecution of my journey
through his dominions.

H.R.H. Prince Devan introduced me into the presence of the sovereign, who, as he shook hands with me,
congratulated me on my return, though, he added, I
had become so thin that I was only the half of my former
self. Though only half of my body might be there, I
could assure his Majesty that all my soul was in the
thanks which I desired to offer him for the very generous assistance he had extended to me during my stay in
his kingdom. He asked to see my sketches, and, sitting
down at a table to examine them carefully, showed that,
if not himself an artist, he is a competent art-critic,
for he readily noticed points in some of them in which
they were out of drawing. His Majesty said he did not
think I had chosen very good-looking women as subjects;

but I answered that I had endeavoured to select good types of the characteristic features of the people in different parts of the country. As for the women, it was always a matter of difficulty to get a woman to sit for her portrait at all, as they were afraid of evil spirits, and, I always thought, still more afraid of the foreigner, whom they probably considered to be a fiend incarnate.

In reply to his Majesty's questions I gave a short *résumé* of my journey, and of the many obstacles placed in my way by the natives, on which he remarked that many of my troubles were no doubt due to the faults of my interpreter. This suggestion, coming voluntarily from the king, more than confirmed my own opinions on this point, for I felt sure that Kao, good servant though he was, did not always interpret my words correctly. Almost more than anything else, the success of a traveller in a strange land depends upon the use made of the tongue of his interpreter.

The King very kindly presented me with the portraits of himself and his Queen and of the Crown Prince, copies of which adorn the pages of this book.

Before leaving Bangkok I had the pleasure and privilege of being conducted within the precincts of the king's harem by His Royal Highness Prince Diss, his Majesty's aide-de-camp, to whom I am indebted for many acts of courtesy and kindness. The permission to enter the harem was a very special favour, which is granted to very few men. Certain men trusted by the king are allowed to enter the harem at certain times to perform the necessary work incidental to the cleaning and repairs of the rooms, but the presence of mankind is rigorously interdicted at all other times, and, I believe, no eunuchs are in attendance. At the same time I was permitted to visit the Wat Putta Niwet, or Buddha's Palace, which might be termed the private chapel of the king, and the privilege of entering which is accorded only, with the king's special permission, to favoured visitors.

The "chapel" is a very small apartment, but is noted as containing a matchless crystal figure of Buddha, placed on the top of a magnificent altar of carved ivory, with the upper portions gilt or of solid gold. The beautiful transparency of the crystal figure lends to it a peculiar charm which it is difficult to describe in words. Before this unique representation of the lord Buddha, the queen and the court ladies offer their devotions. On either side were two gold trees, part of the tribute from Chengmai or one of the Lao states, while near at hand were two smaller figures of Buddha.

Adjoining this Buddha's palace is the monastery, a small carpeted room, in which the king served his priesthood. The most striking objects in this chamber are a series of native wall-frescoes, in the peculiar perspectiveless style of art of the country, illustrating various episodes in the king's life; among others being his first audience given to European ambassadors, and the regent paying homage—an incident in the king's childhood in which his governess, droll Mrs. Leonowens, figures.

But the time for bidding good-bye to Bangkok and to Siam was rapidly drawing near, and, after a round of visits to bid farewell to the many friends who had conspired together to render my stay there so pleasant, and whose names have been recorded in these pages, I left the city on the 2nd of August, on board the S.S. *Ban Jong Hu*, for Singapore, whence in due time I took passage for Europe.

APPENDIX.

APPENDIX I.

NOTES ON THE CUSTOMS OF THE ROYAL FAMILY OF SIAM, AND
THE POSITION OF PRINCES, ESPECIALLY OF THOSE STYLED
" CHAOFA,"¹ " PRA ONG CHAO," AND " KROM."

THE royal family of Siam observes customs many of which
appear to be peculiar to the country, differing even from the
customs of the neighbouring Laosians; as for example in the
provision made in Siam for the rapid descent from princeship to
commonership which prevents a surplusage of princes, while, in
Lao, sons all take their father's title, and consequently throughout Cheng-Mai and Hluang Prabang there are so many princes
that they are often grateful for employment as corporals in
charge of nine or ten men.

If the customs of Siam are viewed with such light as the
accepted histories, since 1351, throw upon them, they will be
found to have changed much and often in names and in matters
of individual precedence, but not in important principles.
They were modified from time to time by the reigning sovereign for the better governance of his kinsmen in days when the
country was little civilized. During the two hundred years from
about A.D. 1350 to 1550 very few changes were made. Then
followed a period of transition, during which the customs gradually
became very similar to those which now prevail. The most
reliable evidence extant of the customs of precedence, dignity,
and privilege during the first two hundred years is afforded by
the book of royal edicts, " Kot Montieraban," laws for the regu-
lation of the royal palace, enacted by King Ramathibodi I. in

¹ " Chao " is the official orthography of the Siamese word for prince,
which is popularly spelt " Chow," the method adopted in the foregoing pages. The information in this appendix being derived from
a distinguished source, the official or court orthography is retained.

1359, eight years after he had founded the old capital Ayuthia.
In these edicts the dignity and prerogatives of the king, and the
rank and privileges of princes and officials, high and low, are all
set forth in order, but the expressions used are so antiquated that
none but unusually well-read Siamese can understand them.
Hence, although every Siamese knows the edicts by name, very
few indeed have read them. These laws define four ranks of
princes, sons of the king :—

1. King's sons by a royal queen (Akkamahesi) were styled
Somdet No Putthi Chao, " most excellent buds of the wise lord."
These princes were on no account allowed to leave the capital
city.

2. Sons of the king by a princess, herself daughter of a king,
were styled Luk Hluang Ek, " first-class royal children." It
was usual to appoint them to rule over first-class provinces, such
as Pitsanulok, Sukothia, and Nachou Rachasima or Korat.

3. Children of the king by a princess, granddaughter of a
king, were also called Luk Hluang, " royal children," and were
actually appointed rulers over second-class provinces, such as
Sarwankalop and Supau.

4. Children by concubines were styled Pra Yaowarat,
" royal youths ;" they were not appointed to governments.

Each of these classes took precedence of the class below it, the
young child of the higher class had precedence of aged men of
the class next below. The princes appointed to govern provinces
were no mere titular chiefs, but really governed their territories,
hence the people applied to them the title Chaofa, that being to
this day the term by which the laws speak of all their prince-
rulers, both in large states and small ones. In the correspondence
with Lao and other up-country chieftains during the war for the
suppression of the Haw marauders, the term Chaofa is frequently
used, and applied not only to the rulers of every petty district,
such as Niut and Senni, but also to the kings of Siam and
Annam. It means and should be translated as nothing more
than " prince-ruler," literally, " prince from the skies," a grandi-
loquent expression implying a descent from angels, in accordance
with the Indian belief in the divine or angelic ancestry of kings
and princes. It is to be noticed that the title Chaofa was ap-
plicable to two grades of princes only, and was given neither to
the highest nor to the lowest, but only to those princes whose

mothers were daughters or granddaughters of kings. The custom of appointing princes to govern provinces prevailed for about two hundred years; then successive kings ceased to make appointments, and let the custom fall into disuse. No proclamation of intention was made, but the system was changed quietly, for the old system had often brought misfortune on the country when Chaofa princes fought among themselves for the kingdom, or leagued with the enemies of Siam against some royal brother by a different mother.

Although the reason for the title Chaofa was thus removed the title remained, and was persistently applied to those two classes of princes, and as the kings, for political reasons, exalted no ladies to the overpowering rank of queen, no sons were born to them of higher rank than these Chaofas, and the term came to signify prince of the highest degree. Then when again some of the ladies were styled queens, their children were called Chaofas also, and so Chaofa became, and has remained, the term applied to the best-born princes of Siam. The Chaofas when they ruled in almost royal state over the first-class provinces had the right of being preceded by a band of spearmen, and when going in state on the river of having an escort of long boats, and boats with men standing and beating time with flagstaves. Both these royal prerogatives they have continued to enjoy, though they have no territory to rule over. They alone, among the princes, can be anointed with water from the coronation-vase, which the Brahmins would decline to use for any one whose parents were not both of royal blood, in the belief that it would certainly bring calamity upon them. It could not, for instance, be used for the present Wangna, whose maternal ancestry is not royal. Chaofas can, however, receive from the Brahmins offerings made to Vishnu at the annual swinging festival (Piti Tri Yampawai), which none but Vishnu, the King, or a Chaofa, could receive without bringing destruction upon themselves.

From their birth Chaofas are distinguished above other princes; they have special musicians, with special instruments, who play to them the music reserved for kings; and singers, who sing to to them in high-flown language used for no others; Brahmins place them in their cradle chanting odes from the Ranaxana; their male and female nurses are honoured with the title Pra, and styled Pra Pidieng Pra Nom; a full establishment of officers of the household is assigned to them, and they all have their pages and their tutors. On reaching their ninth year, they are taken to the river, and, seated on a raft under a four-sided spire (mandop), go through a great bathing ceremony. When the time arrives for a Chaofa's topknot to be cut, there are grand festivities and processions, lasting six days; an artificial hill is built to represent Mount Krailat, by the side of which the Chaofa sits enthroned on a lion's skin, covered by a carpet having a dragon embroidered on it. The topknot is shaved, not in three tufts as in other persons, but in five tufts. Chaofas use trays, teapots, boxes, and other insignia of gold enamelled, while other princes and officers can only appear in the royal presence with plain gold insignia.[2]

As at birth a Chaofa has his appointed servants, so on death official mourners are appointed to sing dirges, day after day, until his cremation, which does not take place in an ordinary building, but in a lofty and gorgeous pavilion, of a special design, the very floor of which is raised high above the ground.

A Chaofa if appointed as Krom to the charge of a department cannot take the lower rank of Krom, but must at least be Krom Khun, and in the scale of relative importance, called " Sakna," or marks of dignity, he is more highly regarded than other princes are.

	Dignity marks.
A Chaofa brother of the king has	20,000.
If he takes office as Krom he has	50,000.
A Chaofa son of the king has	15,000.
If he takes office as Krom	40,000.
An ordinary prince brother of the king has. . .	7,000.
„ „ „ son „ „ „ . . .	6,000.
Either of these taking office has	15,000.
An ordinary prince grandson of the king has . .	4,000.

This scale, which was fixed nearly 500 years ago, shows the high regard in which Chaofas are held by law. When ordinary sons of a king are appointed to take charge of departments or

[2] His late Majesty, Pra Chom Klao, permitted a very few who were not Chaofas to use enamelled boxes, &c., on a plain gold tray. This refers only to the official style of enamel called Ya Rachawadi. Two or three favoured noblemen are permitted to use gold with Chinese enamel.

Kroms, they cease to use their own name, and become known only by the name of their department; but Chaofas retain their own name, or, more properly speaking, the title conferred on them in their ninth or tenth year, which is engraved on a plate of gold presented to them by the king.[3]

Besides their official name or style, Chaofas have a title given to them by the people ; as Phyas are addressed by their equals and inferiors as Chao Khun, "lord of benefits," so Chaofas are addressed and spoken of as Tun Kramom : neither word is official, and to speak of a Phya to the king as Chao Khun would be a violation of court etiquette, which requires that full official titles should be used. So in public audience the use of the words Tun Kramom is inadmissible, and the Chaofa's full style must be given, but in private audience, although a Phya may not be spoken of as Chao Khun, a Chaofa may be referred to as Tun Kramom.

The title of the present king of Siam while still a Chaofa was as follows : " Somdet Pra Chao Luk Ya To, Chaofa Chulalonkorn Bodinthara Thipaya Maha Mongkut Burutsaya Ratana Rah Rawiwongs Wurutana Pongs Boriphat Sri Watana Racha Kuman."

The title of a Chaofa always contains his father's name, or rather a portion of the name indicating his father. Thus the words Maha Mongkut, in the above name, are the principal words in the style of the late king, his Majesty's father. But the reference is not always very clear to foreigners ; thus his Majesty's brother's name is related to that of his father by the word Makut, a form of the word Mongkut. In the style of the Chaofa Maha Mala, again, the word Mahisarthirat refers to that of his father King Pra Putthi Lot La, one of whose names was Isara.

Chaofa princesses have only short names, not including any portion of the name of their father.

A Chaofa succeeding to the throne is said to be Upato Siyati Sansutta Khroni, or " pure," that is, well-born paternally and maternally, " the offspring of a pure womb."

Sons of a king address their father as Tun Kramom Keon, or Tun Kramom, and children of Chaofas address their fathers in the

[3] A Chaofa in charge of a Krom adds the style of the Krom to his style of Chaofa.

same way.   The use of this word was approved of by King Pra
Chom Klao.

The customs above mentioned date from the first 200 years after
Ayuthia was founded, and have been steadily observed ever since,
excepting on occasions when the ceremonial haircutting had to be
reduced in pomp owing to state necessities.   The Montieraban
edicts contain many other particulars, the relation of which would
be tedious, the more so as the observances are mostly obsolete.   The
customary use of the title Chaofa during the 300 years next
following the period above spoken of, and up to the present day,
must be deduced from the precedents of history.

During this period we first find Chaofas whose rights to that
title depended on seven different contingencies : —

1. Chaofas by creation on the first establishment of a dynasty.
A king seating himself on the throne by the conquest of his
enemies may raise to the rank of Chaofa those princes and
princesses among his relations who would have been Chaofas by
birth if he had been a Chaofa and purely born.

Thus King Pra Putthi Yot Fa, on taking the throne, raised
his two elder sisters and four of his children by Somdet Amarundr
Ammat to the rank of Chaofa, creating the mother a princess.
King Pra Nang Klao, coming to the throne by ordinary family
succession, not by conquest, did not elevate his brothers to the
rank of Chaofa.

2. Chaofas by right of birth, children of a king by the
daughter of a king, such as Chao Fa Maha Mala, son of King
Pra Putthi Lot La, by the Princess Chaofa Kunkan, daughter
of Pra Putthi Yot Fa.

3. Children of a king by the granddaughter of a king are
Chaofas if their mother is promoted to the rank of Pra Ong Chao,
but not otherwise, so that their right depends on the king's
pleasure, except in the case where their mother has herself by
birth the right to the title Pra Ong Chao, which she will have if
both her parents are children of a king—a very rare case.   King
Pra Chom Klao promoted Mom Chow Ying, a daughter of Prince
Lakkana Ruman, to be a Pra Ong Chao, and she bore him a child
a Chaofa.   He also promoted Mom Chao Ramphoi, as granddaughter of King Pra Nang Klao, to be Pra Ong Chao, made her
queen consort, and had by her four Chaofas.

4. Children of a foreign princess, the daughter of an indepen-

dent king, or of a king dependent on Siam but not stripped of his rank, may be created Chaofa. Thus it was that the Princess Kunkan, daughter of the King Vunchan, was created a Chaofa. A Chaofa of this class is thought less of than a Chaofa whose parents are both of the king's own family. In King Pra Chom Klao's reign, the Princesses Nak Emm and Tuanka Suphea, daughters respectively of the king of Cambodia and the sultan of Linga, were inmates of the royal harem, and his Majesty announced that any children they might have would be regarded as Chaofas. This declaration of his Majesty was disapproved of by many persons.

5. Children of a Chaofa princess are Chaofas by courtesy. But Chaofa princesses cannot marry any one below their own rank, not even a Pra Ong Chao son of the king. Hence they cannot marry a foreign prince, and are limited to the choice of their closest relations, to the Chaofas Wangna, or to the king himself. And as princes and princesses generally decline to marry each other, there is very seldom born a Chaofa of the second degree.

6. Children of the Wangna have on two occasions been Chaofas by creation, by special favour of the supreme king. These were the Princess Pi Kun Tong, whose mother was a princess of Chengmai, and the Prince Isarapong, whose mother was a Wangna's daughter, and who, after remaining a simple Pra Ong Chao until his thirtieth year, was promoted to be a Chaofa. Other children of the Second Kings by princess-mothers were not allowed to rank as Chaofas. Even those created Chaofas are not styled Somdet, but have the inferior title of Pra Boworawongs, &c. The son of a Wangna by a mother, herself a Chaofa, would be a Chaofa by right under class five.

7. There is one instance of an appointment of Chaofa not consistent with the principles which hold in all the above six cases. In the reign of Phya Taksin, King of Ianaburi, one of the generals (afterwards King Pra Putthi Yot Fa) held an extraordinary position as Maha Krasat Suk, " great king of war," with full royal power during war, and war was incessant. He married the king's daughter, who bore him a son, and this son was created Chaofa by an extension of the prerogative of a king by conquest.

During 300 years there have been Chaofas of the above classes only. The laws are silent as to the relative rank of Chaofas among each other, but indicate age as giving precedence. In the opinion of the present king of Siam, elder brothers and uncles of the king, if Chaofas, would rank above Chaofas who are younger brothers of the king, but the public does not judge between Chaofas by any rule of age, but by the descent of their mothers; the more unmixed the royal blood of the mother, the more intimately related she is to the king, the higher is the public estimation of the Chaofa.

We will now look at the position of the princes styled in the old palace "Laus Pra Yaowarat," and other princes of inferior degree :—

1. All offspring of the king by his concubines Pra Sanom also called Chao Chom Manda, are equal and have the title Pra Ong Chao.

2. In the times when Ayuthia was the capital of the empire, the offspring of Wangnas (Second Kings), were sometimes styled Pra Ong Chao, sometimes Mom Chao, but since Bangkok became the capital the supreme king, in consideration of the services of Wangnas in war, has always allowed all their sons the title of Pra Ong Chao.

3. The children of the Wang Lang (duplicate second king) have in like manner the title Pra Ong Chao.

4. Grandchildren of the king, when both father and mother are children of the king, are also Pra Ong Chao.

5. Grandchildren of a king, being elder sons, or in consideration of having done good service, may at the king's pleasure be raised to the dignity of Pra Ong Chao. But grandchildren of a Wangna or a Wang Lang are not eligible for that promotion.

The above are the five classes of Pra Ong Chao princes, but their rank depends on quite a different classification and is indicated by the first words of the style of each prince as follows :—

1. Pra Chao Borom Anjaka-*to*, the grandfathers and grandmothers of "*to*," that is, of *him*, the only reigning king.

2. Pra Chao Boroma Wongs-*to*, the uncles and aunts of *him* the king.

3. Pra Chao Pi Ya-*to*, elder brothers of *him* the king;
Pra Chao Pi Nang-*to*, elder sisters of *him* the king;
Pra Chao Nong Ya-*to*, younger brothers of *him* the king;

Pra Chao Nong Nang-*to*,. younger sisters of *him* the king.

All these three grades have equal " Sakna " or dignity marks, that is, 7000 when not in charge of a Krom, or 15,000 when in charge of a Krom.

4. Pra Chao Luk Chai-*to*, sons of *him* the king ;

Pra Chao Luk Ying-*to*, daughters of *him* the king.

5. Pra Chao Rachawongs-*to*, a special title instituted in the reign of King Pra Chom Klao, in favour of the sons of his brother and predecessor, Pra Nang Klao, who, under the usual rule, would by his succession have sunk from the dignity of king's son to that of king's nephew. The king to prevent this hardship created this new style, with rank equal to that of ordinary sons of the king. These two grades have equal Sakna or dignity marks, that is, 6000 if not in charge of a Krom, and 15,000 if in charge of a Krom.

All the above five grades are first-class Pra Ong Chao princes.

There are seven grades of second-class Pra Ong Chao princes, as follows :—

1—4. Pra Chao Worawongs-*to*, of four grades, first, the sons of the Wangna of King Pra Putthi Yot Fa's reign ; second, the sons of the Wangna of King Pra Putthi Lot La's reign ; third, the sons of the Wangna of King Pra Nang.Klao's reign ; fourth, such sons of the Wangna of King Pra Chom Klao's reign as are older than the reigning king.

5, 6. Pra Chao Boworawongs-*to* of the first class, viz. children of the Wangna of King Pra Chom Klao's reign, younger than the reigning king, and Pra Chao Boworawongs-*to* of the second class, viz. the children of the present Wangna.

7. Pra Chao Lan-*to*, viz. nephews and grandsons of the king who are entitled to Pra Ong Chao rank, being sons of a Pra Ong Chao princess, or by promotion from the rank of Mom Chao.

All the above seven grades have 4000 Sakna, when not holding a department, and 11,000 when holding a department.

There are three grades of Pra Ong Chao princes of the third class :—

1. Pra P'rap' ant' awongs-to, children of the Krom Mum Mataya Pitak, maternal grandfather of the present king.

2. Pra Wongs-to, grandsons of former kings who are entitled

to Pra Ong Chao rank by being sons of a Pra Ong Chao princess, or by promotion from the rank of Mom Chao.

3. Pra Samp' ant' awongs-to, sons of a Wang Lang by a Pra Ong Chao princess, or of Chaofas sons of the elder sisters of King Pra Putthi Yot Fa.

These three grades have never had Sakna assigned to them beyond the 1500 which they were entitled to as Mom Chao. This is an omission of the law, for decidedly their Sakna ought to be higher. When appointed to the charge of a Krom, they have 11,000 Sakna assigned to them, and are equal in rank with princes of the second class.

Such are the three classes and fifteen styles of Pra Ong Chao princes, and it is manifest that, as the dynasty continues, new complexities of relationship continually arising will in each reign give rise to one or two new styles. Chaofas use whichever of the above styles expresses their relationship to the reigning king, prefaced by the word "Somdet."

The relationship is in many cases directly expressed in the style, as "Pi Ya," elder brother, &c., but in most cases it is only inferred, the terms used being simply honorary, as "royal race," for cousin, "grand race," and "effulgent race," for Wangna kindred (second and third cousins of the king), &c. The most significant part of the style is the word *to* (*him*) at the end; it implies the relationship to the supreme king, and cannot be applied to any other, but ignorant Siamese sometimes mistake it, and several times in the late reign petitioners were flogged for presenting petitions in which children of the Wangna were styled children of To.

Special permission to use certain of these styles is occasionally granted by the sovereign to those whose style would otherwise be lower. Thus in the present reign the style of Pra Anjaka-to (grandmother of the king) has been granted to her Royal Highness Krom Somdet Pra Suda Ratana Rat Prayun, the king's grandmother on the mother's side, who acted as guardian from the time of his mother's death, and so from his earlier years has been regarded by the king as grandmother. Also in the present reign the style of Pra Chao Boroma Wongs-to (uncle of the king) has been conferred on the Krom Pra Pawaret Waruja Longkorn, the head of the priests, and the king's teacher, who is by birth only a second-class prince, entitled to be styled Warawongs-to of the second grade (*i.e.* he is a son of the Wangna of the reign of Pra Putthi Lot La).

The prince by title next below that of Pra Ong Chao is Mom Chao, which is the title of the children of Chaofas and Pra Ong Chao princes, by mothers who are not themselves Pra Ong Chao princesses. Their dignity marks are 1500. The children of Mom Chao are Mom Rachawong, with 500 dignity marks. The children of Mom Rachawong, are Mom Hluang, with 400 dignity marks. The children of Mom Hluang are commoners.

When Mom Rachawong or Mom Hluang hold an office of any note, they are generally styled Mom Rachanikun. Certain of them formed a body-guard for the king in the old war-system, riding the elephants which protected the royal elephant, and these had 1000 dignity marks. These posts are no longer filled up, and Mom Rachawongs now often drop their princely title, and take that of the office they may hold. Even in old times their court-dress was the " pa-som-phak " (figured waist-cloth) expressive of office, such as noblemen wear, with a plain white silk sash. Princes of higher rank could wear any colour they pleased.

There are seven grades of official promotion, which the king may confer on princes from Mom Chao upwards, all involving the chiefship of a Krom or department :—

1. The dignity of Krom Pra Rachawong Bowara Tatham Mongkon fai ha, chief of the vanguard, called by foreigners second king. To this dignity two may be appointed. When only one is appointed, he is generally known as Krom Pra Rachawong, or as Pra Bant'un. When two are appointed, they are called, respectively, the greater and the lesser Pra Bant'un. Bant'un is an office of a prince of this grade, and so is commonly used for the prince himself.

2. The dignity of Krom Pra Rachawong Bowara Sathan Pimuk fai Lang, chief of the rearguard, a duplicate second king. To this dignity two may be appointed at one time, but there is only one instance of this double appointment, and as a rule there is but one, who is styled Pra Racha Wang Lang.

3. The dignity of Krom Somdet Pra.

4. „ „ „ Krom Pra.

5. „ „ „ Krom Hluang.

6. „ „ „ Krom Khun.

7. The dignity of Krom Mun.

In most cases a prince on taking charge of a department with any of these ranks ceases to be addressed by his name as a prince, and is called by the style of his department. Formerly the prince's name preceded the style of the department, as still is customary in the case of Chaofas, but as the princes' original names were often very short and common, and Siamese are fond of high-sounding, long names, it became a matter of courtesy to drop the name altogether, and now the style of the department is used, with the prefix " Nai," which means " sir," or he who is in such a Krom (office). Krom may be translated " department," or " body of men," and a Krom originally was the whole body of retainers and dependants of a prince, formed into an organized regiment, with officers, of whom the three chief ones were the Chao Krom, Palat Krom, and Samubanchi (manager, deputy, and registrar). The Chao Krom, or manager, has a title identical with the name of his department : thus in the Krom Mun Waret Racha Wararit, the Chao Krom (manager) has the title Mun Waret Racha Wararit, and the prince has the title Nai Krom (or Kromma) Mun Waret Racha Wararit.

In the case of the Kroms of the Wangna and Wang Lang (the second kings), there is no manager bearing the title of the Krom as above, but the title is in itself different in its nature, signifying " the department of the royal palace " named so-and-so ; and the organization is also different, the retainers being far more numerous, and the officers many and high in rank.

In respect of the title being taken from the palace, it is to be noted that certain old palaces have names better established than those of their occupants, and, in such cases the occupants are very likely to be called after their residence, while in the case of new palaces, the residence is generally called after the occupant.

Thus the palace of the prince last referred to by name is known simply as Wang Kromma Mun Waret, but the palace where the Chaofa Maha Mala, Kromma Pra Bamrap Parapax lives, is called the " Wang Nok " (outside palace), and that prince is often referred to as " Wang Nok."

At Ayuthia, the palace of the Wang Na was on the eastern front or face of the city, and therefore called " Na." The Wang Lang's palace was below or behind the city, and was therefore called "Lang." The Wangnas have each a distinctive name added to that part of their title which expresses their office. They are all Krom Pra Rachawang Bowara, and the subjoined list shows the personal affix during the last three reigns :—

Wangna of King Nang Klao's reign was Maha Sakdi Polla Seph.

Wangna of King Chom Klao's reign had a higher dignity than his predecessors or successor, and was really a king—King Pra Pin Klao.

Wangna of the present reign is Wichaichan.

When the prince holding the office of Wangna gives an order, it is called "Bant'un," except in the case of the King Pra Pin Klao, whose commands were "Ongkan" (king's command).

A command of a Wang Lang is called "Bancha."

Commands of princes of lower degree are called "Rap Sang."

The third grade of dignities in the above list is that of Krom Somdet Pra, and after it Krom Pra. In speaking of a prince of the Somdet Pra grade, some words must precede the word "Somdet," implying the degree of relationship to the sovereign as before explained. If "Somdet" were used as first word in the style it would imply, not that the Krom was of Somdet Pra rank, but that the prince who directed the Krom was a Chaofa. The manager (Chao Krom) of a Krom Somdet Pra has the rank of Phya. The manager of a Krom Pra has the rank of Pra; the manager of a Krom Hluang has the rank of Hluang, and so on.

It very rarely happens that the higher Kroms are conferred on any except first-class Pra Ong Chao princes of the reigning king's family ; but in the reign of King Pra Nang Klao, a son of the Wang Lang was appointed Krom Hluang Seni, for distinguished military service ; and in the present reign a prince, son of the Wangna of the reign of Pra Putthi Lot La, has been, on account of his high standing in the priesthood, appointed Krom Pra Pawaret. Two or three princes of Wangna descent have been appointed Krom Khun, but in general they are not appointed to a higher office than Krom Mun.

Precedence among princes depends on the family grade of the prince, not on the Krom or official position, and, when other things are equal, seniority in age gives precedence ; an elder brother not holding a department precedes his younger brother, though a Krom.

E e

All princes with departments, and almost all Pra Ong Chao princes, sons of a king, receive similar gold insignia teapots, &c., and now all receive the Commandership of the Chula Chom Klao Order. Princes with Kroms use at their appointment a pointed, gold, enamelled crown, with a tuft of bird of paradise feathers; they have a sword with gold or pinchbeck sheath, and they ride in a covered litter.

The topknot-cutting ceremony [4] of princes, not being Chaofas, is not defined by law, and its grandeur depends on the king's pleasure; so also does the amount of state with which they enter the priesthood.

[4] The ceremony of " topknot-cutting " is an important event in the life of every Siamese, and occurs at the age, according to circumstances, of eleven, thirteen, fifteen, or seventeen years—the girls undergoing the operation somewhat earlier than the boys. Up to the period of " topknot-cutting," the head of a child is shaved, with the exception of the crown, where the hair is twisted into a coil, fastened with a gold pin, and surrounded with a wreath of flowers. The dispensing with this topknot is a sign that the young person has arrived at the age of puberty.

The popular name for the ceremony is *Koan Chuck*, but the festival with which the event is celebrated in the case of a member of the royal family is called *Sokan*. Europeans are not allowed to witness the ceremonies, which are very elaborate, especially in the case of a Chaofa; and the following particulars were furnished to me by a Siamese official. An auspicious day having been appointed by the astrologers, the priests are invited three days beforehand to read prayers morning and evening, and every afternoon a procession is formed, the prince or princess being carried round the palace, seated on a carved and gilt litter borne by eight men. This chair is called in court language *Phra Sareang*, and the eight carriers, *Ratee yan*. Immediately behind the prince comes the umbrella-bearer with a seven-storied umbrella, called *chat*. As the procession proceeds it is greeted at intervals by musicians placed along the route. Presents are offered to the prince or princess, the minister of war, or Kalahome, and the Kromatah, or minister for foreign affairs, each offering 100 ticals, and the other officials in proportion. The priests are feasted every day, and offerings of yellow robes, &c., are made to them on behalf of the child. On the fourth day the actual ceremony of cutting off the topknot is performed by the chief Brahmin, who for the purpose sits on a throne, called *Bencha*, and who afterwards gives the child a bath.

At death all princes above the rank of Mom Chao have certain allowances for the due conduct of mourning and cremation and a cremation urn suitable to their rank. Mom Chao princes (generally grandsons of a king) have the privilege of a state top-knot-cutting ceremony, in the royal palace. They are admitted to monk's orders under royal auspices at the chief temple in the palace; they have the right of audience as princes, a yearly pension allowance, and are entitled to certain royal gifts for their cremation, among them a white coffin.

Mom Rachawongs and their children, Mom Hluangs, have no princely privileges or advantages, except a trifling pension. When they desire to enter the service of government, they must offer themselves, just like the sons of noblemen, as pages (Mahat Lek), and they take audience, not among princes, but among pages.

The precedence of princes is thus tabulated:—

1. Pra Bant'un Nai ⎱ both are Wangnas.
2.   „   „   Nok ⎰

3.   „   Bancha Crot ⎱ The Wang Lang.
                      ⎰ First-class sons of a king.

4. Somdet Pra Chao Boromanjaka-to Chaofa—Chaofas who are grandparents of the king.

5. Somdet Pra Chao Boromawongs-to Chaofa—Chaofa uncles and aunts.

6. Somdet Pra Chao Pi Ya-to Chaofa—Chaofa elder brothers and sisters.

7. Somdet Pra Chao Nong Ya-to Chaofa—Chaofa younger brothers and sisters.

8. Somdet Pra Chao Luk-to Chaofa—Chaofa children.

9. Pra Chao Boromanjaka-to Pra Ong Chao—Grandparents.

10. „   Chao Boromawongs-to Pra Ong Chao—Uncles and aunts.

11. „   Chao Pi Ya-to Pra Ong Chao—Elder brothers and sisters.

12. „   Chao Nong Ya-to Pra Ong Chao—Younger brothers and sisters.

13. Pra Chao Luk-to Pra Ong Chao—Children.

14. „   „   Rachawongs-to Pra Ong Chao—Cousins.

(Princes of the thirteenth and fourteenth degrees take precedence by age only, their rank is the same.)

15. Somdet Pra Chao Lan-to—Chaofa grandchildren of the king.

16. Pra Chao Worawongs-to of the 1st class ⎫
17. „   „   „   „ „ „ 2nd „ ⎬
18. „   „   „   „ „ „ 3rd „ ⎬ Pra Ong
19. „   „   „   „ „ „ 4th „ ⎬ Chao.
20. „   „ Boworawongs-to of the 1st „ ⎬
21. „   „   „   „ „ „ 2nd „ ⎭

(All these six are princes of Wangna descent.)

22. Pra Chao Lan-to Pra Ong Chao—Grandsons or nephews of the king.

23. Pra Prap'antawongs-to Pra Ong Chao—Princes of the family of the king's maternal grandfather, Krom Mun Mataya Pitak.

24. Pra Wongs-to Pra Ong Chao—The Mom Chao princes who have become Pra Ong Chao by promotion.

25. Pra Samp' antawongs-to Pra Ong Chao—Grandchildren of the elder sisters of King Pra Putthi Yot Fa.

26. Mom Chao—ranking according to the rank of their fathers.

On formal occasions princes of the highest rank, such as Chaofas, sometimes, out of respect to their uncles and other elder relatives of lower rank, will insist on giving them precedence, but indeed it only makes the elder relatives uncomfortable, and on state occasions it cannot be done. The style of Krom, in all its grades, is conferred upon princesses as well as princes, but seldom on princesses of Wangna birth, unless their mothers are princesses.

APPENDIX II.

To those not acquainted with the geography of Siam, a short description of the country may be interesting.

Name.—The word " Siam " is derived from the Malay *Sayam* which means " brown," and refers to the colour of the race.

The native name for the country is " Thai," which means " free," and it is sometimes called " Muang Thai," or the " kingdom of the free."

Position.—Including its dependencies, the Lao States in the north, and the Malay States in the south, Siam extends from latitude 20° 20′ N. to nearly 4° S., and, including the dependent Cambodian Provinces on the east, its extreme breadth is from about 99° E. to 105° E.   The northern frontier of the Lao States has not been defined, but may be said to be formed by the River Mekong and its tributary the Mekok, which divide it from the Ngiou or Shan States.   On the west it abuts on British Burmah and Independent Burmah.   On the east Cambodia is its neighbour, with the River Mekong or Cambodia as its approximate boundary.

Political Divisions.—Siam proper is divided into forty-one provinces, viz :—

Northern provinces, five : Sang Kalok, Phitsanulok, Kampheng Pet, Phixai, and Raheng.

Central provinces, nine : Nantaburee, Pak Pret, Patummatanee, Ayuthia or Krung-Kao, Ang-Thong, Muang Phrom, Muang Inn, Xainat, and Nakhon Savan.

Eastern provinces, ten : Petchaboon, Bua-Xum, Saraburee, Nophaburee, Nakhon-Nayok, Pachin, Kabin, Sasong-Sao or Petriu, Battabong, and Phanatsanee Khom.

Western provinces, seven : Muang Sing, Suphan or Suphanaburee, Kan-chanaburee or Pak-Phrek, Raxaburee, Nakhon Xaisi, Sakhonburee or Tha-Chin, Samut Songkhram or Mei-Khlong.

Southern provinces, ten: Paklat, Paknam, Bangplasoi, Rajong, Chantaboon, Thung Jai, Petchaburee, Xumphon, Xaiya, and Xalang.

MOUNTAINS.—Through Siam and Lao run two great mountain-chains, both radiating from Yunnan through the Ngiou States. The eastern chain stretches in a S.S.E. direction, from Kiang Tsen right down to Cambodia, while the western chain extends in a southerly direction right through the Malay Peninsula. Their height seems not to exceed 5000 feet. Limestone, gneiss and granite I found throughout to be the main composition of the rocks.

RIVERS.—Between these two chains of mountains, with their ramifications, lies the great alluvial plain watered by the River Menam, a magnificent river of which the immortal Portuguese poet, Camoens, has sung in his Lusiad X. cxxv..—

> " Olha e rio Menao que se derrama
>
> Do grande lago que Chiamai [1] se chama."

which has been translated:—

> " The Menam now behold, whose waters take
>
> Their sources in the great Chiamai lake."

In this, however, the poet was wrongly informed. The source of the river I ascertained to be a mountain-stream on the borders of the Ngiou States,[2] but within the Lao territory, and not, as is generally marked on charts, in Yunnan.

At Raheng the main stream is joined by the Menam Vang, flowing from a N.E. direction from Lakon; and above this junction the larger river is called the Meping. The other great tributary of the Menam is the Paknam Po, or Menam Jai (Great Menam), which joins it in latitude N. 15° 18′ after flowing also in a S.W. direction.

To the annual inundation of the Menam and its tributaries, the fertility of the soil is due. Even as high up as in the Lao States, the water rises from eight to ten feet during the rainy season. A failure of these inundations would be fatal to the rice-crop. From Bangkok to Raheng, crossing three degrees of lati-

---

[1] Could this have been a mistake for Chengmai? There is, however, no lake there.

See p. 357.

tude, the alluvial plain of the Menam may be said to be one of the most fertile valleys in the world.

The second great river of importance is the Bang-Pak-Kong, which has its source in a barrier-range of irregular mountains separating the elevated plateau of Korat from the alluvial plains extending to the head of the Gulf of Siam. The river meanders through the extensive paddy-lands and richly cultivated districts of the north-east provinces, and falls into the sea twenty miles east of the Menam. Another great river is the Meklong, which falls into the sea about the same distance to the west of Bangkok; at its mouth is a large and thriving village of the same name.[3] This is a great rice-district, and from Meklong all up the river to Kanburee a large number of the population are Chinese. In the valley of the Meklong are salt-pits, on which the whole kingdom depends for its supply. The Meklong is connected with the Menam river by means of a canal, which is a short cut to Bangkok, avoiding the sea-passage. I have done the journey both ways, but I prefer crossing the gulf, as the mosquitoes in the canals are a terrible pest.

I must not omit the Mekong—the largest of all the rivers in Indo-China—which, however, only partly runs through Siamese territory in the extreme north. I have only seen the stream up at Kiang Tsen, some 1500 miles from its mouth, and that was during the dry season, but even then it had a width twice that of the Menam at Bangkok. It was then, however, very shallow, and only navigable for small boats, being interrupted by many sand-banks. The river is historically celebrated, for at its mouth the immortal poet Camoens was wrecked in 1560. He mentions the river in the tenth canto of " Lusiadas," wherein he pours out the bitterness of his soul against his ungrateful country.

The coasts of Siam are rocky, with numerous islands.

Towns.—Next to Bangkok, and lying to the south-east of it, the most important port is Chantaboon or Chantaburee, built on the banks of the river of the same name, and some seven miles distant from the mountain-range so famous for its precious stones, especially sapphires, zircons, and rubies.

There are numerous other smaller villages on the coast of the Gulf of Siam, which in course of time will no doubt become

[3] The town of Meklong is noted for being the birth-place of the ' Siamese twins."

leading ports, as the fertile soil gets cultivated and commerce increases, for instance :—

Anghin, fifty-eight miles from Bangkok, is a favourite sea-side resort for both Siamese and Europeans.

Ban Pla Soi is another large village close by, whence fish and salt (procured from fields by evaporation) are exported.

Ban Pak Kong is an extensive fishing-village situated about a mile inside the mouth of the River Pak Kong. The inhabitants are mostly Chinese, who are busily engaged in the prawn and mussel fisheries, large quantities of which are dried and exported. A good supply of oil is also extracted from mussels by a boiling process.

TRIBUTARY STATES.—The tributary Lao States have already been described in the body of this book.

Of the Malay States, the most important is Quedah, or, in Siamese, Muang Sai. The Malay population of this province is about 500,000; the Chinese muster 20,000; other races about 5000—total 525,000. The country is said to be level and covered with vast forests, where elephants, tigers, and rhinoceros abound.

The principal town of Quedah is situated on a fine, deep, and navigable stream, with, however, a bad bar.

A high range of mountains separates Quedah from the provinces of Patani—which has over 200,000 inhabitants, who export rice and tin—and Songkhla.

These, again, are divided from the province of Kalantan by the Banara river, and from Tringanu by the Batut river. Tringanu is well wooded and fertile, and exports gold and tin.

In Ligor province, called by the Siamese Lakhon, three-fourths of the population are Siamese. The gold and silver-smiths of Ligor have a considerable reputation for their gold and silver vessels, inlaid with a black enamel.

Of the Cambodian provinces under Siamese rule but little is known. The following particulars are extracted from a paper by M. Victor Berthier.

The most important provinces are the most westerly, Battambang and Korat.

Battambang is situated on the west of the Grand Lake, and has a population of about 70,000. The principal exports of this province are salt, fish, rice-paddy, bees'-wax, cardamoms, hides, and horns. The wild bullock, buffalo, elephant, and rhinoceros are found in the forests which cover the mountains in the south of the province. According to Mouhot, the present town of Battambang dates only from the time the Siamese took the province; the old town was situated some nine miles more to the east, on the banks of a river whose course has been changed. In the neighbourhood of Battambang are the remains of the great temples of Baset, Banom, and Vaht-Ek.

Two days' march from Battambang is the village of Angkor Borey (the royal town). It is the great centre of the production of bees'-wax, of which 24,000 pounds are sent yearly to Siam. Thirty miles E.N.E. of Angkor Borey is situated the auriferous country of Tu'k Cho. It is only a few years since that two Chinese companies bought the monopoly of the mines. The metal is obtained by washing the sand extracted from wells of about twenty feet deep. The auriferous sand is extracted during the dry season, and washed during the rainy season. The deeper the wells the more considerable is the return. M. Brossard de Borbigny, in the *Revue Maritime*, affirms that at the above-mentioned depth auriferous quartz is met, and working as they do with primitive appliances, the miners have no means whatever of extracting the ore from the quartz.

Korat is the largest province and is peopled almost entirely by Cambodians. Its chief town bears the same name, and is the centre of a very important trade. According to Mouhot, this town has only a population of 5000 to 6000 inhabitants, including some 600 Chinese, a great part of whom came direct from the Celestial Empire. The whole province contains a great number of villages, and more than eleven towns or centres of districts, at an average distance one from the other of from four to eight days' journey, which, allowing the same population to each as to the principal town, would give at least 50,000 to 60,000 inhabitants to this large and rich province.

Of the other provinces the most noted is Angkor, which, however, is now of small importance, being thinly populated, and is chiefly renowned for the splendour of its ancient capital, whose remarkable ruins left are the silent witnesses of a glorious past. The present capital of the province is Siem Rep, a few miles south of which is the hill called Phnom Krom (Inferior Mount), which becomes an island during the annual inundation.

North-west of Angkor is the province of Choukan, of which very little is known. It is said to be fertile and well cultivated, and contains several ruins, amongst which is the great bridge of Stung Sreng, visited by M. Garnier. In the north of this province are the important ruins of Bantey Chumar, among the largest and most remarkable to be found in Cambodia.

North of Choukan lies Souren, covered with large forests. The population is thin and scattered. To the eastward are Sankea, Koukau, Melu-prey, which has not been explored and is totally unknown by Europeans; and Touly-repou, of which also very little is known. This province, which owes its name to a fine but small river, was once rich and populated, but Garnier says that since its separation from Cambodia, it has been partly deserted, and its mountains serve as refuges to bands of thieves.

THE CLIMATE.—Siam is considered, for the tropics, a healthy country, and this opinion is endorsed by European and American residents of long stay. Of course in such an extensive country the climate varies greatly. In the low lands it is hot, sometimes intensely so, but those residing in the low alluvial parts, say for instance at Bangkok, need not travel very far before reaching a cooler climate. A few hours' steam or rowing in a travelling-boat, will bring them to the coast, where at Koh Si Chang, a small island on the east coast, they can enjoy sea-breezes and sea-bathing, while on the hills at Radburee and Petchaburee, a few miles inland on the west coast, there is a salubrious air.

The rainy season begins in April. Though the beginning of this month is the hottest of the year, with easterly and southerly winds prevailing, towards the latter part of the month showers of rain relieve the intense heat of the day, and the nights are cool. This period is generally unhealthy for Europeans, as dysentery is very common. In May the heaviest rainfall of the year occurs. It seldom rains all day, but the showers are heavy and frequent. This is the month when the Siamese prepare the ground for planting rice, and the minister of agriculture has a day devoted to him in honour of the commencement of seed-time, which is called " Wan-kam-takh."

In June the wind varies from S. to S.W. with abundance of rain. Intermittent fevers prevail in the jungles, and it is fatal for Europeans to travel in the forests and prairies.

In July pleasant weather is the rule, and unpleasant weather is an exception; although more rain falls than in June, refreshing breezes come in from the south and west. In August the rain begins to abate, while in September the rainfall is almost as heavy as in May, often more so; streets and roads are inundated, the rivers and canals overflow their banks, and locomotion on shore is difficult. This continues throughout October when, with November, the N.E. monsoon begins to blow and the Siamese complain of the cold, but, to the joy of the Europeans and Americans, the " hot season " is over, and the " cool season " has set in, to last till the end of February. The rivers are now full of water, and boat-travelling is a pleasure, though sometimes showers of rain fall with a change of the wind to S.W.

In December the N.E. monsoon prevails, and January is the coolest month of the year. Mists are common in the mornings, and the thermometer registers 68° Fahr. The rivers now begin to fall, the foot-paths become dry, and there is no danger of fever.

February is one of the best months for travelling through the jungles and over the vast prairies, as the ground is perfectly dry, and the river-banks are high above the water.

In March, though usually dry, it is beginning to get hot, the thermometer marking generally 93° in the day, with E.N.E. and S.S.W. winds blowing. The Siamese, young and old, are much engaged at this time in playing games with kites, which are fitted with whistles, and the air resounds with the noise produced by the toys and the shouts of the multitudes of people engaged in the sport. Two or three smart showers of rain usually fall about the time of the vernal equinox, attended with much lightning and heavy thunder.

POPULATION.—The total population of Siam is estimated at 7,000,000, but there are no means of proving the correctness of the estimate. I am inclined to believe that this is only the male population, women and children under age not being counted. I saw it stated in a Singapore paper (the *Daily Times*, I believe) that there were 7,000,000 Chinamen alone in Siam, but this is as palpably an exaggeration as the other is an under-estimate.

APPENDIX III.

SIAMESE MODE OF RECKONING TIME.

THE Siamese language contains no word for *week*. The days of the week, however, have specific names derived from the names of the planets :—

> Wan-aht'it = Sunday.
> Wan-chan = Monday.
> Wan-angk'ahn = Tuesday.
> Wan-p'ut = Wednesday.
> Wan-pra-hat = Thursday.
> Wan-suk = Friday.
> Wan-sow = Saturday.

N.B. *Wan* means day.

The following are the names of the months :—

> Du'-an ai, first month.
> Du'-an vee, second month.
> Du'-an sahm, third month.
> Du'-an see, fourth month.
> Du'-an hah, fifth month.
> Du'-an hok, sixth month.
> Du'-an chet, seventh month.
> Du'-an paat, eighth month.
> Du'-an kow, ninth month.
> Du'-an sip, tenth month.
> Du'-an sip-et, eleventh month.
> Du'-an sip-saung, twelfth month.

N.B. *Du'-an* means a lunar month.

The Siamese month is lunar, and, as this is nearly 29½ days, the Siamese make the odd months contain 29 and the even months 30 days, to complete 59 days in two months; thus the year has only 354 days. To compensate for this deficiency, they introduce in nineteen years seven or eight intercalary months, and, in addition, sometimes three or four intercalary days.

When the intercalary month is introduced, the eighth lunation of that year is doubled, making two consecutive months of thirty days each. The first of these two eighth lunations is called *Burap'ah-saht* or *Pat'oma-saht*, i.e. first eighth lunation. The second is called *Utarah-saht* or *Tutiyah-saht*, i.e. second eighth lunation.

When the intercalary day is introduced, the seventh lunation is prolonged a day, and it becomes a month of thirty days, instead of one of twenty-nine days as is usual. In this way the Siamese contrive to bring their months and years and seasons in unison with the yearly revolution of the earth round the sun.

In dates, the age of the moon, either waxing or waning, is reckoned by the evenings, designated *k'am*, and hence the day of twenty-four hours is always considered as beginning at sunset. The waxing (*K'ahng-k'ɯn*) and the waning (*K'ahng-raam*) are always specified.

The waxing of the moon of every month is invariably reckoned fifteen days. The waning of the moon in the odd months consists of only fourteen days, except of course when the intercalary day occurs in the seventh month, when, as in the even months, it consists of fifteen days.

The quarters of the moon are called *Du'an K'ruing seek*, but this distinction is not required in dates.

The years are distinguished in the following manner :—

Each year has a specific name in a cycle of twelve years, as follows :—

1. Pee Ch'u-at, rat.
2. Pee Ch'alu, cow.
3. Pee K'ahn, tiger.
4. Pee Tau, rabbit.
5. Pee Marohng, major dragon.
6. Pee Maseng, minor dragon.
7. Pee Mammee, horse.
8. Pee Mammaa, goat.
9. Pee Wauk, monkey.
10. Pee Rakah, cock.
11. Pee Chau, dog.
12. Pee Kun, hog.

The years are reckoned successively in the order of the above list, in groups of ten. Each of these decades is called *Sok*, the names of the years composing them being distinguished as follows, in addition to the name given in the above list :—

Eka sok . . . 1st of the decade

Toh sok . . . 2nd „

Tree sok	.	.	.	3rd of the decade
Chatawah sok	.	.	4th	,,
Bencha sok	.	.	5th	,,
Chau sok	.	.	6th	,,
Septa sok	.	.	7th	,,
Atta sok	.	.	8th	,,
Noppa sok	.	.	9th	,,
Samreth sok	.	.	10th	,,

Thus in every cycle of sixty years each year in the first list returns to the same position in the decade which it originally held, to pass through the decades again in the same order as before.

The first of the Siamese lunations or months is usually the moon of November or December. Popularly the Siamese year closes with the last day of their fourth lunation, and New Year begins with the first day of the fifth lunation. This popular New Year's Day may fall on any day between the 9th of March and the 7th of April.

The astronomical and official New Year's Day always occurs on either the 11th or 12th of April.

The Siamese reckon three seasons of four months each. The seasons are called *Radu.*

1. Radu raun, or K'imhan, hot season.
2. Radu fon, or Wasan, rainy season.
3. Radu now-a, or Heman, cold season.

The Siamese have two eras, which are made use of in dates; the one a civil, and the other a sacred, era.

The sacred era is called *Putta-sakaraht,* and is reckoned from the death of the last Buddha. At the full moon of the sixth Siamese lunation, i.e. on April 21st, 1883, this era closed its 2426th year. It antecedes the Christian era 543 years. This era is used in religious matters. Every time a Siamese priest reads or recites one of his homilies, he is very particular to state the number of years Buddhism has existed up to date, and how long it will continue after that date. Buddhists believe it will exist 2574 years after the above-mentioned date.

The other is the civil era, and is called the *Chula-sakaraht.* The commencement of this era was fixed by a distinguished king, and on the last day of the fourth Siamese lunation, i.e. March 8th, 1883, it closed its 1244th year, and is subsequent to the Christian era 639 years.

INDEX.

INDEX.

F f

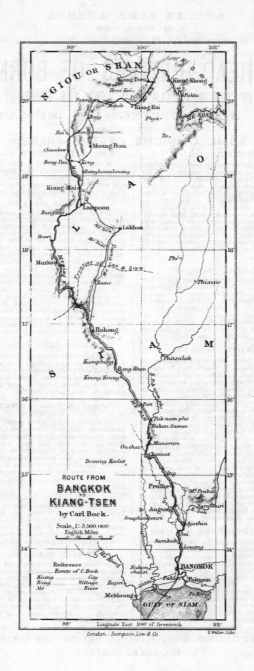

ROUTE FROM
BANGKOK
TO
KIANG-TSEN
by Carl Bock.

Scale, 1: 3.500.000
English Miles
0   10   20   30   40   50

Reference
Route of C.Bock .....
Kiang   City
Bang   Village
Mé   River

London : Sampson Low & Co.

E.Weller, litho.

**Some other Oxford Paperbacks for readers interested in Central Asia,
China and South-East Asia, past and present**

CAMBODIA

GEORGE COEDÈS
Angkor: An Introduction

CENTRAL ASIA

PETER FLEMING
Bayonets to Lhasa

LADY MACARTNEY
An English Lady in Chinese
Turkestan

ALBERT VON LE COQ
Buried Treasures of Chinese
Turkestan

AITCHEN WU
Turkistan Tumult

CHINA

HAROLD ACTON
Peonies and Ponies

ERNEST BRAMAH
Kai Lung's Golden Hours

ANN BRIDGE
The Ginger Griffin

PETER FLEMING
The Siege at Peking

CORRINNE LAMB
The Chinese Festive Board

W. SOMERSET MAUGHAM
On a Chinese Screen*

G. E. MORRISON
An Australian in China

OSBERT SITWELL
Escape with Me! An Oriental
Sketch-book

INDONESIA

S. TAKDIR ALISJAHBANA
Indonesia: Social and Cultural
Revolution

DAVID ATTENBOROUGH
Zoo Quest for a Dragon*

VICKI BAUM
A Tale from Bali*

MIGUEL COVARRUBIAS
Island of Bali*

BERYL DE ZOETE AND
WALTER SPIES
Dance and Drama in Bali

AUGUSTA DE WIT
Java: Facts and Fancies

JACQUES DUMARCAY
Borobudur

JACQUES DUMARCAY
The Temples of Java

JENNIFER LINDSAY
Javanese Gamelan

EDWIN M. LOEB
Sumatra: Its History and People

MOCHTAR LUBIS
Twilight in Djakarta

MADELON H. LULOFS
Coolie*

ANNA MATHEWS
The Night of Purnama

COLIN McPHEE
A House in Bali*

HICKMAN POWELL
The Last Paradise

E. R. SCIDMORE
Java, Garden of the East

MICHAEL SMITHIES
Yogyakarta

LADISLAO SZÉKELY
Tropic Fever: The Adventures of
a Planter in Sumatra

EDWARD C. VAN NESS AND
SHITA PRAWIROHARDJO
Javanese Wayang Kulit

MALAYSIA

ABDULLAH ABDUL KADIR
The Hikayat Abdullah

ISABELLA L. BIRD
The Golden Chersonese: Travels
in Malaya in 1879

PIERRE BOULLE
Sacrilege in Malaya

MARGARET BROOKE
RANEE OF SARAWAK
My Life in Sarawak

C. C. BROWN (Editor)
Sejarah Melayu or Malay Annals

COLIN N. CRISSWELL
Rajah Charles Brooke: Monarch
of All He Surveyed

K. M. ENDICOTT
An Analysis of Malay Magic

HENRI FAUCONNIER
The Soul of Malaya

W. R. GEDDES
Nine Dayak Nights

JOHN D. GIMLETTE
Malay Poisons and Charm Cures

JOHN D. GIMLETTE AND
H. W. THOMSON
A Dictionary of Malayan
Medicine

A. G. GLENISTER
The Birds of the Malay Peninsula,
Singapore and Penang

C. W. HARRISON
Illustrated Guide to the Federated
Malay States (1923)

TOM HARRISSON
World Within: A Borneo Story

DENNIS HOLMAN
Noone of the Ulu

CHARLES HOSE
The Field-Book of a Jungle-Wallah

SYBIL KATHIGASU
No Dram of Mercy

MALCOLM MacDONALD
Borneo People*

SOMERSET MAUGHAM
The Casuarina Tree*

AMBROSE B. RATHBORNE
Camping and Tramping in Malaya

ROBERT W. C. SHELFORD
A Naturalist in Borneo

J. T. THOMSON
Glimpses into Life in Malayan Lands

RICHARD WINSTEDT
The Malay Magician

PHILIPPINES

AUSTIN COATES
Rizal

SINGAPORE

PATRICK ANDERSON
Snake Wine: A Singapore Episode

ROLAND BRADDELL
The Lights of Singapore

R. W. E. HARPER AND
HARRY MILLER
Singapore Mutiny

JANET LIM
Sold for Silver

G. M. REITH
Handbook to Singapore (1907)

J. D. VAUGHAN
The Manners and Customs of the
Chinese of the Straits Settlements

C. E. WURTZBURG
Raffles of the Eastern Isles

THAILAND

CARL BOCK
Temples and Elephants

REGINALD CAMPBELL
Teak-Wallah

MALCOLM SMITH
A Physician at the Court of Siam

ERNEST YOUNG
The Kingdom of the Yellow Robe

Titles marked with an asterisk have restricted rights